Governance in the Asia-Pacific

This book is part of a series produced in association with The Open University. While each book in the series is self-contained, there are also references to the other books. Readers should note that references to other books in the series appear in bold type. The list of other books in the series is:

Asia-Pacific in the New World Order, edited by Anthony McGrew and Christopher Brook

Economic Dynamism in the Asia-Pacific, edited by Grahame Thompson

Culture and Society in the Asia-Pacific, edited by Richard Maidment and Colin Mackerras

The Asia-Pacific Profile, edited by Bernard Eccleston, Michael Dawson and Deborah McNamara

The books form part of the Open University course DD302 *Pacific Studies.* Details of this and other Open University courses can be obtained from the Course Reservations and Sales Office, PO Box 724, The Open University, Milton Keynes MK7 6ZS, UK. For availability of this or other course components, contact Open University Worldwide Ltd, The Berrill Building, Walton Hall, Milton Keynes MK7 6AA, UK. Alternatively, much useful course information can be obtained from the Open University's website: http://www.open.ac.uk

Governance in the Asia-Pacific

Edited by Richard Maidment, David Goldblatt and Jeremy Mitchell

London and New York

in association with

The Open University

First published 1998 by Routledge
11 New Fetter Lane, London EC4P 4EE

Simultaneously published in the USA and Canada
by Routledge
29 West 35th Street, New York, NY 10001

© The Open University 1998

Edited, designed and typeset by The Open University

Printed in the United Kingdom by Alden, Oxford, Didcot and Northampton

British Library Cataloguing in Publication Data
A catalogue record for this book is available from The British Library

Library of Congress Cataloging in Publication Data
A catalogue record for this book has been requested

ISBN 0-415-17275-6 (hbk)
ISBN 0-415-17276-4 (pbk)

1.1

CONTENTS

Series preface

The five volumes in this series are part of a new Open University course, *Pacific Studies*, which has been produced within the Faculty of Social Sciences. The appearance of *Pacific Studies* is due to the generous and enthusiastic support the course has received from the University and in particular from colleagues within the Faculty of Social Sciences. The support has been especially remarkable given that this course has ventured into relatively uncharted scholarly waters. The potential risks were readily apparent but the commitment always remained firm. I am very grateful.

There are too many people to thank individually, both within and outside of the Open University, but I must record my appreciation for some of them. Within the University, I would like to acknowledge my colleagues Anthony McGrew and Grahame Thompson. *Pacific Studies* could not have been made without them. Their role was central. They were present when the course was conceived and they lived with it through to the final stages. They also made the experience of making this course both very enjoyable and intellectually stimulating. Christopher Brook and Bernard Eccleston made an enormous contribution to the course far beyond their editorial roles in two of the books in the series. They read the successive drafts of all chapters with great care and their perceptive comments helped to improve these volumes considerably. David Goldblatt and Jeremy Mitchell, because of their other commitments, may have joined the Course Team relatively late in the production process, but their contributions, especially to *Governance in the Asia-Pacific* have been much appreciated. Michael Dawson played an especially important role in the production of *The Asia-Pacific Profile* and his calm and genial presence was valued as always. Jeremy Cooper and Eleanor Morris of the BBC were responsible for the excellent audio-visual component of *Pacific Studies*. Anne Carson, the Course Manager of *Pacific Studies*, was consistently cheerful and helpful. All of the volumes in this series have been greatly improved by the editorial craftsmanship of Stephen Clift, Tom Hunter and Kate Hunter, who have been under great pressure throughout the production of this course, but nevertheless delivered work of real quality. The striking cover designs of Richard Hoyle and Jonathan Davies speak for themselves and the artwork of Ray Munns in all five volumes has been most impressive. Paul Smith, whose recent retirement from the University will leave a very real gap, made his usual remarkable contribution in providing unusual and interesting illustrations. Giles Clark of the Copublishing Department was a constant source of encouragement and in addition his advice was always acute. Our colleagues in Project Control, especially Deborah Bywater and David Calderwood, were far more understanding and helpful than I had any right to expect. Lene Connolly of Print Buying and Pam Berry of Text Processing did all that was necessary to ensure that this series was produced on schedule. Anne Hunt and Mary Dicker, who have been responsible for so much of the work in this Faculty over the past several years, performed to their usual exacting standards by preparing the manuscripts in this series for publication with remarkable speed and accuracy. They were very ably assisted by Chris Meeks and Doreen Pendlebury.

Pacific Studies could not have been made without the help of academic colleagues based in the UK as well as in the Asia-Pacific region. This series of books has drawn on their scholarship and their expertise but above all on their generosity. I must record my appreciation to all of them for their participation in this project. The Course Team owes an especially large debt to Dr Gerry Segal, Director of Studies at the International Institute of Strategic Studies, who was the External Assessor of *Pacific Studies*. He was both an enthusiastic supporter of this project as well as a very shrewd critic. His wise counsel and tough advice have greatly improved the volumes in this series. It has been a pleasure to work with Professor Colin Mackerras, Director of the Key Centre for Asian Studies and Languages at Griffith University in Australia. Griffith University and the Open University have collaborated over the production of *Pacific Studies*; an arrangement that has worked extremely well. The success of this collaboration has been due in no small part to Colin. Over the past three years I have come to appreciate his many qualities particularly his immense knowledge of the Asia-Pacific region as well as his patience and courtesy in dealing with those of us who know far less. I would also like to thank all of those colleagues at Griffith who have helped to make this collaboration so successful and worthwhile, especially Professor Tony Bennett, who played a key role during the initial discussions between the two universities. Frank Gibney, President of the Pacific Basin Institute, was always available with help, advice and encouragement. It was one of the real pleasures of this project to have met and worked with Frank and the PBI. This series has also benefited considerably from the enthusiasm and insight of Victoria Smith at Routledge.

The production of *Pacific Studies* was helped greatly through the assistance of several foundations. The Daiwa Anglo-Japanese Foundation awarded this project two grants and its Director General, Christopher Everett, was a model of generosity and support. He invited the Course Team to use the attractive facilities of the Foundation; an invitation which was accepted with enthusiasm. The grant from The Great Britain Sasakawa Foundation was also greatly appreciated as was the advice, encouragement and the shrewd counsel of Peter Hand, the Administrator of the Foundation. Mr Tomoyuki Sakurai the Director of the Japan Foundation in London was always interested in the development of *Pacific Studies* and I have no doubt that this resulted in a generous grant from the Foundation. Mr Haruhisa Takeuchi, formerly Director of the Japan Information and Cultural Centre, was most supportive during the early stages of this project and his successor at the Centre, Mr Masatoshi Muto has been no less helpful. Finally, I must record my thanks to the British Council in Australia for their assistance which was much appreciated.

Richard Maidment
Chair, *Pacific Studies*
Milton Keynes, March 1998

Governance in the Asia-Pacific: preface

We would like to thank all the contributors to this volume for their enthusiasm and generosity with their time and effort. We would also like to record our appreciation to Bernie Eccleston, Anthony McGrew and Grahame Thompson for reading and improving the book as it went through several drafts. We would also like to thank Gerry Segal, the External Assessor of *Pacific Studies*, who was as insightful a critic on this volume as he has been for the entire series. Annabel Caulfield joined the Course Team at a point where she was able to assist with the production of this book and we are grateful for her help. Stephen Clift and Tom Hunter edited this volume with their usual sensitivity and style. Finally, Anne Hunt and Mary Dicker, it goes without saying, did all that was required, plus a bit more, to prepare the manuscript.

Richard Maidment
David Goldblatt
Jeremy Mitchell
Milton Keynes, May 1998

CHAPTER 1

Politics and governance in the Asia-Pacific: historical and thematic overview

David Goldblatt

1.1 Introduction

This book deals with politics and governance in the Asia-Pacific region since the end of the Second World War, however, despite the apparent narrowness of its coverage, this volume is premised on a broader model of politics and governance than its subject matter might initially imply. Four arguments run throughout the chapters of this book.

- The first is that the study of contemporary politics requires an historical perspective. Unquestionably, an immense gulf separates the politics of the Pacific before and after the Second World War, but this book takes the position that the nature of the region's political cultures and political values, the territorial reach of its states, and the form and character of its political institutions can only be properly explained by delving into their long and complex pre-war history.

- Second, that the distinctive arena of politics is not captured by the study of the state or governments alone, but by processes of governance: the collective processes of rule-making, monitoring and implementation conducted by many intertwined social actors and institutions. While casual inspection of the contemporary and historical record suggests that in most of the region, most of the time, states have been an indispensable element of the process of governance, they have no monopoly. Collective rule-making has also been undertaken by the stateless indigenous societies of North America and Oceania and the assemblies of the Japanese feudal village, while political power has been wielded by military forces, economic institutions and theocratic bureaucracies.

Two aspects of the notion of governance are developed in this book. First, the notion of governance requires us to focus on active processes rather than passive, static accounts of institutions. While an understanding of the structure of political institutions is indispensable, we have tried to look at the ways in which key actors have used those structures and institutions: what resources, options and strategies do different institutional structures make available to those actors? Second, the notion of governance suggests a process of rule-making in which government and political elites are locked into economic and social networks – these may be formal or informal, vertical hierarchies or more horizontal egalitarian relationships, co-operative or conflictual. While politics and governance constitute a distinct realm of human actions and institutions, they cannot be understood independently from their interaction with military power and inter-national affairs, economic power and institutions, cultural beliefs and social structures.

- Third, the study of politics in the Asia-Pacific is necessarily interdisciplinary and in this book you will find a diversity of social forces at work in almost every chapter. This is reinforced with links to the other books in the *Pacific Studies* series which focus on other dimensions of life in the Asia-Pacific – international relations, economics and social and cultural life. (Where possible we have referred you to these volumes, which are referenced in bold.)

- Fourth, many of the key questions and issues that political life in the Asia-Pacific has thrown up can usefully be approached thematically. Three themes run through the chapters of this book: *difference*, *dynamism* and *disjunctures*. *Difference* points to the enormous variations in political life in the Asia-Pacific. *Dynamism* focuses our attention on the rapid and intense processes of social change that have convulsed the polities and societies of the region. *Disjunctures* point to the complex interaction of different forms of social change, focusing our attention on the side-effects, contradictions and conflicts that emerge in response or opposition to those changes.

This introductory chapter is intended to serve as a stepping stone to, and route guide through, the rest of the book. The interdisciplinary approach to politics is not dealt with explicitly but informs the general approach of the chapter. The structure and purposes of this chapter spring from the historical and thematic elements of our approach to studying politics and governance. In Sections 1.2–1.5 I outline the essential elements of the historical background to politics and governance in the contempor-ary Asia-Pacific. This does not constitute a comprehensive history. Rather these sections serve to orientate you within the basic co-ordinates of the region's political history prior to the Second World War. In Section 1.2 I have chosen to begin that history in 1500 to signify an era in East Asia, Oceania and the Americas just before the arrival of Europeans. It is central to the argument of this chapter that this historical experience – the demographic, military, political and cultural conflict between Europe, its North American offshoots and the indigenous states and societies of the region – has been central to the character of politics and the fate of states for most of the subsequent four and a half centuries.

In Section 1.3 a fundamental line is drawn between the Asian and the American-Oceanic experience of European imperial expansion. In the case of the latter, Europeans achieved a total victory and set about the erection of new states on the demographic ruins of indigenous societies. However, in East Asia Europeans encountered a much more complex, dense, and entrenched set of societies whose total defeat was impossible. Indeed, prior to 1800, the impact of Western imperial power was minimal. At best, on the coasts and island chains of South-East Asia, Europeans had managed to construct fragile parasitic colonial polities whose realm consisted of little more than chains of ports, forts and trading stations, tiny garrisons, and pockets of plantation agriculture. In China and Japan, the West reached the limits of its colonial power if not its ambitions. The Chinese still viewed the European presence with a mixture of disdain and indifference, while Japan remained almost entirely cut off from European encounters since its expulsion of Christian missionaries in the seventeenth century.

However, as Section 1.4 seeks to demonstrate, after 1800 the balance of power between European imperialism and the great powers of Asian antiquity shifted massively in favour of Europe and the USA. South-East Asia, apart from Siam, was eventually directly colonized. European colonialism did not leave the political and social life of its fragile Asian colonies untouched, initiating processes of momentous economic, social and cultural change; change that would lay the basis for national independence movements, new state borders and territories, and the institutions of post-Second World War governance. By contrast, Japan and China, falteringly, and in their different ways, were able to muster sufficient political and military power to resist Western occupation and begin their own processes of political and economic modernization. Of all the responses to the threat and presence of the West in the Pacific by far the most successful was the Japanese. Indeed so swift and so impressive was Japan's reconstruction of itself in the late nineteenth century that the early twentieth-century politics of the region would be shaped by the emergence of a powerful, aggressive and effective Japanese imperial project. It was this that ultimately led to the conflagration of the Pacific War, discussed in Section 1.5, as Japan sought to both replace European imperial powers in the region and destroy the potential imperial power of the USA across the Pacific. Thus my narrative, which begins in 1500, ends in 1945.

Having taken that narrative up to the end of the Second World War, I turn from *historical* to *thematic* questions. In Section 1.6 I unpack the meaning of our three *themes* in terms of governance and political institutions. While there is a distinctive political dimension to all of them, I argue that *difference, dynamism* and *disjunctures* come in many forms; political, economic, military and cultural. I then explore the ways in which the individual chapters of this book draw upon historical argument and engage with our themes in pursuit of exploring and explaining governance in the contemporary Asia-Pacific.

1.2   The state in the Asia-Pacific in 1500

The contrasts of political life in the Asia-Pacific five centuries ago with political life in the 1990s are instructive. The gulf is enormous and illustrated by two key differences.

- First, the idea of the Pacific or the Asia-Pacific as a region, in which political life could be viewed as a whole, would have made little sense given the absence of traffic across the ocean, and the effective social and political separation of Asia, Oceania and the Pacific coast of the Americas. In any case, any political observer of the time would not have looked to the Pacific Ocean and the ring of states and societies around it to construct a mental and political geography. In 1500 there was only one centre of political life: the vast and ancient Middle Kingdom, Ming China.

- Second, we view the political life of the Pacific today predominantly in terms of nation-states. States that possess an impersonal legal existence independent of the incumbents of offices and the households and personal retinues of monarchies. States that possess an entrenched and regularized bureaucracy and possess a monopoly of legitimate force evenly across a demarcated and internationally recognized territorial area. No such states existed in the Asia-Pacific in 1500 and no single state form predominated. Political life displayed an unparalleled diversity.

At the centre of that diversity was the great and ancient Chinese empire – self styled as the Middle Kingdom. It considered itself the centre of the known civilized world, the sole site of legal and moral sovereignty to whom all other states owed allegiance and tribute. In 1500 the empire was controlled by the Ming dynasty who had expelled the Mongol invaders and usurpers in the mid fourteenth century. In 1500 the Ming state seemed secure and powerful, despite the immense demographic losses of the fourteenth-century plagues and the subsequent slow down in economic and technological innovation. Yet as with almost every other Chinese dynasty, the Ming fell – not to internal revolt but to conquest by nomadic warriors, in this case the Manchu, from the northern borders beyond the Great Wall of China. The Ming finally fell in 1664 inaugurating the last dynasty of imperial China the Manchu or Qing. As with earlier cycles of imperial history, the nomadic barbarians may have had the military capacity to destroy a Chinese dynasty at a moment of internal weakness, but they lacked any distinctive cultural weight or depth of their own. In a matter of a generation the Manchu elite had become entirely Sinicized, that is, absorbed by the dominant Chinese culture. The culture of elite China and the membership of the Mandarinate – the Confucian imperial bureaucracy – remained unchanged. Qing China retained all the strengths and weaknesses of its Ming forerunners. On the one hand it possessed an organized and regularized administrative and bureaucratic system stretching across an enormous territory with a huge population that could generate the necessary surplus for elite cultural development and military success. On the other hand the Qing state remained dependent on a decentralized landlord class whose interest in seeing power flow to the centre was minimal and whose capacity for developing innovative economic relationships was very low. Qing China's capacity for economic development and the centralization of political and administrative power – essential when threatened from without – was constrained by the stand off between central state and local landlord.

In the shadows of the great Middle Kingdom stood a wide range of other political forms. In Japan a weak and declining feudal monarchy had been displaced some time before 1500 and the turn of the century saw Japanese society enmeshed in conflict and civil war that was to last for over 100 years. Isolated and protected by its island geography, Japan's political development could proceed unthreatened until the basic conflicts between the centralizing tendencies of would-be feudal monarchies and powerful local lords and barons was resolved in favour of the former. The Tokugawa Shogunate was established in the early seventeenth century. A small central state was created around the wealth and domestic administration of the Tokugawa family. They set about the destruction of local feudal powers, the imposition of civil order and the neutralization of the ancient imperial house in whose name they ruled, but whose power was rendered nugatory. Increasingly successful, Tokugawa Japan was able to expel the few Christian missionaries who had made it onto the mainland, impose a rigorous peace, and effectively close the country to outside influence. Two and a half centuries of peaceful internal development, some economic growth and considerable cultural achievement followed, but, when the outside world did arrive, it would provide a very sharp political awakening.

In Vietnam the Le dynasty had come to power half a century or so earlier and had by 1500 established a stable and entrenched Confucian monarchy that paralleled Chinese social and political organization as well as being rooted in Chinese philosophy and culture. Yet its core areas of control were small and petered out as soon as one moved inland from the Mekong delta and the long coastline. In Korea, the Yi dynasty had consolidated control over the peninsula even earlier, in the late fourteenth century, and ruled a similar, if more insular, Confucian kingdom. In what is now contemporary Burma/Myanmar a variety of different small Buddhist kingdoms existed, each reflecting variations in the theological tradition and all with a narrow area of actual political control, vying with each other for a wider regional hegemony. This region of inland South-East Asia, over the next two centuries, came to be contested between the Buddhist kingdoms of Ava, centred in Burma, and Ayudhya, centred in contemporary southern Thailand. Between these kingdoms and the expansionary Vietnamese to the east, the remaining independent princi-palities of Phnom Penh, and the Lao and Shan peoples, were squeezed out of existence. To the south, the Malay peninsula was a complex patchwork of tiny kingdoms, emerging trading city states and Islamic sultanates whose spheres of control did not penetrate much beyond the ports and river estuaries and deltas on which they prospered. A similar patchwork was developing across what has become the Indonesian archipelago, but in 1500 no state of any consequence had emerged in the area outside of the Buddhist kingdoms of Java. The region remained populated by stateless societies of hunter-gatherers and subsistence agrarians. Beyond the ancient and densely populated civilizations of East Asia and its off-shore islands, the stateless societies of Oceania and the Pacific coasts of North America remained untroubled by the states, armies and bureaucracies of either Asia or Europe.

1.3 Early European colonialism

The Americas: democracy and oligarchy

As Section 1.2 made clear, in 1500 the Pacific may have been an ocean but it did not in any sense provide a point of reference for discussing politics. The worlds of East Asia, Oceania and the Pacific coasts of the Americas remained separate. What ultimately brought them together was the creation of a state on the American continent of sufficient power that its reach could be felt across the ocean: the USA. How did such a state emerge and why should it have become the earliest if incomplete liberal democracy? European colonialism in the Americas begins with the Portuguese, Spanish and Dutch in the Caribbean and Latin America. From the early sixteenth century onwards successive waves of colonial adventurers and Jesuit missionaries landed on the Latin American mainland encountering and then waging war on the indigenous societies. In the centre of the continent the Spaniards blundered into the Aztecs while in the south all along the continent's Pacific coastline they encountered Inca civilization. Within a generation these societies had been decimated by the ravages of European diseases and succumbed to a combination of military power, bravado and brutality. Over the next century Spanish control was consolidated along the Pacific coastline and into the interior, where it met Portuguese control spreading out from the Atlantic coastline. Spanish power was extended northwards into what is now Mexico – then called New Spain – as well as into the Florida peninsula, while claims of sovereignty and control were made over much of the western half of North America (see **Eccleston *et al.*, 1998, Figures 2 and 3**). However, the immensity of Spanish and Portuguese conquests never corresponded to the real reach and power of the colonial admin-istration established in the Americas. The Spanish empire was never able to secure any of its claims to territory north of Mexico and none of the independent states that emerged out of the collapse of the empire in the nineteenth century were able to muster sufficient power to reach across the Pacific. Over the vast territories of the Spanish and Portuguese crown there was perhaps no more than ten million people in 1600. Despite some European immigration, large-scale imports of slaves from Africa, and some local population recovery, the territories remained very thinly populated for three centuries. It is hardly surprising that colonies, and then states, which could barely define their own borders and build more than the most rudimentary social and political infrastructures, should have such a minimal international reach. Nor is it surprising that societies so systematically reliant on the use of repressive labour (slave plantations, metal mining) and so dominated by an ersatz and implanted military-aristocratic class, should be fertile soil for the emergence of elite-dominated oligarchic politics.

Along the Atlantic seaboard in the north of the continent the dominant colonizing powers were Britain and France. Steadily displacing the native American tribes of the east coast by a mixture of disease and war, British colonies were founded from Virginia in the south to the Great Lakes in the north, from the early seventeenth to the early eighteenth century. Simultaneously French adventurers, colonists and fur trappers were establishing themselves in Quebec, along the Great Lakes and across a whole swathe of the middle-west of North America south to New Orleans. Despite the smallness of the European populations and their distance from Europe, the fate of the continent and the basic division of the land was decided as part of a series of intra-imperial European wars. The decisive culmination of over a century of skirmishing was the North American dimension to the Seven Year War in Europe. Between 1754 and 1763 British colonial forces successfully defeated the French, the Spanish and their indigenous allies, at almost every turn. At the Peace of Paris in 1763 Britain took possession of all of North America east of the Mississippi. French, Spanish and indigenous populations remained and the African slave population was growing – but culturally, politically and demographically, North America would be ruled by Anglo-Saxons.

What turned this collection of colonies and this immense mixture of peoples into a powerful, liberal democratic state was the American revolution. Though it did so at the cost of dividing North America between an independent USA and the northern remnants of British and French colonial ambitions which would become Canada in the following century. In Britain's American colonies in the 1760s, where property qualifications for the vote were low and wealth, especially land, was much more evenly dispersed than in Europe, as much as 50–80 per cent of the adult male population was on the electoral register. However, less actually voted, and this takes no account of the 20 per cent of the population who were totally disenfranchised slaves. Government was conducted by elected state assemblies, London-appointed governors, and networks of patronage amongst large landowners and the urban middle classes. Actual parliamentary or representative control of state executives and legislation was minimal. The American revolution, which ran from the beginning of the War of Independence in 1776 to the establishment of the new American constitution in 1787, changed all of this. What began as a predominantly anti-imperial struggle became entwined with a national struggle for democratization. One of the central slogans under which the

American War of Independence was fought was 'no taxation without representation', for the imposition of British fiscal demands on the colonies – unrepresented at Westminster – had fuelled the conflict. Consequently, in the post-war era, when the new American political constitution was being discussed, there were strong calls for a suffrage of taxpayers at the very least. In many states there was a poll tax in place which therefore made such a call equivalent to one for white male suffrage. The constitution of 1787 established a popularly elected federal (national) legislature and executive, alongside a powerful system of decentralized state (local) governments, a powerful and independent judiciary and entrenched a series of universal civil and political rights into the American polity.

However, property qualifications for the vote remained in the USA at a state level for another 60 years with only small advances in the post-constitutional era and in the 1830s. Women, native Americans, and black Americans remained overwhelmingly excluded from the democratic process. Indeed, as literacy tests were introduced as part of the voting registration process, illiterate, poor immigrants to the northern states also found themselves excluded. It was the American Civil War (1861–65) that was the next crucial stage in American democratization. The war ended slavery in the south, politically it broke the back of the southern plantation aristocracy, maintained the territorial integrity of the nation and curtailed the development of an explicitly anti-democratic coalition of northern and southern elites. However, in the reconstruction period after the Civil War enough space was left to southern elites to maintain the exclusion of black Americans from the political process. It was not until after the First World War that women finally achieved the vote. The inclusion of black Americans would await the passage of the Civil Rights Act and the Voter Registration Act in 1964 and 1965 (see Chapter 5). Thus a combination of liberal ideology and a relatively egalitarian social structure, radicalized and organized by a war of colonial independence were the foundations of a democratic America. The contrast with similar struggles in a radically different sociological and cultural context in post-Second World War Asia are instructive (see Chapter 4). While the depth and economic weight of southern slavery constituted a major authoritarian element in America, it was ultimately defeated by the industrialized north and the independent agrarian politics of the west. Thus it was a relatively democratic and rapidly industrializing America which finally reached and embedded itself on the Pacific coast of the continent in the middle decades of the nineteenth century (see **McGrew and Brook, 1998, Chapter 1**).

Prior to the First World War American politics was overwhelmingly domestic in its orientation and what energies were expanded on foreign policy were focused on America's backyard: the Caribbean and Latin America. None the less in two bursts of almost effortless imperial expansion the USA stretched its Pacific coastline and acquired its first Pacific island colonies. In 1867 the USA acquired the apparently barren state of Alaska from Russia and annexed the Midway Islands in the north-central Pacific. Following the defeat of the Spanish in the war of 1898, American control

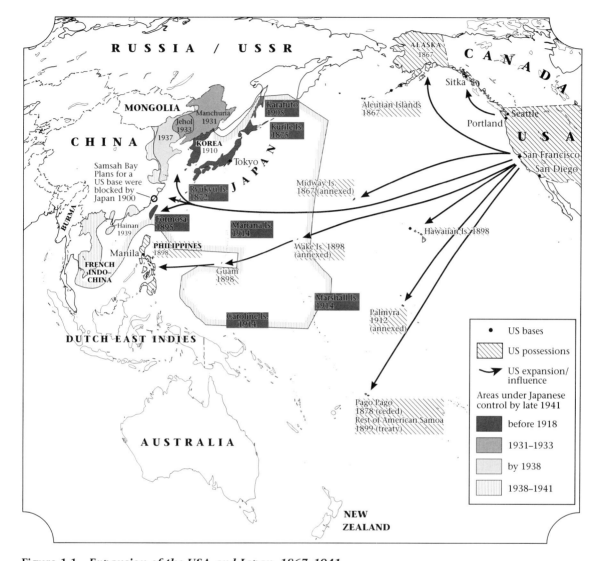

Figure 1.1 *Expansion of the USA and Japan, 1867–1941*
Source: Thomas, A. *et al.* (1994); see also **Eccleston *et al.* (1998, Figure 4)**

extended to the Hawaiian Islands, the Wake Islands, Guam and the Philippines. Henceforth politics in the Asia-Pacific would be an American as well as an Asian affair.

Oceania: late colonialism, early democracies

The American revolution had almost run its course by the time British ships first landed on the Australian shore in 1778 and the colonization of New Zealand would not begin for another 60 years. Yet both of the British settler colonies had, before the First World War, established independent and reasonably democratic states based on a wider franchise than that of the

USA. The story of state formation in Oceania is one of late colonialism and early democratization.

Britain's Australian colony was, for the first five decades of its existence, essentially a military dictatorship. The state transported a small fraction of the metropolitan lumpenproletariat and rural unemployed that commercial agriculture and urbanization had generated in Britain and Ireland. On the back of this extraordinary display of a global imperial, penal and social policy, the British built a wool economy that steadily displaced and disempowered the indigenous aboriginal peoples of the continent. At the apex of the emergent social structure were a small number of colonial landowners who made extensive use of government supplied and organized convict labour. In the late eighteenth and early nineteenth centuries these penal latifundia were supplemented by the emergence of a second distinct rural upper-class strata – the squatters who ran great sheep herds on unfenced crown land. In addition a small holding farmer class of ex-convicts and new immigrants emerged in the countryside. In the small towns industries grew up to service the wool economy and nascent labouring and middle classes developed. These groups remained on the margins. Political power was concentrated within landlord classes economically dependent on repressive labour relations and then politically dependent on the state for unimpeded access to the land. Neither of these needs disposed them towards a democratic politics.

The early representative state assemblies and legislative councils operated on a restricted property franchise which suited them well, but as the colony moved towards self government Australia's rural oligarchies were not able to manage the transition from British to local rule in their favour. The suffrage was successively widened in struggles throughout the 1840s to the 1860s led by urban Australian liberals. In the 1890s the rise of an indigenous labour movement in the cities raised the social and political weight of a labour–liberal coalition to the point at which universal suffrage was forced onto the political agenda and successfully implemented during the transition from separate colonies to an Australian federation in 1901. However, it was a federation in which the political representation of the indigenous peoples of the continent was almost totally absent.

In New Zealand a much later process of colonization, uncomplicated by the use of penal labour, encountered an indigenous Maori people whose social and political organization far exceeded that of Aboriginal Australians and whose capacity to make war and treaties forced a different kind of ethnic and political settlement. None the less, despite achieving some recognition of their political and land rights, Maoris remained a minority force in the creation of a New Zealand polity. From the beginning that polity was almost democratic if not universal in character. In part, this reflected the enormous social and political shifts within Britain in the 60 years since the foundation of colonies in Australia. The policy of the colonial office was to create self-government on the back of a broad suffrage. It did so in a settler society that was unencumbered by large landlords, large inequalities of wealth and power or the need for repressive labour and landlord control of the state. Thus, in New Zealand, it was possible to create early representative government and an early transition to universal male suffrage and then early female suffrage. In contrast to the Australian experience, this was achieved in the absence of a politically significant urban working class. It can be argued that New Zealand was almost born democratic, but its egalitarian social structure ensured that it would remain that way.

1.4   Late European colonialism and Asian responses

The contrasts between European imperial expansion in the Americas and Oceania and the same process in East Asia are threefold. First, while Europeans encountered vast and thinly populated territories in the Americas and Oceania, they encountered densely populated societies in East Asia. Second, Europeans had the decisive epidemiological and demographic edge in the Americas. Conquest and colonization was greatly facilitated by the devastating impact of Eurasian microbes on the indigenous population. In East Asia, the balance of epidemiological power lay with Asians who proved both resistant to European microbes and whose gene pool protected them against local disease strains that were rare or non-existent in Europe. As a consequence, while European colonies were established in Asia, none was able to maintain more than the thinnest layer of European migration. Third, while resistance had been fierce from both the stateless peoples of North America and the settled agrarian states of the southern half of the continent, neither possessed the kinds of organizational and military powers and technologies that could have generated any significant long-term resistance. In East Asia, Manchu China and Tokugawa Japan were very different prospects, possessing large populations, tax raising bureaucracies, gunpowder technologies and capable of widespread social and military mobilization. It was only very late in the day that Europeans acquired a decisive edge in these fields.

Imperial expansion in East Asia and the consequent reshaping of political life in the region can be seen in three waves. First, in a period running from around 1500 to the early nineteenth century European arrivals were rebuffed and ignored at the centre of East Asia. Pushed to the periphery the Portuguese, Spanish and Dutch were only able to establish the merest toe-holds of economic engagement, religious ascendancy and political control in the island archipelagos of South-East Asia. The Portuguese, after being expelled from Canton and Ningpo in the early part of the sixteenth century were allowed by the Ming dynasty to settle in the walled and encircled micro-territory of Macau down river from Canton. The Dutch constructed a precarious infrastructure of control and extraction – The Dutch East India Company – that controlled the spice trade in what is now Indonesia, but it barely penetrated the interior of the islands. The Spanish, after much struggle, held the isolated and underdeveloped Philippine islands.

Beyond these outposts and entrepôts European power was nugatory. The Tokugawa state oversaw the systematic repression and liquidation of indigenous Japanese Christianity, while Spanish, English and Portuguese traders and missionaries were expelled from Japan in the first half of the seventeenth century. Only the Dutch were allowed to remain and then only on the condition that they renounce missionary work and publicly tread on the cross. China, revived under the Qing dynasty, continued to hold both a formal and informal suzerainty over the patchwork of states and societies that made up mainland East Asia, as well as dominating the Korean peninsula, the Mongol steppes and expanding westward into the Islamic lands of Singkiang and the Buddhist societies of Tibet. Although Christian missionaries had more success in China than Japan it was accomplished by Sinicizing theology and practice. While some degree of local accommodation had been acceptable to the Vatican, this appeared to be more of a cultural rout than a tactical feint; Chinese missions and their practice suffered repeated papal condemnation. Territorially and culturally China and Japan remained untroubled by Western adventurers.

However, from the early nineteenth century onwards there was a wave of renewed imperialism driven, in part, by inter-imperial struggle within Europe and equipped more effectively by the military and economic fruits of European industrialization. This second wave of expansion came in two forms: the struggle for territory and military security, and the struggle for trade and market access. The struggle for trading rights and access to markets was the main arena of conflict between European imperial powers and China and Japan. Neither state could actually be defeated, but significant openings and concessions could initially be forced through the display, and if necessary the deployment, of the massively increased naval power that iron ships and new gunnery had equipped Western states with.

The struggle for territory was played out across South-East Asia and the Pacific Islands, as well as in the far north of Asia. In South-East Asia the Dutch consolidated and attempted to deepen their rule in the Dutch East Indies. The French, until then almost absent imperial players in the region, took successive colonial possession of Cochin China, Cambodia, Tonkin, Laos and scattered Pacific Islands. Entwined in the same dynamic struggle Britain sought to defend its Indian imperial possessions from the French and Chinese by successive expansion into the Malay peninsula, Singapore, Sarawak and the rest of north Borneo and Burma in the latter half of the nineteenth century. In the north the Tsarist regime of imperial Russia pushed on from its Siberian hinterlands and their Pacific coastline and began challenging for territorial and trading rights in the northern Pacific Islands, Mongolia, northern China and Manchuria. While from the east, American power had steadily advanced from the Californian Pacific coast to Hawaii and the Philippines. Even the Germans, Europe's most landlocked major imperial power, took what tiny possessions it could in the Pacific Islands and on Papua New Guinea.

The third and final wave of imperial expansion and conflict in the Asia-Pacific is defined less by dates and more by the rise of a powerful and indigenous modern Asian imperialism. For out of the maelstrom of European colonial expansion and the fires of forced industrialization and modernization arose imperial Meiji Japan. While the Chinese empire shrank in both territory and prestige and the Siamese royal state survived only as a useful buffer zone to warring imperial powers, Japan affected a political, social and economic transformation of immense proportions. Able not only to protect the territorial integrity of the state, Japan was able to defeat the Chinese in the wars of the mid 1890s and by the early years of the twentieth century to defeat the Russian imperial fleet in the Russo-Japanese War of 1905. On the eve of the First World War Japan had become a serious contender and player in the progressive dismantling of China, while Formosa/Taiwan and Korea had already succumbed to Japanese imperial control (see Figure 1.1).

So why was it that the Japanese state was able to respond with such vigour to the threats from European states while the Chinese state would eventually be consumed and fragmented by domestic revolution and civil war? The answer in part lies with the state and politics in these societies. In Japan, the response to Western threats was the Meiji Restoration. An apparently conservative move in which the Tokugawa Shogunate was overthrown and replaced by a revamped and strengthened Japanese monarchy. But appearances can be deceptive, while the ideological and ceremonial superstructure of Japanese political life was changed in this way the Meiji Restoration in fact serves as shorthand for a far more revolutionary transformation in the form of state power, the distribution of power amongst Japanese elites, and the ways in which that power was constructed and deployed.

From the perspective of 1800 there were few obvious warning signs that the imperial Manchu state was about to embark on a long drawn out death. Chinese power remained unquestioned on the Asian mainland, foreign traders and missionaries were accepted from a position of strength; their movements controlled, their ideas rejected by the Confucian elite. Indeed, Chinese power had been expanding as the empire pushed out into the west over the eighteenth century and while peasant uprisings and brigandage occurred within the empire, they hardly constituted a loss of control by the state and gentry. By the first decades of the twentieth century these twin forces – external imperial pressure and internal revolt – had brought the Qing dynasty to its knees. The shift in the balance of power between European and Asian states was decisively signalled by the Opium Wars. The details of both the war and its origins need not concern us here (see **McGrew and Brook, 1998, Chapter 1**). In essence, they were the result of a trade dispute between China and Britain. The British, mainly through the old East India Company, had found that the only goods they could sell on a regular basis to China – an indication of the advanced quality of Chinese production at the time – was opium. Intensely addictive and socially disastrous for many Chinese communities, the imperial state sought to control and ban the trade. This initiated four years of warfare between Britain and China, in which British naval power and Chinese weakness saw the British obtain control in Hong Kong, take Shanghai and Jinjiang and ultimately reach Nanjing. Forced to capitulate to the barbarians, the Chinese initiated the first of many unequal trading treaties with foreign powers in which open trading agreements and provision for special status for foreign nationals, merchants and missionaries were made. Over the next 60 years Chinese sovereignty and control of trade was progressively lost to the British, French, Russians, Japanese and Germans. Moreover, in conflicts over Indo-China with the French, over Korea with the Japanese and northern Manchuria with the Russians, the Chinese state proved incapable of mustering sufficient strength to win.

Pu-yi (1906–67) – the last Emperor of China as Xuan-Tong (1908–12)

This external weakness was matched by a growing incapacity to maintain domestic order and control. Throughout the late nineteenth century wave after wave of general social disorder and organized rebellion swept across the empire fuelled by the increasingly desperate situation of the Chinese peasantry. As population levels rose, food production and economic development stagnated and the tax and conscription demands of the state increased, peasant unrest grew and the legitimacy of the ruling order, locally and centrally, declined. The Taiping rebellion raged from

1850 to 1864, the Nien rebellions ran from 1853 to 1868 and Islamic separatists rose in the west throughout the 30 years after 1850, while the century closed with the Boxer Rebellion in northern China. Why was it that China experienced such a wave of social disquiet and why was the Chinese state unable to meet either the threat of foreign powers or the aspirations and needs of an unruly populace? In short, the answer is that the Chinese state and its ruling elites were unable to sufficiently mobilize enough of the country's existing resources, nor were they able to initiate a successful programme of modernization – industrialization, economic development, military reform, etc. – which might have made those resources available. Throughout the nineteenth century the Chinese state was unable to capture more than a fraction of the potential tax resources of the countryside, nor was it able to field armies with sufficient discipline, training and modern military technology to match foreign threats or internal uprisings. When attempts at reform came – particularly in the late nineteenth century after defeat at the hands of the Japanese in the Sino-Japanese war of 1894–95 – they were too little and too late, failing to appeal to resistant social structures and entrenched attitudes. The Chinese state was always dependent on an entrenched local landlord class for most tax collecting and judicial functions and a literate class of Confucian scholars as the mainstay of a very thinly spread imperial bureaucracy. Over this period, attempts to raise more taxation, centralize control away from landlords, initiate processes of rural economic development from the centre, or use the imperial bureaucracy to promote social and intellectual change, all failed.

With the collapse of the Qing dynasty and the proclamation of the first Chinese Republic in 1911, politics in China rotated around three key social forces: the nationalist KMT (Kuomintang) party and movement, the Chinese Communist Party, and the many warlords whose personal territories and retinues functioned as their claim to political power in the absence of any other political or administrative machinery. These three forces contested a civil war of varying levels of intensity throughout the 1920s. By the time of the Japanese invasion of Manchuria in 1931, the KMT had acquired a temporary ascendancy, driving the communists into fighting a guerrilla war and subduing most warlords, but it had yet to consolidate its rule in any meaningful way and it had yet to embark on any kind of programme of social renewal or economic transformation. As we shall see below, any possibility of doing so was terminated by the advent of the Pacific War. It would take another two decades of struggle for the final form of the post-imperial Chinese state to emerge (see Chapter 2).

The contrast with Japan could not be more striking. Again, the trigger for social and political change came from outside. In 1853 Commodore Perry and a small squadron of US warships arrived in Japan, demanding that the country open itself up to trade with the West. The experience of China in the Opium Wars and the evident inequality of naval firepower left the Tokugawa Shogunate little choice but to reluctantly agree to the demands. In doing so, they demonstrated both the Japanese state's international weakness and exposed their own domestic failings. But while defeat at the hands of foreigners was part of the reason for the flood of opposition that the Shogunate faced, there were long-term domestic grievances as well. The warrior or samurai class in Japanese society had long been descending the social scale; excluded from the central institutions of wealth and power, they had been living on declining fixed incomes, unable to pursue their historic martial role. They provided a reservoir of thwarted ambition. External weaknesses and domestic rigidity helped force a coalition of some of the great lords or *Daimyo* – particularly in the distant provinces of Choshu and Satsuma – with restive and ambitious samurai and some court nobility around the emaciated royal house. This fragile and complex coalition eventually forced the resignation of the last Tokugawa Shogun in 1867 and by 1869 had both restored the prominent place of the imperial household and taken the vast majority of senior political and administrative positions within the government. It was only at this point that a more strategic vision of social change was elaborated and embarked upon (see Chapter 3).

The vision combined cultural, political, military and economic elements. In the cultural field the Meiji state set about the transformation of national identity and national purpose. The royal house was both economically and ideologically refurbished at the summit of the new Japanese nation. Massive educational programmes controlled by bureaucrats in Tokyo and compulsory military conscription provided the government with vital instruments for systematizing language and literacy, creating new notions of national identity, and curbing local affiliations and regional dialects which had previously divided the population. Economically, the government initiated, supported and helped co-ordinate a programme of industrial and economic development harnessing a small indigenous business class to programmes of banking and finance reform, heavy industrial investment, shipbuilding and armaments production. Foreign loans, which had bedevilled China, were avoided, taxes were raised and efficiently collected. Militarily, on the back of conscription and the development of industry, the Japanese state set about constructing a navy and army of sufficient size to both protect Japan and explore imperial ambitions in East Asia. Like their economic and social programmes, the military programme of the Meiji Restoration combined an indigenous and imported component, modelling the new Japanese armed forces on foreign forces and importing and developing foreign military technologies. Political development was perhaps the weakest element of the reform programme for Japan. Despite a very gradual expansion of the franchise and the development of parliamentary institutions and political parties, Meiji Japan failed to generate a stable and lasting democratic polity. The oligarchic control of the late nineteenth and early twentieth centuries gave way to a limited parliamentary regime in the 1920s. The latter, buffeted by the social turmoil of a rapidly industrializing society and the concomitant hardships and dislocations of the global economic downturn of the early 1930s, succumbed to an increasingly dictatorial coalition of the military and right-wing politicians. The Meiji Restoration had certainly produced a Japanese state capable of surviving in the modern imperial era; it can be argued that the same trajectory also brought about its own destruction in the imperial adventures of the 1930s and 1940s.

1.5 The state and the Pacific War

1945, like 1500, marks a fundamental dividing line in the international relations and domestic politics of every state in the Asia-Pacific. While 1500 signalled an era before the arrival of European empire, 1945 signals an era in which European empire in Asia was finally defeated and forced to retreat. While convention dates the beginning of the Second World War in Asia on 7 December 1941 – the date of the Japanese attack on the US naval and air base at Pearl Harbor, Hawaii – it is more accurate to date the beginning of the war to 1937 and the renewed onslaught of Japan on China. Japan was already in occupation of Manchuria in the north of China after military victory in the early 1930s. Military and diplomatic skirmishing continued until full-scale fighting broke out again in the north of China in the summer of 1937. When the main Japanese offensive began in late 1937 its impact was devastating. The corrupt, poorly led, demoralized and ill-equipped nationalist Chinese armies – despite their massive size and the recklessness of their generals with life – crumbled in the face of ferocious

Victorious Japanese forces march under the ancient Chungshan gate, Nanjing, China, January 1938

Japanese attacks. The whole north of the country and the eastern seaboard fell, as did the main navigable rivers, southern ports and other centres of population. However, by 1939 the Japanese advance had been quelled. In part because they held nearly all of China that seemed worth taking. Nevertheless, both nationalist and communist forces in China held significant territories in the south and east, and showed no signs of accepting a Japanese-imposed peace treaty. They continued to conduct a guerrilla war with the Japanese. A military and political stalemate had developed.

Japan's attempt to break the stalemate turned on a policy of southern advance. If Japan could weaken or expel the European and American imperial presence in Pacific Asia, it could force the Chinese to sue for peace. If Japan could take control of a huge swathe of territories and resources in East Asia, that would release it from economic dependence on the West and force the Europeans and Americans to leave it as the local hegemon in a reshaped New East Asian Order. The main lines of that southern advance are well known. The attack on Pearl Harbor delivered a significant but not a crushing blow to US air and naval power in the Pacific. It was significant enough to allow the Japanese army to progress almost unmolested across much of the Pacific, but it was not sufficiently crushing to terminate US power in the region. In December 1941 American bases in the Philippines were simultaneously bombed and landings initiated all across the northern part of the island chain. American and Philippine resistance had all but collapsed by the following March. America's other island possessions in the Pacific – Guam and Wake Island – fell almost instantly. At the same time as the attack on Pearl Harbor, Japanese forces took Hong Kong from bases in occupied China, while troops stationed on territory already extracted from the Vichy French regime in Indo-China marched into Thailand and the Malay states. Fighting down the western coast of the Malay peninsula they overwhelmed British imperial forces and took the strategic kingpin of the British Empire in the East – Singapore. A similar fate awaited the Dutch East Indies which fell to the Japanese in early 1942. In around 100 days four and a half centuries of European and American imperial power in the Pacific had been summarily dismissed. The Japanese held most of China, Manchuria, Korea, Formosa, Indo-China, the Malay Peninsula and the Dutch East Indies and all the significant island chains of the western Pacific. They had also invaded Burma, threatening British India, and Papua New Guinea threatening mainland Australia.

The story of the war after this is relatively straightforward. In China, battle continued to rage between the Japanese and Chinese and between Chinese nationalists and Chinese communists. While Japanese rule was harsh and arbitrary in many areas of South-East Asia and the Pacific, local nationalists flourished, either supported by the Japanese and co-opted into governing (Burma, Indonesia) or in opposition to the Japanese (Korea and Vietnam). On the fringes of their initial advance Japanese forces were halted: in the Pacific Ocean the Japanese navy's victories in the Java Sea and at Guadalcanal were reversed at Midway by the still considerable might of

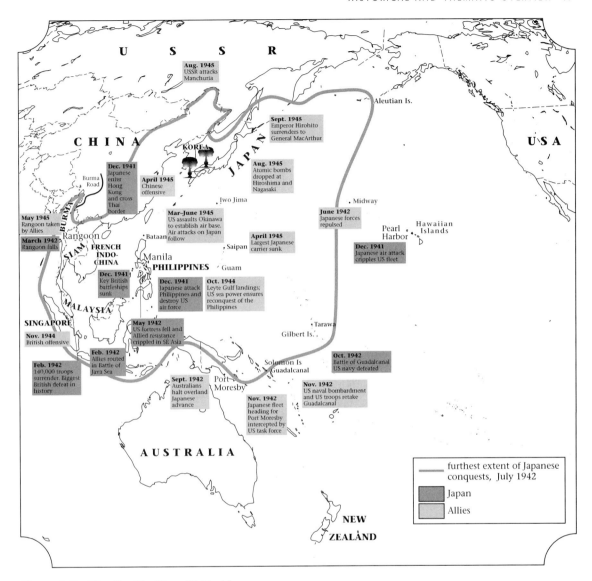

Figure 1.2 *The Pacific War, 1941–45*

Source: Burns (1991); *The Times Atlas of World History* (1978); see also **Eccleston *et al.* (1998, Figure 7)**

US naval power. On land, Japanese expansion was finally halted, in Papua New Guinea by combined Australian and American forces and in Burma on the Indian border by combined British and Indian armies. Unable to close and secure their borders, unable to match the ferocious pace of American military production and unable to protect and supply their immensely long and complex supply lines, the Japanese were forced to gradually retreat. The main thrust came from the Americans in the south; island hopping through the Solomons and across the Pacific until their air and naval forces were sufficient to protect large-scale landings and ground forces in the heart of the new Japanese empire. In late 1944 and early 1945 American

Tokyo's industrial area after saturation bombing, September 1945

forces advanced towards Japan through the Philippines, Iwo Jima and Okinawa. Whilst increasingly isolated, Japanese ground forces on the Asian mainland remained in notional control of huge areas of the continent, but the Japanese war machine, domestically and industrially, was shattered. The navy and the air force had been effectively extinguished as fighting forces by the massive naval engagements of 1943 and 1944 and the relentless American bombing of Japanese urban areas. Hiroshima and Nagasaki brought a final Japanese surrender, but as the following chapters acutely demonstrate there would be no going back to 1937. Politics in the Asia-Pacific had been irreversibly changed.

The legacies of the Pacific War were many, but four stand out in this book. First, the total military defeat of Japanese imperialism and the subsequent American occupation transformed the character of the Japanese state and military. Second, after defeat at the hands of the Japanese, the victorious European imperial powers suddenly found themselves facing restive and mobilized colonial subjects. Busy dismantling Japanese imperialism, American power was not available for the re-establishment of European empire and within a decade European imperial power in the region had shrunk to a few scattered micro-states, islands and mini-colonies. Across South-East Asia an entirely new swathe of independent nation-states had emerged. Third, as both of these legacies show, and Hiroshima and Nagasaki had announced, the awesome power and reach of the American state stretched right across the Pacific Ocean. Fourth, the war directly contributed to the collapse of the Chinese nationalists and the victory of the Chinese communists in 1949. Successful revolutions in Korea and Vietnam heralded further advances for Asian communism. It was this that brought the USA permanently into the web of Asia-Pacific politics; a web that would eventually ensnare the whole of American society and political life in the Vietnam conflict of the 1960s and 1970s.

1.6   Contemporary politics and governance: difference, dynamism and disjunctures

Any account of politics and governance in the Asia-Pacific must begin with the issue of *difference*. In a region as huge as the Asia-Pacific it is hardly surprising that political life should exhibit enormous differences and variations, but as the earlier sections of this chapter have argued, it is the region's history rather than simply its size that has created such a plurality in the forms of political life and the structures of political institutions. Prior to the arrival of European imperialism the states and societies of the Asia-Pacific showed considerable differentiation. The might of Confucian Ming China sat alongside the fragile Buddhist kingdoms of Java, the isolated island feudalism of Shintoist Japan, the Islamic city states of the Indonesian archipelago. To the south lay the isolated stateless societies of Oceania. With the arrival of European colonists this initial diversity was supplemented and transformed by the contrasts of political life in European colonial states. In the post-Second World War era these long-standing differences have been overlain by two other sources of variation. First, the different political trajectories of communist states. Second, the radically different forms that politics has assumed in non-communist polities, a group that encompasses the federal liberal democracy of the USA, the military authoritarianism of Burma/Myanmar and the partial democracies of volatile Thailand and more stable Malaysia. I return to these differences below when exploring the individual chapters of the book.

If imperial, ideological, ethnic, and religious history divides the Asia-Pacific, there is a case for arguing that in the post-Second World War era many societies are comparable, if not united, by virtue of their experience of *dynamism*. In most conventional discussions of the region dynamism has been taken to refer to economic development in the post-war era and more particularly the dynamism of Japan and capitalist East Asia. In this book we qualify this picture in a number of ways. We argue that dynamism – rapid and structural social change – can spring from economic, political and social sources and that these forms of dynamism intertwine with each other. Second, we argue that economic dynamism as well as political dynamism comes in many forms. Third, we argue that dynamism is not a spontaneous or unregulated phenomenon – processes of governance can initiate and seek to manage dynamism. Finally, we recognize that contemporary concern with dynamism can ignore the many states and societies that have experienced periods of stagnation or experienced these changes at the periphery.

Dynamism is typically associated with capitalist industrialization in East Asia, beginning with Japan and spreading first to the four 'little tigers' – South Korea, Taiwan, Hong Kong and Singapore – and then to other South-East Asian states. However, two other trajectories of rapid economic change can be seen in the region. The advanced capitalist states of North America and Australasia have, since the end of the Second World War, undergone very large-scale economic change. In the three decades after the war all enjoyed historically high rates of economic growth and technological innovation that took them to historic heights of personal income and productivity. As they started from a higher base than the growing East Asian economies of the recent era, the raw growth data and sense of economic dynamism appears muted. However, in the USA in particular, economic success has spawned structural economic transformation as well as raw economic growth. Industrial development has given way to a postindustrial service-dominated economy that has become the norm in the West. All the advanced capitalist states of the region have seen the rise and fall of core industries – cars, heavy engineering, textiles – and a huge growth in public sector employment, jobs in finance, banking and real estate, the health and education sectors, the culture industries, microelectronics, etc. The communist states of the Asia-Pacific, until the 1980s, took a third path. In the absence of conventional markets and private property, industrialization has been conducted under the auspices of state and party. While the results of that economic change were less successful than those of Japan and the 'little tigers', the immensity of economic change and the enormous social transformation wrought by, for example, Mao's Great Leap Forward and five-year plans, should not be diminished. While there is considerable diversity to the characteristics of economic dynamism in the Asia-Pacific there is also a shared element; all the region's economies, to a greater or lesser extent, have become increasingly enmeshed with both each other and a wider global economy (see **McGrew and Brook, 1998, Chapters 4, 8 and 12**). While earlier books in this series have explored the economic origins (**Thompson, 1998**) and cultural consequences (**Maidment and Mackerras, 1998**) of these various forms of economic dynamism, we pay particular attention in this volume to their governance. What coalitions of political and economic actors have combined, and in what way, to shape these changes? How have the costs and benefits been distributed, by whom and on what grounds?

The experience of Mao's China points to a very different source and form of dynamism in the post-war era, a political dynamism in which the main energies and forces for social change have come from states, parties and political actors. This is most obviously the case during and immediately after the great political revolutions of the era. Even after the initial breakthrough to independence or communist rule, politics and politicians have been able to mobilize sufficient social enthusiasm and power that politics rather than economics or religion can actually be the decisive force in social change. In China the Cultural Revolution of the 1960s, which initially sprang from ideological and personal conflict within the communist party leadership, consumed the country for a decade. In Indonesia the creation, diffusion and struggles over a state-led nationalist identity and ideology dominated the first decade and a half of the nation's history. In the Anglo-American states of the region, politics has been the leading force less often in the post-war era. Politicians have often found themselves riding and adapting to the waves of economic change. However, on occasion, on specific issues, political power and political motivations have been the leading force in social change. For example, in this book we look at the rise of the Civil Rights movement in the USA in the 1960s which not only brought about a change in the political structures of the US state but helped initiate an entire generation of cultural and ethnic tumult (see Chapter 5). But the capacity of Western civil societies to maintain the kinds of ecstatic and regularized political mobilizations experienced in post-colonial and communist Asia seem limited. More often, a source of political dynamism has been more diffuse and decentralized changes within the social structures and cultural values of these societies. For example, the forces that have amassed behind the environmental and women's movements in the Anglo-American societies have grown out of deeper shifts in cultural values and needs, as well as changing patterns of social stratification.

Not surprisingly the common experience of economic, political, and social dynamism has created great differences in political and cultural regimes in the Asia-Pacific. But perhaps the greatest differences, and certainly some of the greatest political challenges, emerge from what we have called *disjunctures* – the contradictions and conflicts that have occurred within and between the main institutions and social structures of the region during this process of tumultuous change. In this book, we look at how a number of disjunctures have erupted in the political realm, and the modes of governance that have emerged to cope with them. First, the costs of economic development and economic change that receive so much attention in studies of the Asia-Pacific have consistently come into conflict with values of social stability and social solidarity. The destruction of older patterns of employment and family life have created new problems of unemployment and under-employment, urban poverty amongst the elderly and those with disabilities, and wide-spread ill health. This disjuncture has surfaced in the political realm as the struggle to create and transform systems of collective welfare provision. Chapter 5 looks at these struggles in the post-war era in the Anglo-American states of the Asia-Pacific while Chapter 9 provides a suitable contrast looking at the emergence of welfare systems in East Asia. Second, a similar disjuncture between economic development and other needs and values has erupted in the region around environmental issues. It has become clear that the model of economic development pursued in the region has immense environmental costs, locally, regionally and globally (see **Thompson, 1998, Chapter 12**). Moreover, it is equally clear that the current systems of economic organization and the dominant motivations of economic actors consistently come into conflict with the desire to preserve valued landscapes, limit environmental externalities and politically regulate economic production and consumption. The ways in which different societies and different states have tried to respond to these issues, and the practice of governance that has grown up around these struggles are dealt with in Chapters 8 and 10. Third, and perhaps the key disjunctures that the region faces, are in the political realm itself. In the Asia-Pacific, particularly in East Asia, the main political instrument of economic development and social change has been the strong state governing in the context of authoritarian political relationships. However, the very process of economic success that this combination has initiated has also generated new social classes, with new demands that threaten the continued existence of both. We return to the fate of the strong state and the democratic challenge to authoritarianism in Chapters 11 and 12.

How then do the chapters of this book relate to our themes and to the history of the region? The book is structured in three parts. In Part 1, 'State forms and political struggles' (Chapters 2–5), the main lines of political life and the formation and disintegration of states is examined from the end of the Second World War. This provides much of the broad institutional and structural context within which contemporary processes of governance occur. In Part 2, 'Policy, politics and governance' (Chapters 6–10), the focus shifts from particular states or groups of states to particular areas of governance and the social forces that have mobilized to contest them. Finally in Part 3, 'Riding the Juggernaut: political change' (Chapters 11 and 12), two of the key patterns of change and conflict – the disjunctures of politics – in the region are examined: the future of the strong state and the challenge of democratization.

In Chapter 2, Colin Mackerras examines the tidal wave of communist revolution that swept the Asia-Pacific in the immediate post-war era. It provides the closing chapter to the story of China's titanic battle with the West, Japan and itself, and explains the origins of one of the key forms of contemporary diversity in the Asia-Pacific: communist and non-communist states and societies. While explaining the origins and success of the Chinese revolution he also compares it to other successful revolutions – in Korea and Vietnam – and the communist defeats and failures in the Philippines, Indonesia and Malaysia. His account of politics in China since the revolution is an excellent illustration of our idea of political dynamism, for it was the enormous mobilizing energies of Mao's Marxism and the Chinese Communist Party that drove the social and economic transformations of China in the 1950s and the whirlwind of the Cultural Revolution in the 1960s. Only in the late 1970s and early 1980s has political dynamism given way to economic dynamism. It is left open at the end of the chapter as to whether the economic dynamism of contemporary China (and other communist states) will spill over into political, cultural and social change. It is a disjuncture that has yet to fully emerge.

In Chapter 3, Frank Gibney takes up the story of Japanese dynamism in more depth. As I have argued in this chapter, political and military forces provided considerable dynamism in Japanese life before the Second World War, though the impact of capitalist industrialization in the inter-war era itself was beginning to transform the Japanese social landscape. However, it required total defeat and American occupation to tame the military and political dynamism of imperial Japan and for a liberal democratic constitution to be imposed. Subsequently economic dynamism has driven both social change and much of Japanese political life. Gibney seeks to explain the origins and role of the dominant force in post-war Japanese political life – the Liberal Democratic Party (LDP) – and how, in alliance with elite economic bureaucracies and big business, it effectively governed Japanese political and economic life until the end of the Cold War when Japanese politics was thrown into turmoil (see **McGrew and Brook, 1998, Chapter 6**). In the aftermath of this crisis it appears that the LDP has remained stronger than their new challengers and seems poised to be the main force once again in Japan's political life. Yet this is at a time when the social and cultural fabric of Japan has been transformed and the patterns of deference and patronage on which their earlier mode of governance was built seem much more shaky. Once again, the disjunctures between cultural, social and political life are opening up possibilities for political uncertainty and political change.

Bob Elson takes up the story of politics and state building in East Asia outside the two main Asian powers and looks at the processes of decolonization and early state formation from the ruins of European empire in Chapter 4. Not surprisingly, imperial polities left behind innumerable complex problems: underdeveloped economies, simmering ethnic tension and hostilities. The final ejection of imperial power often required prolonged and draining warfare. Elson provides a narrative account of these processes in Indonesia, Vietnam, Thailand, Cambodia, Laos, Malaysia, the Philippines and Burma/Myanmar. In each case he seeks to explain how and why independence came about, what the pattern and balance of indigenous force was at the end of imperial rule, how the conflicts and compromises between those forces generated such a diversity of outcomes, and how so many of these states succumbed to or actively chose restricted democracy or authoritarianism as their mode of rule.

In Chapter 5, George Lafferty and Jacques Bierling offer an instructive contrast to all three of the previous chapters by looking at the main lines of political life and conflict in the Anglo-American states of the region: the USA, Canada, Australia, and New Zealand. While most of the Asia-Pacific has been engaged in the momentous process of political reconstruction and reinvention, all four Anglo-American states came through the war relatively unscathed – both economically and politically. Combined with their great wealth and radically different historical origins this has produced very different politics and modes of governance, and a sharp contrast to those looked at in Chapter 4. In these states, where liberal democracy has been the norm for some time, politics has turned on issues of economic policy, welfare policy and identity politics, and governance has been conducted by a complex mixture of weak states and diverse and active civil societies displaying great inequalities of power. Lafferty and Bierling examine the different fortunes of welfare state institutions and the position of indigenous minorities and women. They argue that some of the differences in modes of governance and the resulting political agendas and public policies can be accounted for in terms of three key factors: the relative strength of the labour movement in these states, their radically different state structures, and the peculiarities of their colonial and ethnic histories.

While Part 1 provides much of the historical and structural context of governance in the Asia-Pacific, Part 2 focuses more closely on who is occupying and using those institutions and what modes of governance arise. The first two chapters deal with the configurations of political forces that exist in the post-war Asia-Pacific. In Chapter 6, Duncan McCargo looks at the relationship between the key elites of the Asia-Pacific: business, bureaucracy and the military. In Chapter 7 William A. Callahan looks at the movements for change from below: amongst agrarians, urban workers and the urban poor, the new middle-class pressure groups and indigenous peoples. Both chapters illustrate the extent to which the governance of the region is contested by state and non-state actors, different state institutions, and different elite and popular groupings. The last three chapters in Part 2 examine the ways in which these forces have attempted to govern and organize their societies in specific policy areas. In Chapter 8 David Martin Jones looks at the governance of the process of economic development. In Chapter 9 Gordon White, Roger Goodman and Huck-ju-Kwon examine the struggles over welfare policy in East Asia, while in Chapter 10 Rowland Maddock looks at the governance of environmental issues across the region.

The issue of difference is addressed across all of the chapters in Part 2. In Chapter 6, the relationships of elites to each other and to the state is contrasted in the classical strong states, such as Japan, with what has come to be known as the bureaucratic polities of Thailand and Indonesia. The chapter also contrasts the complex interrelationships of elites and state systems in capitalist Asia-Pacific with the important role of bureaucrats and the military in the People's Republic of China. Similar contrasts are drawn in Chapter 7, where Callahan seeks to explain the apparent diversity of new social movements and oppositional politics across the region. The issue of dynamism is most centrally addressed in Chapter 8 where David Martin Jones seeks to explain the different political routes to economic development taken in East Asia, while Chapters 9 and 10 compare different modes of governance established in response to the social and environmental costs of that development.

Many of the themes and issues raised in the first ten chapters of the book are brought together in Part 3. Chapter 11 by William Case examines the fate of the strong state in the Asia-Pacific, and Chapter 12 by Jacques Bierling and George Lafferty examines the fate of democracy and democratic politics. The strong state – internally, tightly organized and technocratic; externally, insulated from popular and sectional pressures – has already featured earlier in this book. In Part 1 the account of Japanese and South-East Asian political history explores the strong state's historical and structural origins, while the account of politics in the Anglo-American states in Chapter 5 provides an excellent corrective to the image of a strong state all across the Pacific. Chapter 8 on economic development shows the strong state in action, while Chapter 6 on Asia-Pacific elites explores the social origins and connections of the elites that inhabit and drive those strong states. However, as the struggles over the environment and welfare have shown, the strong state has already begun to be challenged. In Chapter 11 Case reviews the multiple pressures that economic, political and social dynamism in the region are placing on these strong states, and examines how modes of governance are consequently changing. Perhaps the greatest threat to these strong states does not come directly from economic change however important the rise of a global economy has been in diminishing the powers available to national bureaucrats. Rather, the greatest threat has come from the domestic social and cultural transformations wrought across the region by national economic development. For the states of the region face societies and publics that are radically different from those that existed 50 years ago. In Chapter 12 Bierling and Lafferty explore the social forces that have emerged in the Asia-Pacific in the extraordinary half century since the end of the Second World War, social forces which are no longer content to live under unaccountable elites, however benign and however successful they have been at promoting and governing economic growth.

References

Burns, R. (ed.) (1991) *War in the Pacific, 1937–1945*, London, Bison.

Eccleston, B., Dawson, M. and McNamara, D. (eds) (1998) *The Asia-Pacific Profile*, London, Routledge in association with The Open University.

McGrew, A. and Brook, C. (eds) (1998) *Asia-Pacific in the New World Order*, London, Routledge in association with The Open University.

Maidment, R. and Mackerras, C. (eds) (1998) *Culture and Society in the Asia-Pacific*, London, Routledge in association with The Open University.

Thomas, A. *et al*. (1994) *Third World Atlas*, 2nd edn, Buckingham, Open University Press in association with The Open University.

Thompson, G. (ed.) (1998) *Economic Dynamism in the Asia-Pacific*, London, Routledge in association with The Open University.

The Times Atlas of World History (1978) London, Times Books.

Further reading

The following texts all provide good introductions to aspects of the history of politics and governance in the Asia-Pacific.

On democratization and state formation:

Moore, B. (1967) *Social Origins of Dictatorship and Democracy: Lord and Peasant in the Making of the Modern World*, London, Allen Lane.

Rueschemeyer, D., Stephens, E. and Stephens, J. (1992) *Capitalist Development and Democracy*, Cambridge, Polity Press.

Skocpol, T. (1979) *States and Social Revolutions*, Cambridge, Cambridge University Press.

General histories:

Cummings, B. (1997) *Korea's Place in the Sun: a Modern History*, New York, Norton.

Gray, J. (1990) *Rebellions and Revolutions: China from the 1800s to the 1980s*, Oxford, Oxford University Press.

Jansen, M. (ed.) (1989) *The Cambridge History of Japan, Vol.5: the Nineteenth Century*, Cambridge, Cambridge University Press.

Steinberg, D. *et al.* (1987) *In Search of South East Asia: a Modern History*, Honolulu, University of Hawaii Press.

Totman, C. (1993) *Early Modern Japan*, Berkeley, University of California Press.

On the Pacific War:

Calvocoressi, P., Wing, G. and Pritchard, J. (1989) *Total War: the Causes and Consequences of the Second World War*, Harmondsworth, Penguin.

PART 1

State Forms and Political Struggles

CHAPTER 2

Red star over East Asia: communist states and communist parties

Colin Mackerras

2.1 Introduction

One of the most important features of post-Second World War politics in the Asia-Pacific has been the rise of Asian communism. In the inter-war period Asian communism seemed a peripheral political player. Mao and the Chinese communists had withdrawn to remote parts of Jiangxi in south-east China, unable to take on either the Japanese occupiers or the Chinese nationalists. Nascent communist parties in Korea, Vietnam and elsewhere were in their infancy, often no more than small groups of colonially educated intellectuals. By the early 1950s, communist parties had ridden a wave of decolonization, civil war and peasant revolution, that took them to power in North Korea, North Vietnam and China. Communists were active political players in the Philippines, Malaya, Indonesia and Japan. In the following decades, national communist movements were defeated, marginalized and sometimes exterminated in all of these states but continued to win victories in Vietnam, Kampuchea and Laos.

We cannot survey the entire history of East Asia's communist movements in a single chapter, so I have chosen to focus on the three earliest and most successful communist revolutions and communist states – China, North Korea and North Vietnam. In Section 2.2 I consider some of the reasons that explain the success of these communist revolutions, and some of the reasons for their failure in South-East Asia. One of the key reasons for the success of these movements was the appeal of the Asian communists' own brand of Marxism. But why should this uniquely European body of thought be translatable into the societies of post-war East Asia? In Section 2.3 I examine the legacies of Marx and Lenin and their translation into a successful political idiom in East Asia. With the assumption of power, Asian communists soon set about creating a very distinctive form of politics and government. In Section 2.4 I examine how, in the post revolutionary era, the party-states of communist East Asia were created. In Section 2.5 I explore the distinctive institutions of the People's Republics – the Communist Party and the government apparatus built alongside it. Then in Section 2.6 I examine how the process of governance emerges from within these complex institutions and explore the similarities and variations amongst communist states. Finally in Section 2.7 I ask how it is that these communist states have been able to survive despite the unleashing of economic reforms and the end of the Cold War – events that were sufficient to destroy the regimes of Central and Eastern Europe and ultimately the Soviet Union itself.

2.2   East Asia's communist revolutions: successes and failures

Among those many countries of North-East and South-East Asia occupied by the Japanese during the Second World War communist parties came to power in all (or almost all) of two, China and Vietnam, and the northern half of one, Korea. In several others, notably Malaya, Indonesia and the Philippines, communist movements were strong for a time, but ultimately failed to make a successful revolution. Why should communism have proved so successful in the region? Anti-imperialist, and especially anti-Japanese nationalism played a role in the politics of all these countries, and mostly it favoured the communists. Indeed, the bitter anti-communism of the Japanese and popular reaction against them were major factors in communist successes almost everywhere in East Asia. Another factor assisting the communists in most countries was landlordism. The Asian countryside displayed enormous inequalities of land holdings, as well as other social inequities. This provided rich soil for the egalitarian politics of communist parties. The charismatic leadership and political guile of men such as Mao Zedong in China and Ho Chi Minh in Vietnam were yet further factors assisting communism. That leadership was both ideological and military. The strategies of guerrilla warfare pursued by Asian communists, in which the fighters are more or less indistinguishable from ordinary people, proved very difficult to combat. Of course, the precise course of communist victories showed considerable variation in the different countries of East Asia. In China, the Chinese Communist Party (CCP) went through a long and tortuous history before coming to power. Holding its First Congress in the middle of 1921, it did not actually gain victory against the ruling Nationalist Party (Kuomintang) until 1949. The Japanese invasion, apart from giving the CCP the chance to exercise real nationalist leadership, also exhausted the Kuomintang. By the end of the war, the Kuomintang was also internally corrupt and economically incompetent. Spiralling inflation destroyed what was left of the economy.

Mao Zedong's reputation and legacy are complex to assess but his political fortunes can be clearly linked to his understanding of nationalism, his awareness of the importance of the social revolution and his sheer persistence. The Long March of 1934–35, which brought the CCP forces from near defeat and total exhaustion in Jiangxi in the south-east of China to northern Shaanxi in the north-west, would have spelt the end of most parties. Huge numbers of troops were lost and party organization was shattered. But Mao refused to give up and even used the experience to gain new supporters and to develop his strategic and theoretical ideas, so that the CCP could actually benefit from the war against Japan. In the communist bases in northern Shaanxi and elsewhere he was able to carry out land reform, and thus appeal to the serious poverty and exploitation which the peasantry suffered at the hands of landlords. His appeal to women's equality, in the slogan that 'women hold up half the sky', also assisted him in his revolutionary endeavour, for they were the victims of serious discrimination, especially in the countryside.

Wu Yinxian portrait of Mao, 1945

By contrast, the Nationalist Party, led by Chiang Kai-shek, failed to live up to its nationalist tag. It was slow to resist Japan, allocating more effort to destroying the CCP, which, for all its faults, was at least Chinese. It was not until the Xi'an Incident of December 1936, when two of his subordinates actually arrested him outside the Shaanxi provincial capital Xi'an for his passivity towards Japan, that Chiang was persuaded to go all-out to resist the imperialists to the east. Even then his record of resistance was less effective than it should have been and his claims to nationalism were undercut by the extent to which he came to rely on the USA in the last few years of his rule. In addition, Chiang Kai-shek held no appeal for the poor peasantry, since his rural alliances were mostly with the landlord class, the very people who were exploiting the peasantry so savagely.

As Japan capitulated, the Soviet Union occupied Manchuria and the northern part of Korea in August 1945. In the case of Manchuria historians still debate as to the real contribution of the Soviets to the final victory of the CCP, but in the case of Korea they were undoubtedly crucial to communist success. Although the communists in Korea relied heavily on the Soviet Union to come to power, they helped their own cause considerably. Kim Il Sung and the elite of the North Korean left could call on a significant reserve of political and ideological support and internal coherence from their long fight against the Japanese in Manchuria and elsewhere. This legacy was supplemented in the first years of his regime by carrying out thorough-going social reform, equalizing land holdings and raising the status of women. The victory of the communists in Vietnam did not come immediately after the end of the Second World War, but in 1954 in the north of the country and not until 1975 in the south. There is some detail of this long and extraordinarily painful process in **McGrew and Brook (1998, Chapter 2)**. Just as in Korea, the USA made a major troop commitment. But in contrast to Korea, where it succeeded in preventing the communists from taking over the whole country, in Vietnam the communists were able to reunite the country under their control. Why did the economic and military colossus of the USA fail to defeat the technologically backward peasant country that was Vietnam? It is notoriously difficult for formal armies to cope with guerrilla warfare. The protest movement in the USA and other Western countries also produced an enormous effect on American determination to win. But the most important reason was probably the nationalism of the Vietnamese. The armies of the Americans and their non-Vietnamese allies were not too different from a foreign occupation, whereas the North Vietnamese were fighting for their own people. Their nationalism gave them the incentive to accept casualties, however great, and never to give up, however difficult the struggle.

In Malaya, the main support for communism came from the Chinese, with many Malays actually collaborating with the Japanese. The Malay Communist Party was thus largely Chinese and lacked the nationalist ethnic credentials to appeal to the Malay population. Armed insurrection began in mid 1948, but soon began to lose support. There were several reasons for this, including anti-Chinese feeling, the ability of the British to bring a degree of economic prosperity depriving the communists of appeal for their radical programme, and the effective British anti-guerrilla strategies. With the substantial defeat of the guerrillas, the British granted Malaya independence in August 1957.

Finally, in the Philippines, the anti-Japanese cause became interwoven with the peasant struggle against rampant landlordism that had thrived under US colonialism. Nationalism and the land revolution thus combined to strengthen the Hukbalahap (People's Anti-Japanese Army). Although the Huk rebellion continued to do well in the first years after the war, the election of Ramon Magsaysay in 1953 reversed their fortunes. His ability to carry out land reform cut the ground from under the feet of the Huks, and the fact that the Philippines were islands prevented allies from sending them effective support.

So there was a range of reasons why communist parties were victorious in China, North Korea and Vietnam, but failed in Malaya and the Philippines, amongst other places. Nationalism, directed mainly against the Japanese and the Americans, was a central factor in all cases. The appeal to social justice, especially land reform, carried weight in favour of the communists in several cases but was undercut in others. The skilful use of guerrilla warfare and outside support were reasons for their success in some countries but in others opponents succeeded in negating both factors.

2.3   Asian communism and Marxism-Leninism

The ideology of Asian communist parties derives from very particular readings of Marx and Lenin. The appeal of Marx's work to Asian radicals in the early part of the twentieth century is not immediately obvious. Marx argued that socialism and communism could only be built in the most advanced capitalist states. In the absence of rapid and sustained capitalist development, no mature working class could emerge to challenge the ruling classes. Moreover, socialism could not be built in poor countries. Capitalism was to furnish not only a revolutionary class but the expansion of the means of production to the point where material abundance could underwrite a free and egalitarian social and political utopia. Neither of these conditions existed in East Asia. If they did anywhere it was Japan rather than China, Korea or Vietnam. The impact of Marxist thought in East Asia was mediated by Russia and then the Soviet Union. Lenin, recognizing that the same arguments that limited Marx's relevance to East Asia could be applied to Tsarist Russia, made a number of decisive innovations in Marxist thought. First, he argued that revolution was possible in more backward countries. But the agent of that revolution could not be tiny and politically immature working classes but a vanguard party of disciplined intellectuals and activists. Second, he argued that capitalism could stimulate the emergence of these movements but not directly. Imperialism, which was the international expression of the growing conflict and competition amongst capitalist states, could provide the social transformations which could initiate social protest. If guided by the party correctly they could produce a revolution. The task of the party would then be to leapfrog the process of capitalist development and initiate a process of rapid industrialization and modernization but under the auspices of a communist party and radical egalitarian ideology. Thus, European Marxism was made relevant to both Russia and East Asian societies.

Lenin's notion of the party required a highly disciplined and tightly knit organization. It must network in cells which would reach to every corner of the land. Despite the emphasis on equality which characterized Marx, the party must be strongly hierarchical and Lenin was a great advocate of strong leadership. At the top the leadership must be united and able to prevail everywhere. It must be assisted by a central committee and be able to pass its views and dictates downwards through a network of party committees at lower levels.

It was Lenin's model of the party that really captured the imagination of East Asian communists, and was even highly influential in the Chinese Kuomintang. However, Mao Zedong was always ambivalent about Lenin's views on the party. Asian communists have exalted the party but placed a stronger faith in the mobilization of the masses than Lenin. During the Cultural Revolution Mao was to appeal directly to the masses of Chinese youth over the heads of his own CCP stalwarts. He encouraged the active humiliation of party leaders and attacks on bureaucracy in the name of revolutionary purity. He was prepared to throw the CCP and the country into turmoil in the hope that it could eventually lead to a more just, more equal and more revolutionary society. Mao found very little support for his views among other senior communists, most of whom thought the Cultural Revolution both crazy and destructive. In conclusion, the communist parties which came to power in East Asia were not just Marxist, but Marxist-Leninist. Leninism provided a bridge between European Marxism and Asian conditions. It allowed for nationalism and a major role for the peasants. It also stressed the key role of the party in the revolution.

2.4   The development of the party state

The establishment of new states in the People's Republic of China (PRC), the Democratic People's Republic of Korea (DPRK) and the Socialist Republic of Vietnam (SRV), involved a tight relationship between the ruling party and the government it led, in which charismatic leaders dominated while at the same time encouraging mass participation in what the party-dominated state was trying to achieve.

The most important example of the Asian communist state is the PRC, founded by Mao Zedong and the CCP in 1949. In September 1949, Mao and the CCP he led held a large-scale meeting of a body called the Chinese People's Political Consultative Conference consisting of a united front of the various forces opposed to Chiang Kai-shek, it adopted an interim constitution called the Common Programme and determined to establish the PRC with its capital in Beijing. In consolidating his new state in the early 1950s, Mao carried out an intensive land reform programme throughout the country which was aimed at destroying the landlord class and distributing land among the peasantry. In May 1950 his state adopted a new Marriage Law, which aimed to promote the status of women and abolish such practices as arranged marriages which had discriminated against them in the past.

From the beginning, the PRC was designated as a unitary and centralized state. Although minorities were allowed to control autonomous places, in fact Mao's state had no time at all for secession, any attempts at which it suppressed quickly and brutally. In 1950 Mao's troops re-established Chinese control over Tibet, the new regime signing an agreement in May 1951 with that of the Tibetan spiritual and temporal ruler, the Dalai Lama, by which Tibet would be reincorporated into the PRC but allowed to remain autonomous politically and socially. When a rebellion broke out against Chinese rule in March 1959 it was put down speedily but brutally, with the Dalai Lama fleeing to India and later establishing a government-in-exile there. The Chinese carried out reforms in Tibet and established the Tibet Autonomous Region in 1965. Meanwhile in Xinjiang, home to the Uygurs and other Muslim minorities, the Nationalist Party-appointed governor had cabled his surrender to the CCP in September 1949. Although the Uygurs had for decades been trying to set up an independent Islamic republic in the region, secessionism proved a less serious problem in Xinjiang than in Tibet, enabling the establishment of the Xinjiang Uygur Autonomous Region in 1955.

A vitally important feature of the PRC which Mao established was his own near total domination of the party and state and the series of mass campaigns he carried out as a way of implementing his reforms. Although these measures proved effective in many ways, and they did indeed go a long way towards eradicating corruption as well as beginning the establishment of a modern industry and adding to China's infrastructure, they also brought serious instability to China and were extremely traumatic not only to the designated enemy classes, such as the landlords and big bourgeoisie, but also to any intellectuals, journalists or artists who stepped even slightly out of line with the prevailing Mao-dictated orthodoxy. In 1958 Mao Zedong launched his Great Leap Forward, in which he tried to involve the masses in a large-scale programme to industrialize and establish the communist society (see also **Eccleston et al., 1998, pp.360–2**). A major part of the programme was the establishment of people's communes in the countryside. This proved disastrous in practice, coinciding as it did with very unfavourable seasons which combined serious flooding in some parts of China and catastrophic drought in others. The result was a major famine which, even Chinese official sources now concede, killed many millions of people.

Although Mao's star declined in the early 1960s as a result of the failure of the Great Leap Forward, he staged a comeback in the Cultural Revolution. In theory this was an attempt to reshape Chinese society in a more egalitarian mould, based on the theory that class struggle continued into the socialist period and that the bourgeoisie had 'wormed its way' even into the CCP; two leaders, President Liu Shaoqi and CCP General Secretary Deng Xiaoping, being castigated as the main 'bourgeois' representatives. Mao's notion of mass participation escalated when he set up groups of youthful Red Guards with orders that they should attack his enemies and put his ideas into effect. Most of these young people were so intensely indoctrinated that they responded not only enthusiastically but fanatically. It may be that they were sincere in their beliefs, but their ideological motivation drove them to highly irrational and dangerous behaviour, for instance humiliating their teachers in public, destroying religious buildings and damaging ancient monuments. Another pronounced feature of the Cultural Revolution was a strengthening of the personality cult of Mao himself. His works were quoted endlessly with a little red book of his quotations selling hundreds of millions of copies, badges of Mao circulated in many millions and many statues of him were erected, while 'long live Chairman Mao' became a slogan repeated *ad nauseam*. Perceived in terms of

Red Army soldiers read from the little red book, 1969

struggle in which violence was permissible, the Cultural Revolution threw the country into very serious disorder, even involving short and localized but savage civil wars in 1967 and 1968. Although a kind of political order based on the Cultural Revolutionary ideal was set up briefly, it proved very unstable and required continuing and destructive political campaigns orchestrated by Mao to keep it alive.

No sooner did Mao die in September 1976 than the principal supporters of the Cultural Revolution, termed the 'gang of four', were overthrown, one of the quartet being his widow Jiang Qing. An interregnum followed led by the colourless Hua Guofeng, but at the end of 1978 the reformist Deng Xiaoping rose to power and brought in a completely different kind of Marxist-Leninist regime which gave free scope to the entrepreneurial spirit of the Chinese and propounded that what China needed was not leftist revolution but modernization. The slogan Deng put forward was 'to get rich is glorious'. At the same time China opened itself very deliberately to the outside world, aiming thereby to bring about the kind of technology transfer and modern management and thinking that could industrialize China and raise the standard of living of its people. The effect was to produce a period of very rapid economic growth and social liberalization, but also the major expansion of ills such as widening regional, class, gender and nationality inequalities, and rising crime rates.

Politically, Deng Xiaoping was quite clear that the CCP should remain in power, its basic structure and authority unchanged. At the same time, the processes of the state must rest on law and order, not mass participation. Almost without exception, the leaders who had risen to power during the Cultural Revolution were demoted or dismissed, while the leaders of the new period came from the ranks of those who had

Special trial of the 'gang of four' and their allies, 1981. From left to right: Yao Wenyuan, Jiang Tengjiao, Qiu Huizuo, Wu Faxian and Jiang Qing

suffered humiliation and dismissal as a result of Mao's brainchild. Although Deng never dominated the CCP to the extent that Mao had done, and was never the subject of any personality cult even remotely approaching that given to Mao, he was usually able to get his way on major issues and appointments through his personal authority and networks, especially those with the military. The overall effect of Deng's rule in political terms has been the decline of the CCP's power, with far greater space allowed for alternatives, one of the main ones being a form of grassroots village democracy which has taken root since the late 1980s. There have even been the tentative beginnings of what is often called 'civil society' with its emphasis on non-state, autonomous centres or groups of influence. At the same time, official corruption began expanding as early as the late 1970s to become a serious and growing problem in the 1980s and 1990s.

China remained a unitary state which suppressed attempts at secession. However, the 1980s and 1990s saw an upsurge in ethnic identity and a strong growth in separatism in Tibet and Xinjiang. In Tibet, this began with major demonstrations for independence in September and October 1987 and further such rioting in 1988 and March 1989. This led to the declaration of martial law for the first time in the PRC. In 1990 a secessionist rebellion was staged in southern Xinjiang and disturbances have continued in both Tibet and Xinjiang in the 1990s, the most serious case as of early 1998 being in Yining, north-western Xinjiang, in February 1997. The Chinese state has reacted to these separatist attempts with a carrot-and-stick approach. On the one hand, it has tried to win over the Tibetans, Uygurs and other minorities with major economic infusion which aims to bring about quick and significant rises in the standard of living of the people. On the other hand, the Chinese authorities have suppressed all separatist attempts brutally and quickly.

In Vietnam, the Communist Party won the war against the Americans in 1975, with the country formally reunified as the SRV in July 1976. Reform policies were introduced by a Vietnamese Communist Party (VCP) Central Committee Plenum in September 1979 and, after a great deal of debate, adopted by the Fifth National Congress in March 1982. In the late 1980s free-market reforms were introduced. Although the policies of reform were similar in direction in China and Vietnam, the weight of evidence is that both countries saw the need for reform independently at about the same time. It was for domestic reasons that the SRV instituted reform, and there was no suggestion that it was following China's lead. Indeed, in the late 1970s relations between China and Vietnam fell to such a low ebb that they even fought a border war in February and March 1979. Vietnam had undergone great trauma in the war against the USA and its allies, but it never went through any process even remotely similar to the Cultural Revolution in China and the personality cult of Ho Chi Minh was extremely mild by comparison with that of Mao Zedong, let alone Kim Il Sung. The overall result of the reforms was that economic growth accelerated and the standard of living of most people rose, with political control loosening and opening more interesting and broader life-style possibilities.

Like the Vietnamese leadership, Kim Il Sung was highly critical of the Cultural Revolution, even though the DPRK never actually quarrelled openly with China. In contrast both to China and Vietnam, he never adopted reform policies, and allowed his country to remain isolated from the rest of the world. Although economic growth was good in the 1980s, the long-term effect of his failure to reform was disastrous. In the 1990s economic decline set in, especially after Kim Il Sung's death in 1994. His son Kim Jong Il proved totally unable to control the situation and in 1997 serious famine became apparent in a country which had once enjoyed quite good living conditions. The reasons for the collapse are manifold but the implication seems inescapable that the personality cult of Kim Il Sung had reached proportions so serious as to render it almost impossible for the people to do without him.

2.5   Party and government in communist polities

In the People's Republic of China, the Democratic People's Republic of Korea and the Socialist Republic of Vietnam, the party is regarded as the vanguard of the proletariat and is the organ of greatest power within the state. For example, Article 4 of the Vietnamese State Constitution states that the Vietnamese Communist Party 'is the only force leading the state and society, and the main factor determining all successes of the Vietnamese revolution.' The 1982 Chinese State Constitution has several references to the CCP in its Preamble, but makes no claims for it to be the 'only force' of leadership. The DPRK 1972 State Constitution mentions the importance of Marxism-Leninism in several places, but gives very little space indeed to the Korean Workers' Party (KWP). But the differences in the three constitutions are deceptive. The party is in fact by far the most important power-holder in all three societies. The government, army and other social organizations are all subordinate to it.

The extent of the party's power does not mean that these three countries are necessarily one-party states. In the PRC, for example, there are eight 'democratic parties' which still exist as of the 1990s. These include the Revolutionary Committee of the Chinese Nationalist Party, the left-wing of Chiang Kai-shek's party which went over to the CCP in the late 1940s. The eight democratic parties formed a united front with the CCP in 1948, responding to the CCP's invitation to hold the Chinese People's Political Consultative Conference. This was the body which in September 1949 actually adopted the Common Programme, in effect the interim Constitution of the PRC, and determined to set up the PRC on 1 October 1949. The Chinese People's Political Consultative Conference still exists and meets from time to time. However, neither it nor the democratic parties exercise any really meaningful power. The democratic parties make no pretence to being 'opposition' parties in the Western sense. However, the CCP still undertakes to consult with them, and to accept political supervision from them. In return they undertake to accept the leadership of the CCP.

The highest organ of the party is the National Party Congress. These congresses summarize achievements since the last congress through extensive reporting, lay down the party line for the next period, and may adopt a revised constitution. They also elect the Central Committee for the following period. The number of people taking part in national party congresses is about 2,000 or more. The Central Committee of a communist party is supposed to run the affairs of the party while the congress is not in session. The number of people belonging to the Central Committee varies according to the time and country, but is of the order of 200 to 300. The Central Committee tends to meet every year or so in plenary session. These sessions are termed plenums and frequently reach decisions of critical importance for the future of the party and the country which they rule. For example, in China the Third Plenum of the Eleventh Central Committee (December 1978) saw the adoption of the reform and modernization programme which has characterized the Chinese governmental process ever since. It was also the meeting at which Deng Xiaoping began his rise to positions of such enormous power in the 1980s and early 1990s. The Sixth Plenum, held in 1981, issued a long document which summarized and evaluated the history of the CCP to that time. In particular, it denounced the Cultural Revolution in extremely strong terms, declaring it both destructive and fraudulent, in effect a massive con job on the Chinese people. In addition, it downgraded the status of Mao Zedong in the history of the CCP: he was a great leader until 1957 when he began to go down the false ultra-leftist path; by the time of the Cultural Revolution, for which he bears major responsibility, he had gone crazy and abandoned Marxism. The Sixth Plenum document describes his misunderstanding of his own position and abilities as 'his tragedy'.

Plenums of the party are not open to the public in any of the three countries under discussion here. The media hardly mention them, sometimes not even their existence, until they are over. The conclusion of these plenums is always considered a great success or victory and is followed by extensive coverage in the press. Such coverage includes the full text of the communiqué and the speeches by the main leader or leaders, as well as laudatory editorials and discussion in the official press. When the plenum is not in session the party's work is carried on by its Political Bureau (Politburo for short). This consists of the most important leaders of the Central Committee and meets on a regular or frequent basis. In China the most powerful body is the Standing Committee of its Politburo, an extremely elite group which, as of 1998, had only seven members. In mid 1996 the Vietnam Communist Party's Eighth Congress set up a five-person Standing Board of its Politburo, arousing concern over the implied concentration of power.

Although it is the party which wields the greatest power, there is in fact also a nominally separate government structure in communist countries. It mirrors the party structure in a great many ways. For instance, in China the highest non-party body is the National People's Congress, which elects a Standing Committee equivalent to the Central Committee. The Chairman of the National People's Congress Standing Committee is one of the highest government members in the country. In the SRV the equivalent body is called the National Assembly, and in the DPRK the Supreme People's Assembly. In all three countries the highest non-party congress is generally subordinate to the Communist Party. However, there are gradations here. In the DPRK, despite its near total absence in the state constitution, party power is greatest. In Vietnam in the 1980s, the National Assembly took quite deliberate measures to expand its own functions, especially in matters of law, with the aim of reducing its reactive rubber-stamp image. These moves were resisted by VCP conservatives, but did make a difference to the country's administration anyway. In China, the National People's Congress was regarded as merely a rubber stamp of the CCP until the early 1990s, when it showed quite clear signs of much more open debate than had been the case before. At the March 1993 Opening Session of the Eighth National People's Congress, Premier Li Peng's report excited far more intense debate than anybody expected. It was adopted in the end, but only after quite a few amendments had been made.

The non-party congress can adopt or amend the constitution, which in communist countries is much more flexible than in Western states. In China there have been four, adopted in 1954, 1975, 1978 and 1982. These constitutions lay down the structure of the state governance and define the rights of the citizens, among other matters. Although the constitutions of communist states are very democratic in their rhetoric, they have not been adhered to rigidly. For instance, the DPRK Constitution adopted at the end of 1972 lays down 'genuine democratic rights and liberties', equal rights for all, and 'the freedoms of speech, the press, assembly, association and demonstration'. In fact, few would argue that any of these freedoms exist in the DPRK. In China in the days of Mao, it was possible for the party to ignore or override the state constitution very easily. Although things have improved enormously in this regard since 1978, it still remains possible to bypass the constitution if state elites feel themselves under serious threat. For example, during the student demonstrations of 1989, when Deng Xiaoping used his power as Chairman of the Military Commissions of the State and of the Central Committee to suppress the demonstrations, he argued that he was in fact quelling a counter-revolutionary rebellion.

There is a government structure at various levels of the community in communist states. In each case it mirrors the central government structure very closely. In China there is a considerable degree of autonomy in economic matters, and the minority nationality areas are called autonomous. In cases of emergency, however, the central state can, and does, exert very considerable power. None of the Marxist-Leninist states is in any way comparable to a federation in terms of the extent of autonomy enjoyed. In 1988, following the adoption of a law encouraging village elections the preceding year, a form of grassroots democracy was initiated in China's Shandong Province and subsequently spread to most other provinces. Villagers elected a council to take charge of business formerly decided by the local party secretary. The significance of this was that it transferred some of the grassroots power of the CCP to elected representatives. Most of the council members are senior citizens, who enjoy the most prestige and respect in Chinese society and have more organizational experience. They are supposed to consult with other villagers before making decisions. A spokesperson for the Chinese Ministry of Civil Affairs, quoted in the *China Daily* (29 September 1995, p.3), claimed of this grassroots democratization programme that it had helped maintain public order and narrowed the gap between officials and the public, as well as freeing authorities to pay more attention to economic development.

There is a process for joining the CCP and other communist parties. It is necessary to be screened, to believe in Marxism-Leninism and to pay dues. For the government, however, there are elections. These are not general elections in the sense of everybody being able to vote on one day for the national government. Instead the elections take place over a period, and are based on a tier system. What this means is that people vote at the lowest level, after which the elected representatives vote for the next layer up, reaching finally to the national level. Under the PRC Electoral Law of 1979 anybody may stand for election and be elected. While most of those elected are in fact members of the CCP, it is possible for members of other parties, or indeed no party at all, to stand for election. There is virtually no possibility under this system of groups opposed to the Communist Party gaining enough power to overthrow the communists in China, North Korea or Vietnam. However, in China it is certainly possible for people with views alternate to the CCP to stand and win.

In summary, it is the party which holds greatest power in East Asia's communist states. Although there is a government structure it is subordinate to, and dependent on, the party. The party has a pyramidal structure which places power at the top, while allowing for very substantial, even mass membership at the bottom.

2.6 Government and governance in communist states

What are the likely implications for the mode of governance in communist states given the ruling party's adherence to Marxism-Leninism? One would expect that the public sector of the economy would be substantial and that private ownership of the means of production would be sparse and government control of the economy intense. Private enterprise and the workings of the market, including market determination of the prices of commodities, especially essential ones, would be very highly restricted. One of the core aims of such a system of governance is to move towards social equality. Thus social welfare should be good and public facilities should receive a great deal of attention.

One would expect very substantial state intervention in the economy, society and politics, much more than in a free enterprise system. There is a widely held view that states run by communist parties are not as free as others, the word totalitarian being frequently applied to them, with its implications that the power of the state is total, and ordinary freedoms of thought, religion, the press, association and public expressions of dissent banned or suppressed. Therefore one would expect the legal system of these states to be more or less totally subordinate to the party, with no hint of an independent judiciary.

To some extent these phenomena are indeed found in the PRC, DPRK and SRV. All three have undertaken land reforms, and instituted policies in favour of equality between the sexes and other measures promoting social equality. However, it is not possible to make blanket distinctions between states run by communist parties, and those by other systems. Furthermore, the three countries under discussion here are themselves very different from each other, despite their common Confucian culture and communist rule. Other states in East Asia share cultural heritages with the communist states which, in many cases, unite them more strongly than the political system divides them. Thus the Republic of Korea and Taiwan both have traditions as Confucian and authoritarian as do the DPRK and the PRC.

The country which fits the above description of a communist state most nearly is the DPRK. There is very substantial state intervention in the lives of the people in all kinds of ways, economic, social and political. The public sector of the economy is large, with private ownership of the means of production extremely sparse. Certainly the polity is extremely authoritarian, but in theory humane. Kim Il Sung was regarded as the great and fatherly leader, who cared for his people as a parent does a child. Social welfare was egalitarian with free health and education and very cheap housing available to all, as well as an excellent pension system. Freedoms are not widely enjoyed, with virtually no non-party, let alone anti-party, expressions of opinion in the media or published works, very little open religious life and ubiquitous spies ensuring loyalty to the KWP. Article 140 of the constitution specifies that the courts are independent. However, my enquiries about an independent legal system during visits to the DPRK in 1981, 1982 and 1986 drew more or less complete blanks. There is a legal system, I was told, 'but our society is so free of conflict that it is hardly ever used'.

During the time that the CCP has been in power, China is probably next to the DPRK in corresponding to the features listed earlier for communist party rule. However, in the period since 1978 it has diverged increasingly from that model. Moreover, China's history under the CCP shows far more internal variation than Korea's under Kim Il Sung and his son. As a country it is incomparably larger and more diverse and its political leadership more various. Under Mao the degree of state control over the economy and society was considerable. Freedom of religion was strongly restricted but at least mosques, monasteries and churches operated in the early years. Almost all were closed down in 1966 during the Cultural Revolution. The press did not express anti-CCP opinion in the 1950s, but some newspapers did put forward a variety of opinions on matters about which the CCP was neutral. However, the Cultural Revolution saw a degree of aridity and uniformity worse than at any time since the beginning of a modern press in China. Social welfare was reasonably good in the state-owned enterprises, health services were available free to workers and at half price to their dependants. Female workers got two months off on full pay to bear children and excellent and comparatively cheap child-minding services were available. Housing was extremely cheap in the state enterprises, although commodities like electricity and gas were not free. There was a legal system, and the 1954 Constitution laid down its independence. But in any matter where politics entered into the case even remotely, the CCP exercised fairly tight control.

In the 1980s and 1990s, the system has changed drastically, despite the retention of the CCP in power. Although the state sector still includes the most important industries and other enterprises, such as the railways and iron and steel industry, the private sector has grown enormously since the period of reform began at the end of 1978. Joint enterprises with foreign companies have become increasingly important in the economy. Moreover, there is a widespread view, both in the West and in China itself, that the state-run enterprises are far less efficient than the private, collective or joint Chinese-foreign ones. Freedoms have increased enormously, although they are still less clear even than in authoritarian capitalist countries in East Asia. Religions are widely practised and tolerated, provided they pose no threat to Chinese unity or to CCP rule. In particular, Tibetan Buddhism has frequently suffered repression due to its links with Tibetan nationalism and separatism. Ordinary people talk far more openly than they did in the 1970s. Although the press cannot, and does not, openly express opinions which threaten CCP rule, it is incomparably more varied, free and interesting, and less rigid and strident than was the case in the 1970s, let alone the 1960s. One observer writes aptly: 'This is not Western freedom. But it is a different world from the effort at total control of people's thought which used to be the defining characteristic of Chinese communism' (Overholt, 1993, p.88).

The legal system has developed enormously. Although the control of the CCP remains tight in highly politicized trials, in the run-of-the-mill cases the law operates reasonably fairly. Since the early 1990s, there have even been a few cases where individuals have taken state organizations to court and won. While this remains abnormal, such an eventuality would have been completely unthinkable even a few years before. Change in the direction of the rule of law, as opposed to the law of rule, has proven more rapid than most people expected. On the other hand, social welfare has declined greatly with the rise of the market economy. In the 1990s, fees have been, and are being, introduced at all levels of the education system, even including the primary level. Although they are still quite moderate, they are quite high enough to turn away very poor people. While members of state organizations can still get free health care, it is not widely available elsewhere. Housing is increasingly something purchased on the market, with even state enterprises no longer feeling the need to supply cheap accommodation to their workers. Although even now the disparities in wealth in China are probably nowhere as large as in many other East Asian countries, such as the Philippines, inequalities have widened enormously since the late 1970s. There is definitely an emergent wealthy middle class with considerable disposable income, a phenomenon which simply did not exist in China in the late 1970s.

Turning to the third country, Vietnam, we find similarities with China amid substantial differences. Vietnam's socialist system was developed under Ho Chi Minh from 1954. It had a great deal in common with China during the 1950s when the two countries were on very good terms with each other. However, the Vietnamese system was also much influenced by its own culture, which is somewhat more relaxed in style than the Chinese, and in particular by the fact that the country was at war for most of the period before reunification.

A major point of interest concerning Vietnam after 1976 is that sharp differences have persisted between the north and south, despite the fact that the country had been formally reunited and the SRV founded. The south has remained far more free-wheeling in its approach to commerce, industry and social life in general. Although there were restrictions on freedom everywhere, there was a far more vigorous religious life in the south than the north, with a more varied press. Saigon, or Ho Chi Minh City as it was renamed, remains a more lively city than Hanoi, with far more signs of capitalism. The result of the reform policies adopted in March 1982 has been to lift many of the state-imposed restrictions and move the economy in the direction of free enterprise. Social welfare has never been as good in Vietnam as in the DPRK, and poverty is very widespread. However, while the reforms have given overall economic performance an enormous boost, they have also been injurious to the social welfare system. When the mid-term conference of the Seventh National VCP took place in January 1994, it opted in favour of continuing the move in the direction of a market economy. At the same time, anxiety was expressed over the decline in health care and education, with a stress laid on the need to fight unemployment and poverty. Vietnam and China thus share quite a few major reform policies. Their models of development also have one other feature in common, namely the accent is on economic rather than political reform. In this they have differed very sharply from Gorbachev's Soviet Union, which gave earlier priority to political democratization while keeping the old communist patterns of economic development. In both cases economic reform has brought widespread corruption in its wake, a problem about which the authorities of both countries are quite open.

2.7   The survival of Asian communism

In 1989, the communist parties of Central and Eastern Europe all collapsed. The Communist Party of the Soviet Union followed suit at the end of 1991. One of the most interesting questions this raises is why the communist parties of China, Vietnam and the DPRK resisted the trend. Is it that East Asia is different after all? Are there special characteristics applying to the communist parties of East Asia which separate them from those of Europe? Possibly the most important reason for the endurance of the communist parties of East Asia is that their nationalist credentials were firmer. All three parties showed leadership against the Japanese occupation, especially the CCP. Both the CCP and the Vietnamese Workers' Party came to power after very long and intensive nationalist wars against very strong enemies. These two parties were not simply put in place by Soviet troops, as was the case with almost all the communist parties of Europe, they were not imposed by force on peoples unwilling to accept their rule. In the case of the KWP, while it is true Soviet troops put it in power in the first place, it acquired nationalist credentials during the Korean War which were not matched by any counterparts in Europe.

The nationalist credentials of communist elites have been strengthened by leadership, or attempted leadership, in the reunification of divided countries. In the case of Vietnam this has proven to be successful with the establishment of the reunified SRV in 1976. In Korea, the KWP places enormous weight on national reunification, even though this has yet to occur and will probably never do so in a way it favours. In the case of China, reunification is less important than in Vietnam or Korea simply because of the extreme unevenness in size of the two divided parts. Yet, national unity and the Taiwan issue loom very large indeed in the ideology, policy and nationalism of the CCP. This was displayed with great clarity by the anger shown by the PRC government when the USA allowed the Taiwan President Lee Teng-hui to visit in June 1995. The PRC government stated repeatedly in its propaganda that this was tantamount to a threat to undermine Chinese unity.

A second major reason why these three parties have outlived the other communist parties is the Confucian tradition shared by all three countries (see also **Maidment and Mackerras, 1998, Chapter 11**). There are several relevant points in this tradition. The first is its authoritarianism. This feature sits very comfortably with the communist parties' own ideological make-up. It can be agreed that people accept the ruling power more readily than might be the case in Europe. 'Tremble and obey' was how the emperors of China formerly ended their edicts, and the Confucian imperial system was mirrored and copied both in Korea and Vietnam. A second feature of Confucianism is the desire for stability, and dislike of chaos. 'Women zui pa de shi luan' ('what we most fear is confusion') is a phrase sometimes heard in China, and it results directly from the Confucian distaste for rebellion and social disorder.

Of course in this context one cannot avoid noticing that, despite this Confucian tradition, all three countries have undergone violent upheavals and revolutions in the twentieth century. But two points are notable here. One is that, beside the Confucian authoritarian tradition of stability, lies one of resistance to outside invasion. This is strong in China, Korea and Vietnam, and, especially, for Vietnam, it has on several specific occasions been directed against China itself. The second point concerns the Chinese people: generally docile to authority but when really stirred up against it becoming like an irresistible torrent of opposition. The stability of everyday Chinese life, interspersed with repeated rebellions and revolutions in the nineteenth and twentieth centuries appears to bear out this generalization.

A third reason for the durability of the three parties is that all have produced effective, even great, leaders. In the case of the CCP there have been several of these, but two stand out: Mao Zedong and Deng Xiaoping. Both have, quite reasonably, come under attack over time for various reasons both in their own country and outside. But few would challenge their ability to impose their will on the CCP, Mao from the mid 1930s until his death in 1976, and Deng from the end of 1978 until shortly before his death. The DPRK leader Kim Il Sung bestrode the North Korean state like a colossus from late 1945 until his death in July 1994. He outlived all other leaders of the Second World War generation and showed himself capable of dealing with any challenges. He established a personality cult of extreme proportions which, although offensive to many outside the DPRK itself, did have the effect of inculcating the people with the strength and marvels of his leadership. In his late years, he succeeded in establishing his son Kim Jong Il as his successor. Although the younger Kim remains in power as of early 1998, his position does not seem entirely secure. The tight relationship between the Kim dynasty and the DPRK state may eventually result in a source of weakness and a reason why it does not survive as long as the PRC or SRV. In the case of Vietnam, the Marxist-Leninist party has produced a number of leaders of great stature, among whom the nationalist Ho Chi Minh is the foremost. Since his death in 1969 it is true that there has been no successor of even comparable stature. But, in contrast both to China and the DPRK, Vietnam has coped very well with collective leaderships and been remarkably free of the power struggles which have characterized the history of the CCP.

Mass memorial rally for Kim Il Sung, Pyongyang, July 1994

The economic factor is certainly a reason for the resilience of the Chinese and Vietnamese parties, but this factor is less clearly relevant to the Korean. China and Vietnam both adopted policies placing the emphasis on economic reform but with far less enthusiasm for basic change in the political system. From the end of 1978, China's policies of reform and opening to the outside world have yielded tremendously fast economic growth of almost 10 per cent per year. Both China and Vietnam have been much more enthusiastic for economic than political reform and far more flexible in economic terms than any of the East or Central European communist states. This does not mean that there has been no political reform. For instance, China in the 1990s is a far more open place politically than it was in the 1970s or 1960s.

It seems then that the communist parties of China, Vietnam and North Korea will not necessarily follow their Eastern and Central European counterparts into oblivion. Of course, this is not to declare their rule permanent or to predict the future. The CCP has entered a period of uncertainty in the post-Deng Xiaoping era, and even its long-term survival in power is by no means certain. But as of 1998 it appears strong enough to stay in power for quite a few years yet. The rule of the KWP appears considerably more tenuous. Kim Jong Il lacks the flair of his father and his rule is hardly likely to be long-lasting. Any reunification with the south is almost certain to resemble a takeover, just as happened in the case of Germany, resulting in the demise of the DPRK and its ruling Communist Party. Moreover, several of the reasons suggested above for the survival of the East Asian communist regimes simply do not apply to the DPRK. As for Vietnam, the intensity and length of the struggle which brought its Communist Party to power may well keep it in power for many years, even if it in fact adopts capitalism in all but name.

Are the reasons advanced here peculiar to East Asia? The answer is that some of them are, but the majority are not. The particular ways in which nationalism operated in the three countries under discussion may be different from most European countries, but they do not have to be, since nationalism is in no sense peculiar to Asia. On the other hand, Confucianism is peculiar to the societies of East Asia and so, therefore, is the particular brand of authoritarianism and the quest for stability. Although there are highly authoritarian European societies, the history of the twentieth century has seen authoritarianism challenged and defeated in a way which has appeared only much more slowly in Asia. Whether economic backwardness keeps authoritarianism alive, and whether rises in the standard of living will bring democracy to East Asia in the same way as it has done in Europe is an important question to be taken up in other chapters.

2.8   Conclusion

Strong nationalist credentials are the prime reason why East Asia's communist parties both rose to power and have stayed there. The suggestion that traditions of Confucianist authoritarianism has helped keep these parties in power is ironic for communists, in the name of modernization, once violently opposed that legacy. Their elitist pyramid-like structure is in some ways similar both in nature and *modus operandi* to a latter-day Confucian bureaucracy. The fact that Confucianism has always placed emphasis on the secular state links it to modern political forms, including those deriving from Marxism-Leninism. Finally, the retention of communist parties in power has not prevented rapid and radical change in China and Vietnam. Both are countries which are reforming in directions favouring market economies and rapid economic growth. Communism is likely to continue losing influence in both cases. Nationalism may be the ideological force that sustains economic growth and modernization.

References

Eccleston, B., Dawson, M. and McNamara, D. (eds) (1998) *The Asia-Pacific Profile*, **London, Routledge in association with The Open University.**

McGrew, A. and Brook, C. (eds) (1998) *Asia-Pacific in the New World Order*, **London, Routledge in association with The Open University.**

Maidment, R. and Mackerras, C. (eds) (1998) *Culture and Society in the Asia-Pacific*, **London, Routledge in association with The Open University.**

Overholt, W.H. (1993) *China, the Next Economic Superpower*, London, Weidenfeld & Nicolson.

Further reading

Christiansen, F. and Rai, S.M. (1996) *Chinese Politics and Society, an Introduction*, London, Prentice Hall.

Hoston, G.A. (1994) *The State, Identity, and the National Question in China and Japan*, Princeton, Princeton University Press.

Lieberthal, K. (1995) *Governing China: From Revolution through Reform*, New York, W.W. Norton.

Mackerras, C. and Knight, N. (eds) (1985) *Marxism in Asia*, London, Croom Helm.

Ok, T.H. and Lee, H.Y. (1994) *Prospects for Change in North Korea*, Berkeley, Calif., Institute of East Asian Studies.

Overholt, W.H. (1993) *China, the Next Economic Superpower*, London, Weidenfeld & Nicolson.

Scalapino, R.A. (1992) *The Last Leninists: the Uncertain Future of Asia's Communist States*, Washington, DC, Centre for Strategic and International Studies.

Scalapino, R.A. and Kim Dalchoong (eds) (1988) *Asian Communism: Continuity and Transition*, Berkeley, Calif., Institute of East Asian Studies.

Turley, W.S. (ed.) (1980) *Vietnamese Communism in Comparative Perspective*, Boulder, Col., Westview Press.

CHAPTER 3

Politics and governance in Japan

Frank Gibney

3.1 Introduction

In some ways, Japan is the most modern of all countries, creator and prototype of the East Asian 'economic miracle'. Japan's resurgence from defeat and devastation in the Second World War is unique. Yet the current politics of this singular modern democracy cannot be understood without going back to the Meiji Restoration, that extraordinary cultural revolution in which the Japanese modernized their feudal society within three decades. This Meiji revolution brought the seeds of democracy to Japan; but also contained within itself some tragic flaws – resulting from the disjuncture of a Western-style nation-state supported by the revival of ancient Japanese racist Shinto ideology. Japan is a remarkably cohesive society – quick to accept innovations in a pragmatic way, yet at the same time extraordinarily protective of ancient customs and social behaviour. The tremendous resurgence of the Japanese economy in the post-war era was matched by a spreading lassitude in politics. The result was an odd kind of one-party government. None the less, the reforms of the US occupation, which revived the earlier impetus of Meiji days, have left Japan as an undoubted democracy where basic personal freedoms and guarantees are uncontested.

Japan's economic ascendancy, however, was based on an export-oriented development model, a partnership of big business and a powerful bureaucracy. This has proved to be something of an anachronism in an era when knowledge industries have taken priority over older forms of production. Since the bursting of an over-expanded financial 'bubble' at the beginning of the 1990s, Japan has fallen prey to a kind of political malaise, where the curious combination of one-party politicians and over-protective bureaucrats has called the country's basic democratic credentials into question. A study of these Japanese modern political problems is impossible without reference to the extraordinary strides in self-modernization dating from the latter part of the nineteenth century.

3.2 The Meiji Restoration

Modern Japanese politics began with the Meiji Restoration of 1868. Without some knowledge of this 'first opening' of Japan, as it is frequently called, it is impossible to understand, let alone to evaluate, the complex web of democratic impulse, primitive factionalism, pragmatic functionalism, respect for authority and populist discontent of which Japanese politics is made. Meiji is best described as the dramatic self-modernization of a compact and ancient Asian nation society, under intense pressure from an aggressive and technologically superior West. As such its achievement remains unique in world history. Meiji set a paradigm which other nations in Asia and elsewhere have attempted to follow, with varying degrees of success. Although the immediate cause of the Meiji revolution was the intrusion of Commodore Perry's well-armed 'black ships' into Japanese waters, internal forces had long been at work to reform, if not to destroy, the crumbling Tokugawa Shogunate. A whole generation of young students broke out of the Shogunate's long-imposed isolation to learn Western languages and study Western 'science and civilization', which they saw was already colonializing China. By 1868 a small group of low-ranking samurai teachers, scholars and bureaucrats, backed by some of the powerful 'outside' clan (*tozama*) leaderships, succeeded in forming a new national government. They acted in the name of the young Emperor Mutsuhito, who was brought from his secluded court in Kyoto and after a triumphal progress installed in the renamed capital of Tokyo. He took the official name of Meiji, meaning 'enlightened rule', for his era, in line with long-established practice. He was greeted by tremendous popular enthusiasm.

Meiji's young samurai handlers, haunted by possible aggression from America and Europe, were anxious to build up a viable modern state. Beginning with purchased ships and guns for national defence and universal conscription for military service, they set out to construct all the complicated furnishings of a modern polity. Attendance at a new network of national schools was compulsory. There followed the Gregorian calendar, new banks and a stock exchange, railways and steel mills, to be supported initially by government investment and all based on a new system of tax collection. Western technicians and teachers were imported, albeit on a temporary basis. The Hong Kong mint was purchased and shipped intact to Tokyo for Japanese use. The old feudal codes of Tokugawa times were abolished by fiat, along with its Confucian class distinctions. Scholars began work on translations of European legal codes to replace them. There was no part of Japanese life that was not touched, twisted, altered or destroyed. This included cancelling the ancient perquisites of the samurai class from retainers' rice subsidies to abolishing the hallowed samurai top-knot (*chonmage*) in favour of Western-style haircuts – probably the world's most sweeping barbering reform since Peter the Great made his noblemen shave their beards.

To secure widespread popular sanction for these changes, the young reformers – the oldest among them was 43 in 1868 – brilliantly channelled the swirling currents of militant anti-foreignism, resentment of new invention and protest against Tokugawa arrogance and corruption into a revived cult of the Emperor as living symbol of Japan's ancient and singular society. By bringing the Emperor out of the closet, turning him into a political as well as religious leader, they revived a spirit of aggressive racist insularity which was to bring war and destruction and continues to plague Japan to the present day. None the less their enforced modernization worked. It succeeded by implanting in future generations four factors which Irokawa Daikichi, for one, holds critical:

1   a feeling of 'democratic self-awareness' and respect for human rights,

2   a dawning of individual consciousness,

3   an attraction for the 'elements of capitalism' – materialistic values, utilitarianism and practicality, and

4   the nationalism of what he terms 'a strengthened ethnic and national self-consciousness' (Irokawa Daikichi, 1985).

For all the flaws that developed in their polity, this achievement of Japan's modern 'Founding Fathers' was extraordinary and unprecedented. In little more than a generation they took a country, steeped in its own variety of feudalism, into the modern world of nation-states and industrial technology, compressing more than two centuries of Western political development into a fraction of that time. In 1905, a country that built its first railroad in 1872, defeated Russia in a major European-style war. The same country produced several novelists whose writings ranked with the first-class literary talent of Europe and the USA.

The human transformation involved in the Meiji achievement might be epitomized in the work of Fukuzawa Yukichi, who taught his countrymen elementary geography and chemistry, double-entry book-keeping and the handling of modern rifles, and founded a large national newspaper and Keio University. After beginning adult life as a two-sworded samurai with a standard Confucian education he described the learning experience of his first trip to Europe in 1870:

> ... when I saw a hospital, I wanted to know how it was run – who paid the operating expenses; when I visited a bank, I wished to learn how the money was deposited and paid out. By similar first-hand queries, I learned something of the postal system and the military conscription then in force in France, but not in England. A perplexing institution was representative government.

> When I asked a gentleman what the 'election law' was and what kind of an institution the Parliament really was, he simply replied with a smile, meaning I suppose that no intelligent person was expected to ask such a question. But these were the things most difficult of all for me to understand. In this connection I learned that there were different political parties – the Liberal and the Conservative – who were always 'fighting' against each other in the government.

> For some time it was beyond my comprehension to understand what they were 'fighting' for and what was meant, anyway, by 'fighting' in peacetime. 'This man and that man are "enemies" in the House', they would tell me. But these

Admiral Togo's victorious return to Japan after the Russo-Japanese War, October 1905

'enemies' were to be seen at the same table, eating and drinking with each other. It took me a long time, with some tedious thinking, before I could gather a general notion of these separate mysterious facts ...

(Fukuzawa Yukichi, 1992)

However well the Meiji reformers assimilated the science and technology of the West, they inevitably retained the mind-set of their background and tradition. They were after all samurai, loyal retainers brought up in the Confucian world which Tokugawa Ieyasu had created within the Shogunate. Their loyalties were now transferred from allegiance to local clan-leaders to the patriotism of the new imperial nation-state. In this sense they revived the earlier cosmos of the Heian days. But they kept a strong sense of *noblesse oblige*. The same people who formally abolished class distinctions remained an elite band of brothers, convinced that they and they alone knew best what was good for the polity. As the young reformers became bureaucrats, they increasingly thought of themselves – to borrow the images of Plato's Republic – as 'guardians of the state'. Since most of the old-fashioned Tokugawa traders and money-lenders seemed ill-equipped to handle modern business dealings, some of the reformers took over management of the mines, mills and railways of the new order, with the co-operation of those who remained in government. In this way began the symbiotic relationship of business, banking and bureaucracy which would become a prominent feature of Japan's new capitalism.

3.3   The Meiji Constitution

In 1889 the Meiji reformers unveiled their new constitution. This was partly in response to a groundswell of public demand, stimulated and led by liberals like Nakae Chomin, who had first translated the works of Rousseau into Japanese, and populist politicians like Itagaki Taisuke, who wished to see a modern Japan with a parliamentary government. Local committees worked on their own ideas of a constitution, against a background of mass meetings, demonstrations and considerable political protest against this modernization by fiat. The constitution which resulted created and institutionalized a system of representative government for the first time in the history of East Asia. A Diet of two houses was established to pass legislation, a judiciary to enforce the laws and an executive arm with a premier and cabinet, representing the party in power in the Diet, responsible for initiating legislation and enforcing it. Safeguards for individual human rights and property rights were written into the constitution. Its promulgation was followed by the general election of 1 July 1890. Some 300 representatives were elected to the Lower House of the National Diet (*kokkai*) with primary responsibility for making laws to govern the polity. An Upper House of Peers was added. It was composed of the clan leaders (*daimyo*), members of the court nobility and leading bureaucrats who were fashioned into a European-style peerage, with newly minted titles ranging from Baron (*danshaku*) to Prince (*koshaku*). Only about 450,000 out of a population of some 40 million were authorized to vote, due to qualifications of age, property-holding and sex. In later years, qualifications were steadily widened and more voters added to the rolls – a feeling of public responsibility developed among the people – although women did not receive the right to vote until after the Second World War. The system of national public education, from primary school to university, produced a kind of meritocracy, in which bright students could advance whatever their social backgrounds. The writings of leading Japanese intellectuals reflected the turmoil of a nation struggling to graft a whole new set of modern, materialist ideas onto long-established nativist and

Confucian tradition. With new factories and a network of nation-wide communications Japan began its long forced march from a network of isolated communities to a unified industrial society.

None the less the Meiji Constitution was far from a guarantee of popular sovereignty. It produced a government that was 'given' to the Japanese people, with a constitution neither demanded by the people nor in fact written by them. Despite the agitation of the more democratic reformers, the government, now led by Meiji's long-time Prime Minister, Ito Hirobumi, set out to create a law of the land that would be democratic without being dangerous or disorderly, representative without being in the least republican. Ito, who was entrusted with framing the constitution, travelled at length in Europe, examining the parliamentary systems of the West before he put pen to paper. Interestingly, American democracy had been ruled out for model purposes by the Japanese reformers as too unruly. Ito's handiwork most closely resembled the modified parliamentary government of Bismarck's Germany. But it was even more vulnerable to capture by anti-democratic forces within its structure. The Preamble to the Meiji Constitution made no pretence at sovereignty being a right of the people: 'The rights of sovereignty of the State, We have inherited from Our Ancestors and We shall bequeath them to Our descendants. Neither We nor they shall in future fail to wield them, in accordance with the provisions of the Constitution hereby granted.' Accordingly, in Article XXVIII, for example, Japanese subjects would enjoy freedom of speech and the press *within the limits of law.* In Article XXVII, they would enjoy freedom of religion *within limits not prejudicial to peace and order, and not antagonistic to their duties as subjects.* As for the armed forces, they reported to the Emperor, or whoever managed to wield power in his name.

In a speech to some constituents at Otsu, in the year the Meiji Constitution was promulgated, Prince Ito elaborated on the somewhat contradictory aspects of Japanese representative government. 'It will be evident', he explained, 'that as the supreme right is one and indivisible, the legislative power remains in the hands of the Sovereign and is not bestowed on the people ... But the Sovereign may permit the representative body to take part in the process of practically applying the legislative right ... Nothing being law without a concurrence of views between the Sovereign and the people, the latter elect representatives to meet at an appointed place and carry out the views of the Sovereign'. For the next 50 years just what was the view of the sovereign and how it made itself known, remained a baffling and unsolved problem in Japanese politics.

3.4   Taisho democracy

In the late nineteenth century the slogan *Fukoku Kyohei,* literally 'rich country, strong army', guided Japanese politics. The government developed a central banking system to fuel its plans for capital formation. Foreign capital investment, however, was severely restricted. Where industry was not well developed – or in some cases did not exist – the government fostered it. The Yahata Steel Works, for example, was established in 1901 as a state industry. Some 40,000 miles of track now linked Japan's major cities in a national railway system. By the turn of the century Japan's economy was at the 'take-off' stage. With the government's benign backing the *zaibatsu*, which were family conglomerates, took a leading role in the procurement of raw materials and the production and export of finished products. But the rush of new sights and new ideas in the pell-mell industrialization was beyond bureaucratic control. Private enterprise capitalism had come to Japan in Meiji days. In fact, the Meiji bureaucrats' rapid sell-off of early government-owned industrial assets foreshadowed the 'privatization' of a far later time. Expanding Japanese capitalism mirrored the excesses as well as the successes of its European and American models. Long hours and low wages were the rule. Inevitably, newly urbanized workers in the cities and the new factories began to organize to protect their rights. In December 1911, Tokyo's tram workers went out on a successful five-day strike, paralysing the city's fast growing commerce. Proletarian political parties were formed, fuelled by the spread of Marxist ideas after the Russian Revolution. As newsprint increased and multiplied, the reporting and editorials in a relatively free press often helped mobilize popular discontent. As a counterpoint to the growth of the cities, there were urban rice riots in 1918 and spasmodic uprisings in the countryside, whose farmers had suffered both from the new tax and conscription policies of the government.

In 1920, 24,000 workers went on strike in the steelworks in Yahata, protesting against cruel labour conditions. After battles with police reserves and hastily called out troops, the workers received huge increases in wages, while their working day was cut to eight hours from the original twelve. The following year 30,000 went out in the Kawasaki shipyard strike. By the beginning of 1926 fully 200 unions were active in Japan. While their membership did not begin to include all of Japan's industrial labour force their rise reflected the new sense of freedom and civic rights which was slowly stirring among the Japanese people. Until the 1920s, conditions in Japanese factories had been almost as brutal as the first sweatshops of Europe's Industrial Revolution. Once the workers and some liberal capitalists had begun to change these conditions themselves, the government gradually responded. A labour bureau was set up in the Ministry of Commerce and Industry. The Diet began to pass laws such as the Health Insurance Act of 1926. However, the pioneers of women's rights found the going tougher. Although Meiji reformers like Fukuzawa and the liberal Education Minister, Mori Arinori, had spoken out against the traditional Confucian disparagement of women, progress was very slow. Higher education for women, however, was established by the early 1900s; and the emergence of female publicists and political activists like Fukuda Hideko, Yamada Waka and Hiratsuka Raicho at least suggested the beginnings of a new consciousness.

In 1918 Hara Takashi became premier, the first commoner – that is to say, a public figure outside of the ennobled Meiji oligarchy – to head the government. In 1925 Prime Minister Kato Takaaki, another liberal statesman, put through the Diet a law granting universal male suffrage, with no property qualification. Throughout the 1920s the country was run by party governments. Although the two major political parties, the Seiyukai and the Minseito, were ultimately dominated by rival business and financial interests, they were not unresponsive to popular pressures. The civilian population seemed to have come into its own, and the Kato Cabinet even succeeded in chopping four divisions from the army. Taking its name from the short reign of Meiji's son, the Taisho Emperor, the 1920s became known as the 'Taisho democracy'. A wave of Western pop culture swept across Japan's cities, as a new generation of *mobo* and *moga* – 'modern boys' and 'modern girls' – danced the foxtrot and flocked to see Harold Lloyd and Charlie Chaplin movies. New university graduates competed for jobs in international companies or the new stock exchange at Tokyo's Kabuto-cho. Reflecting the democratic spirit at home, Japanese statesmen abroad strongly supported the post-war League of Nations and pledged their support to an Open Door policy for their Chinese neighbour. Nothing better symbolized the drive towards internationalization than the six-month visit and study trip of Crown Prince Hirohito to Europe in 1926 – the first time an heir to Japan's throne had ventured abroad.

In altered circumstances, the Taisho democracy might have continued and grown stronger. A sense of democracy and respect for human rights was indeed an integral part of the Meiji heritage. A rough sort of party politics had been functioning since the 1890s. But during its apparent triumph an undertow of basic weaknesses and unhappy events had already begun to carry the Japanese democracy off course. There were capable men in the Diet, sincere believers in democracy like Okuma Shigenobu and the old-fashioned liberal Ozaki Yukio. Okuma, in particular, twice Prime Minister and founder of Waseda University, was the most consistent supporter for people's rights among the original Meiji reformers. Yet most elected officials readily absorbed the bureaucrat's conviction that public office was a right and prerogative of the official, given him by the Emperor. Once elected to the Diet or prefectural assembly, the average politician all too often succumbed to the network of favours given and received, resulting in the corruption of 'money politics'. Politicians soon acquired a bad name. By contrast, bureaucrats and administrative technicians by and large remained faithful to the 'guardians of the state' tradition of Meiji days.

Another cause of democracy's failure lay in the doctrinaire type of Japanese liberal, the product of a university system infatuated with nineteenth-century German philosophy. The Japanese liberals tended to fall into Marxist, socialist or communist extremes. To be a real *interi* – the borrowed word for Japan's intelligentsia – some Marxist beliefs were virtually mandatory. Although the Communist Party of Japan was not founded until 1922, the archetypal socialist Katayama Sen led a Japanese delegation to the first Moscow conference of the Comintern in 1919. Labour demonstrations and student protest rallies showed a strong Marxist flavouring but public support was limited. In fact, agitators and activists played into the hands of governments like the Tanaka Cabinet of 1928, which could silence ten honest trade-unionists for each communist who publicly provoked it. In 1925, ironically the same year that suffrage was extended, government bureaucrats drew up the infamous Peace Preservation Law, ultimately to be used by later regimes to stifle political discontent.

Another blow to democracy came with economic depression. Trouble began at the close of the First World War. The rice riots of 1918 were an explosion of popular indignation against the hoarding of wartime profiteers. Starting with a housewives' protest in Toyama Prefecture, hundreds of thousands took to the streets throughout the country. Worse yet for the economy was the collapse of the wartime export boom, after Japan's European allies moved to regain the markets lost to Japan during the war. As a nation now dependent on its export trade, Japan became very vulnerable to changes in the world economic system. A fall in the New York price of silk – in those days 40 per cent of Japan's exports – meant hardship for thousands of rural families. The financial panic of 1927 was followed by the after-shocks from depression in Europe and the USA. Between 1929 and 1931 Japan's GNP fell by almost 20 per cent. While big business weathered the storm, hardship and insecurity pressed upon small farmers and factory workers. Economic depression produced great political discontent.

3.5   The militarized state

Into this charged atmosphere marched a revived Japanese militarism. Its guiding spirit had been Yamagata Aritomo, the most conservative of the Meiji reformers. General, Field Marshal and Prime Minister at various times in his career, Yamagata despised party politics and did his best to strengthen the bureaucracy, the armed forces and the police. The architect of the national conscription system, Yamagata also saw to it that the military chiefs of staff reported directly to the Emperor. In 1900 he had pushed through the fateful law mandating that the war and navy ministers in any cabinet had to be serving officers – a move that could and often did put civilian cabinets at the mercy of the military. Yamagata died in 1922, but his legacy lived on. Unlike the old samurai elite who led Yamagata's turn-of-the-century victories over China and Russia, the officer corps of the twentieth century included many sons of poor farm families who had passed the military academy examinations on their merits. This new generation of military populists nursed deep grievances against their own capitalists as well as foreigners. Their racist chauvinism had been amply fuelled by word of the anti-Japanese Exclusion Act in the USA and, earlier, by the Western Allies rejection of Japan's proposed 'racial equality' clause for the 1919 Versailles Treaty. They steeped themselves in the eclectic doctrines of national socialist theorists like Kita Ikki who espoused a weird combination of Marxism, intensified Shinto loyalty to the Emperor and a destined expansion into the Asian continent. This was to be 'Asia's Monroe Doctrine', as Ikki put it. They thought of themselves as leaders of a 'Showa Restoration' – named after the new Emperor Hirohito's reign. First they would move into China. Ultimately, they looked to a military showdown with the West.

On the night of 18 September 1931 a bomb exploded on the tracks of the South Manchurian Railway near Mukden, in an area occupied by Japanese troops under a long-term agreement. Within two days after the explosion, Japanese troops had occupied all of southern Manchuria, and by January of the following year all of Manchuria was under Japanese occupation. The smoothness of the take-over left no doubt that it was carefully planned and executed by young troop commanders on the scene, with the benign acquiescence of the general staff in Tokyo. The leaders of the Kwantung Army speedily organized the puppet state of Manchukuo under the nominal rule of Pu-yi, the surviving Manchu Emperor who had been deposed by the Chinese in 1912. The civilian government in Tokyo, thoroughly brow-beaten, acquiesced. Right-wing zealots in various patriotic societies had already assassinated two Prime Ministers, Hara and Hamaguchi, then in 1932 they murdered Dan Takuma, the head of the Mitsui companies. Later that year, in the infamous May 15 Incident, a band of young navy and army officers and cadets killed Prime Minister Inukai Tsuyoshi, who had tried unsuccessfully to halt the army's adventurism. Four years later 1,400 troops of the First Division, led by another clique of fanatical young officers, briefly staged a revolt in Tokyo, as a protest against civilian government. They murdered three government ministers, including Finance Minister Takahashi and narrowly missed killing Admiral Okada Keisuke, who was then premier. They were brought under control by army authorities on direct orders of the Showa Emperor Hirohito and their leaders executed or allowed to commit suicide. This marked the first and, until the end of the Second World War, the only occasion on which Hirohito used his direct imperial authority. Having punished the young officers for their disobedience, the Emperor did little or nothing to restrain their superiors; later research has left little doubt about his complicity in leading Japan towards war. Real civilian government had died with the assassinated Prime Minister Inukai and succeeding cabinets were largely in the service of the military. Police censorship intensified – even foreign words were discouraged in conversation. Where government action was lacking, the militarists used force and intimidation, for example the free press of Japan received its death-blow in 1937 when troops moved into the offices of the Osaka *Asahi*, Japan's most respected newspaper, and smashed the printing presses. The total weight of the armed forces was now put behind the troops in China, while the strategists at Imperial Headquarters (*Daihonei*) began to draw up plans for the conquest of South-East Asia and, ultimately, the show-down with America and the Allies. Soon to become a full partner in the tripartite Axis alliance with Nazi Germany and Fascist Italy, Japan began national planning for a general war.

Emperor Hirohito in military uniform, c. 1926

In 1937 the Kwantung Army, now ensconced in north China, provoked a fight with Chinese troops on the Marco Polo Bridge outside Beijing. By the end of that year more than 200,000 Japanese soldiers were in action and a war begun that was to last until August 1945. The Japanese military tried its best to force a general Chinese surrender. The 1937 Rape of Nanjing, in which an estimated 200,000 Chinese soldiers and civilians were killed, with tens of thousands tortured and raped, was something more than a spontaneous outbreak of cruelty. It was an effort dictated by high-ranking officers to terrify the Chinese into submission. But the Chinese continued a stubborn resistance. The attack on the USA and the Allied powers in 1941 was the immediate result of their embargo on the export of oil, rubber and other raw materials to Japan. But at Imperial Headquarters in Tokyo it had long been planned. Japan's entrepreneurs were indecently eager for expansion in Asia. With the labour movement crushed and politicians no longer a factor, the military ruled to its liking. On 12 October 1940 premier Konoye Fumimaro presided over the establishment of the Imperial Rule Assistance Association, a totalitarian kind of structure that superseded all the old political parties. The following July Japanese troops disembarked at Saigon to take military control of what was then French Indo-China. In October 1941 Konoye, after failing in a variety of attempts to head off war with the USA, was replaced by the Minister of War, General Tojo Hideki, who presided over what was little more than a military junta in the war years that followed.

Why did they get away with it? One reason was general public approval. The bureaucrats in Tokyo did not mind having a rich dependency. Leading capitalists had welcomed the Manchurian annexation and the later thrusts into China as essential to the economy. Many thoughtful people opposed the war – diplomats, businessmen, academics, even some military men – most particularly among navy officers, who had all too good an idea of the military force and industrial power Japan would ultimately confront. Each month, however, it took more courage to speak out, and few possessed that courage.

To record the history of what the Japanese originally called the Greater East Asia War (*Dai Toa Senso*) is outside the scope of this chapter. What concerns us here is the effect which this war and the preparations for it had on Japan's body politic. Some results were immediate and transitory, whilst others have lasted to this day. By the mid 1930s Japan had largely recovered from its earlier economic depression, thanks largely to the efforts of Finance Minister Takahashi (the same man who was assassinated by the young officer rebels in 1936). With the yen devalued, exports had hugely increased. Japanese products – textiles in particular – were pushing out foreign competition. With the military heading the country into a long war, it fell to the bureaucrats in the Tokyo economic ministries to produce a unified national effort that would last as long as possible. Within the framework of a National Mobilization Law enacted in 1938, followed by a host of supplementary decrees and ordinances, civilian economists, under pressure from the military, turned what had been a reasonably standard *laissez-faire* capitalist economy into what amounted to a new kind of developmental state. As the Duke University sociologist Bai Gao recently summarized:

> ... the Japanese state emerged as the 'economic general staff'. It not only started making long-term plans to promote production and upgrade the industrial structure of the economy, it also exercised tight control of resource allocations, adopting a discriminatory policy to ensure the supply of materials and capital to the munitions industries. [The National Mobilization Law] gave the state bureaucracy unprecedented power to shape the managed economy by using administrative decrees. From then on, the state bureaucracy could issue orders directly to the private sector without consulting with the Diet. This has had a long-lasting impact on the post-war Japanese economy.

> (Bai Gao, 1997)

This '1940 system', as Japanese economists call it, included wage controls, company employee work councils and a network of business consultative committees and cartels – all of them destined to play a prominent role in the post-war 'economic miracle'. The system of seniority pay and guaranteed employment was also stimulated by wartime urgencies. For while Japan's military defeat left the generals and colonels thoroughly discredited, the capitalist developmental state constructed under military urgencies remained more or less in place after 1945. Indeed, it provided the industrial policy responsible for Japan's post-war high-growth period. However, its economic justification no longer exists, and de-velopmentalism as such will probably not survive the changed economic climate of the coming century. None the less the political power of the bureaucracy, thus fortified, remained. The bureaucrats' governance has persisted for almost a half-century – an ironically successful by-product of a disastrous war.

3.6   The 'second opening'

When General Douglas MacArthur and his staff officers landed on Atsugi airfield at the end of August 1945, they found a country on the verge of mass starvation – the result of the long American submarine and air blockade of the archipelago. Its industries were smashed, its cities were levelled and millions had been left homeless. In addition, seven million Japanese, military and civilians alike, were stranded in China, Manchuria, Korea and elsewhere in Asia. Within a year most of these people had been repatriated, to return to bombed-out homes and workplaces. By the end of 1946 there were some 13 million unemployed. The occupation, long planned in Washington, was not to be punitive. By 1952, the USA had spent US$2 billion on Japan. Although at first charged only with maintaining order in an occupied enemy country, the Supreme Commander for the Allied Powers (SCAP became the familiar acronym) interpreted his directives broadly. After taking care of Japan's de-militarization and drawing up a vast 'purge' list that included regular officers, former government officials and leading executives of banks and corporations involved in the war effort – about 180,000 people were excluded from participating in public life – he turned the occupation towards a loftier objective: the complete 'democratization' of Japan.

In this effort he was assisted by a hastily assembled staff of army and navy officers, transplanted Washington bureaucrats, and experts recruited directly from the USA. Their one common denominator was enthusiasm for the job. In the best traditions of Wilsonian idealism and New Deal reform SCAP's youthful officials, backed by the troops and military government teams of the Eighth Army and a small British Commonwealth force, set out to transform the ancient island society into an American-style democracy. To attempt a peaceful political transform-ation on such a sweeping scale was unique. So was its relative success, for all its flaws and stumbling. Small wonder that Japanese historians generally refer to it – harking back to the early days of Meiji and Commodore Perry – as the 'second opening' of Japan.

At this low point of their national fortunes, the Japanese were oddly receptive to drastic changes. They had never before lost a war. It was a war moreover that had mobilized almost every aspect of their racial and national identity, only to end in destruction and defeat. Japan was morally exhausted and spiritually bankrupt – not least of all through the appalling atrocities its troops had committed under arms. Yet the people remained resilient and adaptive, particularly when the occupation showed itself to be benevolent. MacArthur was a classic American idealist, with all the virtues and defects of that breed. 'Politically', he once remarked, 'the Japanese are young and plastic enough to copy anything'. In the event, he was not far from wrong. The first problem the occupiers had to solve was how to deal with the Emperor. At the very beginning of the occupation, Hirohito had driven to MacArthur's residence at the American Embassy to pay his respects. (It was the first time since his European trip as Crown Prince that he had gone calling.) On 1 January 1946, on order from SCAP, the god-emperor had sent down to his people an Imperial Rescript the like of which no Emperor of Japan had ever written. 'The ties between us and our people', he wrote, 'have always stood upon mutual trust and affection. They do not depend on mere legends and myths. They are not predicated on the false conception that the Emperor is divine and that the Japanese people are superior to other races and fated to rule the world.' Many Americans, as well as some of the Allied leaders, had thought that the Emperor should be tried as a war criminal. So did quite a few Japanese, disillusioned by the deaths of so many in a war fought in Hirohito's name. Ideally, he should have at least been forced to abdicate. But Washington decided otherwise. Hirohito's words ending the war in August had enforced a total cease-fire when there was real danger of a fanatic last-ditch resistance by the Japanese military. His retention, it was thought, would have a calming effect on the public. Since SCAP was occupying an entire country with only a few under-strength divisions, immediate security concerns carried the day.

At first the reforms planned by the occupation were far from drastic. But SCAP officials quickly discovered that ensuring a democratic future in a heavily militarized country was no easy thing. One revision of law and practice soon led to another, like links in a chain. Try to destroy the cartels, then something must be done to the investment laws; reform the investment laws and you must overhaul the stock market; overhaul the market and you need to encourage new investors. Inevitably, some of the reforms attempted were more successful than others. Overall the SCAP planners had to deal with the fundamental contradiction of trying to establish a working democracy by military fiat – even when working through the civilian government. There were three notable successes. The first was land reform. Absentee landlords were forced to sell their lands to the government and even resident farmers were limited in the size of their holdings. The law was a sweeping one, based on considerable research done by Japanese agronomists and bureaucrats. It inevitably caused hardships, but it corrected a major social and economic injustice in rural areas where more than half of the cultivated land had been owned by only 7 per cent of Japan's farmers. By 1951 less than 2 million acres of land were operated by tenants, as compared with 6.3 million acres pre-war.

The second success was in the area of labour relations. SCAP's Labor Division, staffed largely by young American labour economists and union organizers, set out with some enthusiasm to restore Japan's shattered trade union movement. A trade union law, borrowing heavily from America's Wagner Act, set forth basic guarantees for union rights. It was followed by labour standards and labour relations laws, enacted by occupation directives and ultimately passed by a reluctant Japanese Diet. Most of this legislation, which amounted to a Magna Carta for a reviving labour movement, remains on the books today. By the beginning of 1949, some seven million Japanese workers belonged to the revived unions. Inevitably, many of these unions were heavily politicized, dominated by communist and socialist activists. (In 1947 the anti-government general strike they called was, ironically enough, suppressed by MacArthur's decree, in the interests of public order.) In the end, after some bitter and well-justified strikes during the 1950s, Japanese labour and management worked out a mutually profitable coexistence, which played no small part in the success of the high-growth economy. Its model on the labour side was generally the single-enterprise company union, in contrast to the national union patterns developed in Britain and the USA. Given initially strong management resistance, however, and the anti-labour stance of conservative cabinets, the continued vitality of Japan's unions was made possible only by the occupation's labour laws.

The occupation's third great achievement was the new post-war constitution. For four months, at SCAP's behest, Japan's most eminent legal scholars worked on the draft of a document. The product which Prime Minister Shidehara's Cabinet presented was little more than a modification of Prince Ito's 1889 model. It left intact the same imperial powers which the militarists had exploited. Whereupon Colonel Charles L. Cades, in civilian life a Washington lawyer, was called upon to produce an American alternative. The generals gave him barely a week to do the job. Working with a team of young officers and civilians from SCAP's Government Section, Cades produced a document which, 50 years later, remains the law of the land in Japan. MacArthur offered a few directions. 'The emperor is the head of the state', he wrote, '... his duties and powers will be exercised in accordance with the new constitution and responsible to the basic will of the people as provided therein ... War as a sovereign right of the nation is abolished. Japan renounces it as an instrumentality for settling its disputes and even for preserving its own security ... The feudal system of Japan will cease ...'.

Cades and his young collaborators – most of them in their twenties and thirties – put these basic thoughts into sound Anglo-Saxon legal language and enlarged on them with scores of specific guarantees of individual liberties and safeguards against official abuse. The cabinet was made responsible to the legislature. A supreme court was set up as the capstone of an independent judiciary. 'Academic freedom' was guaranteed and a special section was included on women's rights. The new constitution mandated universal suffrage, thus women voted in the 1946 election for the first time in Japan.

However, there were also faults with the new constitution. It was written by a group of bright and idealistic Americans, most of whom had little more than a superficial knowledge of Japan. It guaranteed individual human rights, as its Meiji forerunner had not; and in this justified the aspirations of the truncated Taisho democracy. The reforms it offered in education, local government and the decentralization of police power, while laudable in principle, paid little heed to the traditions and temperament of the people it was written for. Above all, the uncompromising 'anti-war' statement in Article IX soon came to pose problems in sovereignty and national security for Japanese political leaders, not to mention the Americans who had sponsored it. By the end of the 1940s Soviet encroachments in eastern Europe and the victory of Mao Zedong's militant communism in China had riveted a new Cold War mind-set on American policy makers. Local communists in Japan seemed to be making alarming gains. Predictably, their party line took full advantage of occupation reforms to the detriment of the conservative post-war government. George Kennan, then in charge of the US State Department's policy planning, warned that continued reform 'paved the way for a Communist take-over'. Along with other Washington officials, he advocated that further democratization be abandoned in favour of a programme for economic recovery. In a world of suddenly changed political circumstance, yesterday's Japanese enemy became tomorrow's newly democratized ally.

Led by the Detroit banker Joseph W. Dodge, appointed President Harry Truman's special representative in Tokyo in 1949, American bureaucrats and business experts gave a new priority to putting the Japanese economy back on its own feet and hence off America's back. (Republicans now held a voting majority in the Congress.) The budget-balancing Dodge Plan, largely executed by a new strong-minded Finance Minister, Ikeda Hayato, cut off the network of costly government subsidies, reduced a crippling rate of inflation and enforced a general exchange rate, while maintaining protectionism for Japan's slowly recovering industry. The severe hardships that resulted were, fortunately for Japan, ameliorated by heavy US military procurement spending in Japan during the 1950–53 Korean War. This 'reverse course' in American policy was far from the sudden, total change the name implied. SCAP's various democratization programmes continued until the occupation ended, but they were diluted in the interests of economic recovery.

The 'Made-in-America' Constitution remained. No government has felt strong enough to attempt serious revision – which, practically speaking, means any revision at all. In particular, any plan to revise the 'anti-war' Article IX has provoked outcries of protest, despite the fact that because of it Japanese Self-Defence Force units may not even participate actively in UN peace-keeping operations. Like the later Japan–US Security Treaty and the early occupation acceptance of the wartime Showa Emperor, its pervasive popular acceptance has served to deepen a collective and wilful national amnesia over Japan's real responsibility for the Greater East Asia War in favour of a sanctimonious sense of national victimization over the A-bomb tragedies. Meanwhile, an increasingly powerful bureaucracy in the Tokyo ministries has for practical purposes interpreted the constitution by administrative directives in pursuit of its varying goals.

3.7   Yoshida and the one-party state

In the 1947 elections, the first to be held under the new constitution, the results seemed to justify the hopes of its American drafters for an active multi-party democracy. The new Prime Minister, Katayama Tetsu, was an old-time moderate Socialist who had formed a coalition government with the moderately-right Democrats, strong enough to beat the conservative Progressives and Liberals. He lasted barely a year. His cabinet fell when the left-wing Socialists pulled out to join the Communists in opposition; exhibiting for the first time a political death-wish that lasted until their virtual extinction in the 1990s. Following the shaky, six-month cabinet of the Democrats' Ashida Hiroshi, the conservative parties took over. Yoshida Shigeru, who had inherited the Prime Minister's job in 1946 (after his predecessor, Hatoyama Ichiro, was 'purged' by occupation directive) went back to the Prime Minster's official residence in October 1948 and remained in office until 1954. His successors were all conservatives, formally united in 1955 in the Liberal Democratic Party or LDP (Jiminto). Apart from a brief 'new' party principate in 1993–94, the Liberal Democrats have controlled Japanese politics ever since. No other political party has thus managed to hang on to power for almost a half century, in a democracy where elections are honest and fairly run.

What kept them in office? It was certainly not charisma. Barring a few impressive exceptions, LDP leaders have been colourless political tacticians, who owed their positions largely to money politics and their skill in an archaic system of mutual favour-trading. Most of them – more than half of Japan's 22 post-war premiers – were products of the pre-war bureaucracy. In their governance they relied heavily, if not exclusively, on the guidance of the career bureaucrats in the ministries of Kasumigaseki – that congeries of modest public buildings in the heart of Tokyo where the lights traditionally burn far into the night. Despite their complicity in the war effort, Japan's bureaucrats largely escaped the occupation's purges. For one thing, they were badly needed to keep the machinery of government going. True to the Meiji tradition and the ideals of the Tokugawa *bushi* before that, they were drawn from the best and brightest of Japan's educational meritocracy. Throughout the post-war period, at least until very recently, they retained the subservient respect of a fundamentally conservative Japanese public.

The second great bulwark of the Liberal Democrats was the Japanese business community. As the post-war high-growth economy took off, manufacturing conglomerates and trading companies alike turned towards the government for policy support and administrative guidance in a pattern of dependency that dated directly from the wartime. The industrial policy of Japan's new capitalism was an intensely co-operative effort. The various industry councils and consultative bodies (*shingikai*), working closely with the men in the ministries, lent some truth to the image of 'Japan, Inc.' advanced by frustrated international competitors. In return for the bureaucracy's benign co-operation, the business sector supplied funding for the Liberal Democrats. Until very recently, for example, the main task of the Vice-Chairman of the big business Keidanren (the acronym for the Federation of Economic Organizations) was to channel a huge amount of contributions from its corporate members to the various factions and political leaders of the majority party. Given the increasing amounts of slush funds necessary for winning election campaigns, this business support became essential. Also, by the 1970s, Japan's trade union movement had lost most of its far-left political orientation. Thanks to high wages and good working conditions, most union members were happy to partake of the general prosperity.

The nicely interlocking triangle of politicians–bureaucracy–business remained in place until the troubles of the 1990s. It was supported by the voters, in election after election, on the principle that nobody cuts off the hand that feeds them. The rewards of the nation's rising GNP were relatively well distributed; and economic advancement towards super-power status became a matter of national pride. For most voters there were few reasonable alternatives. A stubbornly left-wing core of the Socialist Party, in the face of rising affluence, continued to advocate some form of Marxist revolution. As a result the Socialists, however well supported by some large unions, never reached more than 30 per cent of the vote, gradually declining in the 1980s to under 20 per cent. The only other large party, the Komeito (Clean Government Party), founded in 1964, at first gained great strength among urban voters. But it was too heavily identified with the Sokagakkai Buddhist religious group to gain widespread acceptance. The Communists, except for some zealous supporters, rarely attracted more than protest votes.

The Liberal Democratic Party itself resembled less a party than an alliance of separate factions. The personal politics of its Diet members ranged from moderate left to far right. Because of the odd proportional representation rule in elections – finally changed for the better in 1993 – the three, four or five candidates who gained the most votes would be elected from a single district. It was thus not unusual under this system for five Liberal Democrats, four Socialists, three Komeito and two each from the Communists and the moderate Social Democrats (Minshato) to contend for the top spots. The resulting competition between rival party factions was often more intense than that between parties. Factions tended to rally around individual leaders and their henchmen, all of whom depended on well-funded local support organizations (*koenkai*) for votes. It is not surprising that many Diet seats turned out to be more or less hereditary. As late as the 1990s some 50 per cent of Lower House Diet members were sons or other relatives of their predecessors.

From the early US occupation days, the Liberal Democrats had solidified their power through a process of gerrymandering, since rural districts – agricultural and conservative – had disproportionate political power as against more liberal urban constituencies. Another variety of political loyalty was shown by the so-called *zokugiin* (literally, family legislators). These were alliances of various business and bureaucratic special interests. For example, construction *zokugiin* were legislators with special ties to the construction industry. Networking with contractors, bureaucrats in the Construction Ministry and construction specialists at party headquarters, they would see to it that government budgets made more than adequate provision for a variety of building projects, generously contracted to favoured firms. (Predictably, foreign competitors were discouraged.) Although similar special-interest politics is attempted by parliamentarians in other countries, Japan's one-party government was raised to a fine art.

One wonders how politicians with such divisive interests could have formulated a national policy – and one which directed Japan's extraordinary rise from destitution to economic superpower. The answer is that they were given one. The blue-print for national governance was outlined in the early post-war days by Yoshida Shigeru and Ikeda Hayato, to be drawn up in detail by their helpers in the ministries. Yoshida established the political paradigm. An old-fashioned Meiji liberal, product and loyal defender of the Emperor system, this retired professional diplomat – an Anglophile who smoked Churchillian cigars, and a vocal anti-militarist who had been jailed briefly for his opposition to the war – was appointed Foreign Minister in the post-war Shidehara Cabinet. At the age of 67 he became Liberal Party leader and hence Prime Minister through a series of accidents. This was a stroke of good luck for Japan. Oddly resembling his two well-aged contemporaries, Konrad Adenauer in Germany and Alcide de Gasperi in Italy, he played a role similar to theirs in bringing back their beaten and demoralized countries to the edge of post-war international respectability. As an ingrained conservative, Yoshida was nervous about the US occupation's reforms, although he could do little to stop them. He welcomed the 'reverse course' in American policy however. Yoshida's first objective was to secure a peace treaty, which would automatically end the US occupation. This he effected, with American help, in 1951 (see **Eccleston *et al.*, 1998, p.341**). At San Francisco, where the treaty was signed, he commented: 'Japan has regained political independence. Now we must see to it that economic independence is achieved. Without this, political independence has little meaning'.

In fact, Yoshida gained American approval for the treaty at the cost of pledging Japan as a faithful ally of US foreign policy. The other side of the bargain proved to be whole-hearted American support for Japan's economic renewal, then just beginning. A firm supporter of the 'anti-war' clause in the new constitution, Yoshida was quite content to leave Japan's security to the Americans. Without wasting any money on rearmament Japan would concentrate on building up its economy with the same single-minded zeal in which the militarists and the bureaucracy had waged war. The doctrine of *seikei bunri* – the separation of economics and politics – became government policy, with politics very much in second place. Practically speaking, the economic ministries – principally the Finance Ministry and MITI (Ministry of International Trade and Industry) – were to serve as Japan's Pentagon; and bureaucrats, rather than politicians, were to be its generals. Yoshida's skill at statecraft, however, did not duplicate itself in the give-and-take of domestic politics. His strong personality came on as autocratic and abrasive. After a total of six years in office, he had to give way in December 1954 to the veteran conservative politician Hatoyama Ichiro, now 'unpurged'. Long after his retirement, however, he continued to exercise great influence over his successors, almost all of whom were, like him, former bureaucrats. They were called, collectively, the Yoshida school. Tokyo wits commented that disciples like Ikeda Hayato and Sato Eisaku (whose eight-year premiership from 1964 to 1972 set a new political longevity record) spent half of their waking hours on the road to Oiso, where Yoshida had his residence, to receive counsel and instruction.

3.8 Money politics in the high-growth economy

The 1950s were a noisy decade in Japan. Labour–management struggles grew more intense. The five-month long walkout at Nissan, the electric power workers' union (Densan Roso) walk-outs, and the bloody battles at Mitsui's Miike coal mines typified the confrontational tactics of both sides. Leftist unions like the public workers' Sohyo attacked the 1952 Security Treaty with the USA as a revival of militarism, while the press and the intelligentsia denounced the government's 'Red purge' of union leaders. Left versus right tensions finally exploded in 1960 in huge demonstrations against the impending visit of US President Dwight Eisenhower to Japan. The visit was cancelled. The right-wing Prime Minister Kishi Nobosuke was forced to resign, but only after he and the Liberal Democrats had pushed a revived Security Treaty through the Diet.

His successor was Yoshida's former Finance Minister, Ikeda Hayato. Strongly pro-business and himself a Finance Ministry product, Ikeda had already put in place the Japan Development Bank, the Export-Import Bank and other instruments of an internationally oriented industrial policy. Deservedly called the father of Japan's high-growth economic 'miracle' Ikeda encouraged the economic ministries to use all the resources of government – tax breaks, foreign exchange controls, technological imports and protection against other foreign imports – to support the export drive of Japan's expanding international marketers. Various advisory boards and committees were set up to keep communication channels open between business people and their guardian ministries. Communication was furthered by the fast developing practice, known as *amakudari* (literally, descent from heaven), where senior officials on their retirement took up directorships and managerial jobs in the private sector.

Ikeda's administration tried to downplay left–right confrontation, and he proposed a long-range plan to 'double your income' (*shotoku baizo*)

Students clash with police outside the Diet in protests against the Japan–US Security Treaty, June 1960

through sustained economic growth. Intensive money-making proved a marvellous cure for political tension. An increasingly affluent public took pride in their country's soaring GNP increases and export surpluses, now reported in the daily press with the same enthusiasm once given to the chronicles of military victories. For the most part, the history of Japan under the LDP – familiarly called the '1955 system' – is best recorded by economists.

However, some political problems remained, or recurred. Campus unrest heightened throughout the 1960s. Students showed their distaste for the business society, American imperialism and capitalism in general by noisy demonstrations. At one point more than 70 universities were disrupted by protest. Marxist or Maoist splinter groups, such as the infamous Kakumaru faction of the nation-wide leftist students' organization Zengakuren, sometimes engaged in destructive violence. Demonstrators regularly turned out to picket American air-bases outside Japanese cities, while the visits of US Navy aircraft carriers to their bases in Yokosuka or Sasebo, particularly during the Vietnam War, regularly provoked 'anti-nuclear' demonstrations. The Communist vote remained relatively small, however, and most student demonstrators cheerfully put on suits after graduation, to take the company examinations for Sumitomo or Mitsubishi.

Internationally, Japan's position steadily improved. The USA returned the captured Ogasawara (Bonin) Islands to Japan in 1968. After long discussions, Washington agreed to return sovereignty over Okinawa and the other Ryukyu Islands to Japan. Tokyo agreed for its part that the

Americans could retain the disproportionately large number of US Air Force bases and Marine staging areas on Okinawa, thereby perpetuating an unhealthy relationship which would cause problems for all concerned. By contrast, the Soviet Union refused even to consider returning the islands off the Hokkaido coast which it had occupied along with the Kurile Islands at the end of the Second World War. This would remain a festering area of disagreement between Japan and Russia. It was made all the more painful since neither the Soviet Union nor the People's Republic of China had yet signed a peace treaty. Relations with the southern portion of Japan's former Korean colony – the Republic of Korea – were normalized in 1965, although the communist Democratic People's Republic in the north remained aloof and hostile. In 1972 Prime Minister Tanaka Kakuei led a mission to Beijing, following the informal re-opening of relations between the USA and the PRC.

Although junior members of the 'Yoshida school' continued to staff cabinets and ministries, the balance of Japan's ruling 'triangle' began to shift away from the bureaucrats. Big business grew more independent with prosperity. It became increasingly difficult for the ministries of Kasumigaseki to enforce their 'guidance' on international conglomerates like Toyota, Fujitsu or Sony. A generation of experience in power had developed a new, more confident race of Liberal Democrat politicians. Two classic, if in many ways dissimilar, examples were Tanaka and Nakasone Yasuhiro. Unlike most post-war Japanese premiers, well-mannered products of Tokyo University's elite law faculty, Tanaka, known familiarly as 'Kaku-san', was rough, tough and commercial. A foreign biographer aptly called him 'Japan's first true, successful populist' (Schlesinger, 1997). Going straight from high school into the contracting business, he proved himself an alert and ruthless competitor. Swimming in the muddy waters of construction industry politics, and getting richer by the day, he soon became one of the LDP's big decision makers. His efficiency was legendary. He was known widely as the 'computerized bulldozer' for his quick decision making and became hugely popular with his northern Japan constituents. Like most Japanese voters in an age of increasing affluence, they were untroubled by his loose money politics. (He had already been indicted for bribery in 1948, when serving as Vice Minister of Justice.) Meanwhile, he smoothed his way to the party presidency through lavish pay-offs provided by a network of shadowy influence peddlers. The centrepiece of Tanaka's premiership was to be an ambitious and imaginative project, long worked over within MITI, to 'remodel the Japanese archipelago' by moving a good part of the country's industry and work-force from the overcrowded Tokyo–Osaka–Nagoya area to northern and western Japan. The plan proved immensely popular but fatally flawed, since Tanaka's contractor friends had private information about what was to be built and where. Corruption spread, climaxing in the Lockheed scandal of 1974, when influential Japanese officials – Tanaka among them – were paid off by bribes and kick-backs to purchase Lockheed aircraft for Japan's Self-Defence Forces. The resultant investigation, triggered by a comprehensive exposé in the magazine *Bungei Shunju*, disclosed a vast network of cronies and dummy corporations who funnelled some US$250 million to help Tanaka and his faction win elections.

Tanaka resigned at the end of 1974 and ultimately was given a jail sentence which, thanks to long illness and interminable appeals, he never actually served. He was succeeded by the veteran parliamentarian Miki Takeo, one of the 'Mr Clean' types who appear as interval-markers in Liberal Democratic politics. Tanaka's political resilience, however, proved more extraordinary than his disgrace. In a warped imitation of the 'Yoshida school', he continued to dominate Japanese politics behind the scenes, working out of his huge mansion in Tokyo's Mejiro district. Thanks to money politics and his large and well-funded Tanaka faction, the dethroned premier remained his party's decision maker for more than a decade thereafter.

Nakasone earned his popularity more honestly. A Diet member since 1947, he became Prime Minister in 1982, after the usual intra-party horse-trading. Like his fellow Liberal Democrats, he was dependent to a great extent on factional politics and fund-raising. But he was the first of the post-war premiers to go to the people directly rather than rely on the back-room judgements of the party bosses. Gifted with an inborn sense of public relations, plus a flair for self-dramatization, he skilfully used the media to project a strong leadership image. His ratings soared in the public opinion polls, and the press half-admiringly called him the 'presidential Prime Minister'. In the 1986 election his personal popularity helped the Liberal Democrats win a record Diet majority of 300 votes.

The post-war position of the Japanese Prime Minister is structurally weak. Given a small staff, with only indirect authority over the powerful ministries under him, he functions more like the chairman of a foundation. Nakasone expanded this power personally as no one had done before him. He made continual public pronouncements on policy matters, and his various 'personal' consultative committees by-passed the normal party–bureaucrat channels. He also had some policies: he urged constitutional revision on security matters; and privatized some government institutions, the huge, lethargic Japanese National Railways among them. In 1984 he set up a Council on Education, which recommended, among other things, a more internationalized curriculum and modification of the rigid examination system inherited from pre-war days. That same year he organized a blue-ribbon commission, chaired by Maekawa Haruo, former governor of the Bank of Japan, to recommend improvements in Japan's social structure as well as its economy. Its reports contained detailed recommendations for financial liberalization and deregulation of the domestic economy. They were the foundation of the economic reform movement.

A genuine internationalist, Nakasone urged Japan to play the great power role politically that its successful economy warranted. He welcomed the kind of give-and-take with foreigners which most Japanese statesmen shun. In visits to China and the Republic of Korea he tried to further good political as well as economic relations. Instinctively, he knew that the old

Yoshida paradigm, for all the prosperity it had brought, was no longer effective in dealing with the global economy of a post-Cold War world. The protected 'hot-house economy' of Japan would have to go.

Meanwhile the money politics of the majority party continued. A 1988 newspaper article about pay-offs to local officials in Kawasaki by a company named Recruit set off a chain of circumstances that exploded into the biggest national scandal since Tanaka/Lockheed. A large job-placement company, as the name implies, with more than 20 subsidiaries, Recruit had set up a network of bribes, retainers and bargain stock transfers to politicians, principally Liberal Democrats. Its slush fund amounted to more than ¥6 billion. Prime Minister Takeshita Noboru, Nakasone's successor, was among the principal recipients, along with cabinet ministers and a variety of other officials. Takeshita, who had been one of Tanaka's leading henchmen, had to resign the following year and was lucky to escape arrest and trial with Recruit's officers. In 1990 Tokyo's stock market crashed; and the vastly inflated prices of company shares and bank assets collapsed with it. At the height of the crisis, it transpired that Japan's largest broker and investment firm, Nomura Securities and three other brokerage houses had paid no less than US$1.5 billion worth of kickbacks to cover the market losses of favourite big-business clients.

There was yet more work waiting for the prosecutors. In the summer of 1992 the Sagawa Kyubin scandal broke. Sagawa Kyubin, the country's largest private mail and delivery company, had assured its primacy in the market-place with political pay-offs of billions of yen, eclipsing Recruit's excesses. This time the evidence pointed to the leading don of the party's money-dispensers, once Tanaka's chief lieutenant and a former Deputy Prime Minister, Kanemaru Shin, who had taken his faction's money politics and egregiously advanced them – along with his own fortunes. In a raid on his home after his arrest, prosecutors unearthed ¥3 billion in anonymous bond certificates, tens of millions in bank-notes and no less than 100 kilograms in gold bars. Most of the funding, predictably, had come from the construction industry. Dozens of executives from Japan's top builders were subsequently arrested and at least half a dozen received prison terms. Again, most party leaders were implicated, and, as in other recent scandals, so were a growing number of bureaucrats. By the beginning of the 1990s scandals at the Construction Ministry, the Ministry of Health and Welfare, MITI and the Finance Ministry itself had implicated scores of senior officials. Public confidence was badly shaken in a civil service once esteemed as a paragon of rectitude.

3.9 Heisei and the 'third opening'

Emperor Hirohito died on 7 January 1989. His reign had lasted for 62 years – next to Austria's Franz Josef's the longest monarchical tenure in modern history. He had presided over a recently democratized country that plunged into a suicidal militarism, but emerged from total defeat to build itself, albeit with considerable outside help, into an economic superpower. Its developmental brand of capitalism had raised the per capita GDP of its 125 million well-fed people to more than US$30,000, the world's highest. Its trade surplus with the rest of the world exceeded US$140 billion and its manufactured exports constituted 12 per cent of the world's total. Japanese owned and managed banks and factories dotted the world. Its urban society was the world's safest, with enviably low crime rates, and its people's habits, appetites and work patterns largely fixed by community sanctions and the guidance of a sternly benevolent government. Japan's democracy was real. Basic human rights were guaranteed. Popular culture was broadly based, with daily newspaper circulation to 60 per cent of the population, the world's most addictive television audience, and more than 50,000 book titles published annually. Japan's university student population exceeded 2.5 million, about one-third of the age-group, and its national school system was probably the world's most pervasive. In almost every way Japan's people would seem to have become the epitome of modern industrialized progress.

Yet behind the formidable figures there was a deep-seated political, social and indeed economic malaise. The developmental state was already the casualty of what the economist Nakatani Iwao (1996) termed 'institutional fatigue'. In the globalized world of business and, particularly, finance, it was no longer possible for a protective bureaucracy to keep their country a tight mercantilist sanctuary. The political corruption that had long lurked beneath the surface of Japan's '1955 system' of one-party governance had exploded. A depression threatened. Consumers were not buying. The long-standing alliance with the Americans showed signs of intense strain, in both its security and economic aspects. Crown Prince Akihito, his accession to the throne confirmed by traditional Shinto rituals, chose the name Heisei, literally translated as 'the onset of tranquillity', for his reign. A pleasant and well-meaning man, the product of an internationalized education, he found the first years of his new era a legacy of troubles from the past.

For starters, the economic 'bubble' burst. Immediately after the 1990 New Year's holiday the Nikkei index of stock prices began to drop. From an 1989 high of almost 40,000 yen it plummeted to 14,300 yen by the summer of 1992 (Wood, 1992). Land prices, hopelessly swollen, went down proportionately. By 1995 the total value of land and securities had dropped a staggering US$5 trillion in value. Detailed economic commentary is outside the scope of this chapter – suffice it to say that the 'bubble economy' itself was caused by a combination of business greed and the financial bureaucracy's insular over-confidence. After raising the yen's value due to the G5 Plaza Accord in 1985, the Japanese government pumped a flood of cheap money into the economy to ease the strain on Japan's exporters. This, however, provoked a veritable feeding frenzy as businesses and banks recklessly expanded, built and loaned, hugely swelling values in the process. When the Finance Ministry and the Bank of Japan, alarmed, sharply raised interest rates, while the yen continued its ascent in international markets, the result was a rash of business bankruptcies, lay-offs and bank failures, and the annual growth rate sank from 3 per cent to almost zero.

The sudden recession only intensified public concern over political corruption and voting scandals. A clamour arose, at last, for a new electoral system that would end the soaring costs of personal and party electioneering. When the Liberal Democrat bosses resisted, they were finally turned out. New parties arose, augmented by LDP defections. A new government came into office in July 1993, led by Hosokawa Morihiro, leader of the appropriately named New Party. The following year, against entrenched Liberal Democrat and some old-line Socialist opposition, the Diet approved a reformed electoral system. Of 500 seats in the Lower House, 300 representatives would be chosen from single-vote districts. The remaining 200 would be elected from regional constituencies, on the basis of party proportional representation.

Although Hosokawa and his political ally Hata Tsutomu, who briefly succeeded him, were pledged to a wider political reform, they were turned out of office the next year by a surprising coalition of Liberal Democrats and their traditional Socialist opponents. A Socialist leader, Murayama Tomiichi, became Prime Minister in June 1994. But he depended on a large bloc of Liberal Democrats for his support. The Socialists were punished for sacrificing principle to power so flagrantly in the 1996 elections, when their Lower House representation shrank to 15, a far cry from their 1958 high of 166 seats. Despite some losses in the 1996 elections, the Liberal Democrats, assisted by the Socialists and another small party, managed to cobble together a majority in the Diet, sufficient to give their latest party boss, Hashimoto Ryutaro, the office of Prime Minister.

The calls for reform, however, were becoming too insistent to ignore. The domestic economy remained flat; and although car exports continued to grow, electronics manufacturers found themselves upstaged by American advances in the new 'knowledge-business'. Technology experts continued to complain about the lack of creativity in the homogenized products of Japan's school and university system. The perceptive commentator Sakaiya Taichi, himself a former MITI bureaucrat, concisely summarized the basic contradictions overtaking Japan's once-vaunted 'catch-up' economy: 'the imbalance of mass production industries that overwhelm the rest of the world with their volume and efficiency alongside distribution, information and knowledge-value creation industries mired in inefficiency and waste'. The industrial barons of the Keidanren echoed the urgency of freeing the Japanese economy from the carapace of government over-regulation. Early in 1996 Toyoda Shoichiro, Keidanren Chairman (and Chairman of Toyota as well) publicly demanded 'bold and effective measures to stimulate demand and open Japan's markets ... We simply cannot leave reform half-done'. From former premier Nakasone, across the political spectrum, came demands for a 'third opening', with reforms needed to be as sweeping as the edicts of Meiji and MacArthur.

Kobe, January 1995, after the worst earthquake in Japan in nearly 50 years

Two shocking events of 1995 illustrated the scope of Japan's problems. In January the port city of Kobe was savaged by an earthquake that killed 5,500 people and left 300,000 homeless. The reaction of Japan's governing bureaucracy, on both the local and national level, was slow and halting. Summing up the national rescue effort, Nakauchi Isao, chairman of the Kobe-based Daiei retail chain, remarked: 'In emergencies like this, someone must assume the leadership. Yet today's Japan is a country where no one dares take responsibility'. In March 1995 the premeditated explosion of sarin nerve gas in a Tokyo subway station killed twelve and injured more than 5,000 people. It was part of an effort by a religious cult called Aum Shinrikyo to wage a terrorist war on the entire country. The most disturbing thing about the cult was that its membership included not merely malcontent cranks but young people – technical experts and academics among them – from the cream of Japan's business society.

In a sense two generations of Japanese had been living off accumulated social capital. In particular the age group now in its forties and early fifties had lulled itself into a false sense of security by the years of steady growth, rising affluence and protected living. Sakaiya labelled them *dangai no sedai*, freely translated as 'the generation of clods from the government housing developments'. By this term he meant to indicate the political inaction of people who had grown up in the mind-set that an enveloping, yet permissive, government and paternalistic corporations would take care of their big decisions.

At the end of the century Japan stands as a unique product of economic success and social solidarity. Its primacy throughout Asia is unquestioned.

No one can dispute Japan's claim to be the second great superpower in the world. None the less, the political problems of a country too long obsessed with economic gains cannot be denied. The Japanese politicians have yet to solve the problems left them by the ill-fated economic bubble of the early 1990s and the subsequent drastic fall in land and stock prices. The result of a government of bureaucrats and political cronies is a staggering amount of bad loans in the Japanese banking system – which in itself has intensified, if not indeed started, a general economic malaise throughout East Asia. The passivity of voters cannot be blamed on the bureaucrats and politicians. Japan's future now lies in the hands of a new generation, apparently more individualistic and self-confident, who can make some big decisions themselves. There are signs that this generation, untroubled by the inhibitions of its fathers and grandfathers, may be better equipped to bring the country back to economic and social stability, as well as giving Japan the international stature which the diligence of its citizens deserves. But this remains to be seen.

References

Bai Gao (1997) *Economic Ideology and Japanese Industrial Policy,* Cambridge, Cambridge University Press.

Eccleston, B., Dawson, M. and McNamara, D. (eds) (1998) *The Asia-Pacific Profile*, London, Routledge in association with The Open University.

Fukuzawa Yukichi (1992) *Autobiography,* translated rev. edn, Washington, Madison.

Irokawa Daikichi (1985) *The Culture of the Meiji Period,* translated by Jansen, M.B., Princeton, Princeton University Press.

Nakatani Iwao (1996) *Nihon Keizai no Rekishiteki Tenkan*, Tokyo.

Schlesinger, J.M. (1997) *Shadow Shoguns*, London, Simon & Schuster.

Wood, C. (1992) *The Bubble Economy: the Japanese Economic Collapse*, London, Sidgwick & Jackson.

Further reading

Beasley, W.G. (1990) *The Rise of Modern Japan*, London, Weidenfeld & Nicolson.

Gibney, F. (1997) *Japan: the Fragile Superpower*, 3rd edn, New York, Tuttle.

Irokawa Daikichi (1995) *The Age of Hirohito: in Search of Modern Japan*, translated by Hane, M. and Urda, J.K., New York, Free Press.

Lu, D.J. (ed.) (1996) *Japan: a Documentary History, Vol.2*, New York, M.E. Sharpe.

Smith, P. (1997) *Japan: a Reinterpretation*, New York, Pantheon.

CHAPTER 4

Independence: state building in South-East Asia

R.E. Elson

4.1 Introduction

In 1939, Western colonial powers seemed securely, tranquilly and permanently entrenched in South-East Asia. They dominated five of the region's six states: British Burma, with its headquarters in Rangoon; French Indo-China, a collection of states ruled by the French from Hanoi; the Philippines, an American colony; the Netherlands East Indies, a vast archipelagic state managed from Batavia; and British Malaya, a collection of political units controlled, with varying degrees of directness, from Kuala Lumpur and including, for our purposes, the regions of northern Borneo. Only in the Philippines was there any assured prospect of independence in the near future. The Americans – keen almost from the beginning to ensure their rule of the islands was only temporary and facilitative – had begun a period of tutelage in independence with the establishment of the Philippine Commonwealth in 1935. The single large state which had escaped colonization by the West was Siam (renamed Thailand in 1939). It had, since the late nineteenth century, preserved its oft-threatened sovereignty through a programme of careful diplomacy abroad and, much more important, administrative modernization and infrastructural enhancement at home, ironically paralleling Western colonial efforts at state-building.

By the end of 1954, most of these colonized states had secured their independence. The Philippines was the first in 1946. Independence celebrations followed thereafter at more or less regular intervals: Burma in 1948, Indonesia in 1949, Cambodia and Laos in 1953. Vietnam, racked by eight years of struggle against the French, seemed on the verge of establishing its independence, whilst in Malaya independence had been achieved in all but name and detail.

This chapter seeks to answer two major clusters of questions:

- First, how was it that these South-East Asian states achieved their independence in so short a span of time? Was it through the inherent strength of the nationalist movements in the respective states? Was it a function of the relative weakness and war weariness of the colonial powers? Were there larger world forces and tensions at work which served to produce this result?

- Second, how are we to account for the diversity of independent states that emerged: from re-invigorated monarchy to secular republics, from competitive democracies to communist one-party states, and from centralized unitary states to more fragmented federations? Why did some states plump for democratic arrangements which mirrored Western practice, whilst others established frameworks for a more regimented control of society? And why did those democracies that did emerge out of the region's post-war political settlement prove, for the most part, so fragile, giving way to various shades of authoritarianism?

I begin in Section 4.2 by sketching the historical background to the post-war struggles for independence, focusing on the rise of indigenous nationalism and the impact of Japanese occupation in the 1940s. In Sections 4.3 and 4.4 I contrast the two routes to national independence in South-East Asia – independence by violence and independence by negotiation. In Section 4.3 I focus on the Indonesian revolution which illustrates the importance of indigenous nationalism and its internal divisions in shaping the form of post-independence states. Vietnam provides an illuminating contrast. Then in Section 4.4 I contrast Burma, the Philippines, Malaya, Cambodia, Laos, and Thailand. All six produced fragile democracies which, in Burma, the Philippines and Thailand, fell to varieties of personal and military-backed rule, while Cambodia and Laos eventually underwent communist revolutions. Malaya, whilst retaining its democratic forms and a mildly competitive electoral system, took on a more authoritarian bent after 1969. Finally in Section 4.5 I explore some of the reasons for this drift to authoritarianism.

4.2 The historical context of nationalist movements

We need first to appreciate the extraordinary distance these South-East Asian states had to travel, both politically and conceptually, to arrive at their 1954 destination. Most of these states were, in fact, colonial creations. It was the Dutch who contrived the political entity which they named the Netherlands East Indies, the British who constructed British Burma and British Malaya and the French who manufactured Laos. The Philippines, as the name suggests, was a Spanish invention, and its rounding out was the work of the USA. Cambodia, indeed, had been 'saved' in the mid nineteenth century by French intervention in the face of enduring efforts by the Siamese on one side and the Vietnamese on the other to 'protect' it from the other. Of the colonized states, only Vietnam could claim a unity of history and culture which readily gave it a sense of continuity and identity, a feature it shared with uncolonized Thailand.

Equally, independence and nationalism did not emerge out of an ideological vacuum. In most of these colonized states, indigenous figures, starting with intellectuals like José Rizal in the Philippines in the later nineteenth century, had long been contemplating the ideal of independence and debating the forms of state they wished to construct once freedom was achieved. For the most part, these early nationalists assumed that they would take the place of European rulers and occupy the new states they had established. Because nationalist leaders were, without exception, the products of Western education, they relied heavily on Western ideas and discourses. While liberalism made some headway it was Marxist and Leninist thought that attracted many nationalist leaders. Marxism provided a comprehensive and satisfying explanation for the lowly status, material deprivation and suffering of their peoples. There was, however, a deep well of indigenous thinking which also shaped nationalism and politics in the region. Religious thought, usually of Indic or Islamic origin, helped shape political thinking and political identity, and found common ground with German conservatism. This odd intellectual couple shared a preference for ideas of social harmony, hierarchy, and order. Finally, a determined strand of what might be called ethnic nationalism emerged. This owed its vigour and tenacity to the slights endured by the region's minority communities, and especially by the failure of Western state-building and colonial policy to accord them a proper place or, on occasion, to the fear that the privileged place accorded to some minorities by European rule would be lost. The Shan and Karen of 'Burma', the Muslim Malays of southern Thailand and the Moros of the southern Philippines exemplified the first of these categories, the Malays in Malaya the second. Both forms of ethnic nationalism would contribute to the political character of the newly independent states and Thailand.

The ordered and apparently tranquil situation of South-East Asia was demolished with stunning rapidity and thoroughness by the Japanese invasion of 1941–42; 'few historical events of the history of Southeast Asia appear so definitive' (Stockwell, 1992, p.329). By early May 1942, all of Western-controlled South-East Asia lay under direct Japanese rule, save French Indo-China, now ruled by the collaborationist Vichy regime under Japanese monitoring. Thailand, conditioned by long experience of the realities of its international environment, had formally thrown in its lot with the Japanese and declared war on the Allies in January 1942.

A key concern of the Japanese was the mobilization of the peoples and productive potential of South-East Asia in support of the Japanese war effort. In order to promote indigenous enthusiasm for Japan, independence was promised to the nationalist movements which had gradually established themselves in these places from the late nineteenth century. Indeed, before the Japanese surrendered on 15 August 1945, they had sponsored the 'independence' of the Philippines and Burma in 1943, and of Vietnam, Cambodia and Laos in early 1945. More important, they had so destroyed the myths and infrastructure of European colonial superiority that a return to the colonial status quo was unthinkable for the great bulk of its former subjects. With the final defeat of Japan in 1945, a relentless surge towards independence began in earnest across the region. In some places, independence was asserted as a matter of right almost immediately and its seizure entailed widespread violence. In others, it came more gradually as the product of a process of negotiations between Western colonial powers and indigenous leaders.

4.3   Independence by violence

The two great cases of the violent seizure of independence came in Indonesia and Vietnam. In the former, the impeccably credentialled nationalist leader Sukarno proclaimed the independence of the Republic of Indonesia on 17 August 1945. In Vietnam, the proclamation, made on 2 September 1945, came from the veteran nationalist and guerrilla leader, Ho Chi Minh. In both cases, the assertiveness of the nationalist proclamation was met with an obdurate refusal of the colonial powers to assent to what had been proclaimed. That refusal set the stage for a period of sustained violent struggle as both nascent nations sought to free themselves from the bonds of colonialism, a struggle that was to shape fundamentally the nature of the independent states that finally emerged. I begin with Indonesia because its experience embodied many of the vital themes of post-independence state formation: conflict over the form of the state, the trials of democracy, the search for an appropriate guiding ideology, the emergence of militarism, and the problems of accommodating religious and ethnic/regional sentiment.

Indonesia

The Indonesian revolution of 1945–49 was a contest on two fronts. On the one hand, there was the struggle of Indonesians against the reimposition of Dutch rule. On the other, there emerged serious and continuing conflicts amongst Indonesians themselves about what form their state would take. We can deal with the first of these stories in a straightforward and rudimentary way. In Indonesia, the British forces which landed in late September 1945 decided to adopt a *de facto* recognition of the newly-proclaimed Indonesian Republic. This gave the Republic an important breathing space in which to consolidate its control and administrative operations. When Dutch forces began to return in late 1945, they found a functioning and confident nationalist government in control. The Dutch response to this alarming discovery had both a political and military dimension. The political dimension involved, from mid 1946, the Dutch establishing puppet states outside Java and Sumatra. These were in areas that were not under the complete control of the Indonesian Republic and where peoples with entrenched regional and ethnic identities feared the prospect of a centralizing, Java-focused Republic. The Dutch hoped to use these regimes as a counterweight in negotiations with the Republic. Essentially, the Dutch were seeking to establish a federal state of Indonesia, in which the Republic would be just one of the component parts. By manipulating the states they had created, the Dutch planned to water down the Republic's demands for complete independence so that what might finally emerge would be a weaker state still politically and economically tied to the Netherlands.

The negotiations between the Dutch and the Republic were concerned with establishing some sort of federal Indonesia in an equal partnership with Holland. An agreement was signed at the end of 1946, but the two sides had very different understandings of its substance and purport. The Dutch lost patience in July 1947 and initiated what they called a 'police action' to bring the Republic to heel through force. The police action achieved significant military success, but although the Republic lost large amounts of territory it managed to survive. Moreover, the outbreak of hostilities brought the conflict into the glare of world publicity. Both India and Australia lodged complaints with the UN about the Netherlands' action, and the UN Security Council intervened to halt the fighting and get the parties talking again. Another agreement was signed between the two sides in January 1948. Again it was no real solution, since it masked radically different understandings of how the dispute might be resolved. At the end of 1948, frustrated by the lack of progress, the Dutch launched a second 'police action'. Again, as in the previous year, they enjoyed military success. The Republic's territory was overrun and its leaders, Sukarno and Hatta, were captured. But Dutch successes were illusory. The Republic's armed forces fell back into a pattern of guerrilla harassment of Dutch troops, making the conquered areas, and even Dutch areas, impossible to govern. Moreover, the fighting again brought the dispute onto the international scene. The USA was increasingly embarrassed by its seeming support for the Dutch, a function of its desire to promote post-war reconstruction and an anti-Soviet security alliance in western Europe. When finally assured of the non-communist credentials of the Indonesian leadership, the USA in early 1949 brought irresistible pressure to bear upon the Dutch by suspending Marshall Plan aid to the Netherlands East Indies and threatening to remove aid from Holland itself. Under this pressure, and unable to make further military headway against the determined guerrilla opposition of the Republic's army, the Dutch were drawn back to the negotiating table. They restored the Republican leadership in May 1949, and in December 1949 transferred full sovereignty to a federal Republic of the United States of Indonesia, a combination of the Dutch-created states and the Republic. The Republic's military and political strength, and the respect and legitimacy it drew from its stubborn struggle against the reimposition of colonial rule, assured its dominance in the new arrangement. Indeed, Republican leaders' deep-seated antipathy and suspicion of the federal scheme made its retention impossible. By August 1950 most of the other states had voluntarily integrated themselves with the Republic, and the fractious remainders were incorporated by means of force, to form a unitary and independent Republic of Indonesia.

So much for the struggle between Dutch and Indonesians. Let us now look at the more interesting strife amongst Indonesians themselves during this period. This was a struggle over the ideological vision that would shape the new state, and how that vision might be put into constitutional practice. A fruitful way of examining this conflict is to outline the major ideas about the nature of the state that emerged around 1945, and to evaluate the success (or otherwise) they enjoyed in the course of the revolutionary period. Feith (Feith and Castles, 1970, pp.12–17) isolated five major strands of political thinking in the revolutionary period which, in an adapted form, provides a useful way forward.

- First, *integralism*, which emphasized a centralized, patrimonial, and statist style of politics. It drew its inspiration from allegedly indigenous modes of customary behaviour which emphasized the community over the individual, although it was strongly influenced by Western conceptions of conservative organicist politics. Sukarno, the President of the new Republic of Indonesia, was the major representative of this group.

Sukarno, the President of the new Republic of Indonesia, November 1945

- Second, *Islam*, which, in general terms, sought the establishment of Indonesia as an Islamic state, or at least an Islamic society, and wanted for itself as a minimum a strong formal position in the structure of the state.

- Third, *democratic socialism*, which was the preserve of Western-educated intellectuals, especially those like Sutan Syahrir, the Republic's first Prime Minister, and Mohammed Hatta, its Vice-President, who had studied abroad. Their ideological viewpoint treasured parliamentary democracy as a political system, and rationalist thinking as a political virtue. It was heavily influenced by Western socialist and populist ideas, and found its fullest embodiment in the PSI (Socialist Party).

- Fourth, *Marxism*, most unambiguously manifested in the Indonesian Communist Party (PKI), and which saw the revolution in terms of a struggle against imperialism and capitalism, and as a means to reshape Indonesian society and radically free it from its colonial and feudal relationships.

- Fifth, *perjuangan* (struggle), not, properly speaking, an ideology at all, but rather a certain orientation or cast of mind which sprang up and spread rapidly, especially amongst youth, in the months before the Japanese surrender and the first year of the revolutionary period. It was, in a sense, the consequence of the social dislocation of the Japanese period, Japanese mass mobilization techniques and style of rule, and the general feeling of crisis and the exuberance of the early period after the proclamation of independence. It embodied the idea that struggling for independence and a new beginning was a virtue and a glory in itself; independence had been proclaimed, and there was no need for negotiation with the Dutch. *Perjuangan*, as a set of ideas, was extremely vague. There was a clear sense about the way forward, but no one had a very precise notion about precisely what the goal was or what was to be done once it was achieved.

What happened to these five positions during the revolution? Only one of them was destroyed – *perjuangan*. The *perjuangan* forces were mostly localized and uncoordinated, with no one to guide them and organize them into a coherent movement. For a brief time in late 1945 and early 1946, following a series of turbulent social upheavals in parts of Java and Sumatra which saw the temporary overthrow of traditional modes of rule, Tan Malaka, an old communist leader of the 1920s, threatened to lead the *perjuangan* forces on to something more substantial. However, poor organization and the decisive opposition of Sukarno destroyed the movement in mid 1946.

Supporters of the other four viewpoints survived the revolution, some better than others. The two biggest losers were Islam and communism. The Muslims lost out badly before the revolution had even begun. In the political debates of mid 1945 which resulted in the drafting of the 1945 constitution, and which were dominated by secular nationalist politicians like Sukarno who had benefited from Japanese patronage, Muslims failed to secure a prominent position for Islam. The PKI was disadvantaged because of the pounding it had taken during the period of colonial rule. It took some time to make up lost ground following the proclamation of independence, and when it had done so other ideas and leaders were already in the ascendancy. It was not until 1948 that it had developed into a significant force, and it made the mistake of attempting an ill-organized rebellion against the Republican leadership in late 1948, centred on the East Java town of Madiun. Suffering an embarrassing defeat at the hand of Republican forces, and portrayed as having stabbed the Republic in the back just at the time when it needed the undivided support of all Indonesians, the party went into partial eclipse until it was rebuilt again in the early 1950s.

Of the two remaining points of view, the democratic socialist model gained most from the period of revolution. The most skilful, experienced and able politicians – with the notable exception of Sukarno – came from this tradition. Its liberal and democratic values were the ones most acceptable to the USA which, as we have seen, placed crucial pressure on the Dutch in 1949 to give up their attempt to reassert their sovereignty. The result was that when Indonesia secured its independence, most of its senior leaders were of this particular persuasion, and the form of government adopted was a Western-style parliamentary democracy with the Cabinet responsible to Parliament, and a figure-head President.

It is important to note, however, that none of these viewpoints, with the exception of *perjuangan*, were decisively defeated. All of them were still vital elements in the Indonesian political scene, and none of them had anything like an assured dominant position. Moreover, the revolution had seen the further development of a powerful new force in Indonesian politics – the armed forces. Unlike the situation in China and Vietnam, where communist parties had emerged firmly in control, the revolutionary period in Indonesia had not really resolved fundamental issues of state formation. Notwithstanding the temporary dominance of democratic socialists, there was no general consensus among political leaders about the form of the state and the dominant political values. The succeeding fifteen years after 1950 can perhaps best be seen as a struggle between contending forces in the Indonesian Republic – including Muslims, communists, regionalists, the army, and Sukarno himself – for dominance. Parliamentary democracy was in the ascendancy in 1950, but by the late 1950s integralist and communist elements had moved to the apex of politics, and Western-style democracy – 'an imported democracy, a democracy which is not Indonesian' (Sukarno, 1970, p.84) – with its multiplicity of parties, its institutionalized conflict, and its apparent inability to solve the nation's pressing social and economic problems, was in retreat. Only in the years after 1965 was the debate finally resolved in favour of the armed forces and their integralist views of statecraft.

Vietnam

The story of the post-Second World War struggle and eventual triumph of the Vietnamese communist nationalists was addressed in Chapter 2 and does not need recounting in detail here. However, the decisiveness of the communist victory over competing nationalist forces, providing a striking contrast with the Indonesian case, does warrant further comment. Amongst the great variety of pre-war Vietnamese nationalist groupings, which included religious sects, traditionalists, Trotskyites and leftovers from the Vietnamese Nationalist Party destroyed by the French in 1930, it was the communists who best turned the circumstances of Japanese occupation and post-war disarray to their own ends. They did this by their steadfast attachment to the concept of unalloyed independence and their judiciously selective programme of social change which avoided alienating powerful elements of Vietnamese rural society, winning them prestige and legitimacy in the eyes of ordinary people. Even if, by the mid 1950s, the decolonization process in Vietnam was only half completed, Ho's regime was in undisputed control in the north; there, with an intensity of vision which rivalled Mao's progress in China, it began a revolutionary process of agricultural, industrial and social change.

4.4   Independence by negotiation

The prolonged violence and conflict associated with independent state formation in Indonesia and Vietnam was the exception rather than the rule in South-East Asia after the Second World War. For the most part, other colonial states attained their independence through negotiations with the former colonial power, a process which, however, was just as strongly characterized by robust and fissiparous debate amongst indigenous leaders about the spirit, form, substance, and direction of the new creations.

Burma

Britain's initial political intentions in Burma, announced in May 1945, were to reassert its rule in the form of executive government until the end of 1948 and move only gradually towards granting Burma dominion status within the British Commonwealth in the distant future. In the circumstances, this scheme proved unrealistic in the face of the strikes and turmoil raised by the Anti-Fascist People's Freedom League (AFPFL) led by the charismatic military hero Aung San, leader of the 'Thirty Comrades' who had originally accompanied the Japanese in their conquest of Burma and who then, in March 1945, turned against them to support the Allies when the Japanese had refused Burma real independence. Agreement about Burma's independence was achieved through a process of negotiation in January 1947 between Burmese nationalists led by Aung San and the British. This was a process in which 'the most intractable issues were not between the Burmese and the British but between the Burmans and various other ethnic groups' (Kratoska and Batson, 1992, p.284). These arrangements allowed for the election of a Constituent Assembly and the drafting of a constitution of an independent Burma, which created separate states within the union for the Shan, Karen-ni and Kachin peoples, but not for the Karen. Burma achieved its independence on 4 January 1948.

Burmese independence was faced with the dual challenges of a communist movement, which took no joy in the style of independence which the British had granted, and an ethnic diversity. Suspicion of the Burmese majority was sharpest among the Shan and the Christianized Karen peoples, but was also strong among such groups as the Karen-ni (who already thought themselves independent), Chins and Kachins. These peoples were accustomed to separate political status as they lived in 'excluded areas' under British colonial rule. Ethnic hostility, intensified by conflict between Burmans and other ethnic groups during the period of Japanese occupation, saw the mounting of various new challenges for separate statehood or, at least, guarantees of substantial autonomy. Indeed, a Karen delegation travelled to London in August 1946 to put its views for separate statehood, and the Karen refused to take part in discussions between Aung San and the Shans, Chins and Kachins which led to the signing of the Panglong Agreement in February 1947. This agreement granted 'full autonomy in internal administration for the Frontier Areas ... in principle'. Elections for a Constituent Assembly took place in April 1947, and were dominated by the AFPFL; the constitution was approved in September.

The country's ability to negotiate these different visions was severely compromised by the assassination of Aung San in July 1947. The not-quite federal Union of Burma which emerged in 1948 was republican, ideologically statist, and socialist – 'the hallmark of political and economic legitimacy in Burma since the 1930s has been socialism' (Steinberg, 1989, p.36). It was also economically nationalist in orientation, unwilling to make compromises to its programme, determined to forge a centralized, Burman-dominated state. Its greatest compromise was the extraordinary provision that allowed the Shan and Karen-ni states to secede after an initial period of ten years. 1948 saw the new state plunged into grave crisis by rebellion. On the one hand, the communists, expelled from the AFPFL coalition in October 1946, and disaffected by their inability to secure greater leverage in the construction of the new state, went underground in March. On the other hand, the Karen, who had taken no formal role in the negotiations leading up to independence, sought to bring into being their desire – at least two decades old – for their own independent state.

By 1949, the embryonic Union look set for stillbirth. The government, now headed by U Nu, controlled only a small segment of its purported territory. The Karen National Defence Organization, the military arm of the Karen National Union, seized the town of Insein, just 12 km north of Rangoon, early in 1949. By August, the communists claimed a liberated area of almost 200,000 square km containing more than six million people. It took until 1951, with the development of a strong Burmese Army under Ne Win (assisted by the provision of military *matériel* by India, Britain and the USA), before a measure of political stability was established. None the less, the communist and regional rebellions endured, albeit in severely contracted forms, despite the Union's best efforts to quash them.

Thereafter the AFPFL government suffered a steady diminution of its support, notwithstanding U Nu's invention of amalgams of Buddhism and Marxism to provide ideological direction and inspiration. The economy lagged steadily, undermined by declining international prices for the rice exports on which its health depended. U Nu's romantic and utopian welfarist ideas had little purchase and he presided over an increasingly divided and corrupted polity. In the end, the AFPFL's attempt to be all things to everyone cost it its legitimacy and ran the country into problems that the fledging democracy, already battling against the centrifugal forces of ethnicity, could not solve. The result – after a final split within the AFPFL in May 1958 – was a voluntary and temporary hand over to the military in September 1958. A restoration of civilian rule in December 1960 fell to a full-blooded military take-over by Ne Win in 1962.

The Philippines

The period of Japanese occupation saw the opening of an ideological chasm amongst Filipinos. The conservative and privileged landed elite which had served as the vehicle for American plans in the islands lost little time in entering into collaboration with the invading Japanese. The leftist anti-Japanese guerrilla forces, the Hukbalahap (People's Anti-Japanese Army), fought strenuously against the invaders. On their return, the Americans quickly reached agreement with the collaborationist elite and refused to countenance their punishment. From the American perspective, the old elite was the best means through which social order might be maintained and the Americans might mediate their continuing economic and strategic interests in the Philippines. The Americans supported Manual Roxas, a key figure in the Japanese-sponsored 'Republic'. He was elected President of the independent Republic of the Philippines in 1946. Not one important member of the elite was convicted of collaboration. In 1948, Roxas gave an amnesty for all those involved in collaboration during the war years. The same elite which had dominated Filipino politics since the early twentieth century remained in control. There was no social change; nor, indeed, was there any sense that the elite of vast landholders saw any need for change. What emerged on 4 July 1946 was a state closely modelled on the forms of American democracy; a House and Senate, with an executive President elected every four years. The survival of the old Filipino oligarchy, its attachment to its old privileges, and its continuing espousal of clientelist politics, together with the tightness of the American economic embrace and American failure to reward wartime anti-Japanese military activity, saw the re-emergence in 1948 of the Hukbalahap movement. This was now a fully-fledged communist-sponsored agrarian uprising, in open revolt against the government. In 1950 the Huks, as they came to be known, for a time threatened to take Manila. They were gradually brought down by a combination of fortunate intelligence and coercive force. The charismatic Ramon Magsaysay succeeded, as Minister of Defence and, from 1953, President, in reorganizing and invigorating the security forces, sustaining a hard-driving military offensive and weaning many Huks from the movement through promises of amnesty and favour. By the mid 1950s, the Huk rebellion had been brought to an end, the hold of the landowning oligarchy of the Philippines consolidated.

Malaya

Malaya was subject to direct British colonialism from the mid 1870s. The Malayan indigenous elite had been co-opted into the British administration, but for the most part Malays were isolated from the economic development of the country, which rested upon the twin props of tin and rubber. Immigrants from southern China had come in large numbers to work the tin mines, while Indians were imported as workers on the rubber estates. The result was that twentieth-century Malaya became a plural society, its various racial groups operating within communal boundaries. In 1947, about 50 per cent of the population was Malay, about 38 per cent Chinese, and about 12 per cent Indian.

In British Malaya before the Second World War, nationalism remained muted, partly a consequence of British policy of privileging the Malay elite in terms of status and administrative position, but in no small measure a result of the divided nature of Malaya's society. The different communal groups had tended to pursue their own specific interests rather than a notion of an independent Malaya for all. The Japanese conquest of Malaya in 1942 saw a pattern emerge quite similar to that in Indonesia. The traditional rulers and the educated Malaya elite agreed to collaborate with the Japanese and provide the legitimacy and administrative wherewithal which the Japanese needed to run the country. The Chinese, however, were treated harshly by the Japanese who had, of course, been fighting on the Chinese mainland for nearly a decade. The result was that opposition to the Japanese tended to coalesce around the Chinese-dominated Malayan Communist Party (MCP), which made up the backbone of the Malayan resistance force, the Malayan Peoples' Anti-Japanese Army (MPAJA). This resistance force was supported by the Allies who supplied its 6,000 fighters with arms and money. The Japanese interregnum in Malaya provided the MPAJA and the MCP with legitimacy, arms, members, and organization. The MCP emerged from the war as the strongest political force in the country.

The communists' hopes of playing a political role in post-war Malaya were quickly dashed with the resumption of British colonial rule. The British returned with plans to construct a more broadly-based multiracial society, which involved placing limits on the privileged and protected status they had historically granted Malays, and removing the traditional powers of Malay rulers. Strident Malay opposition to these plans for a 'Malayan Union' which would grant citizenship to all on an equal basis, were articulated and led by Dato Onn bin Jafaar's United Malay National Organization (UMNO). The British were forced to recast their plans. The Federation of Malaya which emerged in February 1948 reaffirmed the sultans' authority, as well as other aspects of Malay pre-eminence and privilege.

Around the same time, the British began to apply increasing pressure to the MCP, which had achieved a dominant position in urban and rural trade unions. In 1948, the MCP abandoned the relatively peaceful political strategy it had been pursuing since the end of the war and, operating through its Malayan Races Liberation Army, took up a strategy of armed struggle against British colonialism. This began the period euphemistically known as the Malayan Emergency. The communists' tactics involved the use of the jungle as a sanctuary and a guerrilla offensive against the Malayan political, security and economic system, in an attempt to promote the maximum possible disruption. The party apparently hoped that, having secured large liberated areas, it could surround the cities and envelop them. It managed, for a couple of years, to go close to achieving some of its objectives with its force of around 8,000 guerrillas, although it was unable to create the administrative breakdown it had sought to achieve. The MCP reached a high point in 1951, during which it inflicted more than 1,000 casualties on the security forces, including the assassination of the British High Commissioner, Sir Henry Gurney. Then its fortunes began to decline. The appointment of Sir Gerald Templer as High Commissioner and Director of Operations in early 1952 helped turn the tide the way of the British, reviving the efficacy of both military and civil administration and successfully carrying through the New Villages project aimed at separating the guerrillas from their sources of respite and supply amongst the Chinese population which lived in squatter settlements on the fringes of settled areas. These very poor and underprivileged Chinese were a vital part of the communists' ability to keep the struggle going. In a massive operation, nearly half a million Chinese were relocated into new villages which were 'defended' by security forces. This tactic distanced the villages from the insurgents who made very few inroads into the overwhelmingly ethnic Malay rural population. A concerted military campaign destroyed the MCP as an effective threat by the mid 1950s.

All the while the struggle was going on, the British were cutting the ground from under the communists' feet by negotiating the granting of independence to the Malayan elite in the form of the UMNO. Between 1952 and 1954 the UMNO had allied itself with two smaller communal parties, the Malayan Chinese Association (MCA) and the Malayan Indian Congress (MIC). The success of the alliance strategy was such that in the 1955 federal elections, the Alliance won 51 of the 52 seats. After much subsequent negotiation between the British and the Alliance government, under Tungku Abdul Rahman, a constitution was drafted which provided some concessions to non-Malays on the question of citizenship, while protecting the interests of Malays in such matters as royal authority, religion, land, government service, business, language and education. Independence was finally granted to Malaya, led by this conservative grouping of bureaucrats, politicians and businessmen, on 31 August 1957.

First anniversary of independence, Kuala Lumpur, Malaya, September 1958

The great paradox of the situation, of course, was the way in which communal politics worked during this period. The MCP had sought independence on the basis of armed struggle against imperialists and class enemies, in other words, by trying to move above communal politics. However, they were never successful in broadening their membership beyond the poor Chinese community. By contrast, successful politics was communally based; the UMNO was established to protect Malay privileges and interests, and much the same applied to the MCA and MIC, which campaigned under the banner of looking after their own. These tactics made much more sense to Malayans than the effort to stand above the ethnic politics which were so much a part of people's experience of life in British Malaya.

Cambodia

Before the Second World War, nationalist sentiment in Cambodia was minimal, and restricted to a tiny number of intellectuals and Buddhist monks. The most notable of these early nationalists was Son Ngoc Thanh, a librarian at the Buddhist Institute in Phnom Penh and founder of the first Cambodian language newspaper, *Nagara Vatta*. The French countered these intimations of disloyalty by strengthening the prestige and visibility of the young King, Norodom Sihanouk, who had come to the throne in 1941; Son Ngoc Thanh took refuge in Japan in 1942. The 'independence' granted by the Japanese on 12 March 1945 lasted only until the French returned in mid October, but the French themselves found that circumstances had changed in Cambodia, and allowed political parties and an elected consultative assembly to emerge in 1946. A constitution promulgated in 1947 under the auspices of the strongest party, the vaguely republican Democrats, sought to relegate Sihanouk to the background, but the National Assembly, first convened in 1948, found itself unable in practice to exert its authority over the King or over the still-dominant French. In 1952, in an atmosphere of rising tension, Sihanouk sacked the Cabinet and took over the reigns of government. In early 1953 he dissolved the Assembly and instituted rule by royal decree.

Thereafter, a series of deft political manoeuvres by Sihanouk secured all his major objectives. A personal campaign to embarrass the French into granting independence was successful in August 1953. In February 1955 Sihanouk sought a *post-factum* mandate for his independence strategy and, unsurprisingly, won the wholesale endorsement of his people. Then, in March 1955, he abdicated from the throne to enter politics more wholeheartedly, and neutralized that institution by putting his complaisant father, Norodom Suramarit, in his place. Finally, he created a vehicle for the 1955 elections, the Sangkum Reastr Niyum (Popular Socialist Community) party, which romped to a victory of such proportions as to raise suspicions about the fairness of the electoral process. By 1955, Sihanouk dominated the Cambodian state root and branch. Indeed, he had become the state.

Laos

Notwithstanding French rule, Laos had remained politically undeveloped, partly because of the French preference for employing Vietnamese administrators. Politics, construed here in the narrow sense of administration, remained restricted to the activities of the King of Luang Prabang and his family and relatives. Colonial efforts to provide a French education for this tiny ruling caste saw no move towards a national consciousness nor the development of any sense that the future would not involve the French. Encouragement by some French officials of Lao nationalist sentiment amongst the elite during the Japanese period (a measure designed to neutralize Thai designs on Lao territory) bore some fruit, creating an enhanced Lao cultural consciousness and a seminal desire for independence. The Japanese grant of 'independence' to the King of Luang Prabang on 8 April 1945, and the fact that the French did not return in force to Vientiane until April 1946, saw the courtiers who supported independence expand their control of much of north and central Laos through the vehicle of the Lao Issara (Committee for a Free Laos), a provisional Lao people's government created in October 1945. In the south, however, the Prince of Champassak supported the French. As the French returned in numbers, courtly pro-independence figures fled Vientiane for exile in Thailand in April 1946 and established a Lao Issara government in exile. Other members of the anti-French elite retreated to eastern Laos where they gained the support of the Viet Minh. In 1949, most Lao Issara members decided to return to Laos as a result of French concessions to Lao independence. But the figure who was later to assume greatest prominence, Prince Souphanouvong, fell out with his Issara colleagues and took to the hills where, connecting with the groups in eastern Laos, he formed a resistance movement called the Pathet Lao (Land of the Lao), in alliance with the Viet Minh fighting the French in the northern region of the Lao–Vietnamese border. The French, as in Cambodia, were not so obstinate about independence as they had proved to be in Vietnam – a testimony to their long history of indifference to the place. They assured a grateful court at Luang Prabang of its place in a Lao state which would itself be assured a degree of autonomy within the French Union – a state of affairs which formally came to pass in 1949 – and granted Laos independence in October 1953. Around the same time, however, the Pathet Lao, in alliance with the Viet Minh, had gained control of much of northern Laos.

Under the terms of the Geneva conference, the Lao communists were allowed to regroup in the two northernmost provinces of Laos, where they remained in effective control. Elections held by the Royal Lao government in 1955 were boycotted by the Pathet Lao, unable to reach agreement about their re-integration into a post-Geneva Laos. A settlement was finally brokered in mid 1956 by Prince Souvanna Phouma, Prime Minister of the Royal Lao government, and in late 1957 a coalition government was formed. By mid 1958, however, with increasing American hardline pressure, the coalition had dissolved and, within a year, armed conflict resumed between the Royal government and the Pathet Lao. The conflict was further confused by the entrance into the fray of a neutralist force led by a young paratroop commander, Kong Le. In Vientiane, the divided, snarled, inept and corrupt non-communist forces were sustained only by generous American military, political and monetary assistance. A second Geneva conference, occasioned by American apprehension at the prospect of a communist take-over in Laos, and Soviet fear that Laos might become the site of a superpower conflagration, created the conditions for the construction of a second neutralist coalition government in 1962. Like its predecessor, this government soon dissolved, a victim of the tensions spun off by the emerging American war in Vietnam. The USA and the northern-based Democratic Republic of Vietnam (DRV) had radically different ideas of what Lao neutrality meant, especially in relation to the use of the Ho Chi Minh trail in south-eastern Laos; 'neither the United States nor the DRV had any intention of permitting the neutrality of Laos to interfere with their prosecution of the war in South Vietnam' (Stuart-Fox, 1986, p.28). Not until the effective conclusion of that war was a third temporary coalition constructed in 1973 which was itself to give way, finally, to communist rule at the end of 1975.

Thailand

Thailand, of course, had remained free from direct colonization by Western powers. None the less, since a military–civilian coalition had conspired to destroy the absolute monarchy in 1932, Thailand's progress towards constructing a stable and legitimate state system had been plagued with the same sorts of agonies of identity, struggle and partisanship which affected its colonized counterparts. In the Thai case, the particular problems of the post-Second World War era revolved around the difficulties of accommodating the democratic and sometimes socially radical tendencies of the country's civilian intellectuals, led by Pridi Phanomyong, with the strong state control desired by the military who, under the leadership of Phibun Songkhram, had effectively controlled affairs since the late 1930s. Initially, it was the civilians who held supremacy, trading on the soft terms of war settlement provided by the Allies (who sought to encourage the hopeful signs of emergent democracy in the country), and the stigma attached to the military for its wartime partnership with the Japanese. Drift and indecision followed. This was a function itself of divisions amongst civilian politicians and bureaucrats on such issues as the ambit of popular sovereignty and the proper place of the monarchy. The shock and recriminations occasioned by the mysterious fatal shooting of the King in 1947 saw the re-emergence of military rule under Phibun by the late 1940s, albeit cloaked in a façade of democratic institutions. Through the 1950s Phibun himself gradually found himself hemmed in by military opponents, notable army strongman Sarit Thannarat, and was removed in a 1957 coup. This was itself a harbinger of the full-scale military authoritarianism imposed by Sarit in 1958.

Thereafter, through the 1960s, in a context of continuing American support for Thailand's robust anti-communism and the emergence of a threatening communist insurgency in the north and north-east of the Thai state, now ruled by Thanom Kittikachorn following Sarit's death in 1963, military rule was consolidated. The only significant interruption came in 1973, when student demonstrations sent Thanom fleeing the country and opened the way for a brief, confused, contentious and socially polarizing return of civilian democracy which lasted only until 1976, when the military again seized power.

4.5   State formation: the drift towards authoritarianism

The first decade or so of independence in South-East Asia were years of political experimentation, frustration and continuing crisis. In Indonesia, the lack of a firm commitment to parliamentary democracy amongst important sections of the political elite, the difficulties of administering a state riven with ethnic and regional differences, and the heightened expectations aroused by the attainment of independence saw parliamentary democracy totter and then fall. It fell, first to the episodic authoritarianism of Sukarno's Guided Democracy and later, and more definitively, to the Pancasila democracy of Suharto's purposefully authoritarian New Order. In Malaya, the arrangements which had allowed a political solution in the 1950s broke down in the late 1960s with the flaring of violent ethnic unrest in Kuala Lumpur. The New Economy Policy, together with a more circumscribed and paternalist version of democracy was introduced to enshrine Malay political dominance and enhance its commercial interests. In Vietnam, the persistence of the Viet Cong in the south, and the DRV more generally, finally defeated the Americans in 1975. Deepening economic problems, however, would later bring substantial changes to the economic style, if not the form, of what was now the Socialist Republic of Vietnam. In Burma, the inability of the combination of statist intervention and democratic forms to deliver anything but economic decline and enhanced separatist sentiment led, finally, to the intervention of a highly authoritarian and unimaginative military in 1962. In the Philippines, too, the failure of a democratic model to deliver both economic prosperity and security from communists and southern separatists brought on the long years of the Marcos dictatorship. In Cambodia, as Sihanouk's efforts to create a royally directed and neutralist state fell foul of American interests in the region, the final result was the horror of the Khmer Rouge years. Laos, similarly caught up in the Cold War in Asia, suffered from American efforts to create a non-communist regime, and two unsuccessful efforts to create a coalition government, before the Pathet Lao rode the communist wave to power in 1975. The story of politics in postwar Thailand was one in which Western-style democratic politics were increasingly seen as both inappropriate to Thai culture and interests and singularly unable to provide the strong and effective governance the country needed.

In almost every case, the state building which accompanied and followed the attainment of independence by South-East Asian nations was a failure, at least in the short term. In no single instance did it provide the bridges – ideological, structural, economic – to the golden futures which independence had seemed to promise to pre-war nationalist leaders. The reasons for these failures, and especially the failure of Western-style forms of democracy to take solid root, are complex. At the purely domestic level, they reflected the most fundamental legacy of colonial rule: the shaping of economies to provide an abundance of simply produced tropical goods for the world economy, and societies accordingly frozen to keep that mode of production in place. The fruits of this policy were societies with little modern education and small Westernized and urbanized indigenous elites of a bureaucratic rather than an entrepreneurial cast of mind. The latter had neither the need nor the desire to respond to broader political constituencies. Ethnic division, cultures dominated by ideas of hierarchy, order and authority and glued together by patrimonialism, made for difficult democratic territory. Western modes of democracy were imposed in soils too thin and arid to support them in the context of the social strains and demands generated by independence. From a wider perspective, the imperatives imposed by the Cold War placed a premium on order and social control; the jostlings, wranglings, disorder and unexpected outcomes which inevitably accompany the exercise of popular sovereignty were too risky to win the approbation of the Great Powers. Both sides in the Cold War struggle found themselves supporting and rewarding authoritarian rather than popular regimes in the name of a purportedly greater good. In such context, varieties of authoritarian and semi-democratic regimes were easier to attain, made more immediate sense, and guaranteed more certain outcomes than the painful, sweaty work of democracy.

Notwithstanding the fact that the shadow of authoritarianism fell longer and more widely across South-East Asia as the 1950s gave way to the 1960s, there were more positive stories to tell. In a longer perspective, and in the context of the extraordinary problems of identity and ideology these entities faced in making themselves states – and the much more subtly difficult job of creating themselves as nations – we can only marvel at the general outcome. For example, in all this turmoil it is easy to lose sight of the fact that Indonesia had survived as a unity, and that there had never been a significant attempt from within that recent construction to form separate, ethnically-based states. This was an extraordinary achievement. Equally, there is the realization that, at least in some cases, authoritarianism has been usefully employed to provide a sound basis for successful economic development. Half a century on from their creation, after many vicissitudes, much trial and error, and sometimes much bloodshed, we may be permitted to indulge in a more realistic hope of a stable, and increasingly prosperous and democratic collection of states in South-East Asia.

References

Feith, H. and Castles, L. (eds) (1970) *Indonesian Political Thinking 1945–1965*, Ithaca, Cornell University Press.

Kratoska, P. and Batson, B. (1992) 'Nationalism and modernist reform' in Tarling, N. (ed.).

Steinberg, D.I. (1989) 'Neither silver nor gold: the 40th anniversary of the Burmese economy' in Silverstein, J. (ed.) *Independent Burma at Forty Years: Six Assessments*, Ithaca, Southeast Asia Program, Cornell University.

Stockwell, A.J. (1992) 'Southeast Asia in war and peace: the end of European colonial empires' in Tarling, N. (ed.).

Stuart-Fox, M. (1986) *Laos: Politics, Economics and Society*, London, Frances Pinter.

Sukarno (1970) 'Saving the Republic of the Proclamation' in Feith, H. and Castles, L. (eds).

Tarling, N. (ed.) (1992) *The Cambridge History of Southeast Asia, vol.2*, Cambridge, Cambridge University Press.

Further reading

There is a surprising dearth of studies which use a comparative approach to modern South-East Asia. By far the greatest number of studies focus on the specific countries of South-East Asia, which makes the study of the region as a whole time-consuming and sometimes tedious. The most useful of the comparative works are:

Jeffrey, R. (ed.) (1981) *Asia – the Winning of Independence*, London, Macmillan, chapters by McCoy, Reid, Marr and Lee, and comparative analysis by Low.

Osborne, M. (1995) *Southeast Asia: an Introductory History*, 6th edn, Sydney, Allen & Unwin, chapters 10 and 11.

Steinberg, D.J. (ed.) (1987) *In Search of Southeast Asia: a Modern History*, rev. edn, Sydney, Allen & Unwin, part 5.

Tarling, N. (ed.) (1992) *The Cambridge History of Southeast Asia, vol.2*, Cambridge, Cambridge University Press, chapters by Kratoska and Batson, Stockwell, Owen and Yong.

Politics and governance in the Anglo states

George Lafferty and Jacques Bierling

5.1 Introduction

This chapter examines the recent politics and governance of the Anglo, or English speaking states, of the Asia-Pacific. The USA, Canada, Australia and New Zealand share a number of important characteristics, apart from their common language. Each has a long tradition of political democracy and each is a mainly migrant society, with a substantial indigenous population. There are also, interestingly, significant differences between these four nations and the non-English speaking nations of the region. The differences are particularly notable in the domain of governance and political culture. The Anglo nations draw on a shared colonial political heritage, although there are differences between them, plus a marked attachment to liberal democracy, although the institutions and mechanisms of government vary (see Chapter 1). This chapter takes a close look at the political debates that have animated each of these nations over the past decades: focusing on the debates over the size of the public sector and the provision and governance of welfare. Interestingly, all four countries have had broadly similar experiences although there have been significant local variations.

In Section 5.2 the chapter looks at the broad economic and political background in which the debates over the role of the state have been conducted in each of the four nations. The subsequent four sections look at the politics of the USA, Canada, Australia and New Zealand respectively, whilst Section 5.7 looks at the patterns across all four nations.

5.2 The state, markets and political change

The USA, Canada, Australia and New Zealand are the predominantly English-speaking states of the Asia-Pacific. They were first colonized mainly by people from Great Britain and Ireland. However, they are not simply 'Anglo' states. Each country has its indigenous peoples, who settled there many centuries prior to the arrival of the Europeans. These countries have also been the destination for millions of migrants from around the globe ever since. Therefore, these are, to varying degrees, ethnically diverse societies. For example, Canada has a very large French-speaking minority and the USA has a substantial Hispanic population, with Spanish being the main language in some areas.

Each of these countries is among the world's wealthiest nations, although there are significant differences between them in terms of per capita gross domestic product (GDP). In 1995 the USA (population 263.1 million) was the country with the highest per capita GDP in the world, apart from some micro-states, while Canada (population 29.6 million) had the 5th highest per capita GDP. Australia (population 17,483 million) was 9th and New Zealand (population 3,433 million) was in 21st position. The USA also has the largest economy of any single country in the world, by far – over US$6 trillion – more than twice as large as Japan. Canada ranks 11th, Australia 14th and New Zealand 44th.

As in other countries, the distribution of wealth and income is a key political issue in each of these four nations. The historical development of market economies has been characterized to some extent by conflicts over how economic resources are allocated, who controls them and the extent to which private or public goals are given priority. The role of the state has occupied a central role in political debates in each of these countries over the past century. The 'state' includes the complex of institutions and agencies funded through government expenditure. They provide a variety of services – for example, education, transport, health and the maintenance of social order.

These debates have involved two main forces. On the one hand, those on the political right, which includes conservatives and 'free market' liberals, have mainly argued for limited state intervention, except in the areas of defence and 'law and order'. They claim that political freedoms are best guaranteed through the pursuit of individual interests and the operation of a market economy. On the other hand, those on the political left, including socialists, social democrats and 'social' liberals, have typically maintained that substantial state intervention is required to ensure sustainable economic development, social equity and the expansion of citizenship rights. They argue for a greater emphasis on the social welfare role of the state.

The welfare state has developed unevenly in the four nations. There are certain approaches to the welfare state which envisage the provision of little more than a 'safety net' for those who have failed in, or have been excluded from, the labour market, to be sufficient. Arguments for a more extensive welfare state and greater government intervention are based on egalitarian arguments that there should be greater socio-economic equality and more equitable access to such public goods as education, housing and health. The notion of 'universal' rights is crucial in this context: all citizens it is argued, should have access to certain basic rights. However, some would argue that, even in a more extensive welfare state, women and minority racial or ethnic groups continue to be disadvantaged through socio-economic inequalities. Therefore, further state intervention is required; for instance, affirmative action programmes for women and racial or ethnic minorities so that they can achieve equality of opportunity.

National Guard and Civil Rights protester, Maryland, USA, 1964

Following the Second World War, state expenditure and the welfare state expanded in most industrialized countries. In a period of relative economic stability, full employment and rising living standards, the size of the state also grew; a process generally supported by mainstream political parties, as well as by trade unions and business. However, this consensus broke down in the early 1970s, with the onset of recession, higher unemployment levels 'stagflation' (the combination of high inflation and low growth) and a general sense that the expansion of the welfare state had not succeeded. In this atmosphere conservative or neo-liberal policy prescriptions become increasingly influential, particularly in the Anglo countries of the Asia-Pacific. Both right-wing administrations in the USA and Canada, as well as governments of the left in Australia and New Zealand, instituted programmes of deregulation, privatization and reductions in public sector expenditure. However, political outcomes varied from nation to nation depending on differences in their economic structure, historical development and the balance between contending political forces. This chapter assesses these variations.

Liberal democracies, such as those in the USA, Canada, Australia and New Zealand, are often described as pluralist. Pluralism is characterized by the existence of a variety of political positions and organizations and a decentralized and fragmented distribution of political power. There is no single focus or concentration of power. Pluralist societies are characterized by interest group participation; by a political culture in which citizens are at liberty to be involved in those issues that affect them most deeply plus a 'free' news media in which important issues are debated. However, some radical analysts have argued that these societies are actually characterized by substantial socio-economic inequality, the dominance of certain interests, notably big business, the concentration of media ownership in a few hands, political corruption and widespread political apathy. Political democracy is a relatively recent phenomenon even in these countries. Until the late nineteenth century, access to the vote was mainly confined to white males. It was only after the rise of the labour movement, the women's movement and the Civil Rights movements that the adult population of these four countries eventually became enfranchised. Although as late as the 1960s, Australian Aborigines and African Americans in some US states still had restricted political rights.

Martin Luther King delivering his 'I have a dream' speech, Washington, 28 August 1963

In each of these countries, as in other Western nations, recent decades have seen the rise of 'new social movements'. The political landscape has been transformed by the women's movement, gay and lesbian movements, environmentalism, peace campaigns, civil rights organizations and indigenous peoples' campaigns. On the political right, there have been significant popular movements, such as the 'Moral Majority' in the USA, and various groups with 'fundamentalist' Christian allegiances. These changes have also broadened the scope of politics in the four nations. A particular feature of politics in recent years has been the growing importance of indigenous peoples' movements, such as Native Americans in the USA and Canada, Aborigines in Australia and Maoris in New Zealand. In many cases, indigenous peoples, for example the Inuit in the Arctic region, populate areas that cross national boundaries. Campaigns for self-determination among indigenous peoples, including the creation of various cross-national indigenous peoples' organizations, have strengthened considerably in recent years.

Several themes run through this chapter, these include:

- the growth of the welfare state and challenges to it,
- the changing role of government and attempts to reduce public expenditure,
- the differences between federal and unitary political systems,
- citizenship rights and what it means to be a 'citizen' for various social groups,
- political campaigns to eliminate poverty and the growth of an 'underclass',
- the spread of political cynicism and apathy, and
- the impact of economic 'globalization'.

These themes are relevant to each of these countries, in an era of increasing political and economic interdependence, in which the role of the nation-state is being rapidly redefined.

5.3   The USA: the 'New Deal' and its legacy

American federalism

The sheer size of its population, as well as its economic, political and military power distinguishes the USA from the three other nations discussed here. Yet, despite its international pre-eminence, poverty is the lot of millions of its citizens. US governments have rarely been prepared to commit substantial expenditure to the reduction of poverty. In international terms, US spending on social welfare is relatively low. It is also uneven due to its federal system of government, which allows significant policy variations between the 50 states. The dominant political and public culture has generally stressed individual and family self-reliance, rather than a collective, national governmental responsibility to ensure the economic and social well-being of all citizens.

However the limits of the US welfare state cannot be accounted for in terms of political culture alone: the structure of the US state and party systems has also been important. One of the most important restraining influences on all political projects in the USA has been the complexity of the political system and the manner in which responsibilities are divided between national, state and local tiers of government. The system of 'checks and balances', written into the Constitution, makes it significantly more difficult than in most Western nations, to pass reform legislation, especially if it is contentious. The federal nature of US government does place a brake on radical changes to existing practices and to some extent restricts the development of coherent policy frameworks and patterns of governance.

There are notable differences between the US presidential system and the Westminster-style parliamentary systems of the other three countries discussed here. In Canada, Australia and New Zealand governments are usually identified more with the parties than with individuals, and individual prime ministers can be replaced while the same party remains in government. Individual presidents in the USA only cease to occupy the office in exceptional circumstances (such as death or impeachment), in which case they are replaced by the vice-president. In the USA, terms of office are fixed and presidents since Harry Truman, who left office in 1953, are only able to serve a maximum of two four-year terms, whereas in the other countries, a single party and/or prime minister can remain in power for several terms, and governments can also have very short periods in power. The USA does not have the same level of party discipline found in the other countries. US political representatives can and do frequently vote against their own party leadership, making implementation of an overall party platform difficult.

US politics is dominated by the two major parties, the slightly left-of-centre Democrats and the usually right-of-centre Republicans. The 'centre' in US politics, however, is typically more conservative than in the other Anglo countries. The USA has lacked a significant socialist or labour party due to its distinctive and singular history, which is one of the reasons it is the home of 'interest group' politics. Interest groups include ethnic, religious, labour, women's and environmental organizations, as well as single interest groups such as the National Rifle Association, or the pro-life or pro-choice organizations. Most interest groups mobilize on specific issues rather than across the entire political agenda.

The multiplicity of interest groups and their actions often produces political stalemate and unsatisfactory compromises, but over the span of time, legislation is enacted, and reforms turned into law. Welfare legislation has been passed, particularly in the north-east, where more extensive welfare programmes have been enacted. The poorest states, mainly in the south, are those with the worst problems and the fewest resources to deal with them. The degree of economic inequality between the different US states, is greater than exists in either the Australian or Canadian federal systems and has meant that states often compete in terms of low taxation and cheaper labour, in order to attract investment. Overall, the USA has lagged behind Australia, Canada and, until recently, New Zealand, and even further behind the more generous west European welfare systems of Sweden and the Netherlands.

National responsibility vs. small government

The Great Depression of the late 1920s and early 1930s was a watershed for all industrialized societies. President Herbert Hoover (1929–33) clung to the belief that the economy would right itself and remained committed to restraining Federal spending during a period of rapidly contracting income tax revenues. Yet it became increasingly evident that, contrary to their current economic orthodoxy, the national government was the only institution able to ensure some social and economic stability. The Depression undermined the notion of a self-regulating market economy and the advocates of trusting the market, notably President Hoover, were soundly defeated. Franklin Delano Roosevelt's victory in the 1932 presidential campaign ushered in the period of the 'New Deal', during which the national government assumed a much more significant role in areas such as employment, housing and social welfare. While the New Deal altered the landscape of governance in the USA and introduced new programmes and policies, the power of business in the USA was only lightly regulated; and the ownership of industry was left in private hands. The New Deal did not go down the road of social democracy like other Western nations, notably those in western Europe.

Under the New Deal, federal expenditure increased from under US$4 billion in 1931 to almost US$7 billion in 1934 and over US$8 billion in 1936. The states nevertheless retained a key role in implementing new programmes, which meant that the outcomes varied considerably across the country. However, the New Deal did introduce a national Social Security system, but it was contributory, and consequently excluded many of the poorest citizens. The National Labor Relations Act (1935), gave workers the right to unionize and to bargain collectively, and the Fair Labor Standards Act (1938) enforced minimum wage legislation to cover all (legally-employed) workers. The New Deal shifted the US political balance dramatically in favour of the Democrats, who captured working class and ethnic support, and were able to control both houses of Congress for most of the next 60 years. In terms of social welfare, it did create a safety net, but by the standards of the other Anglo countries, it was a somewhat basic version.

Following the Second World War and until the early 1970s, the USA, along with other developed countries, experienced economic stability and growth. This was accompanied by increased government spending and more generous welfare benefits. Although governments, both federal and state, still continued to spend a lower proportion of GDP than their industrialized counterparts, they spent considerably more than previously on health, education, social welfare, employment and the environment. During the 1960s and 1970s, significant inroads were made in reducing poverty in the USA, partly through such programmes as the War on Poverty initiated by President Lyndon Baines Johnson (1963–69). In 1959, there were 40 million Americans living in poverty, over 22 per cent of the population. By 1969, the poverty rate had fallen to 10.1 per cent and total numbers to 27,124,885, and they continued to remain around these levels during the 1980s.

Despite the anti-centralist rhetoric of his 'New Federalism', President Richard Nixon (1969–74) was quite interventionist. For example, he imposed prices and wages controls and introduced legislation on occupational health and safety, consumer protection, the environment and a minimum income for the poor. However, Nixon, as did Gerald Ford (1974–77), turned more responsibilities and funding over to the states and local governments. Jimmy Carter (1977–81), in contrast to other post-war Democratic Presidents, reduced expenditure and gave more control to state and local governments. During the 1970s, disenchantment with Federal programmes grew, and the election of Ronald Reagan as President in 1980 signalled the onset of a prolonged assault on welfare expenditure.

One of the aims of the Reagan years was the dismantling of the New Deal legacy, particularly welfare programmes. Welfare has been a target of the US right since the 1960s but the disenchantment has not been limited to only conservatives. It is argued widely that welfare encourages dependence, that it gives unmarried women an incentive to bear more children because they know they will be supported by the state. Further, it is argued, welfare assistance has contributed to a decline in the nuclear family. These accusations are often given a racial edge, since there are more single-parent black families headed by women and yet many more white people receive benefits.

Budget cuts were aimed directly at the poorest sections of US society. The states were encouraged to tighten controls over welfare recipients and entitlements for recipients were reduced. The Reagan administration tried to turn the responsibility for welfare back to the states, as in the pre-New Deal era. However, these efforts met with limited success, largely due to opposition from Democrats and even some Republicans, although enthusiasm for the existing welfare arrangements was limited. Welfare in the USA was problematic but there did not appear any obvious solutions. Public expenditure continued to grow.

Poverty increased during the 1980s and 1990s. In 1994, the number of people officially living in poverty reached 38.1 million people, the highest figure since 1959. There has been a decline since then, principally due to the strength of the US economy. Nevertheless, an 'underclass', characterized by high, chronic unemployment, limited education and welfare dependency, is a feature of inner US cities. There is evidence of such a growth in parts of the other three countries, particularly among minority groups. The political right attribute the growth of the 'underclass' to the moral failings of welfare recipients and excessively generous government payments. In order to end the 'culture of poverty', they argue, welfare recipients should be compelled to accept low-paid jobs through reduction or even withdrawal of welfare benefits.

In 1992 Bill Clinton became the first Democrat since Jimmy Carter to win a presidential election. However, US national politics in the 1990s has continued to move in a generally conservative direction, particularly following the 1994 Republican election success giving them control of both houses. During 1995, the situation of a Republican majority in the Congress and a Democrat President led to a protracted period of 'gridlock', in which the government of the country came to a standstill, over the issue of public expenditure.

Although the Republicans were more aggressive in their assaults on welfare recipients the President, reflecting a widespread disenchantment in the electorate, also committed himself to cut welfare spending and make welfare benefits more difficult to obtain and welfare recipients subject to tighter control. During the 1992 presidential campaign, Clinton promised a system of universal health care. However, the proposals formulated by the First Lady, Hillary Clinton, and proposed by the President, were defeated. There were numerous reasons for the defeat. There was opposition from the private health care industry and its supporters. In addition, the changes proposed were too complex and while there was universal agreement that medical care in the USA was too expensive, President Clinton's proposals were also viewed as flawed. Belatedly, in August 1996, a very limited bill was passed with bipartisan support, guaranteeing employees who switch jobs the right to continuing health care cover, regardless of any health problems. There were also tax breaks for people taking out private health insurance. Yet the bill did not deal with the approximately 40 million Americans who have no health insurance nor with the rapidly rising costs of health care.

In August 1996 Clinton signed into law a welfare reform bill which introduced radical changes. In spite of some Democratic opponents in the Congress who pointed out the likelihood that many more people, particularly children, would be reduced to poverty, the President declared that the bill was acceptable. The new welfare legislation is projected to save the Federal Government between US$55 billion and US$56 billion over six years. It requires all adults to find paid work after they have spent two years receiving welfare payments and also limits lifetime welfare entitlements for any single family to a total of five years. Under the new legislation, responsibility for the administration of welfare is turned back to the states through the Federal provision of block grants. Currently there are a number of new programmes initiated at state level which are attempting to deal with the restructured system of welfare provision. It is too early to judge the impact of these programmes, but there are fears that the American welfare safety net will not provide as much 'safety' as it once did.

Issues in the 1990s

The 1996 presidential campaign was characterized by a sense of inevitability, since President Clinton held a substantial lead in the polls over his Republican challenger, Senator Bob Dole, in the months leading up to the election. Also, and much more critically for the future of US democracy, the campaign was characterized by a lack of debate over important issues such as poverty and inequality, racial tensions, urban decay, economic 'globalization' and the environment.

President Clinton, by adopting a very centrist agenda, such as smaller federal government, balanced budgets, welfare cutbacks and tougher criminal sentencing, effectively defused the Republican threat to his re-election. On the other hand, those on the political left had no other viable presidential candidate. A right-of-centre consensus has been established in Washington, but a percentage of the American people have become effectively disenfranchised. Although they have the formal right to vote, they see no value in exercising that right. On election day, 5 November 1996, Bill Clinton received the votes of fewer than half of the 49 per cent of voters who cast a ballot, although the margin over Bob Dole was substantial due to the presence of several minor party candidates. The turnout was one of the lowest ever and compared unfavourably with the 1992 figure of 55 per cent. The presidential campaign highlighted the disenchantment and cynicism felt by many Americans towards their political system and politicians. Across the political spectrum, Washington politics is widely viewed as remote and corrupt, accessible only to insiders. Commentators have popularized the idea of the 'real government' (major corporations, powerful interest groups and their lobbyists) as distinct from the 'show government' (politicians and a series of stage-managed media events, in which even television stations have lost interest). America's crisis of democracy continues.

5.4   Canada: the competing dynamics of integration and separation

Canadian federalism

Since the American Revolution, when tens of thousands of United Empire Loyalists fled north to British-controlled territory, Canada has been defined, to a considerable extent, in relation to the USA. Early fears of US military invasion gave way to long-standing concerns over being overwhelmed by the USA economically, politically and culturally. However, with Britain's international decline, Canada's relationship with its superpower neighbour became increasingly crucial.

Like the USA and Australia, Canada has a federal governmental structure, with governments at the provincial and national levels. Like Australia and New Zealand, it has a parliamentary political system. The relationship of the provinces to the national government is a constant feature of Canadian politics. Several of the provinces in this huge country are often grouped during political discussion and debate into informal 'regions' sharing broadly similar political and economic interests, despite substantial differences between the respective provinces concerned. The four provinces to the west of Ontario, British Columbia, Alberta, Manitoba and Saskatchewan, are often referred to as 'Western Canada', while the four considerably smaller and less populous provinces to the east of Quebec, Nova Scotia, New Brunswick, Newfoundland and Prince Edward Island, are often referred to as 'Atlantic Canada' or 'the Maritimes'.

Canada has a 'first past the post' electoral system. The candidate who polls the most votes wins the seat in each single-member constituency in the House of Commons. As with all Westminster systems, the government must be able to control a majority in parliament in order to govern. From the mid 1930s, Canadian national politics has been dominated by the left-of-centre Liberal Party, although before that the right-of-centre Conservative Party, which became the Progressive Conservative Party in 1942, had been the dominant force in Canadian politics. Unlike the USA, Canada has a significant, left-oriented third party, the New Democratic Party (NDP).

The Canadian federation has always been under some stress, with the provinces retaining, to varying degrees, strong distinct identities and conceptions of their political and economic interests which often may conflict with those identified by national governments. The political representation of each province in Canada's upper house, the Senate, is complex and potentially confusing. Since Senators are appointed by the Prime Minister, not elected, the Senate does not provide the same degree of 'checks and balances' present in either the US or Australian federal systems. Nor is there much consistency in terms of representation per state or per head of population. Senate reform has been of particular concern to Western Canadians and the idea of a 'Triple-E Senate' (equal, elected and effective) has gained popularity in the west, where there have been occasional separatist campaigns. However, by far the most important separatist movement in Canada has stemmed from the French-speaking population, concentrated mainly in Quebec.

The distinctiveness of Quebec and 'French Canada'

Canada is distinctive among these 'Anglo' states in that a substantial minority of its population, varying historically between a quarter and a third, has always been linguistically and culturally French. While French speakers have been a minority in Canada overall, in Quebec, the second most populous Canadian province, they have constituted a substantial majority. This situation has contributed to movements for greater *Québécois* autonomy, or even independence. While Canada outside Quebec is usually referred to as 'English Canada', this term understates both the numbers of French speakers in other provinces, approximately 20 per cent of the French-speaking population lives outside Quebec, as well as the increasing diversity and ethnic heterogeneity of Canadian life.

The 'Quiet Revolution', which began in Quebec in 1960 with the election of the Liberal provincial government of Jean Lesage, marked the onset of a major reorientation of Quebec politics and the national political landscape. Previously, Quebec's francophone population, most of whom were regular churchgoers, had been encouraged by the Catholic Church to maintain their culture, while avoiding active participation in business and politics. Largely as a result, the small anglophone community dominated the province's business life. Before the 'Quiet Revolution', the French population of Quebec had been governed (1936–39 and 1944–60) by the isolationist, conservative Union Nationale led by Maurice Duplessis. However, Duplessis's death in 1959 and the Liberals' victory in the Quebec election of 1960 ushered in a new political era, encapsulated in their 1962 provincial election slogan, *'maîtres chez nous'* (masters in our own house).

In order to advance the interests of the French-speaking majority in Quebec, the new government sought to increase the jurisdictional powers of the province, thereby questioning the structure of Canadian federalism. If *Québécois* were to become 'masters in their own house', more decision making and funds had to be concentrated in Quebec, which could not be regarded as a province like the other Canadian provinces. Major goals of the 'quiet revolution' were to achieve equal status with English for the French language and to eliminate the economic inequalities favouring English-speaking over French-speaking Canadians. New laws and regulations were introduced to advance the French language and French became Quebec's only official language, although Canada was officially bilingual.

There was also a general shift in Canadian life during the 1960s away from 'English' symbols, as in the replacement of the Red Ensign (with the Union Jack in the corner) by Canada's new, red maple leaf flag. Such changes were critical to the maintenance of the French-speaking population within Canada, preventing the break-up of the nation. However, the problematic relationship between 'French' and 'English' Canadians has remained a central feature of Canadian politics. In 1980, Quebec had a referendum on independence with resulted in a decisive victory for the 'no' campaign, with 59.56 per cent of voters rejecting independence. However, the *Parti Québécois* continued to press the separatist cause. In July 1990, the *Bloc Québécois* was formed, to campaign for Quebec independence in national elections. Led by Lucien Bouchard, the Bloc won 54 seats in the 1993 election. This enabled it to become the Official Opposition, and it could pressure for Quebec independence within the federal House of Commons. Again, in 1995 there was a referendum on independence for Quebec. The result this time was extremely close, with 49.44 per cent (2,308,072) of the Quebec electorate voting for an independent Quebec, while 50.56 per cent (2,360,717) voted to stay within Canada. The margin for the 'no' campaign was only 1.12 per cent, or 52,645 votes. The closeness of the results indicates that the divisive issue of Quebec's position in, or apart from, Canada will remain a critical area of political conflict and debate.

Welfare expansion and contraction

As in the other countries, the Great Depression had a tremendous impact on the Canadian political and economic landscape. Policy makers generally accepted that unemployment and poverty could no longer be attributed to individual moral failings. Governmental action was necessary if the worst effects of the cyclical nature of capitalist economies were to be avoided. The development of the welfare state and the application of a mild version of Keynesian economic policies in Canada gained momentum after the Second World War.

There had been some piecemeal welfare initiatives in the earlier part of the century, such as the federal Old Age Pensions Act (1927), which was very limited in its provisions, and the establishment of a national insurance scheme in 1941. However, following the war, there was a series of substantial reforms. These reforms included: Family Allowance payments (1945); a universal old age pensions scheme (1951); national hospital insurance (1958); national medicare (1968); expanded entitlements to unemployment benefits and workers' compensation; the Canada Assistance Plan (1996), which provided for several categories of people in need; and a massive expansion of the education system.

The areas in which the welfare state expanded were mainly under provincial, rather than national, jurisdiction. Public sector growth occurred mainly at the provincial and local levels. Increases in welfare spending were largely conducted through combined federal-provincial programmes, rather than through the implementation of uniform national policies. However, the Canadian federal government sought to minimize inequalities between the provinces by providing more resources to the poorer ones, leading to a considerably more generous and even welfare system than exists in the USA. However, during the 1980s, the national government began to reduce its social welfare role.

In September 1984, the Progressive Conservatives under Brian Mulroney won a massive victory against the Liberal Government led by John Turner, who had only recently taken over from Pierre Trudeau. The main priority of the Mulroney government was the reduction of inflation and public sector debt, through a monetarist emphasis on tightening the money supply. However, although the mid 1980s saw significant prosperity, the economy slid into recession towards the end of the decade. Unemployment increased and public sector debt grew substantially, largely due to declining tax revenue. The government's popularity slumped.

In response, Prime Minister Mulroney pursued two main issues in the run-up to the 1988 federal election: constitutional reform and North American free trade. The Meech Lake Accord, between the federal government and the ten provinces, was set up to deal mainly with the issue of Quebec's place within the federation as a distinctive province, and to shore up support in Quebec for the federal government. However, it also contained several measures addressing particular concerns of the other provinces. The Accord was signed by the federal and provincial governments on 2 June 1987, but was defeated at a subsequent referendum. In broad terms many *Québécois* felt the Accord did not give them enough, while many anglophone Canadians felt it gave Quebec too much.

The Free Trade Agreement between Canada and the USA produced even greater political conflict. Big business and some small business organizations, along with several pro-free trade provincial governments and the federal government, supported the agreement. Its opponents included trade unions, women's organizations, indigenous peoples' organizations, some sections of business, as well as the federal Liberals and the NDP. The 1988 Canadian federal election was widely dubbed the 'free trade election'. Although there was considerable popular disquiet concerning the agreement with the USA, the Conservatives won the election with 169 seats (43 per cent of the national vote). The Liberals won only 83 seats (32 per cent) and the NDP made a creditable showing in third place, with 43 seats (23 per cent).

The subsequent establishment of the North American Free Trade Agreement (NAFTA), signed in 1992 between the governments of the USA, Mexico and Canada, signalled a victory for 'continentalism' (see **Eccleston *et al.*, 1998**, p.315). This is the argument that Canada should benefit from being part of a broader North American economy, rather than being protected by tariffs and other trade restrictions. In a globalized economy, trading blocs have become increasingly important, and Canada is in danger of being left out if it is not part of a trading bloc.

Recession hit Canada particularly hard during the early 1990s. The official unemployment rate rose from 7.5 per cent in 1989 to 11.7 per cent in 1992. Governments reduced levels of welfare payments, while tightening eligibility criteria. Canada suffered a contraction of its economy over the first three years of the 1990s. The Free Trade Agreement did not stimulate the jobs growth predicted by the government. The introduction of the contentious Goods and Services Tax in 1990 merely exacerbated the Mulroney government's unpopularity.

On 22 August 1992, after negotiations following the failure of the Meech Lake Accord, the federal and provincial governments struck a deal on several measures. These included: reform of the federal Senate; decentralization of powers to the provinces (in areas such as housing, tourism, forestry and mining); elimination of inter-provincial trade barriers; recognition of Quebec as a 'distinct society'; and acknowledgement of the rights of the Yukon and North-West Territories to lobby the federal government for provincial status. This agreement led to the Charlottetown Accord, signed on 28 August. However, despite having the support of federal and provincial governments, the Accord was defeated at the referendum in October 1992, with 54 per cent rejecting it.

Issues in the 1990s

Following this further setback, Brian Mulroney eventually resigned as Prime Minister in February 1993. Kim Campbell defeated Jean Charest in the contest for the Progressive Conservative leadership, to become Canada's first woman Prime Minister. However, the Canadian Federal election on 25 October 1993 saw the decimation of the Progressive Conservatives and the rise of the New Right-wing force whose centre of political gravity lay in western Canada. The Reform Party was committed to an agenda of small government, deficit reduction, lower taxes and an ideological emphasis on the self-reliance of individuals and families. The overall outcome of the federal election was that the Liberal Party became the government, with 177 of the total 295 seats in the House of Commons, having received 41.6 per cent of the national vote. The *Bloc Québécois* won 54 seats, the Reform Party 52, the New Democratic Party only 9 and the Progressive Conservative Party, although it polled 16.1 per cent of the national vote was left with just 2 seats. Jean Chrétien, the Liberal leader, became Canada's new Prime Minister.

Although it rejected 'New Right' policies, the Chrétien government has cut approximately CAN$7 billion from transfers to the provinces, leading to reductions in health, education and social services, as well as the loss of thousands of public service jobs. Further cuts of approximately CAN$2 billion were scheduled in the 1996 budget. An extensive programme of public sector rationalization has led to a decline in public spending. There has also been a reduction in government subsidies for industry, as well as privatization of major state agencies such as Petro-Canada. Therefore, despite the change of government, reduced public expenditure has remained a priority. Social welfare entitlements have been tightened, although in a less punitive fashion than in the USA.

In the Federal election of June 1997, the Liberals under Jean Chrétien won another term in office, but with a significantly reduced majority. The Liberals finished with 155 seats, to the Reform Party's 60, 44 for the *Parti Québécois*, 21 for the NDP and 20 for the Conservatives. While there was considerable support in the new cabinet for a greater emphasis on social welfare and job creation, the Prime Minister affirmed that the major priority would be to reduce the government deficit to zero within two years. He thereby attempted to defuse speculation of a shift to the left, while rejecting any return to 'New Right' policy prescriptions. Government expenditure, the relationship with the USA, federalism and the future of Quebec, therefore, continue to dominate Canadian politics.

5.5 Australia: citizenship, welfare and diversity

Australian federalism

Like Canada, Australia has a federal political structure with a Westminster-style parliamentary system of government. The Commonwealth of Australia was inaugurated on 1 January 1901, following a series of Constitutional Conventions and electoral approval of a national Constitution in the 1890s. The six colonies of New South Wales, Victoria, Queensland, South Australia, Western Australia and Tasmania became the states of the new country, each with its own state government. Subsequently, two territories, the Northern Territory and the Australian Capital Territory, a small area around the national capital, Canberra, each with its own government but with very limited powers, were established. Australia's Constitution can be changed only through a referendum. To succeed, a referendum proposal must be approved by a majority of voters in a majority of states. Only eight amendments have been approved since Federation, and the Constitution has changed very little since 1901.

Australia has a bicameral parliamentary system. The national parliament's two houses are the House of Representatives and the Senate. The 148 members of the House of Representatives represent single-member electorates with roughly equal numbers of voters. The Senate has 76 members, twelve from each state and two from each territory. Voting in Australian elections is compulsory and fines are imposed on non-voters. Federally and in most states, Australia has a system of preferential voting. Votes for failed candidates are redistributed between the two leading candidates, according to voter preferences, until one candidate obtains a majority.

The Constitution stipulates a division of powers between the national and state governments. However, there have always been significant areas of overlap and occasional jurisdictional disputes. Over the course of this century, the federal government has tended to assume greater responsibilities in most areas. This has been particularly important in the area of revenue-raising capacity. During the Second World War, the federal government in Australia developed greater powers in relation to the lower tier of government than either its American or Canadian counterparts.

Citizenship and the nation-building role of government

The labour movement has played a much more important political role in Australia than in either the USA or Canada, and Australian politics has been more strongly oriented around class-related issues. As early as the 1850s, some trade unions won the right to an eight-hour working day, and throughout the second half of the nineteenth century, unionism expanded and workers achieved significant improvements in pay and conditions. However, during the recession of the 1890s, governments and employers suppressed strikes and sought to limit the power of unions. In response, the union movement established the Australian Labor Party, to promote working class interests in the formal political arena. ALP governments came to power at both federal and state levels during the following decade, and were important in promoting social welfare issues, although 'social liberalism' also played a considerable role. Early in the century, both Australia and New Zealand were widely viewed as 'social laboratories', in which governments assumed an active role in ensuring basic levels of social well-being for all citizens. A less auspicious aspect of these early years in Australia was the establishment, through the Immigration Restriction Act

(1901), of the 'White Australia' policy, which prevented non-European immigration.

The Great Depression hit Australia with particular severity, official unemployment rates rose to over 30 per cent. In contrast to the USA's New Deal, the Commonwealth government practised fiscal restraint and did little in terms of generating employment or providing assistance to the unemployed. Unemployment relief was left mainly to the states, which received little funding from the federal government for this purpose. Many Australians, therefore, experienced severe poverty until the economy recovered during 1937. Virtually full employment returned with the outbreak of war in 1939.

Australia inaugurated an official commitment to full employment in the White Paper of 1945, and for most of the next 25 years unemployment rarely rose above 2 per cent. The years immediately following the Second World War were characterized by an ALP government, led by Ben Chifley (following the death of the country's wartime leader, John Curtin) from 1945 to 1949. During this period, the Commonwealth Bank was established as the central bank, providing low interest home loans, social welfare, and public ownership was expanded. The government began a massive immigration programme, which attracted increasing numbers of people from non-English speaking countries (mainly southern and eastern Europe), who were to transform Australia into a far more ethnically-diverse nation.

This was followed by a long period of conservative coalition government (1949–72) dominated by the Liberal Party, led for most of the period by its founder, Robert Menzies, with the Country (subsequently National) Party as the junior partner. Among the more contentious issues of this period were Menzies' eventually unsuccessful attempts to outlaw the Communist Party and Australia's military involvement in Vietnam. Little was done to expand social welfare provisions. However, Aboriginal people finally achieved the vote through a referendum in 1967. Australia experienced a period of generally steady economic growth, with rising levels of home ownership and consumption of consumer goods.

A split in the ALP during the late 1950s assisted this conservative ascendancy. Eventually, though, the ALP led by Gough Whitlam was elected to power in 1972 under the slogan 'It's Time'. The new government rapidly implemented a quite radical mandate in such areas as provision of universal health care, women's rights and the establishment of Australia as a 'multicultural' society. The 'White Australia' policy was officially laid to rest. In November 1975, the Governor-General, Sir John Kerr dismissed Whitlam, following a crisis caused by the Opposition-controlled Senate blocking the government's money supply. This highly controversial action engendered long-running debate over the Constitution and the future of the monarchy in Australia. At the subsequent federal election, in December 1975, a new Liberal–Country Party government, headed by Malcolm Fraser, came to power. It pursued a 'fight inflation first' strategy, which led to increased unemployment. During this period, Australia shifted towards a more austere fiscal regime, with an increasing emphasis on restricting public sector expansion and less generous welfare provisions. The new government wound back several of the reforms that had been introduced by the Whitlam government.

International competitiveness and national reconciliation

In 1983 another ALP government was returned. However, under both Bob Hawke (1983–91) and Paul Keating (1991–96), it distanced itself from any suggestion of radicalism, operating instead under the banner of responsible economic management and increasing international competitiveness. A consensual approach to policy making was endorsed. An important example of this approach was the Prices and Incomes Accord, struck between the ALP and the Australian Council of Trade Unions (ACTU). It sought to bring closer together the conflicting interests of capital and labour through some form of reconciliation, in order to achieve reduced inflation with greater productivity and employment.

The ALP government sought to reduce public sector spending, deregulate Australia's economy and implement market-driven reforms. This process included the deregulation of the banking and financial system, a shift away from Australia's centralized wage-fixing system towards enterprise bargaining, and the privatization of major public companies such as the national airline, Quantas, and the Commonwealth Bank. None the less, the government retained a commitment to welfare provision, introducing a universal health care system (Medicare), as well as several new benefits, such as Family Income Supplement. Important steps were also made to counteract gender-based inequalities, through such initiatives as the Sex Discrimination Act (1984) and Affirmative Action legislation in 1986, designed to improve the employment prospects of women and socio-economically disadvantaged sections of Australian society.

The issue of land rights for Australia's Aboriginal and Torres Strait Islander peoples also gained considerable prominence. Originally, Australia (unlike the other three countries discussed in this chapter) was colonized under the doctrine of *terra nullius* (uninhabited land) which meant that the country's indigenous peoples were seen as having no rights to land ownership (see also **Taylor, 1998, p.190**; **Young *et al.*, 1998, p.308**). Particularly since the 1960s, Aboriginal and Torres Strait Island peoples have challenged this doctrine and under new legislation passed in the 1970s, have made several successful land claims. In June 1993, the High Court's ruling on a Murray Island land claim (the 'Mabo decision') overturned the *terra nullius* doctrine, giving 'native title' claims greater standing and impetus. On the other hand, fees and charges were gradually reintroduced into higher education, access to unemployment benefits was tightened, with an emphasis on unemployed people taking further training and education. Also, official unemployment rates rose to around 10 per cent and remained around this level, although unemployment has been much worse among the young, Aboriginal people and non-English-speaking migrants.

Aboriginal Land Rights Demonstration at the opening of the Commonwealth Games, Brisbane, Australia, 1988

The ALP won five successive electoral victories between 1983 and 1993, the longest period the party had ever held power. Considerable debate occurred as to whether they could be described as a 'traditional' ALP government, since they pursued quite different policies from those of their predecessors and were explicitly concerned with being a 'catch-all' party, concentrating on winning over 'swinging' voters. This was also important to ensure the support of minor parties, such as the Australian Democrats and the Greens. Although these parties have had no success in winning seats in the House of Representatives, they have frequently held the balance of power in the Senate, and their votes have been crucial to the passage of government legislation.

Issues in the 1990s

A Liberal–National coalition, under John Howard, won the March 1996 federal election with a large majority in the House of Representatives, winning 94 of the total 148 seats. Paul Keating resigned as leader of the ALP, to be replaced by Kim Beazley, son of a minister in the Whitlam government. However, the government failed to win a majority in the Senate, where the Australian Democrats, the Greens and two independents hold the balance of power. The new government, under Prime Minister John Howard, has implemented extensive cuts in expenditure. Their first budget in August 1996 contained a wide array of reductions in public spending, including social welfare, higher education, Aboriginal and Torres Strait Islander funding and labour market programmes.

Although the Australian federal election was decided mainly on economic issues, there was considerable public debate over Australia's constitutional future. The Prime Minister, Paul Keating, assumed a leading role in campaigning for Australia to become a republic by 2000. A Republican Advisory Committee was established in 1993 to investigate the best way of moving towards a republic. There was extensive opposition from monarchists, many of whom are in the Liberal and National parties. Following the ALP's election loss in March 1996, a coalition of the Liberal and National Parties formed a government. The new Prime Minister, John Howard, promised a 'people's convention' on the issue of a republic. The Constitutional Convention was held between 2 and 13 February 1998 and was constituted by 152 delegates from all over the country. 76 were elected under the Constitutional Convention (Election) Act 1997. The other 76 were appointed by the Commonwealth (federal) government. The Convention supported, in principle, Australia becoming a republic and recommended to Parliament 'that the republican model ... supported by this Convention, be put to the people in a constitutional referendum' (Australian Government, 1998). It was further recommended that the referendum be held in 1999 and that if it was 'in favour of a republic, that the new republic come into effect by 1 January 2001' (ibid.).

5.6 New Zealand: from social laboratory to free market experiment

New Zealand's unitary political system

New Zealand differs from the other three countries in having only a single house of parliament and a unitary national political system. This means that new policies can be implemented far more rapidly than in the USA, Canada or Australia, without the 'checks and balances' built into their federal systems. Also, New Zealand politics, due to the small population and relatively small land mass, can have a greater sense of immediacy and community involvement. New Zealanders are less susceptible to the sense of isolation that many people in other countries can feel from Washington, Ottawa or Canberra. It is easier for various interest groups and individual voters to get in touch with their representatives and to have some say in political processes. New Zealand is also more socially and economically homogeneous than the other countries. Despite having a substantial Maori and Pacific Islander population (around 12 per cent of the total population), the great majority of New Zealand's people have British and Irish origins. Economically, New Zealand has always been dependent on its primary industry, mainly dairy products, agriculture and forestry, lacking the levels of manufacturing found in the other three countries.

Political participation in New Zealand provides a remarkable contrast with the USA and, to a lesser degree, both Australia and Canada. Both party political membership and electoral participation are very high. Even without the type of compulsory voting system that exists in Australia, New Zealand elections regularly register turnouts of around 90 per cent. The two main parties, the conservative National Party and the more social-democratic Labour Party (which in recent years, however, has promoted 'New Right' policies) have very high levels of party membership. Also, various surveys have indicated that the New Zealand people feel that their political participation is important, and they tend to be less cynical than voters in most other countries. The national government in New Zealand is relatively close to the electorate, because of the smallness of the country and its population.

Therefore, New Zealand's social and governmental structures permit relatively rapid political fluctuations. Early in this century, New Zealand could become widely known, like Australia, as a 'social laboratory' through its pioneering citizenship and welfare reforms. Yet more recently, in the 1980s, it became a model for 'New Right' economic policies, by embarking on a process of very rapid privatization, deregulation and decentralization.

New Zealand as social laboratory

The most important periods of expansion of citizenship rights and welfare entitlements in New Zealand occurred firstly under the Liberal government of 1891–1911, and subsequently under the Labour government of 1935–49. Under the former, New Zealand became the first country in the world to extend the suffrage to women in 1893. In 1894, it established the Industrial Conciliation and Arbitration Act, instituting a centralized system for settling disputes between employers and ·employees. The Old Age Pensioners Act was passed in 1898, providing a flat rate pension for the aged. Such legislation exemplified the 'social liberal' character of the New Zealand government in these years.

Under the Labour government of 1935–49, New Zealand's Reserve Bank was nationalized, a public health care system was established, the price of basic foods was fixed at a low level, public housing was expanded, low interest loans were provided to home-buyers and a 40-hour working week was introduced. The 1938 Social Security Act provided an array of new welfare benefits, including superannuation and various pensions. This was an important step towards a welfare system based on universal entitlements, with all citizens having a right to basic income security. Although there was a National Government for most of the following three decades, the commitment to the welfare state and full employment policies remained largely intact.

These changes set the stage for the growth of the New Zealand welfare state during the post-Second World War era, based on a relatively high standard of living for most of the population and the widespread ownership of homes and consumer goods. Both main parties, National and Labour, were broadly committed to increasing the provision of services. However, during the 1970s, this consensus broke down. In the early 1980s, the National Prime Minister, Robert Muldoon, resisted 'New Right' arguments from the Reserve Bank, Treasury and a significant section of his own party. Instead, he attempted to solve New Zealand's economic problems by increasing government expenditure and by initiating wages and prices controls to slow inflation. Disaffected free market advocates in the National Party established the New Zealand Party, splitting the conservative vote and increasing the electoral prospects of the Labour Party.

New Zealand as 'free market' experiment

The election of a Labour Party government under David Lange in 1984 saw Roger Douglas appointed as Treasurer. Following bitter debates within the Labour Party and with no electoral mandate, Douglas proceeded to initiate a programme of top-down, market-oriented reforms, including deregulation, privatization and the reduction of the public sector. This programme, far more rapid and far-reaching than anything which has occurred in any other English-speaking country, became widely known as 'Rogernomics'. The government reduced job creation and training schemes, and unemployment was permitted to triple within only four years, from 63,771 in 1985 to 186,630 in 1989. Controls over the exchange rate and interest rates were abolished, within the context of a general deregulation of finance and banking.

The Douglas programme included a campaign to reduce the number of 'undeserving' welfare recipients, through highlighting instances of welfare fraud, which were insignificant in their financial impact but were the targets of media and political outrage. With considerable input from the Treasury and the Business Roundtable, the government instituted extensive welfare cutbacks. Eligibility criteria were tightened and the welfare system moved back from being universalistic to selective, with particular emphasis on discouraging people from remaining on welfare benefits rather than accepting low-paid employment. Targeting and reducing welfare payments would, according to this 'economic rationalist' agenda, increase individual self-reliance and reduce demands on taxpayers. There was, however, no equivalent attack on tax evasion by the wealthy. Whereas equality had been a traditional objective of the Labour Party, inequality under the Lange government was not only permitted to increase but was celebrated, particularly in lauding the activities of business entrepreneurs.

In contrast to Australia under Hawke and Keating, New Zealand's trade union movement was effectively sidelined from the policy process throughout the Lange government's term in office. Also, although there were several women in its Cabinet and important legislation was introduced to increase gender equity, the great majority of women workers, in the lowest paid, least secure employment suffered poorer wages and conditions. While advances were made in relation to Maori Treaty concerns, economically Maori and Pacific Islander people were hit particularly hard by rising unemployment and increasing inequality.

After a brief honeymoon period, disillusionment with these policies set in. New Zealand's inflation rate, economic growth, employment generation and unemployment were all below the average for developed economies. Despite efforts to reduce the public sector, government expenditure as a proportion of GDP also increased, with some fluctuations, over the period of the Labour government. Labour won government again in the 1987 election, but the balance of power within the party had changed. The 'New Right' advocates no longer had the upper hand in economic and social policy. Lange opposed Douglas's proposals to sell off more public assets and cut social welfare. Douglas was eventually defeated and resigned, but the Labour Party had been effectively split. This political unrest encouraged the emergence of important new political forces, such as the New Labour Party, which was subsequently to merge with other groups to form the left-wing Alliance, and the conservative, protectionist New Zealand First. Lange subsequently resigned as Prime Minister, with Geoffrey Palmer leading the Labour Party to a massive defeat in the 1990 election and a new National government taking over, with Jim Bolger as Prime Minister.

The new government took on the role of further reducing the role of government. Various impediments to free markets, such as price controls, subsidies, tariffs, corporate mergers and price-fixing, were eliminated, and New Zealand's system of industrial conciliation and arbitration was virtually destroyed. Through the Employment Contracts Act (1991), national industrial awards were replaced by enterprise-based agreements. At the other end of the income spectrum from welfare recipients, taxation rates on the highest income earners were cut.

Issues in the 1990s

In the 1993 election, the National Party under Jim Bolger won 50.51 per cent of the vote and 50 seats. This gave them an overall majority of one seat in the 99 seat parliament, with Labour having 45 seats and both the Alliance and New Zealand First two seats apiece. In a referendum held in conjunction with the 1993 general election, New Zealanders voted to move from a first-past-the-post electoral system to a Mixed Member Proportional (MMP) system, in which each voter has two votes. One vote (the Party Vote) is for the voter's preferred political party, and the other (the Electorate Vote) is for the candidate they want in their own electorate. This system was used for the first time in the October 1996 election. Under it, parliament usually should (but need not) have a total of 120 members. Various permutations can make it possible that there are either more or fewer than 120 members in the Parliament. These would comprise 60 from General Electorates (voted for by Electoral Votes), five representing Maori electorates, comprising voters on the Maori Electoral Roll, and 55 from lists nominated by the various political parties and decided according to their respective shares of the party votes. (People of Maori descent may choose to be on either the Maori roll or the General roll.) A party requires 5 per cent of all Party Votes or at least one electoral seat to earn a proportional share of the allocation of party seats. This system makes it more difficult for a single party to receive a majority of the seats, and hence be able to form a government, than under the first-past-the-post system.

Following the 1996 election, no single party was able to form a government. The two largest parties, National and Labour, had to negotiate with New Zealand First, the third largest party, in order to form a workable coalition government. On 11 December 1996, after eight weeks of post-election negotiations, the leader of the New Zealand First Party, Winston Peters, gave the party's support to the National government. Jim Bolger remained New Zealand's Prime Minister, with Peters himself becoming the new Treasurer and Deputy Prime Minister. This decision represented a significant turnaround, since several surveys had indicated that a substantial majority of New Zealand First voters were opposed to any coalition with National. The decision of New Zealand First ended the possibility of Labour's Helen Clark becoming the country's first woman Prime Minister. The other minor party, the left-wing Alliance (which polled fourth in the general election), played little role in the negotiations. The new coalition Cabinet, comprising fifteen National and five New Zealand First members, was sworn in on 16 December 1996. The new government is likely to be conservative politically, but less inclined to embark on 'free market' and anti-welfare strategies than its predecessors (both Labour and National) since 1984.

5.7   Conclusion

Despite their great differences in terms of political and economic importance, these four Anglo states in the Asia-Pacific share certain features. Each is a long-standing political democracy, with substantial non-Anglo populations. At various times during this century, governments in all of them have assumed a critical role in creating a more inclusive society through the expansion of social welfare and citizenship rights. Particularly in the 1950s and 1960s, these societies were characterized, to varying degrees, by an accommodation of interests, most notably those of capital and labour, and a governmental commitment to nation building.

In recent years, however, there has been a shift away from the politics of accommodation towards a political agenda, driven ostensibly by the demands of competition in a globalized economy. The nation-building capacity of governments, particularly the reformist potential of social democracy, has declined, as people have come to doubt the capacity of politics to effect change. With the 'freeing up' of international trade, governments have become increasingly reduced to being economic managers, creating the economic conditions demanded by international markets. This shift has been particularly dramatic in New Zealand, indicating how change can occur much more rapidly in smaller, unitary political systems than in larger and more complex federal systems.

Political agendas have been reconfigured in recent decades by the women's movement, civil rights movements, indigenous peoples, gay and lesbian campaigns, environmentalists, peace campaigners and Christian fundamentalists. However, growing numbers of people have become disenchanted with mainstream politics. The poor, in particular, appear to have lost much of whatever political voice they possessed. Regardless of the political complexion of individual governments, a greater emphasis on individual self-reliance and the reduction of public expenditure has emerged. As people have been expected to either sink or swim in the market economy, inequalities of wealth and income have been exacerbated. Governments have diluted any commitment to eradicate poverty, and have instead instigated tougher measures against those people seen as the 'undeserving' poor.

Therefore, we may be witnessing a wholesale transformation from societies with a governmental commitment to increased social welfare and expanded citizenship rights to a new era characterized by a declining role for government, increasing inequality and restricted access to citizenship rights. The future of political democracy into the next century may become less secure if an increasing 'underclass' is excluded from effective political participation and if governments are seen as incapable of responding to the expectations invested in them.

References

Australian Government (1998) *Constitutional Convention 1998: Communique*, available from http://www.dpmc.gov.au/convention/comm3.html.

Eccleston, B., Dawson, M. and McNamara, D. (eds) (1998) *The Asia-Pacific Profile*, London, Routledge in association with The Open University.

Taylor, S. (1998) 'Pacific images' in Maidment, R. and Mackerras, C. (eds) *Culture and Society in the Asia-Pacific*, London, Routledge in association with The Open University.

Young, E., Hunt, C. and Gerard Ward, R. (1998) 'The environment, traditional production and population' in Thompson, G. (ed.) *Economic Dynamism in the Asia-Pacific*, London, Routledge in association with The Open University.

Further reading

Aitkin, D. and Singleton, G. (eds) (1996) *Australian Political Institutions*, Melbourne, Addison-Wesley-Longman Australia.

Dyck, P.R. (1996) *Canadian Politics: Critical Approaches*, Scarborough, Ontario, Nelson Canada.

Fowler, L.L. (1993) *Candidates, Congress and the American Democracy*, Ann Arbor, University of Michigan Press.

LaSelva, S.V. (1996) *The Moral Foundations of Canadian Federalism: Paradoxes, Achievements and Tragedies of Nationhood*, Montreal, McGill-Queen's University Press.

Maddox, G. (1996) *Australian Democracy: in Theory and Practice*, Melbourne, Longman Australia.

Mulgan, R. (1994) *Politics in New Zealand*, Auckland, Auckland University Press.

Patterson, T. (1996) *The American Democracy*, New York, McGraw-Hill.

Russell, P.H. (1993) *Constitutional Odyssey: Can Canadians Become a Separate People?*, Toronto, University of Toronto Press.

Smith, R. (ed.) (1997) *Politics in Australia*, St Leonards, New South Wales, Allen and Unwin.

Woll, P. (ed.) (1996) *American Government: Readings and Cases*, New York, HarperCollins College Publishers.

Wood, G.A. (1988) *Governing New Zealand*, Auckland, Longman Paul.

PART 2

Policy, Politics and Governance

CHAPTER 6

Elite governance: business, bureaucrats and the military

Duncan McCargo

6.1 Introduction

The primacy of elites is a recurrent theme in the study of politics in the Asia-Pacific. A good general definition of an elite is Scruton's (1982, p.143): 'the class of persons within a society who are in a position to view themselves ... as chosen, either by others or by nature, to govern'. Whereas Western liberal democracies are typically characterized by pluralist political systems in which the interests of different groups are checked and balanced by a set of rival competing claims, in many Pacific Asian countries pluralism is quite limited. Instead, governance is the prerogative of a narrow set of interlocking elite interests. Business, especially large corporations and conglomerates, often works hand-in-hand with the bureaucracy. In some cases, public policy is determined by civilian government officials, or by uniformed officers from the armed forces. Although political parties, parliaments, prime ministers, cabinets, and other institutions may enjoy a set of formal legislative and administrative powers, in practice they often have to reflect entrenched bureaucratic economic and military interests. It is not surprising, therefore, that in many Asia-Pacific states the dividing line between the public and private sectors can be extremely blurred: an idea neatly captured by the phrase 'Japan, Inc.', implying a structural integration of business and bureaucratic interests and concerns. The Japanese model, portrayed by analysts such as Chalmers Johnson as a form of command economy which he termed a developmental state, was widely emulated by the first wave of newly-industrializing economies of South Korea, Hong Kong, Singapore and Taiwan (Johnson, 1982). The second wave of newly-industrializing economies – some regions of China, and South-East Asian countries such as Malaysia, Indonesia, and Thailand – have borrowed some features of the developmental state, but often in a more eclectic and less centralized fashion.

Many countries in the region have powerful and well-established state enterprises plus other para-statal organizations which straddle the divide between the public and the private, such as the Indonesian and Malaysian state oil companies. In other cases, the state exerts considerable pressure upon technically private businesses: for example, the way in which South Korean banks were consistently leant upon by the government to provide easy credit for certain sectors of the economy. Rulers such as Indonesia's Suharto or the Philippine's Marcos have at times seemed incapable of differentiating between the public good and their personal financial interests. Another feature of elite governance in many of the region's states has been the extent to which the business, bureaucratic, military and political elites have overlapping memberships. In countries as diverse as Thailand, the Philippines, Indonesia and South Korea, the presidency or premiership has, during certain periods, fallen into the hands of former or serving military officers, usually army generals – in Japan, bureaucrats have routinely pursued a second career in business or politics. Close associates of leading politicians have been rewarded with lucrative monopolies or state contracts in countries across the region. Civilian technocrats have promoted infrastructural development by working hand-in-hand with military officers: strategic highways built in Thailand by the US military during the Vietnam conflict were later used by the Thai military to suppress domestic insurgency, and then by the business sector to support rapid industrialization.

Political realities in the Asia-Pacific sometimes make a mockery of conventional Western-derived categories. If the military are pursuing their own independent policy objectives by political means, how far can they be regarded as part of the state? When the foreign minister and the prime minister of a country have adopted radically different foreign policy goals, which is the authentic national policy? When civil servants are in the pay of capitalist cronies of the president, how can the bureaucracy be distinguished from the executive, or the private sector? One of the most useful ways of seeing elite governance is as a project, the overriding aim of which is to maintain elite power. All the economic and regulatory resources at the disposal of these elites are marshalled for the purpose of minimizing popular input into the political process. The term *governance*, which has bureaucratic and technocratic overtones, may imply a top-down political order. Crawford (1995, p.59) argues that in recent aid policy debates: '"government" constitutes the institutions and personnel; "governance" is the activities and process of governing. To some extent this is a distinction between form and content'. In the Asia-Pacific, the process and activities of governing, or governance, are often far less transparent and clear-cut than the formal power structures of government might imply. The principal aim of elites in many parts of the Asia-Pacific is to contain public demands, especially public demands for political liberalization. Economic growth has served as an ideal carrot to help perpetuate the politics of exclusion.

Where do elites come from? The origins of elites vary widely from country to country. In Japan, for example, elites typically come from a small number of prestigious universities. Although an education system based on competitive examinations appears to offer equal opportunities to all, in practice social mobility is quite limited (Ishida, 1993, pp.247–53).

Politicians may be recruited from the bureaucracy, or they may enter politics as a means of enhancing their social status after growing wealthy from business activities. In South-East Asian countries such as Thailand or Indonesia, political and other elites have a diverse range of origins: some are from 'old' aristocratic families, whereas others come from humble family backgrounds and rise to the top through a career in the military, or as self-made, usually Chinese, entrepreneurs. Senior military officers may feel that political posts such as Defence Minister or Prime Minister are theirs by right. The formation of elites in most Asia-Pacific countries involves a high degree of contestation amongst competing groups such as elected politicians, the bureaucracy, business leaders, and military officers. Senior figures among the elite will typically seek to recruit protégés from similar backgrounds to join their circles. Graduates from the same university or military academy, or business partners with reciprocal links of debt and mutual obligation, will often attempt to help one another gain seniority and elite status. Hence elites are often self-reproducing. At the same time, socio-economic changes also produce changes in the character of elites, as the balance of power among ruling groups alters: for example, economic development in South-East Asia has increased the importance of the business sector, giving entrepreneurs much greater access to electoral politics, and thus to ministerial office, than they previously enjoyed. Such gains by leaders from the private sector have often been achieved at the expense of bureaucrats and military officers. Elites can also be riven by divisions. Ethnicity divides many South-East Asian elites, those of Chinese descent achieving considerable economic power, but important political posts being effectively reserved for those of 'indigenous' ethnicity.

The issues discussed in this chapter relate primarily to the countries of Pacific Asia. The politics of the Anglo-American states, such as the USA, Australia and New Zealand, are very different in character. Although it is possible to argue that phenomena such as the military-industrial complex exist in these liberal democracies, the exclusionary nature of elite governance in the cases examined here differs qualitatively from the governance of liberal democracies.

I begin in Section 6.2 by sketching the historical context of elite governance, with its roots in the pre-Second World War colonial era, its entrenchment during the Cold War and the transformations wrought by the end of the Cold War. In Section 6.3 I sketch the character and institutions of elite governance in North-East Asia, focusing on Japan and its developmental state. This has provided a practical template for both economic policy and elite governance elsewhere in the region, for example in South Korea. I contrast the model of elite governance in the developmental state in Section 6.4 with the bureaucratic polity model that has been used to explore elite governance in South-East Asia, particularly Thailand, Indonesia and Malaysia. Both of these models tend to focus on the interaction between political, bureaucratic and economic elites. In Section 6.5 I look at the role of military elites. The military plays a considerable role in some of the states already examined: Thailand,

Indonesia and South Korea. However, I pay special attention to China, where the military is more deeply enmeshed in elite governance. Finally, in Section 6.6 I examine the ways in which the end of the Cold War and the transformation of the region's economy are undermining the challenging patterns of elite governance.

6.2   The historical context of elite governance

Contemporary forms of elite governance can trace their evolution, in some parts of Pacific Asia, as far back as the mid nineteenth century. Countries like Siam and Japan started to develop centralized state structures in an attempt to ward off European colonial advances, and to catch up, administratively and economically, with the West. Different patterns of elite governance emerged in societies which were the subject of colonization. Despite formal Western control, colonial administrations had to create and rely on a class of indigenous civil servants to carry out much of the routine business of imperialism. The Pacific War brought about an end to both Japanese and European imperialism in the region. Though newly independent nations such as Malaysia, Burma, Indonesia, and the Philippines set about devising new political and administrative arrangements, elite institutions and groups were in part shaped by imperial legacies. Whilst many of these new nations adopted constitutional orders which outwardly resembled liberal democracies, in practice democracy was poorly institutionalized. The independence and nationalist movements which thrived during and just after the Pacific War were often led by military and traditional aristocratic elites. Once their demands for independent national sovereignty were met, these groups moved to secure for themselves the key posts and levers of political power.

Geostrategic concerns helped to entrench the power of these new national elites. As the USA and its Western allies grew alarmed at the prospect of the communist domination of South-East Asia, China, and the Korean peninsula, the USA actively supported sympathetic regimes in the region. During the course of the Korean and Vietnam Wars the USA placed valuable military orders with them which helped kick-start new industries. The existence of a US security umbrella left Japan (and to a lesser extent other countries in the region) free to pursue economic development without having to worry unduly about matters of defence. In many respects, the period of US hegemony in the Pacific during the three decades following the end of the Second World War created an unrepeatable window of opportunity for countries in the region. Bureaucratic, business, and military elites seized this opportunity in order to empower, and sometimes also to enrich, themselves.

From the 1980s onwards, the nature of politics in many Pacific Asian countries became more fluid. Mass demonstrations demanding political liberalization or democratization occurred in several of the region's capitals, including Manila in 1986, Seoul in 1987, and Bangkok in 1992.

The end of the Cold War had an important psychological effect on long-serving regimes such as Japan's Liberal Democratic Party (LDP) government, and Indonesia's New Order. Unable to rely on the Cold War to provide a continuing legitimation for their rule, many regimes were forced to rethink the privileged status which they had long given to bureaucratic and military elites. While these elites did not disappear, many – like the Thai military after the bloody events of May 1992 – were forced to adopt a lower profile, concentrating on rent-seeking business activities, such as smuggling or insider trading, rather than strutting and posturing on the political stage. There were also pressures to curb the privileges of large corporations such as the South Korean *chaebol*, bringing in new regulatory regimes which would protect consumers and the public from the predatory practices of the business sector.

6.3   Elite governance in North-East Asia

Japan

In Western countries, it is often generally assumed that elected politicians play the principal role in devising public policy, and that civil servants are mainly concerned with implementing it. However, this kind of division of labour is often very ambiguous in Pacific Asia. This is especially true in the case of Japan, which has been depicted by Johnson (1982) as a form of developmental state with specific patterns of elite governance. Johnson's arguments are part of a debate in Japanese political studies. On the one side are Johnson and the *bureaucratic dominance* school: they argue that while Japan's elected politicians were nominally superior to their senior civil servants, much of the real power for directing policy and even creating legislation lay in the hands of the bureaucracy. Lacking expert knowledge of policy issues, politicians concentrated on pursuing personal benefit through the system of 'money politics', leaving bureaucrats to do much of the real work of governing the country. On the other hand, this argument has been disputed by the *party dominance* school (for a review, see Koh, 1989, pp.192–218) and studies by political economists (Okimoto, 1989 and Callon, 1995). Johnson's portrait of the Ministry of International Trade and Industry (MITI) as a pilot organization steering industrial development remains a persuasive if sometimes over-simplified account of elite governance in Japan during the 1950s and 1960s. Comparable examples of close collaboration between bureaucrats, politicians and business leaders in other countries of the region illustrate the extent to which Japanese patterns of elite governance have been emulated by Japan's neighbours.

Discussions of Japan's developmental state easily descend into arcane arguments about the precise degree of importance which should be assigned to state agencies, private sector bodies, and market forces (for an overview of this literature, see **Thompson, 1998, Chapter 6**). Regardless of what position is adopted concerning the exact role played by the state in formulating industrial and economic policy, it is possible to sketch out a general paradigm of developmentalism which applies to many countries in the Asia-Pacific. Shibusawa *et al.* (1992, p.53) see developmentalism as a pragmatic policy choice which serves the purposes of state-building and regime survival. Many countries in Pacific Asia have pursued strategies of rapid economic development, not only in order to generate economic growth and enhance living standards, but also to strengthen the state, and the regime which happens to be in power. Bureaucrats, politicians, business leaders, and sometimes military officers, therefore have a shared interest in achieving economic growth. It is possible to see the high growth rates of countries such as Japan, South Korea and Singapore as a direct outcome of attempts by ruling elites to legitimize and extend their rule. Shibusawa *et al.* (1992, pp.54–61) identify five recurrent elements which have tended to characterize these Asia-Pacific developmental states:

- strong government,

- a close public/private sector relationship,

- foreign direct investment,

- deferred gratification in the form of a low wage regime and limited political participation, and

- the American security umbrella.

The combination of these elements produces a pragmatic elite policy community, wedded to neither socialist nor free market dogmas. Whilst unsurprisingly rejecting the developmentalist model and preferring to regard East Asian states as 'market-friendly', the influential World Bank report *The East Asian Miracle* acknowledged that such economies had adopted 'a principle of shared growth' (World Bank, 1993, pp.157–8) which was supported by 'a cadre of economic technocrats insulated from narrow political pressures', along with 'institutions and mechanisms to share information and win the support of business elites'. These two elements may be regarded as a minimum definition of the prerequisites for elite governance in Pacific Asia. First, developmental states require a core elite to undertake the necessary economic planning. Such an elite is typically drawn from one of two sources: career bureaucrats often from core agencies such as Japan's MITI, or South Korea's Economic Planning Board, and technocrats with either a public- or private-sector background, often political appointees. The World Bank has praised merit-based recruitment and promotion procedures for civil servants in Japan and South Korea as a cornerstone of their successful economic growth. A second important element is that of consultative mechanisms for oiling the relationship between public and private sectors, such as Japan's 'deliberation' or consultative councils. These take two main forms: issue-based councils concerned with matters such as pollution or finance, and industry-specific councils for different sectors of the economy (World Bank, 1993, pp.181–7). These councils, of which there were 214 in 1986, exemplify the bridging of the public–private divide common in the Japanese order: attached to and appointed by administrative agencies, they include representatives from relevant producer interests, as well as academics, bureaucrats, Diet (parliament) members and even journalists (Schwartz, 1993, p.219).

How do these elite-dominated institutions interact? How does the process of elite governance actually function in a country such as Japan? Krauss and Muramatsu (1988, pp.208–10) argue that the Japanese system is one of *patterned pluralism*. Patterned pluralism has several features:

1   a strong government and bureaucracy,

2   blurred boundaries between state and society,

3   the integration of social groups into government,

4   political parties that mediate between interest groups and government,

5   government that has been thoroughly penetrated by mediating organizations such as political parties, and

6   interest groups in constant alliances with the same political parties and bureaucratic agencies.

In other words, the central feature of governance in Japan is the unusual extent to which government, bureaucracy, the ruling party, and interest groups have merged their functions and goals. This style of governance emerged during the long tenure of the Liberal Democratic Party, which ruled Japan from 1955 to 1993, and regained much of its control in 1996 following a brief period in the wilderness. It is important to note that the Japanese elite, comprising politicians, senior bureaucrats, and heads of large companies, is unusually homogenous. Most members of the elite are graduates of a small number of prestigious universities: Tokyo, Kyoto, Waseda, and Keio. A handful of faculties from these universities, notably the Tokyo University Faculty of Law, have produced an extraordinary proportion of Japan's leaders. For example, in 1986, of the 22 administrative vice-ministers (the highest-ranking civil servants), sixteen were graduates of Tokyo University Law Faculty, three were graduates from other faculties of Tokyo University, two were graduates of Kyoto University, and one had attended neither university (Koh, 1989, p.141). These universities and faculties in turn obtain most of their students from a small number of elite senior high schools, mostly in Tokyo. Japan's elite, which is almost entirely male, derives largely from a self-reproducing section of the middle class. Its members work assiduously to cultivate personal contacts during their student years which will serve their career interests in later life. Crossing the boundaries between the bureaucracy and business, or from the bureaucracy into politics, are common practices. Senior civil servants often take lucrative jobs in the private sector on retirement. These posts are actually arranged for them by their ministries or agencies – a practice known as *amakudari*, or 'descent from heaven'. Some even enter the Diet, almost invariably under the LDP banner.

How is policy actually made by this governing elite? Nakano (1997) argues that the policy-making process in Japan is actually extremely complex. Different forms of decision-making processes are used under different circumstances, as the different components of the dominant order strive to accommodate one another's interests. A good example is the process of drafting legislation. According to Nakano (1997, pp.14–16): 'policies cause politics'. In other words, a policy agenda requiring legislation which may have been initiated by senior bureaucrats, has the effect of mobilizing a range of interest groups both inside and outside government. The different phases of the legislative process in turn create further political ripples, as various government departments are consulted. Negotiations are held with politicians and political parties. Meetings are held with consultative councils and commissions of inquiry. Parliamentary proceedings are initiated at the committee stage, negotiations are held with the opposition concerning possible amendments. Finally, the legislation is ratified by the Diet. Nakano is critical of simplistic assumptions that participants in the policy-formulation process always pay greatest attention to the interests of their immediate group: that 'bureau comes before ministry', 'section comes before bureau', and in the LDP *zoku* – the policy 'tribes' of elected politicians, who function effectively as parliamentary lobbyists for businesses such as the construction industry – comes before party. In practice there are numerous counter-examples to these assumptions which overlook the importance of personal ties between experts from different sides of the fence. He also stresses that any legislative drafting process will produce a range of political by-products aside from the legislation itself. These by-products serve the function of paying-off or compensating those who have lost out through the legislation itself. The need to satisfy all parties leads to an unpredictable progress for any new legislation, and results in 'accelerations and leaps, stagnations and reverses that sometimes defy logical explanation' (Nakano, 1997, p.16).

Not all elite governance requires parliamentary legislation. In many other policy fields, key decisions involve business leaders as well as politicians and bureaucrats. Nakano identifies two principal patterns of governance here: *elite accommodation politics*, where big business is an important player, and *client oriented politics*, where small business and other interest groups share in the allocation of benefits (Nakano, 1997, p.65). Nakano argues that *elite accommodation politics* brought together the three components of the iron triangle: leading government politicians, the leadership of the Federation of Economic Organizations, the Keidanren, and senior figures from the economic ministries and agencies. The Keidanren primarily represented the iron, steel, banking and electricity industries which were the principal beneficiaries of Japan's depleted financial and energy resources in the immediate post-war period. When Japan was plunged into political crisis by the 1960 Security Treaty riots, industry leaders united with politicians and bureaucrats to pursue a policy of political rapprochement aimed at maintaining the capitalist order in the face of leftist challenges (Nakano, 1997, p.90). Prime Minister Ikeda sought to buy off public dissent with his income doubling plan;

and Japan's big corporations fell in with the strategy of high speed economic growth, forming strong ties with the ruling political and bureaucratic elites, and accepting a higher degree of regulation in exchange for greater involvement in policy formulation. The strategy of rapid economic growth was essentially an elite pact adopted in the interests of mutual preservation. Patterned pluralism was a form of governance which emerged over time, in response to a particular set of political and economic imperatives.

Multiple connections exist between the three components of the triple alliance. LDP politicians influence the bureaucracy through appointments, and by recruiting retiring bureaucrats to become LDP Diet members. Bureaucrats are able to influence business through their authority to offer administrative guidance and to devise secondary legislation of a regulatory nature. Business in turn supplies much of the funding on which the LDP depends. Nevertheless, the economic slowdown of the 1970s led to the emergence of more flexible and less monolithic relationships. In particular the Keidanren experienced a decline in its influence, leaving individual industries and more companies greater freedom to develop direct relationships with politicians through campaign contributions and the emergence of the *zoku*. Nakano (1997, p.91) argues that the triple alliance has now become much less all-encompassing in its influence on politics and policy making.

Under the umbrella of the triple alliance operate a range of what Nakano calls *client oriented politics*: a system which allows the official maximization of private interests in society through the medium of political mechanisms, and in which most of the many kinds of private groups which sprang up in clusters after the Second World War have become clients (Nakano, 1997, p.93). In effect, this form of politics functioned as a non-ideological alternative to the earlier politics of ideological confrontation. Leading participants included the farmers' organization, Nokyo, the Japan Medical Association, and various industrial lobbies. The co-optation of such bodies into the elite-led political order often had negative consequences for the public: for example, the Japan Medical Association has blocked distribution of the contraceptive pill in order to safeguard the lucrative abortion industry, and the Consumers' Union of Japan has helped maintain high food prices by campaigning against the lifting of import restrictions (van Wolferen, 1989, p.53). Below the national level, interest groups included provincial public corporations and regional assembly members, part of a linked network of vested interests feeding off government-related contracts.

A pervasive feature of the patterns of governance described by Nakano is the extent to which they exclude or limit popular participation in decision-making processes. Most policy and legislative decisions are made by closed circles of politicians, administrators and interest groups, with little reference to the public interest. Whilst there are interesting counter-examples – such as a 1989 government climb down over the introduction of consumption tax – which illustrate the potential for public opinion to influence policy outcomes, these instances typically reflect an unusual combination of oppositional forces mobilized over an especially emotive issue. The Liberal Democratic Party has a long tradition of converting opposition groups, like environmental protesters, into loyal supporters through the sharing of spoils. In this vein, Calder (1993, p.246) sees the relationship between the Japanese industrial sector and the bureaucracy in terms of circles of compensation, circles which included both regulators, and the banks and *keiretsu* (industrial groups) they regulate. The state allocated benefits through these circles, which have then offered various forms of support to the bureaucracy. Outsiders and newcomers have found it difficult to penetrate established circles of compensation. The paradox of Japanese elite governance is that it is both inclusionary and exclusionary. Efforts are made to include as many interests as possible in policy, legislative and economic decision making; at the same time, the effect of this inclusionary strategy is to exclude dissident voices and minority views, and often to override considerations of public interest.

South Korea

Many of the features of elite governance in Japan have parallels in the case of South Korea. Following the military coup by General Park in 1960, South Korea pursued a determined policy of export-oriented growth, coupled with tight import controls, a pragmatic blend of EOI (export oriented industrialization) and ISI (import substitution industrialization). Control of the economy rested largely in the hands of the state, but the main agents of economic growth and industrialization were privately-owned companies rather than state enterprises. A distinctive feature of the economy was the pre-eminence of a small group of *chaebol* conglomerates like Samsung, Hyundai, Lucky-Goldstar and Daewoo, which typically had a wide range of business activities. Despite their large size, these conglomerates were generally managed and controlled by the families which owned them. Political connections were an important factor in any *chaebol* growth, since they were essential in securing the all-important investment licences from the government of the day. During the 1970s, the government generally retained the upper hand in setting industrial policy, forcing the *chaebol* to develop heavy industries such as shipbuilding, steel, machinery and petrochemicals. Through its control of the major banking institutions, the government was able to use lending to control corporate strategy. Companies which fell foul of the state could find the rug pulled from under them when banks called in their loans, as actually happened to one of the largest of the *chaebol* (Kukche) in 1985.

Industrial policy in South Korea has been dominated by the President, and a small number of trusted advisers to the President. These advisors 'are often more influential than high ranking public officials, simply because they have greater ease of access to the President' (Luedde-Neurath, 1988, p.94). Guided by his advisors, the President issued directives on policy.

Presidents have tended to use a quasi-military commander-in-chief style of political leadership. Following pronouncements by the President, the content of policy was then determined. This task then fell to governmental organizations such as the Economic Planning Board, and ministries such as the Ministry of Finance, and the Ministry of Commerce and Industry (MCI). Lee (1997, p.131) relates the modern South Korean bureaucracy to Confucian ideals of the scholar-ruler, arguing that these notions are the precursor of the ruling and authoritarian Korean bureaucrat. Government officials effectively monopolized expert knowledge of public policy processes, even serving as policy advisors to the ruling party (Lee, 1997, p.168). The quality of the bureaucracy has been maintained through competitive entrance examinations, and the recruitment of Ph.D. holders and university academics to work in high-powered research institutes affiliated with various ministries (World Bank, 1993, p.175).

An important element in government–business relations in South Korea is the producers' associations, which are controlled by the MCI. Although they are supposed to act as conduits for consultation between manufacturers and the government, in practice they are also used by the government to influence business, and have been described as government watchdogs (Luedde-Neurath, 1988). The associations produce detailed plans of their members' proposed activities, which are then used by the government to monitor industrial production. Where companies propose to undertake activities which do not conform to government plans and priorities, pressure is exerted upon them through the producers' associations to alter their plans. These associations illustrate a highly-developed relationship between the bureaucracy and business. Lee (1997, pp.168–9) argues that it would be wrong to see this relationship as corporatist; therefore he views the South Korean state as a dominant player rather than a partner or neutral arbiter. He argues that despite the articulation of their interests through the Federation of Korean Industries, the *chaebol* were limited in their capacity to check the power of the state, which retained considerable autonomy in matters of economic and industrial policy, even after the political liberalization which began in 1987 (Lee, 1997, p.167). He also argues that policy network theory, according to which policy emerges through close collaboration through merged private and state sectors, is not a satisfactory account of the South Korean case. In practice, the state was often able to impose its will on big business without consulting its views. The autonomy of the South Korean state was reflected in the mechanisms available to the President and bureaucrats who could make use of political and administrative powers to control the *chaebol*, ranging from the Defence Security Command to the police, and even the Office of National Tax Administration. In contrast with the relatively diffuse location of power in Japan, the South Korean President had immense formal and informal powers. These gave him patriarchal capacities to exercise what Lee calls 'political integrating power'. Elite governance in South Korea is dominated by a core group comprising the President, senior bureaucrats and advisors. Lee argues that the distinguishing feature of the

East Asian developmental state is not its monolithic or omnipotent character; on the contrary, there are numerous fissures and conflicts within the state itself. Rather, what distinguishes governance by these states is their capacity to override opposition and bring together competing forces (Lee, 1997, p.14). Armed with two principal advantages – a competent team of bureaucrats and technocrats, and effective mechanisms for handling relations between the public and private sectors – developmental states are able to implement top-down decision-making processes which determine winners and losers among contending interests.

6.4   Elite governance in South-East Asia: Thailand, Malaysia and Indonesia

The models of elite governance in developmental states in North-East Asia can usefully be contrasted with patterns of elite governance in South-East Asia. The concept of the *bureaucratic polity* was developed by Riggs (1966) as an explanation for the elite-dominated political order in Thailand. Riggs (1966, pp.311–66) and others have argued that the early decades of parliamentary politics in Thailand (1932–73) reflected the character of the end of absolutism in 1932: 'the goal of the revolution was not to establish a popular constitutional government but rather to place commoner officials in the cockpit of power and to organize a polity that would rule on behalf of the bureaucracy' (ibid., p.312). In Thailand, the end of the absolute monarchy was not popularly inspired. It was implemented by a small group of bureaucrats, both civilian and military. Whilst Thailand's new power-holders used the rhetoric of constitutionalism, and made use of parliamentary and electoral forms of rule, the masses remained disempowered in the new political order. The military frequently intervened in the political process, regularly staging coups and rewriting constitutions before allowing parliamentary governments to resume.

It is possible to argue that Thailand's bureaucratic polity had the effect of de-politicizing the public sphere, reducing politics to the level of infighting between rival interest groups – for example the intense rivalry between the army and the police in the 1950s. The soft authoritarianism of the bureaucratically-dominated Thai order meant that the Thai electoral process was concerned with mass mobilization rather than popular participation; parties and other non-state political actors were encouraged or compelled to adopt 'acceptable' behaviour which did not threaten bureaucratic dominance (see Girling, 1981, pp.162–75). A second notable feature of the Thai order was the extent of collaboration between the bureaucratic and military elites (mainly of Thai descent) and the economic elite (mainly of Chinese descent). Bureaucrats and military officers commonly served on the boards of business enterprises, providing contracts and protection in exchange for a share of the profits. The Vietnam War, which saw huge US investment in Thailand's strategic infrastructure, helped provide the stimulus for rapid economic growth from the early 1960s, and indirectly further cemented elite alliances. Riggs's characterization of Thailand as a bureaucratic polity has not been universally accepted. Scholars such as Hewison (1996, pp.75–80) have rejected the model as too static, reinforcing the conservative political perspective of Thailand's elites, and downplaying the existence of class conflicts and opposition movements throughout the post-1932 period. None the less, attempts have been made to apply the bureaucratic polity model more widely. Karl Jackson has argued that Indonesia under the post-Sukarno New Order has been 'a presidential variation of a bureaucratic polity' (Jackson, 1978, p.5). Indonesia has also been characterized by a pre-eminent political role for the military, and a top-down, tokenistic parliamentary system under which political parties are given very little room for manoeuvre. Aspinall (1996, p.234) notes the way in which distinctions between state and society are blurred in Indonesia; middle-class intellectuals are provided with positions in government-sponsored research institutes or in universities, where they find themselves well-rewarded for moderating critical utterances.

The idea of the bureaucratic polity may be seen as a South-East Asian variation on the largely North-East Asian developmental state. Many of the five key elements of developmental states (strong government, public/private sector relationships, foreign direct investment, deferred gratification, and the American security umbrella) are also found in bureaucratic polities. Like developmental states, bureaucratic polities are elite-dominated and exclusionary in character. Nevertheless, bureaucratic polities are typically less centralized and monolithic than developmental states, and they are often characterized by greater degrees of corruption and inefficiency. Bureaucratic polities are primarily concerned to serve the interests of public officials rather than the goal of national development, though the rhetoric of development remains an important legitimating discourse for such polities.

There are close parallels in the relationships between business elites and political and bureaucratic elites across South-East Asia. Contemporary Indonesia exemplifies the same kind of mutually beneficial relationship between military officers and Chinese businessmen which characterized Thailand in the 1950s and 1960s. The term *cukong* – boss or master – describes the relationship between a government official and a Chinese businessman. The official provides protection and influence, in exchange for which the businessman raises funds. According to Schwarz:

> The *cukong* relationship repeated itself up and down the bureaucracy, from Soeharto [Suharto] to the top generals to regional military commanders, provincial governors and lesser administration officials. The mutual benefits were obvious: Soeharto wanted to encourage new investment in Indonesia, the military was always short of budget resources, and the Chinese desperately needed powerful patrons.
>
> (Schwarz, 1994, p.107)

The Chinese drew upon their own personal connections and family networks for the resources they required in doing business. These networks sometimes extended beyond Indonesia, to overseas Chinese communities in other parts of the Asia-Pacific.

In cases such as Malaysia, there is an explicit ethnic character to the relationship between the bureaucracy and the business sector. The national bargain provides Malays with preferential access to government jobs as part of a package designed to compensate them for the disproportionate economic power of the Chinese (Means, 1991, pp.310–5; Adam and Cavendish, 1995, pp.13–15). This bargain is predicated upon a set of sensitive political issues, such as the New Economic Policy, being designated off-limits for open public discussion. The spectre of ethnic conflict and unrest – which briefly emerged during the 1969 race riots – is invoked to curtail criticism of the elite-dominated order. Malaysia's democracy remains more of a procedural than a substantive matter; no Malaysian Prime Minister has ever faced the serious possibility of a defeat at the polls. Malaysia is not a bureaucratic polity in the same sense as Thailand or Indonesia, but the recent expansion of the Malaysian bureaucracy has gone hand-in-hand with the emergence of a *patrimonial state* (Means, 1991, pp.297–9). In this state, there is co-operation among different ethnic groups for mutual pragmatic advantages. An example is the way in which Chinese business people have frequently appointed well-connected 'Ali Baba' Malays to positions on the boards of their companies (Means, 1991, p.313). Another example of blurring the distinction between public and private sectors in Malaysia is the intimate connections between government political parties and the corporate sector (Gomez, 1994). Gomez has documented the way in which political parties such as the UMNO, the MCA and the MIC hold huge investments in major companies. He argues that political patronage and money politics have become the norm in Malaysia, to the extent that 'votes have become a marketable commodity during party elections', and the appointment of leaders to top party posts depends on the patronage powers of rival candidates. He highlights the way in which UMNO-related companies, such as the Renong group, enjoy easy access to government contracts (Gomez, 1994, pp.294–5). His conclusion:

> The close alliance between politics and business has led to the emergence in Malaysia of an elite minority in whose hands a disproportionate amount of the country's economic wealth and political power is vested. Equity-based power and hegemonic political position appear to have reinforced each other. With its control of the government through political power, and given the considerable mix between business and politics, this select group has had the capacity to adopt political and economic strategies that ensure the perpetuation of its dominant power base.

> (Gomez, 1994, p.296)

Similar observations can be made about the character of government–business relations in Indonesia, or several other South-East Asian countries. Under conditions such as these, elite governance can all too readily become a cover for elite mismanagement.

6.5   Elite governance and the military

In many Asia-Pacific countries the boundary between civilian and military areas of power and influence is not clearly delineated. In countries as diverse as South Korea, Thailand, Indonesia, and Burma, many national leaders have emerged directly from the armed forces: men such as President Park, General Prem Tinsulanond, General Suharto, and General Ne Win. In some countries – such as Thailand – military intervention in the political process has led to frequent coups and attempted coups. Elsewhere, for example in Burma and Indonesia, the militarization of politics has been associated with long periods of relative political stability, despite considerable tensions just below the surface. It is important to differentiate between direct military rule, and states in which the military plays a dominant or important political role (see Crouch, 1985, pp.287–317).

The reasons for military involvement in the political order vary from country to country but are typically associated with the following historical developments:

1   the central role of the military in a national independence struggle,

2   external support for the military during the Cold War, especially by the USA during the Korean and Vietnam Wars, and

3   domestic political importance of the military as a result of long-standing insurgency conflicts, especially communist insurgency or ethnic unrest.

Where the military (often primarily the army) was a central protagonist in a national independence struggle, it is able to claim a special legitimacy as one of the 'parents' of the new nation in the post-independence political order. Since those who held power in the immediate post-colonial period were often the military officers who had been involved in the nationalist struggle, they were well placed to devise constitutional and other mechanisms which would help ensure their own continuing importance in the political order. In other words, from the very birth of the post-colonial state, the military were intimately involved in politics. During the subsequent process of nation-building, history books were typically rewritten in such a way as to lionize the leaders of the independence movements. Military officers were often able to argue that it would be dangerous for them to withdraw from politics before the task of nation-building had been successfully completed.

Many countries in the Asia-Pacific gained independence in the immediate aftermath of the Second World War, coinciding with the Chinese Revolution and the onset of the Cold War. The USA became deeply concerned that Asia should not fall to communism, and waged two wars in the region to prevent the spread of communism. The Korean and Vietnam Wars led to considerable US investment in the region. In terms of infrastructure the USA constructed massive air, naval, and military bases in Japan, the Philippines, Guam, and Thailand. In addition they supplied training and support for the military in friendly Asia-Pacific states. The CIA and other American agencies sought to prop up governments – often repressive, corrupt, or both – which they believed would act as a bulwark against communism. These policies had the direct effect of bolstering military influence in countries such as Thailand and South Korea, since US support both enhanced the legitimacy of military rulers, and also enhanced their capacity to govern. American political scientists, especially the influential Samuel Huntington, argued that developing countries needed a period of strong government before they would be ready for democratic rule (Huntington, 1968). This argument was partly based on a socio-economic analysis of the countries concerned, which were deemed to lack sufficient countervailing social forces to balance the power of the military. In this absence of a dense civil society, the military had to assume a pre-eminent role in the political order. Whatever their academic basis, arguments of this kind helped legitimate US support for military and authoritarian regimes in Pacific Asia.

The external agency of the USA was, however, only one element in the equation. Indeed, in countries such as Burma the USA played no role at all in the political ascendancy of the military, which seized power in a 1962 coup. Military officers in the region were frequently able to legitimate their rule by reference to both internal and external security threats. Such threats typically took the form of communist insurrections or ethnic unrest. For example, the military rulers of Burma cited threats from the Karen and other sizeable minority groups, which waged war on the Burmese state for decades after independence. In Thailand and the Philippines, communist rebels controlled many remote parts of the country during periods of the 1970s and 1980s, providing a pretext for actions such as Marcos's declaration of martial law in 1972. Events such as the 1966 takeover in Indonesia, or the 1991 coup in Thailand, were frequently justified by the military on the grounds that they had been obliged to intervene to prevent a political crisis. Military regimes often argued that they acted 'for the good of the nation'. Military officers often claimed that the armed forces were closer to the people than civilian politicians. They were often disdainful of the civilian political process, viewing political parties and parliamentary procedures as fraught with corruption and incompetence. Since civilian politicians often *were* corrupt and incompetent, rhetoric of this kind had a degree of resonance with the public, and could provide some degree of legitimacy for military interventions in the political order.

Nevertheless, the citizens of many countries in the region were deeply distrustful of their militaries, and sceptical of military claims to be guardians of the public good. Sometimes the justifications advanced for military involvement in politics seemed more designed to help military officers persuade themselves of their own continuing importance than to win genuine popular support. Military officers were by no means immune from charges of corruption and incompetence. The Thai military, for example, seemed terminally incapable of performing any proper military functions, failing to defend the country's territorial integrity in the face of repeated incursions by Burma, Laos, and Cambodia. From the 1970s onwards, the military found itself increasingly on the domestic political defensive in countries across Pacific Asia. In 1986 the Philippine dictator Ferdinand Marcos was ousted from power by a popular opposition movement which was backed by some elements of the armed forces. In 1987, South Korea's military and bureaucratic elite was forced to embark on a process of political liberalization following huge mass demonstrations, and military influence was drastically reduced. In 1988, the Burmese military faced massive popular protests which reflected public dissatisfaction with its disastrous economic mismanagement. In 1992, similar protests forced Thai army commander and coup leader General Suchinda Kraprayoon to resign as Prime Minister.

Increasingly, military officers in the region have been forced to adopt more pragmatic strategies for participating in political power. No longer able to exercise control by sheer force of arms, they have been obliged to form alliances with civilian politicians, and to engage in the kind of party politicking which they previously despised. Former generals have sought and gained high political office by electoral means: examples include President Fidel Ramos of the Philippines and General Chavalit Yongchaiyudh of Thailand. At the same time, there has not been a one way process of civilianization of politics in the region: Ramos was the first military officer to gain the Philippine presidency, and in Singapore military officers are now being recruited in significant numbers into the previously entirely civilian technocratic and political elite, the most famous being Brigadier General 'B.G.' Lee, son of Singapore's founding father Lee Kwan Yew. The distinctions between military and civilian activities and functions are increasingly blurred, with military units having engaged in rural development activities in countries such as Thailand and Indonesia. The military in Pacific Asia is now engaged in a wholesale process of diversification. As its traditional sources of legitimacy, such as the Cold War, become less significant, it is engaged in a quest for new roles. As economies in the region have grown, so the scope for arms purchases has expanded; militaries have sought to justify arms procurements as a means of becoming more effective and professional fighting forces. The fact is, however, that many military forces in the region continue to hold an entirely unrealistic view of their own relevance and legitimacy.

One state, however, possesses armed forces who are taking an increasingly active role in governance on the basis of a very realistic understanding of their growing power; China's People's Liberation Army (PLA). Shambaugh (1996, p.268) argues that the PLA is both political and professional; according to Joffe (1996, p.300), it is a 'Party-army with professional characteristics'. While the Party has created elaborate mechanisms to control the military, commanders have resisted these controls where they contradicted their sense of professionalism, or challenged the PLA's vested interests (ibid., pp.305–6). Joffe argues that the PLA is essentially non-interventionist politically. By this he means that although the army did intervene in the political upheavals of the Cultural Revolution and was instrumental in ending the Tiananmen Square protests, these interventions were made on the orders of Mao and Deng respectively, rather than initiatives by the military themselves (ibid., pp.307–9). In post-Deng China, the senior Communist Party elites have no military background, nor do they have strong personal networks and authority within the PLA (Shambaugh, 1996, p.269). As Joffe (1996, p.309) puts it: 'the new Party leader will not be able to take for granted that the military will respond unequivocally to his summons for political intervention'. Nevertheless, 24 per cent of the 14th Chinese Communist Party Central Committee were PLA officers, indicating an increasing political role for the military. Recently, some generals are reported to have attended Politburo meetings in an ex-officio capacity (Shambaugh, 1996, p.272). According to Shambaugh (1996, p.274) 'a certain reassertion of the PLA into the political process is evident in recent years. But as the PLA has become more involved in elite politics, there has been a simultaneous effort since 1989 to subordinate the military to Party control.'

Attempts by the Party to impose discipline on the PLA partly reflected the political imperatives of civilian control, but also growing concerns about the scale of corruption in the armed forces, and its potentially corrosive effect on the state's legitimacy. The Chinese military is being pulled in three competing directions: towards increasing professionalism, towards a greater political role, and towards increasing commercialization. Shambaugh (1996, pp.278–9) argues that only internal security challenges and external security threats respectively will test the loyalty of the PLA to the Party, and the level of its professionalism, and speculates that while some units would 'defend the party-state', others would not. Partly as a result of the PLA's extensive business activities, the political and professional reliability of the Chinese military is now open to question. Whereas the ties between the military and business in many countries in the region are clandestine, the Chinese military openly engages in a wide range of business activities. Bickford (1994, pp.460–1) distinguishes between three different types of such business activities. In the first category are enterprises which directly support day-to-day military needs, including food production, equipment repairs, and transportation. Such enterprises date back to the 1930s, and reflect the origins of the PLA as an organization dedicated to self-sufficient revolutionary struggle. This group of businesses was further developed in the 1950s, and by the mid 1990s comprised around 10,000 enterprises with approximately 700,000 employees. A second category comprises collective enterprises, run by individual military units. Some of these enterprises, though run by relatives of service personnel, became independent entities. A third category comprises joint ventures with either local or international partners. During the 1980s, the role of these enterprises grew immensely. Though still providing support for the PLA, military businesses – which include such unlikely ventures as international hotels and Baskin Robbins ice cream franchises – are now highly commercialized, and firmly profit- and consumer-oriented. Nor are they limited to China itself: one of the principal revenue earners for what has been termed 'PLA Incorporated' is the arms export business run primarily by the company Polytechnologies. Income from this company pays for imported technology such as medical equipment. During the Iran–Iraq war, it became evident that both sides had been sold the latest Chinese weaponry (Shambaugh, 1996, p.276). The Saniju Enterprise Group is an example of a PLA-established transnational corporation, with 34 subsidiary enterprises trading in at least six foreign countries including Germany and the USA. Other PLA business activities included medical services, opening military hospitals to the public, factory production of civilian goods, and technology transfer by the navy's scientific research arm. Independently calculated estimates by the CIA and by a PLA research institute concurred on PLA commercial earnings of around US$5 billion in 1992 (Shambaugh, 1996, p.277ff).

Such a large-scale involvement in non-military activities by the PLA has entailed various costs. Corruption is widespread, and some PLA and navy units have crossed the boundary between legitimate business, and illegal businesses such as smuggling, prostitution, and stolen car rings (Shambaugh, 1996, p.227). Because business activities bring personal benefits to those involved, they may lead to the neglect of military duties and training, and consequently to a decline in military preparedness. Bickford (1994, p.470) cites the example of a military medical school so preoccupied with running 73 different businesses that little teaching was being done. Although attempts have been made to curb some of these excesses, they have been largely unsuccessful. It is clearly not in the defence interests of the Chinese state for its soldiers to put so much of their energies into business activities. But China lacks the financial resources to support the vast army it requires. Western estimates put the size of the PLA at around three million in 1994, though the true size may be greater (for a discussion see Shichtor, 1996, pp.340, 346–7). Not surprisingly, the government has no effective means of curtailing the PLA's enterprises (Bickford, 1994, p.471ff; see also **McGrew and Brook, 1998, Chapter 5**). Bickford (1994, pp.472–4) argues that the growth of PLA enterprises illustrates that the army is no longer a bastion of Maoist purity. The army now has a major stake in the economic transformations which are sweeping through Chinese society. The rise of the enterprise army means that the new generation of Chinese army officers will be much more sophisticated in terms of their economic understanding than their predecessors. This trend may help consolidate the transformation of China to a fully-fledged market economy. At the same time, endemic corruption may lead to a worsening of civil–military relations arising from resentment on the part of civilian entrepreneurs, for the PLA's economic activities are now so widespread that it is beyond the capacity of either China's military commanders or its civilian rulers even to monitor, let alone control them.

6.6   The shifting nature of elite governance

Many of the features of state–business relations which characterize both the East Asian developmental states, and the second generation of industrializing countries in South-East Asia, are products of specific historical and geographical circumstances. The collaboration between government and industry in post-war Japan represented a concerted effort to rebuild the country's economy following the calamitous defeat of Japan at the end of the Second World War. Countries such as Malaysia and Indonesia were obvious sites for foreign direct investment by both Japan and the West during the Cold War, and investment patterns helped produce close ties between the public and private sectors. But as international political and economic conditions have changed, so patterns of state–business relations are altering. The very same high levels of economic growth which were associated with these economies during the 1980s and 1990s are weakening the capacity of political and bureaucratic elites to control their national economy. Whereas business communities, notably Chinese minorities, were formerly obliged to play second fiddle to bureaucrats, politicians and military officers, they are increasingly moving into positions of greater power and influence. In Thailand, business people of Chinese extraction have been able to assume important political posts from which they were previously barred; for example, Banharn Silpa-archa, a provincial businessman, served as Prime Minister from 1995 to 1996. In South-East Asia, Chinese business is now firmly regional in character: the Sino-Thai conglomerate CP is reputed to have invested more than US$8 billion in China, for example. Therefore these businesses can escape the dictates of any single national government. The internationalization of finance means that a road-building or power project in Indonesia or the Philippines might be underwritten by a syndicate of ten local and 30 foreign (mainly Western and Japanese) banks, making it difficult for any state elite to retain control of the infrastructure project.

In the light of changing economic conditions, old models for understanding the political economy of states in the region are coming under increasing challenge. South Korea since 1987 has been engaged in a gradual process of structural political and economic reform, which is partly intended to reduce state domination of the economy (see Bedeski, 1994, pp.1–28). Other developmental states, such as Taiwan, are engaged in parallel processes. One major book on Thailand was subtitled *From Bureaucratic Polity to Liberal Corporatism* (Anek, 1992). Its author argued that both bureaucratic and non bureaucratic forces in Thailand were now 'strong and autonomous' and that 'the decision-making of the regime has ceased to be monopolized by the military-bureaucratic elite' (ibid., p.161). Thus a combination of domestic economic and political changes, coupled with international pressures for economic liberalization, and changes in the character of global finance, appear to be eroding the distinctive character of state–business relations in many Asia-Pacific countries.

Hawes and Hong Liu (1993), reviewing seven monographs on the political economy of South-East Asia, note that 'the transformation of these political economies creates tension, and the potential for political instability is quite high'. They caution against over-reliance on general structuralist interpretations of change in the region, since these can easily overlook: 'the periodic succession crises, the idiosyncrasies of individual leaders, and the crosscutting interests typical of the evolving political systems found in the multiracial societies of Southeast Asia' (Hawes and Hong Liu, 1993, p.645). In other words, patterns of elite governance which appear integral to the structure of states and societies in the region are actually less deeply embedded than might appear – a succession crisis or a rise in ethnic tensions could easily upset the political apple cart.

Quite apart from the changing balance of power within the elite itself, Pacific Asian governments are finding themselves confronted by ever-rising non-elite demands. Pressure for increased wage levels, greater political freedom, and reductions in political corruption are examples of issues which have emerged in many countries. The developmental states relied on deferred gratification to keep down economic and political demands during the early phases of rapid industrialization and growth, but increasing income levels – often outstripped by exponential growth in popular aspirations – have led to popular expressions of frustration, even resulting in mass demonstrations which succeeded in ousting unpopular authoritarian governments (see Chapter 12).

Other challenges to elite dominance come from the rise of professional politicians. In several countries in the region, parliaments, elections, and political parties have gained markedly in importance over the past couple of decades. Electoral politics are sometimes compromised by vote-buying and corruption: Thailand and the Philippines are good examples (see Callahan and McCargo, 1996). In other countries, ruling elites use various forms of direct and indirect pressures to ensure favourable electoral outcomes. Nevertheless, the holding of an election offers a means by which opposition to a ruling elite can be demonstrated. Even where the outcome of an election is a foregone conclusion, the election itself offers scope for dissenting voices to be raised (Lev, 1996, pp.248–9).

In conclusion, many states in Pacific Asia have been characterized by elite-dominated political orders, in which the energies of the state have been primarily concerned with economic development and with preserving bureaucratic privilege and military influence. These political regimes relied on close collaboration between the public and private sectors, with the result that popular political participation has often been curtailed, and the interests of ordinary citizens subordinated to those of well-connected political actors and big business. Although these patterns of elite governance have been associated with high levels of economic growth in many of the states concerned, the corporatist arrangements which they reflect are often characterized by internal contradictions. Although elite governance continues to thrive in some parts of the region, elsewhere it faces major challenges from a hollowing-out of the regulatory capacity of the nation-state, and from the rise of popular political and economic demands (see Chapters 11 and 12). It will be incumbent upon elites across the Asia-Pacific to find appropriate ways of responding to these formidable challenges.

References

Adam, C. and Cavendish, W. (1995) 'Background' in Jomo, K.S. (ed.) *Privatising Malaysia: Rents, Rhetoric, Realities*, Boulder, Westview Press, pp.11–41.

Anek, L. (1992) *Business Associations and the New Political Economy of Thailand: From Bureaucratic Polity to Liberal Corporatism*, Boulder, Westview Press.

Aspinall, E. (1996) 'The broadening base of political opposition in Indonesia' in Rodan, G. (ed.) pp.215–40.

Bedeski, R.E. (1994) *The Transformation of South Korea*, London, Routledge.

Bickford, T.J. (1994) 'The Chinese military and its business operations: the PLA as entrepreneur', *Asian Survey*, vol.34, no.5, pp.460–74.

Calder, K.E. (1993) *Strategic Capitalism*, Princeton, Princeton University Press.

Callahan, W.A. and McCargo, D. (1996) 'Vote-buying in Thailand's Northeast: the July 1995 General Election', *Asian Survey*, vol.36, no.4, pp.376–92.

Callon, S. (1995) *Divided Sun: MITI and the Breakdown of Japanese High-Tech Industrial Policy 1975–1993*, Stanford, Stanford University Press.

Crawford, G. (1995) 'Promoting democracy, human rights and good governance through development aid: a comparative study of the politics of four northern donors', Leeds, University of Leeds Centre for Democratization Studies, Working Papers on Democratization.

Crouch, H. (1985) 'The military and politics in South-East Asia' in Ahmad, Z.H. and Crouch, H. (eds) *Military–Civilian Relations in South-East Asia*, Singapore, Oxford University Press, pp.287–317.

Girling, J.L.S. (1981) *Thailand: Society and Politics*, Ithaca, Cornell University Press.

Gomez, E.T. (1994) *Political Business: Corporate Involvement of Malaysian Political Parties*, Townsville, Centre for Southeast Asian Studies, James Cook University.

Hawes, G. and Hong Liu (1993) 'Explaining the dynamics of the Southeast Asian political economy: state, society and the search for economic growth', *World Politics*, vol.45, pp.629–60.

Hewison, K. (1996) 'Political oppositions and regime change in Thailand' in Rodan, G. (ed.) pp.72–94.

Huntington, S.P. (1968) *Political Order in Changing Societies*, New Haven, Yale University Press.

Ishida, H. (1993) *Social Mobility in Contemporary Japan*, Basingstoke, Macmillan.

Jackson, K.D. (1978) 'Bureaucratic polity: a theoretical framework for the analysis of power and communications in Indonesia' in Jackson, K.D. and Lucien, W.P. (eds) *Political Power and Communications in Indonesia*, Berkeley, University of California Press, pp.3–22.

Joffe, E. (1996) 'Party–Army relations in China: retrospect and prospect', *The China Quarterly*, vol.146, pp.299–314.

Johnson, C. (1982) *MITI and the Japanese Economic Miracle*, Stanford, Stanford University Press.

Koh, B.C. (1989) *Japan's Administrative Elite*, Berkeley, University of California Press.

Krauss, E.S. and Muramatsu, M. (1988) 'The Japanese political economy today: the patterned pluralist model', in Okimoto, D.I. and Rohlen, T.P. (eds) *Inside the Japanese System*, Stanford, Stanford University Press, pp.208–10.

Lee, Y.H. (1997) *The State, Society and Big Business in South Korea*, London, Routledge.

Lev, D. (1996) 'Afterword' in Taylor, R.H. (ed.) *The Politics of Elections in Southeast Asia*, New York, Cambridge University Press, pp.243–51.

Luedde-Neurath, R. (1988) 'State intervention and export-oriented development in South Korea' in White, G. (ed.) *Developmental States in East Asia*, Basingstoke, Macmillan, pp.68–112.

McGrew, A. and Brook, C. (eds) (1998) *Asia-Pacific in the New World Order*, London, Routledge in association with The Open University.

Means, G.P. (1991) *Malaysian Politics: the Second Generation*, Singapore, Oxford University Press.

Nakano, M. (1997) *The Policy-Making Process in Contemporary Japan*, Basingstoke, Macmillan.

Okimoto, D.I. (1989) *Between MITI and the Market*, Stanford, Stanford University Press.

Riggs, F.W. (1966) *Thailand: the Modernization of a Bureaucratic Polity*, Honolulu, East West Center Press.

Rodan, G. (ed.) (1996) *Political Oppositions in Industrialising Asia*, London, Routledge.

Schwartz, F. (1993) 'Of fairy tales and familiar talks: the politics of consultation' in Allinson, G.D. and Sone, Y. (eds) *Political Dynamics in Contemporary Japan*, Ithaca, Cornell University Press, pp.217–41.

Schwarz, A. (1994) *A Nation in Waiting: Indonesia in the 1990s*, St. Leonards, Allen & Unwin.

Scruton, R. (1982) *A Dictionary of Political Thought*, Basingstoke, Macmillan.

Shambaugh, D. (1996) 'China's military in transition: politics, professionalism, procurement and power projection', *The China Quarterly*, vol.146, pp.265–98.

Shibusawa, M., Ahmad, Z.H. and Bridges, B. (1992) *Pacific Asia in the 1990s*, London, Routledge.

Shichtor, Y. (1996) 'Demobilization: the dialectics of PLA troop reduction', *The China Quarterly*, vol.146, pp.336–59.

Thompson, G. (ed.) (1998) *Economic Dynamism in the Asia-Pacific*, London, Routledge in association with The Open University.

van Wolferen, K. (1989) *The Enigma of Japanese Power*, Basingstoke, Macmillan.

World Bank (1993) *The East Asian Miracle: Economic Growth and Public Policy*, New York, Oxford University Press.

Further reading

On the Japanese economic model and debates over the developmental state, see especially Johnson (1982) and Calder (1993). Koh (1989) is the best general account of Japanese bureaucracy. On South Korea, see Lee (1997).

For discussions of politics and the military, see Ahmad, Z.H. and Crouch, H. (eds) (1985) *Military–Civilian Relations in South-East Asia*, Singapore, Oxford University Press, and the special issue of *The China Quarterly*, vol.146, June 1996.

On the bureaucratic polity, the classic account is Riggs (1966) while Jackson (1978) applies a similar framework to Indonesia.

For studies which use political economy approaches to understand the changing nature of politics and elite governance in the region, see the Routledge *New Rich in Asia* series, including Robison, R. and Goodman, D. (eds) (1995) *The New Rich in Asia: Mobile Phones, McDonald's, and Middle-Class Revolution*, London, Routledge, and Rodan, G. (ed.) (1996) *Political Oppositions in Industrialising Asia*, London, Routledge.

A good comparative study of electoral processes is Taylor, R.H. (ed.) (1996) *The Politics of Elections in Southeast Asia*, New York, Cambridge University Press, pp.243–51; for a case study, see Maisrikrod, S. and McCargo, D. (1997) 'Electoral politics: commercialisation and exclusion' in Hewison, K. (ed.) *Political Change in Thailand: Democracy and Participation*, London, Routledge.

CHAPTER 7

Challenging the political order: social movements

William A. Callahan

7.1 Introduction

While Chapter 6 focused on the role of political and economic elites in the politics of Pacific Asia, this chapter looks at movements which challenge such top-down organizations of political and social order. Section 7.2 considers definitions of social movements in Pacific Asia in both a practical and a theoretical context. The remainder of the chapter examines specific social movements as case studies of general trends in political opposition in the region. Section 7.3 considers old social movements in terms of nationalist movements in China. Section 7.4 traces the trajectory of social movements from old social movements to new social movements in South Korea. These new social movements, which have their counterparts elsewhere in Pacific Asia, show how the composition, style and substance of popular politics has changed in tandem with industrialization. Section 7.5 examines the fine line that social movements must tread between independence from and co-optation to the state through the examples of anti-corruption movements in Thailand and the Philippines. Thus far the chapter has focused on urban movements. Section 7.6 seeks to balance this by looking at rural social movements that address the issues of development and environmental protest. Section 7.7 concludes the chapter by examining how social movements are increasingly moving from national space to transnational space through an examination of transnational human rights organizations.

7.2 What is a social movement?

Defining terms in political science is often problematic. So, for example, the meaning of the term 'sovereignty' is still contested. Similarly we currently have a slippery understanding of what we mean when we talk of social movements. As Walker writes, they are 'merely social, always moving'; as 'mosquitoes on the evening breeze', some social movements are deadly, but most do not present much of a challenge to the institutionalized power of the sovereign state (Walker, 1994, pp.675, 669). Still, just because of their slippery nature, social movements can pose a challenge, not just to particular regimes, but to any political imagination to which the state is the dominant concern and concept.

Because they are 'social' rather than 'political', social movements can evade state surveillance by creating their own space in a parallel economy and society. Civil society then is the 'sphere of social interaction between economy and state, composed above all of the intimate sphere (especially the family), the sphere of associations (especially voluntary associations), social movements, and forms of public communication' (Cohen and Arato, 1992, p.ix). Social movements constitute the 'dynamic element' that links collective action with the democratic potential of civil society. The political role of civil society is not to seize state power, but to engage in a 'politics of influence' where citizens have a part in the discussion and critique of state policies. Seen in this way, social movements are not inherently anti-state, but rather typically rely on the state to define the legal space for 'civil society' in a dualistic relationship.

Social movements are seen as necessary in Pacific Asia because, in general, the state is often quite strong while non-ruling political parties are quite weak. In countries as diverse as South Korea, the Philippines and Thailand one can see that political parties are personalistic, regional, and generally lack grassroots support and policy-making abilities. Hence even though elections are held, they often have little to do with choosing a government and rarely involve debates about policy issues (Taylor, 1996). Since the formal political system of political parties and parliamentary procedure has not responded to the changing needs of the people, informal citizens' organizations have been growing up to articulate and promote the demands of a broader civil society.

In Pacific Asia a vocabulary is emerging which describes such social movements in various ways to both include and exclude certain actors: old social movements, new social movements, political opposition, civil society, non-governmental organizations (NGOs), and extra-parliamentary activity. And all of these are often subsumed under the title 'democratic movements', though we should be sure to note that these social movements are often looking for alternative notions of 'democracy' and 'development' (Wignaraja, 1993).

Each of these terms – social movements, civil society, NGOs, and so on – poses a slightly different way of framing political and social change. Outright political opposition is often dangerous in Pacific Asia. As the authors of *Political Oppositions in Industrializing Asia* argue, social movements in the region are often at most 'semi-oppositional' in comparison with political opposition as it is known in Europe and North America (Rodan, 1996a). Old social movements of workers, peasants and students which challenge the existing social order are increasingly being overtaken by new social movements led by the middle classes which organize around trans-class issues such as the environment, nationalism, human rights, and socio-economic justice.

Most of the research on social movements in Pacific Asia in the 1990s uses the vocabulary of civil society and the power of non-governmental organizations often interchangeably (Serrano, 1994; Yamamoto, 1995). Both civil society and NGOs are contrasted with the state; they do not make sense unless there is a state. But the political logic of civil societies and NGOs is not radical, they do not seek to overthrow the state, as did the revolutionary social movements of the past. Rather they seek to reform and democratize the state through an indirect politics of influence. These social movements can facilitate the overthrow of an authoritarian regime in the process of reform, but as we will see they do not challenge the logic of state sovereignty (Cohen and Arato, 1992).

Though it may seem daunting to have so many categories for making sense of 'social movements', many see such multiplicity as indicative of power relations (e.g. Foucault, 1980, pp.95–6). The dividing line between the 'oppressive state' and the 'patriotic revolutionaries' is rarely clear or simple. The relation between power and resistance is not clean or pure, but 'sticky'. Resistance to power is already wrapped up in reproducing power for social movements, 'independence' and 'co-optation' are relative terms. The ironic and sticky nature of power comes out well in the workings of social movements in Pacific Asia where the overlap of formal and informal activities, parliamentary and extra-parliamentary politics, and violent and non-violent tactics is quite common. It is also common for NGOs not to fall clearly into a two-sided discourse: in addition to being co-opted, movements can also have a relationship to power where their 'independence' is 'fostered' by the state (Anek, 1992).

The politics of social movements in Pacific Asia then concerns the nature of the relationship between the state and civil society, between ruling parties and opposition, between institutions and social movements. One of the most threatening things that the protesters did in Tiananmen Square was to organize student and labour unions that were both separate from and independent of the Chinese Communist Party's captive organizations. But as we will see, it is not always clear whether certain groups are independent, or whether they have been co-opted by the state.

Before I try and outline the key social movements in Pacific Asia, it is necessary to question the whole project of this chapter. Does it make sense to talk of 'social movements' in Pacific Asia? Or are such descriptions simply a figment of the Western imagination which looks for familiar social forms in the 'exotic East'? To certain bureaucratic and academic elites, asking about 'social movements in Asia' is asking the wrong question. They insist that civil society, opposition and social movements are not universal concepts. They are not phenomena found all over the globe, but merely historical practices that grow out of the peculiarities of European culture.

They look to a developmental state, characterized by an authoritarian government that refers to traditional Asian culture, to argue that in the same way that it is 'natural' and effective for the state to control the economy, it is 'natural' and effective for the state to control society. Democracy and development are separated; rather than being twin goals, they are in conflict. This anti-social movement argument often appeals to corporatist models of an organic state where 'loyal opposition' is an oxymoron; trade unions, business associations and other groups in civil society are creatures of state control. If they resist co-optation, then social movements risk 'extermination' (Wignaraja, 1993).

The means of state control are not just legal or repressive, but ideological. The argument goes that the state gets its legitimacy from the success of economic development, not from the democratic process (Taylor, 1996). More to the point, such corporatist states often appeal to 'Asian values' to deny difference as it is expressed in opposition. Critical social movements are defined as un-Asian, perhaps a product of cultural imperialism, and certainly illegitimate (Lawson, 1996; Mahathir and Ishihara, 1995). Social movements are seen as a foreign practice, part of corrupt Western democracies. Malaysian Prime Minister Mahathir neatly sums up this negative view of social movements when he lists the 'many things wrong with the practice of democracy. The arrogance of power of the media before whom the most powerful politician cringes. The power of trade unions, the power of pressure groups, the lobbyists, the Non-Governmental Organizations, the local party boss' (Mahathir, 1993, p.A6).

This cultural nationalism in Malaysia is not unique; the Chinese government has also been very vocal in redefining topics such as 'human rights', and 'the environment', as Western. Thus when Asians argue for civil society, they are often silenced by being 'depicted as traitors to their own cultures, or not real members of society' (Lawson, 1996, p.110). Indeed, while we might criticize certain social movements for being co-opted by the corporatist state, many national governments charge that critical social movements have been co-opted by foreign governments and/or are captive pawns of external funding agencies; again leading to the conflict between social movements and state sovereignty. (For a further discussion of 'Asian values' see Lawson, 1996; and Rodan, 1996b.)

Regardless of such theorizing and counter-theorizing, recently there have been massive social movements which brought hundreds of thousands of people out onto the streets in countries across Pacific Asia: the Philippines in 1986, South Korea in 1987, Burma/Myanmar in 1988, China in 1989, Thailand in 1992, and Indonesia in 1996. Even in countries that have not experienced massive street demonstrations – such as Singapore and Malaysia – elements of civil society have been struggling to influence the government in more indirect ways (Rodan, 1996a). These various popular movements have challenged authoritarianism not only in different national settings, but also across historical, social, economic, political and cultural differences.

Though democratic movements are not uncommon in Pacific Asia, there is also an uneasy relationship between democracy and social movements. As noted above, many of the mass organizations in Pacific Asia are part of the corporatist state structure, and one of the tried-and-true methods of state power is to organize their own counter-demonstrations with their own 'mobs'. This has happened recently in Thailand, Burma/Myanmar, Indonesia and Malaysia. Furthermore, nationalist and religious groups which are independent of the state can work against democracy.

7.3 Old social movements: nationalism and revolution in China

Though many portray recent democratic movements in Pacific Asia as a new phenomenon, the region has a long history of social movements that have contested power in numerous ways. Indeed, before the current wave of democratization and social unrest there were three other periods where civil society was particularly active in the region: the 1920s–1930s, the 1940s–1950s, and the 1970s (Rodan, 1996a). This section will examine how class-based social movements – of peasants, workers and students – have shaped the politics of the region in the twentieth century.

Nationalism and anti-colonialism fuelled many social movements both before and after the Second World War. Chinese history provides many examples of such social movements in the early twentieth century. The Imperial State was overthrown in 1911, and the 1910s were characterized by broad social movements led by students and workers. The May 4th movement erupted in 1919 in response to the Treaty of Versailles which did not treat China as an equal sovereign state, but simply transferred Chinese territories from the defeated German Empire to the victorious Japanese Empire. These political demonstrations were accompanied by the New Culture Movement which aimed to modernize China by discarding imperial Confucian culture and promoting science and democracy. The 1920s and 1930s were characterized by a very vibrant civil society – including the revolutionary literature of writers like Lu Xun – while the troops of the Communist Party and the Kuomintang (Nationalist Party) battled over Chinese soil (Chesneaux *et al.*, 1977). This period provided a stock of images that were used in Tiananmen Square in 1989: one of the rallying points of this latest student movement was the 70th anniversary of the May 4th movement (Wasserstrom and Perry, 1995).

For China, the Second World War was not a global confrontation of ideology so much as a nationalist war; it is called the 'Anti-Japanese War' in Chinese, and the communists defeated the Kuomintang forces in 1949 in large part because they were able to continue to mobilize people around a powerful anti-colonial ideology. This anti-imperialist nationalism was typical of other mass revolutions that followed the Pacific War. Indeed, the communist insurgencies in Thailand and Malaysia each failed to attract a large following because they were seen to be more Chinese than national. Regardless of their ideology or their methods (violent revolution or elections), groups which held the mantle of nationalism were the most successful in fighting imperial powers: the communists in Vietnam, Sukarno in Indonesia, even the now right wing People's Action Party

(PAP) in Singapore. Anti-American nationalism has been popular in efforts to remove US troops from Thailand, South Korea, the Philippines and Japan.

So where nationalism is now often used (cynically) as a tool of state power in Pacific Asia, in these earlier periods it was very much a rallying point for vibrant social movements. Nationalism remains an important issue in Taiwan where the main opposition party, the Democratic Progressive Party, taps into a Taiwanese nationalism in response to Chinese claims on the island from both the Kuomintang and the Communist Party.

7.4   From old to new social movements in South Korea

The Pacific Asian 'economic miracle' is said to rely on a docile labour force in a corporatist society. But the social and economic dislocations that accompany rapid economic development have also produced class-specific mobilizations of students and workers. The changing pattern of social movements in South Korea provides an example of how revolutionary class-based social movements have been displaced by issue-based reformist new social movements since the 1970s. Labour and student groups in South Korea are more militant than in other countries of the region. But their activities still clearly show the general trends of what has happened in Taiwan, Thailand and the Philippines, as well as pointing out one of the possible directions for social movements in Vietnam, Indonesia and China.

South Korea's democratization process started long before the 'Middle Class Revolution' of June 1987. Social movements in the authoritarian period (1961–87) can be characterized by three distinct stages in the transformation from military authoritarian rule to a liberal democracy (Koo, 1993). The first stage was dominated by students and intellectuals who formed the *minjung* movement in the early 1970s before organized workers' struggles appeared. *Minjung* literally means 'popular masses' and was a populist and nationalist reaction to the bureaucratic authoritarian regime. The *minjung* movement addressed economic and social injustices, as well as raising the national questions of reunification and independence from foreign domination; 37,000 US troops are stationed in bases spread all over South Korea, including Seoul. The *minjung* movement brought together a broad alliance of those who were excluded from the fruits of South Korean economic development and challenged the state-led strategy on the grounds that it was not working for the people. By the 1980s, it would become the most pervasive oppositional political and cultural movement (Koo, 1993).

Such a broad-based movement was possible because during the early period of South Korea's political-economic development, there were no significant class differences. There were severe state controls over civil society in general, and labour in particular. Thus it was tactical to use the more general nationalist language of *minjung* than challenging the hysterically anti-communist state with a class-based movement (Koo, 1993, p.142). In this situation, only intellectuals could criticize the government given the morally superior position of intellectuals in the Confucian tradition. The students also symbolically represented the nation in South Korea, much as they did in Thailand in 1973, Burma/Myanmar in 1988, and China in 1989.

The second stage of social movements involved the emergence of class-based organizations in the 1980s. The three stages that academics use to explain transitions in Pacific Asia are not distinct. These different forms of social movements blend into each other, often co-operating with each other before differentiating themselves. This is particularly true of the emergence of the South Korean labour movement in the 1980s, for it was fostered by the *minjung* movement. This middle-class fostering of labour can be seen in the 1990s in Indonesia where the attempts to form independent labour unions have benefited from the support of middle-class groups. *Minjung* not only politicized the new middle classes, but also provided the working classes with shelter and support, oppositional ideology, politicized language, and organizational networks. Many students concealed their background to get jobs in factories in order to educate workers and help them organize labour unions (Koo, 1993, pp.162, 150). Worker-based opposition rose with South Korea's rapid industrialization in the 1980s. South Korean workers are remarkably defiant compared with other Pacific Asian countries with their frequent strikes and violent expressions of labour activism. This insurgent style is seen as a reaction to the harsh realities of working-class life where the centralized conglomerates (*chaebol*) used militarized management styles and captive labour unions (Koo, 1993; Bello and Rosenfeld, 1992; Dalton and Cotton, 1996). By 1985 the focus of the labour movement had shifted from the economic struggle of workers against employers to a political struggle against the military authoritarian state; as a part of this shift, labour unions increasingly organized at higher levels and formed alliances in umbrella organizations that included a broad swathe of opposition forces.

Things came to a head in 1987 with an explosion of popular frustration. This was sparked by a gross abuse of police power: a university student activist was tortured to death in interrogation. There was a spring offensive by labour unions which is now seen as a watershed of labour power. In April 1987 the middle classes started to join the students and workers, and protests grew to unprecedented levels when President Chun refused to allow even the discussion of an amendment to the constitution to hold direct presidential elections. This finally led to the formation of broad umbrella organizations such as the National Coalition for a Democratic Constitution which organized massive demonstrations in June 1987 and which were supported by labour, students and the middle classes. In the face of such popular defiance, Roh Tae Woo, the presidential candidate from the ruling party who was also Chun's number two, issued the 'June 29 Declaration' which accepted all the demands of the opposition groups. This political opening led to 3,300 strikes in 1987 by industrial workers. The workers demanded to share the fruits of South Korea's economic miracle and set up independent unions. They also made political and social demands which questioned the whole model of capitalist development (Koo, 1993; Bello and Rosenfeld, 1992). The working class was initially stunningly successful: there was a 22.6 per cent increase in blue collar wages in 1988, and by January 1990 an independent democratic labour movement was established at the national level.

But the founding of this national union was also the peak of labour power. The coalition between labour and the middle class defeated Chun's authoritarian capitalist state, but it did not survive after the presidential elections of 1987. The extreme radicalism of violent labour strikes and student demonstrations caused serious disruption to the economy, slowing down GNP growth in 1988. Dominant groups in business and the state manipulated the media to blame the labour movement for wiping out South Korea's competitive edge in world markets. Labour was continuously portrayed as violent, irresponsible, and selfish, while the independent union movement was framed as part of the subversive leftist forces (Koo, 1993, p.158). Thus the middle classes became increasingly suspicious of labour. The middle classes were more interested in the political democracy of elections than the social and economic democracy advocated by labour and students.

Though the confrontational tactics used by (often left-wing) labour and student groups played a crucial role in mobilizing social movements against the continuation of military authoritarianism in 1987, these same tactics did not work in the post-authoritarian era. Political parties also tried to respond to this new situation. Just as labour was establishing its national organization, the ruling military party joined with two moderate opposition parties to found the Liberal Democratic Party in January 1990. But in general, political parties in South Korea are ineffective; they are regional movements headed by charismatic leaders. They lack grassroots support and thus democracy is largely characterized by electoralism. In a passage which characterizes the political situation in much of Pacific Asia, Dalton and Cotton (1996, p.282) argue that 'In the absence of issue-based politics emerging in the legislature, and with the parties slow to seek affiliation with interest groups, a number of new social movements emerged to occupy parts of this political space'.

Hence the 1990s are characterized by the third stage of new social movements which have grown to fill the political space left by deradicalized labour and student demonstrations. As well as having the most militant student and labour organizations, South Korea also has the largest and most dynamic middle class in Pacific Asia (Koo, 1993). Students and labour led the movement in the 1970s and 1980s; but in the 1990s they are increasingly being led by new social movements. Though there were certainly seeds of new social movements in *minjung*, the transition from class-based social movements to new social movements has signified an important change in style and content of civil society and oppositional politics. Since 1987 there has been a mushrooming of NGOs in South Korea and Taiwan; similar mushroomings of NGOs occurred in the 1980s in the Philippines, Thailand and Indonesia.

These changes can best be seen by examining an exemplary case of a new social movement in South Korea: the Citizen's Coalition of Economic Justice (CCEJ). The CCEJ is an NGO, which is typical of new social movements in the region (Serrano, 1994; Yamamoto, 1995). Such NGOs are voluntary, non-profit organizations which are not looking to take state power, but to have a 'politics of influence' in civil society. Though they are typically led by the middle class, they are also known for working on trans-class issues. CCEJ's social justice agenda is issue-based around consumption and quality of life concerns: environmentalism, feminism, consumer and human rights. In countries like Malaysia where old social movements are often organized around ethnicity, NGOs are noteworthy for attempting to transcend ethnic issues and divisions (Jesudason, 1996, p.152).

The CCEJ was founded in July 1989 when it was clear that the government was not meeting popular aspirations for a more balanced approach to industrial growth, social welfare, and the environment. Thus the social costs of rapid development remain an issue, but the focus and methods have changed from an ideologically-charged struggle for economic equity and democracy, to the promotion of diverse agendas which extend beyond strictly economic and political objectives. The CCEJ is typical of NGOs in Pacific Asia; it is more moderate than the labour movement. It is generally not anti-systemic or confrontational. Rather it is reformist, and expressively non-violent, showing a preference for negotiations. Rather than being extremist, one scholar describes them as representing the 'middling grassroots' (Han, 1996). Still, in Indonesia NGOs are denounced as the 'extreme center' (Heryanto, 1996).

CCEJ is one of the largest NGOs in South Korea with 20 regional chapters and over 10,000 members, although the bulk of its membership is drawn from the Seoul middle class. A major part of NGO activity is networking with other NGOs, and the CCEJ has made such linkages with religious groups, academics, farmers, students, and other civic groups. It is important to note that the CCEJ remains independent of labour unions and political parties, which is characteristic of effective social movements in Pacific Asia. It also maintains links with the mainstream media as part of its efforts to develop and mobilize public opinion. In this way it can transcend its middle-class base and speak for marginalized groups: the poor, foreign workers, farmers, and small businesses. But some note an ambiguity in its orientation when promoting the interests of marginalized groups competes with promoting the interests of the privileged (Dalton and Cotton, 1996). This is also the case in Indonesia where in 1994 the NGOs mobilized much more to criticize the government for closing down three weekly news magazines – a middle-class issue – than they did to support independent labour unions – a working-class issue (Heryanto, 1996).

The three stages of social movements outlined in this section trace a familiar pattern in Pacific Asia. In the 1970s there were struggles against the capitalist model of development, first in a general populist mode, and then in a specific class struggle. But once capitalism was firmly established in the 1980s, social movements re-focused on social justice as reform rather than revolution.

The effectiveness of the reform project of the new social movements like CCEJ is still to be tested in South Korea. There is concern that the middle-class membership might not want to challenge entrenched interests; such groups are always susceptible to the 'co-optation' that is a major strategy of authoritarian regimes in Pacific Asia. The strategy of new social movements has been tested in Taiwan, Thailand and the Philippines, and they have been successful in challenging the state and business for various forms of social justice. As we will see in the next section, NGOs and new social movements played an important part in the overthrow of authoritarian regimes in these countries.

7.5 Relations between civil society and the state: anticorruption campaigns in Thailand and the Philippines

The state has dominated the economy throughout Pacific Asia, regardless of whether the ideology was capitalist or communist, and whether the economy was successful or not. Bureaucrats have had not just enormous political power, but also considerable economic power. The technocratic mode of state-led development policies tends to narrow political space, and thus often fosters corruption. Corruption was one of the main issues of the democratic uprisings in the Philippines, China and Thailand, as well as leading to the 'trial of the decade' in South Korea where two ex-presidents and dozens of elite businessmen were tried and found guilty of corruption.

This section examines the workings of two anti-corruption electionmonitoring organizations, National Citizens Movement for Free Elections (NAMFREL) and PollWatch. These two watchdog organizations are not the largest or even the most important NGOs in the Philippines and Thailand, but they are noteworthy because they illustrate how two different relationships between state and civil society have each been successful in pushing for more honest and meaningful elections. When electoral politics did not work, these NGOs transformed themselves into broad-based social movements to overthrow right-wing regimes, only to turn back again into issue-specific groups after the democratic transformation. By comparing NAMFREL and PollWatch we also can see how social movements in Pacific Asia blur the distinctions between formal and informal activity, parliamentary and extra-parliamentary politics, state and civil society, and thus independent and co-opted organizations. Such election watchdog organizations are noteworthy because they also exist in Taiwan and South Korea, while they are being studied and copied in Bangladesh, Cambodia and Indonesia. The phenomenon is not limited to these examples either, for 'During the past decade, non-partisan international and domestic election monitoring has grown increasingly sophisticated' (Garber and Cowan, 1993, p.95).

When social movements are seen in terms of NGOs, then the Philippines has the most active civil society in Pacific Asia, and one of the largest in the developing world. NGOs in the Philippines can also be quite powerful. The 1986 People Power revolution, which ousted President Ferdinand Marcos after a 20-year dictatorship, is the most cogent example of the effectiveness of social movements. NAMFREL was an important part of the People Power movement. It was founded in 1983 as a nation-wide non-partisan umbrella organization of civic, religious, professional, business, labour, educational and youth organizations. It gathered together the 'informed and concerned' citizenry to promote an honest and meaningful election as a citizen's arm of the Commission on Elections, the official election-organizing body in the Philippines. In this way NAMFREL wanted to challenge the Marcos dictatorship through the election process, which is not surprising because the Philippines has a history of meaningful elections; NAMFREL is neither the first nor the last independent election watchdog in the country.

NAMFREL was formed with the co-operation of the Catholic church, which is extremely influential in the Philippines, and the Makati Business Club, which gathers together the economic elite of Manila. These two organizations provided NAMFREL with both the influence and the infrastructure to place 500,000 volunteers at polling stations all over the Philippine archipelago for the 1986 presidential election. The reasoning was that Marcos could only win by cheating: buying votes and manipulating the vote count. The purpose of NAMFREL, therefore, was not to directly oppose Marcos or the state. Rather, NAMFREL is very deliberately positioned as a neutral organization. Rather than supporting opposition candidates or trying to overthrow the state, the logic of NAMFREL is to work for social and political change in an indirect way. By helping to ensure a clean and fair election, it actually is technically aiding the state to enforce the election law. NAMFREL thus uses the law in creative ways to organize two sets of activities. First, during the election campaign NAMFREL engaged in civic education programmes in order to change the election from the patronage of personality politics to a more democratic issue-based politics. Second, on election day, it sought to place a volunteer poll watcher at each polling station in the country to guard against blatant electoral fraud.

Hence, NAMFREL was hardly a radical movement; it did not promote an alternative social order but worked to make the election system work democratically. Actually, NAMFREL was seen as a moderate group in the Philippine context which in 1986 was characterized by a communist insurgency on the left and an authoritarian dictatorship on the right. NAMFREL was composed of people who wished to use elections for peaceful social change; to return to constitutional rule through 'ballots not bullets'.

But when it was clear that Marcos was 'stealing the election' again in 1986, the political struggle was transferred from institutionalized election procedures to the fluid terrain of social movements. People came out in force in Manila and other towns to practice civil disobedience against the

Marcos dictatorship. NAMFREL as an institutional body did not take part in the 1986 People Power revolution. But NAMFREL played an important informal role in the mass movement at various levels. NAMFREL had publicized the Marcos government's corrupt practices, and as the revolution was occurring NAMFREL was working on an alternative vote count which picked Cory Aquino as the winner. Thus it aided in delegitimizing the Marcos dictatorship. The many people who had been politicized and trained by NAMFREL in its civic education campaigns and poll watching used these same skills and experiences in the street politics of the mass movement.

After the People Power revolution, NAMFREL switched back to being one NGO among many in the Philippines. It has monitored each of the elections since 1986, and the 1992 presidential election spawned two other moderate election-monitoring organizations which work in parallel with NAMFREL. Indeed, some argue that moderate groups like NAMFREL were able to control the 1986 revolution, and thus limit it to political democracy as opposed to economic and social democracy (Taylor, 1996).

The PollWatch organization in Thailand engages in many of the same activities as NAMFREL: it both monitors elections and organizes elaborate civic education programmes. But PollWatch's historical circumstances and its relation to the state are much different from NAMFREL's. In the February 1991 coup, corruption was used by the military junta in Thailand to justify overthrowing the constitutional government; so corruption is not just the terrain of social movements but is also used by right-wing elites to seize power.

After the coup there were three stages of social movements opposed to both corruption and military rule, then finally the military dictator was ousted fifteen months later in May 1992. This political process was certainly complex, involving many different groups, but there is a strand of continuity between the three stages. First, soon after February 1991, numerous NGOs and a major labour federation banded together to form the Campaign for Popular Democracy (CPD) to oppose the coup. The CPD's main activity in 1991 was to criticize the new constitution that the military was writing, resulting in a mass demonstration in November 1991.

Once the new constitution was promulgated due to royal pressure, activists in the CPD switched to oppose both the military and the corrupt politicians by forming PollWatch in 1992 to act as a neutral election-monitoring group. Despite their efforts, the March 1992 general election voted back in the same batch of corrupt politicians who were overthrown the previous year. But this time, the coup leader General Suchinda Kraprayoon shamelessly co-operated with his former enemies to form a new government. The public responded to this combination of an un-elected military Prime Minister and a corrupt Cabinet with a series of non-violent protests on the streets of Bangkok and provincial towns. While PollWatch was not institutionally involved in these mass protests – which at their height included 200,000 people in Bangkok – many of the organizers of PollWatch were acting again through the CPD and other groups to organize these demonstrations around the country. After a violent military crackdown in Bangkok, the military government was forced to resign in the face of both elite and popular public opinion (Callahan, 1998a). Elections were scheduled for September 1992, and PollWatch was re-activated to make the elections more fair and issue-based. This election produced a coalition government of political parties which had opposed the military regime, and which were generally much less corrupt. Though this 'pro-democracy' government still did not institutionalize PollWatch, the organization has now become a tradition in Thai politics. PollWatch has been re-activated for each general election and by-election up to the date of writing (early 1998).

Though PollWatch and NAMFREL have similar histories as social movements in democratic revolutions, and both are neutral in the sense that they are not partisan, they occupy quite different positions in relation to state power. Whereas NAMFREL is an independent private organization, PollWatch is an independent state organization. The leaders of the CPD made a deal with the interim Prime Minister in 1992 to form PollWatch to work with the state to push for clean and meaningful elections. So rather than working through business groups or the church as NAMFREL did, PollWatch took advantage of state infrastructure to organize its activities. It received a budget from the Prime Minister's Office. It used office space in government buildings throughout the country. Civil servants and state enterprise workers took paid-leave to work as PollWatch volunteers.

According to theories which divide politics dualistically between the state and civil society, this arrangement is problematic. When does co-operation become co-optation? It appears that PollWatch is a captive of the state. Though PollWatch was often questioned on its neutrality, most would agree that it was quite independent of state power. Indeed in 1997, PollWatch was embroiled in a media event when it tried to press the police to thoroughly investigate electoral fraud charges against the sitting Prime Minister. So PollWatch actually tries to combine the advantages of formal state structures with the creative energy of an informal volunteer organization.

From a structural point of view, one of PollWatch's mandates was to increase popular participation in the election. PollWatch acted as a social movement because it relies on volunteers, recruiting between 50,000 and 60,000 for each general election. Some of the volunteers are drawn by the prestige of a state organization while others by the flexibility of an NGO. Its campaign section also had a budget to make grants to NGOs for independent projects for grassroots civic education. Through its links with NGOs, PollWatch was able to transform the election into a series of social movements addressing the topics of environmentalism, rural development and the rights of women, youth, indigenous people and citizens at large. It thus uses state resources to mobilize the people, and strengthen the network of civil society throughout Thailand. PollWatch volunteers were certainly effective in organizing the demonstration against the military dictatorship in the provinces in May 1992 as part of the basic transformation of politics from clientelism to citizenship.

PollWatch is an example of an organization which traverses the distinctions between formal and informal activities, state and civil society, and parliamentary and extra-parliamentary politics. One common criticism of PollWatch is that it is too weak – a toothless watchdog – and needs more legal and institutional power to address the problems of electoral fraud. But the leaders of PollWatch are also wary of such institutional power; they are afraid that such institutionalization would turn PollWatch into just another bureaucracy, and thus lose the democratic participation that a volunteer social movement entails (Callahan, 1998b).

7.6 Rural social movements: environmentalism and alternative development strategies

The old and new social movements described thus far have largely been urban based. For example, even though NAMFREL and PollWatch were successful in recruiting volunteers in villages through each country, the organization was still top-down, from the capital city down to the local level. This section will consider rural-based organizations which seek to question the dominant modes of development. There are two aspects to social movements in rural areas. On the one hand, rural social movements address the social and environmental fallout from industrialization, demanding that governments and business clean up their act. On the other hand, rural development movements challenge the dominant models of capitalist industrialization and propose alternative routes to prosperity which look to community and culture. These two types of social movements include environmental movements, religious movements, and indigenous rights movements across the region.

The environmental movement is quite strong and successful in Taiwan where the rapid industrialization of the 1960s and 1970s resulted in serious environmental degradation of this once pristine island. This does not just concern the notoriously noxious atmosphere in the main cities of Taipei and Kao-hsiung. The pattern of industrialization in Taiwan is quite different from the centralized conglomerate model of South Korea. Industrialization in Taiwan was decentralized to the small- and medium-sized family-owned enterprises which are often located in rural areas. Economically, this distributed the benefits of industrialization more evenly, but ecologically it distributed pollution to the countryside as well. To counter this, citizens have organized effective environmental movements to address problems both locally on the small scale, as well as nationally for large-scale projects such as the anti-nuclear power plant campaigns (Bello and Rosenfeld, 1992). Environmental movements appeared in the early 1980s when Taiwan was still under a strict martial law regime. Thus they have been an important part of the emergence of a vibrant civil society in Taiwan. Their exercise of the politics of influence has been largely successful; environmental issues have been incorporated into political party platforms as well as drawing positive government responses (Arrigo, 1994).

Farmer's movements have also been quite strong in Japan, South Korea and Taiwan. They have demonstrated against the liberalization of markets which would allow in much cheaper produce from the USA and Australia. They argue that farmers have been left out of the region's model of development, and that the issue is not just economic, but cultural. Using arguments familiar to French farmers, these movements see the family farm as the bedrock of their national culture, and thus insist that it needs special protection (Bello and Rosenfeld, 1992).

Farmer's movements in the poorer countries in Pacific Asia like Thailand and the Philippines are quite different. Though they also state that they have felt the brunt of the industrialization strategy, their criticism is often that the state has been involved too much, or involved in a way that is detrimental to sustainable rural development. The numerous protests against dams in Pacific Asia often point out that the rural areas are being sacrificed to meet the water and electrical power needs of the city. Farmer's movements criticize the technocratic state-led top-down modes of official rural development, and propose grassroots alternatives that are more participatory and bottom-up. For example, the Green Revolution – which relies on the technological wizardry of high-yield varieties of rice which require fertilizer and pesticide – has not led to rural development. Rather, it has often led to the further impoverishment of farmers because it makes them more dependent on costly external inputs.

Alternatives, which have much in common with social movements in South Asia, look to different notions of development and democracy which are based on the needs of the community. These alternatives look to local knowledge as opposed to imported technocracy, and appeal to local culture in its various forms: village culture, indigenous people's culture, Buddhism, Islam, Christianity, and so on (Callahan, 1996). In this way they put the 'culture' back into 'agriculture'. The culture here is quite different from the 'Asian values' that elites refer to; this local culture is directed against the homogenizing effect of official national culture as much as Westernization. The Rural Reconstruction Movement, which was founded by a Chinese doctor in the Philippines, is an example of such an integrated view of development. It frames development in terms of a dynamic interplay between education, livelihood, health and self-government (Serrano, 1994). This approach which looks to sustainable development and sustainable democracy is found in many neighbouring countries and has spread to Latin America and Africa.

These rural development movements straddle the distinction between the old social movements of peasants and the new social movements of local small-scale NGOs. Rather than starting with a national movement, it was common in the 1980s for the small-scale NGOs to band together in networks which gave them a voice on the national and international stage: the NGO Coordinating Committee for Rural Development (NGO-CORD) was formed in 1985 in Thailand, while in the Philippines the Caucus of Development NGO Networks (CODE-NGO) was founded in 1990.

7.7 Transnational social movements: human rights movements

So far, I have framed social movements as a response to the negative aspects of state power and rapid economic development. Examples have all been located in national space: NAMFREL stands for the *National* Citizens Movement for Free Elections, and *Korean* labour unions challenge the South *Korean* state and business. But since the end of the Cold War, the globalization of the economy has been undermining state power both economically and politically. Globalization and regionalization have also affected social movements; the challenge, as the bumper sticker says, is to 'Think Globally, Act Locally'.

Indeed, in its most literal sense, 'social movement' describes the condition of a diaspora, where whole societies have been dispersed around the globe. Exiled activists seek to influence China in a transnational way and diaspora communities have become an important issue in the Asia-Pacific with, for example, the complex Chinese emigration–immigration patterns in Hong Kong and Singapore (Rodan, 1996a; **Maidment and Mackerras, 1998, Chapter 4**). Due to Hong Kong's instability and Singapore's over-regulation, their middle classes have been voting with their feet by migrating in large numbers to Canada, Australia and the USA. Labour has become transnational as well: the Philippines' greatest source of hard currency is the earnings of young women who work as nurses, maids and prostitutes in Pacific Asia and the Middle East.

Such diaspora communities are rarely organized. But with the expanding global power of transnational capital, social movements have responded by increasingly networking around the globe in what many call global civil society (Archibugi and Held, 1995). Unions have been making links across the Asia-Pacific as a way to share experiences for coping with transnational capital (Williamson, 1994). Transnational social movements which have a grassroots base can offer an interesting alternative to both state governments and transnational capital; they can challenge both economic and political power to make development and democracy more sustainable. This has been fostered by the NGO meetings that have run parallel to UN World Conferences on the environment (1992), human rights (1993), population (1994), women (1995), and social welfare (1996).

Amnesty International and Greenpeace are often cited as powerful examples of NGOs working in a global civil society. Free Burma, an organization founded by a Burmese exile in the USA, is an interesting example of a transnational social movement in the Asia-Pacific. Free Burma is innovative because it is organized around a website on the internet. Its homepage states that 'Free Burma is a collection of software, hardware, documentation, and volunteers, all doing what we're best at to hasten the replacement of the current military government who tortures its citizens with one chosen by the people who live there. What Free Burma has to offer is information, and assistance in its dissemination' (http://freeburma.org).

Free Burma, then, is a new social movement involved in transnational politics of influence which relies on the strength of public opinion. One of the main objectives of Free Burma was to persuade the US government to impose sanctions on investment in Burma/Myanmar. Free Burma thus extended the struggle for human rights and democracy from the streets of Rangoon to cyberspace: the Burmese government's American lobbyists responded by setting up their own website which includes information on 'Doing business in Myanmar' (http://myanmar.com). But in its latest battle, Free Burma prevailed. Sanctions on new US investment in Burma/Myanmar were imposed in April 1997, although due to the Burmese government's lobbying, the sanctions had been watered down.

However, looking to groups that are based in the North and West risks universalizing a particular form of civil society which has grown out of European experience and thus might not apply throughout the Asia-Pacific (Walker, 1994). Indeed, some governments such as in Singapore, charge that global civil society is actually a particular form of cultural imperialism: human rights imperialism. And there are persuasive arguments, which cite China's rather successful resistance to international pressure, to say that the human rights diplomacy of the US government is often counter-productive (see, for example, Wessner, 1996; Muzaffar, 1995). During the Asian regional meetings in preparation for the 1993 World Conference on Human Rights, the governments responded to Western criticism by calling the universality of human rights into question on cultural grounds. Asia is peculiar in that it is the only continent that does not have a regional human rights court or convention; though ASEAN stated in 1993 that such an organization was being organized, it has yet to appear.

Since the states in the region are not interested in forming a regional human rights mechanism, a regional civil society has become more active. While the government representatives were gathering in Bangkok to present a cultural relativist 'Asian view' of human rights for the 1993 World Conference in Vienna, national and regional NGOs from Pacific Asia were also discussing their own much broader views of human rights. Hence regional social movements have often been the best strategy for promoting human rights and democratization in Pacific Asia (Serrano, 1994). One example is the Just World Trust (Just), founded in 1992. Rather than being a Western NGO which sets up branches in Asia, it is an Asian NGO which sets up branches around the world including Europe and North America. Its purpose is to challenge the Western discourse of human rights, which privileges the civil and political rights of individuals, and look at a host of issues from the point of view of Asia and the South (Muzaffar, 1995). However, it is hard to tell how independent Just is. It has closely allied itself with the top leadership of the Malaysian government, and many of its statements closely echo the anti-Western themes of Malaysian foreign policy. As one Malaysian scholar comments, this 'Anti-westernism has all the dangers of engendering a new hypocrisy among leaders of NGOs, which allows them to proclaim that they are pursuing a moral cause while directing their attack on safe targets' (Jesudason, 1996, pp.154, 155).

East Timor is another focus of human rights abuse in Pacific Asia. Indeed, world attention recently was focused again on East Timor when the 1996 Nobel Peace prize was awarded to two East Timorese activists. But regional human rights groups had been working on the issue for many years. East Timor is a former Portuguese colony located between Indonesia and Australia (see **Eccleston** *et al.*, **1998, pp.6, 7**). After a hasty decolonization process in 1974, East Timor declared its independence from Portugal. Indonesia invaded the following year, and formally annexed East Timor in 1976. Since then, East Timor has been struggling – both non-violently and through armed insurgency – to re-establish its independence. In the meantime, the Indonesian army has devastated both the population and the environment of East Timor, most recently killing dozens of unarmed people in November 1991 (Inbaraj, 1995).

Since the governments of South-East Asia refuse to condemn or even comment on the Indonesian occupation, regional human rights groups have taken up the issue (ibid.). In the face of state harassment, regional human rights conferences on the subject of East Timor have been held in the neighbouring countries including the Philippines, Thailand and Malaysia. An analysis of the situation in East Timor also forms an important part of a report on Indonesian human rights – *Stability and Unity on a Culture of Fear: Indonesia 50 Years after Independence* – which was published by the Asian Forum for Human Rights and Development (Forum Asia). Forum Asia is one of the first regional human rights groups in Pacific Asia and *Stability and Unity on a Culture of Fear* is the first time that a human rights report concerning an Asian country has been prepared and published by a regional organization in Asia. Forum Asia states that the purpose of *Stability and Unity on a Culture of Fear* is to report on the human rights situation in Indonesia from a regional perspective in an effort to foster solidarity with human rights groups in Indonesia and the region.

In this way, the Forum Asia report on human rights in Indonesia is an example of a new sort of transnational NGO activity in Pacific Asia which aims to support sustainable development and sustainable democracy. The Indonesian government responded to this challenge in predictable anti-Western ways, charging that Forum Asia was 'assess[ing] problems of an Asian country through non-Asian eyes' (Somchai *et al.*, 1995). But actually Forum Asia is part of a growing regional civil society within Pacific Asia that looks to the power of common problems rather than limitation of uncommon traditions. Thus there are many examples of social movements in Pacific Asia which go beyond the limits of the nation-state, while still being critical of a homogenized global civil society which risks promoting a simple Westernization.

7.8 Summary

This chapter has briefly surveyed the terrain of social movements in Pacific Asia. As we have seen, social movements come in a variety of forms: old and new social movements, NGOs, civil society, oppositions. These have been illustrated by particular movements for a range of different political economies and political cultures in China, South Korea, Taiwan, the Philippines, Thailand, Malaysia, Burma/Myanmar and Indonesia. Culturalist objections to the idea of social movements in Pacific Asia were addressed, while noting that regardless of theoretical debates social movements themselves have grown. Not all social movements have been considered; for example, women's and indigenous people's movements in the region are noteworthy, but have only been referred to in passing.

In general, social movements in the twentieth century first mobilized around issues of nationalism in an effort to evict the various colonial rulers. After independence, social movements have addressed the establishment of state power and capitalist hegemony. As the South Korean example illustrated, in the 1970s–1980s there were struggles against the authoritarian capitalist model of development, first in a general populist mode, and then through a specific class struggle. But once capitalism and a substantial middle class were firmly established in the 1980s, new social movements re-focused on social justice as issue-based reform rather than revolution. Still, as the successful labour campaign in South Korea during the winter of 1996–97 shows, the working class remains a movement to be reckoned with; it was able to mobilize considerable mass support for its cause as well. Yet the trend has been moving from the more confrontational (and violent) social movements to non-violent new social movements.

The subsequent sections of the chapter have considered social movements in relation to social theory and different spaces. The examples have shown how new social movements do not neatly fit into the elite–mass notion of society; they are neither top-down, nor bottom-up, but often alongside state power in a parallel civil society. Section 7.5 on election watchdogs sought to demonstrate the ironic nature of many social movements in Pacific Asia as they straddle the conceptual divisions of state and civil society, and the ambiguities of independence and co-optation that such a positioning entails. Section 7.6 on rural social movements argued that environmentalism and rural development pose some of the most significant challenges to the dominant modes of development. Many alternative rural development strategies look to community culture for sustainable development and democracy; this local culture is directed against the homogenizing official national culture of 'Asian values' as much as against Westernization.

The last section re-focused our consideration of social movements from national to transnational space. While economic power is being globalized and states are gravitating towards regional groupings, social movements have responded in kind. The environment and human rights are major transnational issues, and the section pointed out how social movements are starting to address these concerns from the viewpoint of Pacific Asia.

Many of the distinctions made in this chapter between old social movements and new social movements, between urban and rural activity, between human rights and development, have been blurring as networks of a broadening civil society bring such disparate groups into contact. The diversity of activities shows how difficult it is to account for social movements in Pacific Asia: they draw power from throughout society, including both old and new social movements. Rural NGOs which oppose dam construction are increasingly using the language of human rights and co-operating with urban groups. Though NAMFREL and PollWatch were initially top-down organizations, they have become much more grassroots organizations. Social movements that concentrated on political issues in the past are increasingly considering the economic and cultural aspects of democracy and development. These networks developed at the national level in the 1980s, and in the 1990s have been developing in the regional space of Pacific Asia as well as in global space.

Considerations of social movements always risk exaggerating their power and impact; even more so in Pacific Asia where states are often strong and unsympathetic. So we should be wary of romanticizing such popular movements. The language of 'alternatives' speaks to this weakness for it demonstrates how social movements are still generally just responding to the state and business which remain hegemonic. In Pacific Asia, social movements have had notable successes; they have played important roles in both overthrowing authoritarian regimes and in influencing specific public policy plans. Though they are certainly not as powerful as the state or transnational capital, they are more than mosquitoes on the evening breeze.

References

Anek Laothamatas (1992) *Business Associations and the Political Economy of Thailand: From Bureaucratic Polity to Liberal Corporatism*, Boulder, Westview Press/Singapore, ISEAS.

Archibugi, D. and Held, D. (eds) (1995) *Cosmopolitan Democracy*, Cambridge, Polity Press.

Arrigo, L.G. (1994) 'The environmental nightmare of the economic miracle: land abuse and land struggles in Taiwan', *Bulletin of Concerned Asian Scholars*, vol.26, pp.1–2, 21–44.

Bello, W. and Rosenfeld, S. (1992) *Dragons in Distress: Asia's Miracle Economies in Crisis*, London, Penguin.

Callahan, W.A. (1996) 'Rescripting East/West relations, rethinking Asian democracy', *Pacifica Review*, vol.8, no.1, pp.1–25.

Callahan, W.A. (1998a) *Imagining Democracy: Reading the Events of May in Thailand*, Singapore, ISEAS.

Callahan, W.A. (1998b) *Poll Watching, Elections and Civil Society in Southeast Asia*, Aldershot, Ashgate.

Chesneaux, J., Le Barbier, F. and Bergere, M.-C. (1977) *China from the 1911 Revolution to Liberation*, New York, Pantheon.

Cohen, J.L. and Arato, A. (1992) *Civil Society and Political Theory*, Cambridge, Mass., MIT Press.

Dalton, B. and Cotton, J. (1996) 'New social movements and the changing nature of political opposition in South Korea' in Rodan, G. (ed.) pp.272–99.

Eccleston, B., Dawson, M. and McNamara, D. (eds) (1998) *The Asia-Pacific Profile*, London, Routledge in association with The Open University.

Foucault, M. (1980) *The History of Sexuality, Volume 1: an Introduction*, New York, Vintage.

Garber, L. and Cowan, G. (1993) 'The virtues of parallel vote tabulations', *Journal of Democracy*, vol.4, no.2, pp.95–107.

Han Sang-Jin (1996) 'The rush to development and the emergence of "risk society": an exploration of the middling grassroots' orientations and their possible contribution to cross-national solidarity in East Asia' in *Democratization and Regional Cooperation in Asia*, Seoul, Asia-Pacific Peace Press, pp.341–79.

Heryanto, A. (1996) 'Indonesian middle-class opposition in the 1990s' in Rodan, G. (ed.) pp.241–71.

Inbaraj, S. (1995) *East Timor: Blood and Tears in ASEAN*, Chiang Mai, Thailand, Silkworm Books.

Jesudason, J.V. (1996) 'The syncretic state and the structuring of oppositional politics in Malaysia' in Rodan, G. (ed.) pp.128–60.

Koo, H. (ed.) (1993) *State and Society in Contemporary Korea*, Ithaca, Cornell University Press.

Lawson, S. (1996) 'Cultural relativism and democracy: political myths about "Asia" and the "West"' in Robison, R. (ed.) *Pathways to Asia: the Politics of Engagement*, Sydney, Allen & Unwin, pp.108–26.

Mahathir Mohamad (1993) 'Corruption of democracy in the world', *The Nation* (Bangkok), 8 October, p.A6.

Mahathir Mohamad and Ishihara, S. (1995) *The Voice of Asia: Two Leaders Discuss the Coming Century*, Tokyo, Kodansha International.

Maidment, R. and Mackerras, C. (eds) (1998) *Culture and Society in the Asia-Pacific*, London, Routledge in association with The Open University.

Muzaffar, C. (1995) 'From human rights to human dignity', *Bulletin of Concerned Asian Scholars*, vol.27, no.4, pp.6–8.

Rodan, G. (ed.) (1996a) *Political Oppositions in Industrializing Asia*, London, Routledge.

Rodan, G. (1996b) 'The internationalization of ideological conflict: Asia's new significance', *The Pacific Review*, vol.9, no.3, pp.328–51.

Serrano, I.R. (1994) *Civil Society in the Asia-Pacific Region*, Washington, Civicus.

Somchai Homlaor *et al.* (1995) *Stability and Unity on a Culture of Fear: Indonesia 50 Years after Independence*, Bangkok, Asian Forum for Human Rights and Development.

Taylor, R.H. (ed.) (1996) *The Politics of Elections in Southeast Asia*, Cambridge, Cambridge University Press.

Walker, R.B.J. (1994) 'Social movements/world politics', *Millennium: Journal of International Studies*, vol.23, no.3, pp.669–700.

Wasserstrom, J.N. and Perry, E.J. (1995) *Popular Protest and Political Culture in Modern China*, 2nd edn, Boulder, Westview Press.

Wessner, D.W. (1996) 'From judge to participant: the United States as champion of human rights', *Bulletin of Concerned Asian Scholars*, vol.28, no.2, pp.29–45.

Wignaraja, P. (ed.) (1993) *New Social Movements in the South: Empowering the People*, London, Zed Books.

Williamson, H. (1994) *Coping with the Miracle: Japan's Unions Explore New International Relations*, London, Pluto Press.

Yamamoto, T. (ed.) (1995) *Emerging Civil Society in the Asia Pacific Community*, Tokyo, Japan Center for International Exchange/Singapore, ISEAS.

Further reading

Berger, M.T. and Borer, D.A. (eds) (1997) *The Rise of East Asia: Critical Visions of the Pacific Century*, London, Routledge.

Clark, G. (1998) *The Politics of NGOs in Southeast Asia*, London, Routledge.

Diokno, M. (ed.) (1993) 'Special issue: social movements in Asia', *Asian Exchange*, vol.9, pp.1–112.

Dirlik, A. (ed.) (1998) *What is in a Rim? Critical Perspectives on the Pacific Region Idea*, 2nd edn, London, Rowan and Littlefield.

Rodan, G. (ed.) (1996) *Political Oppositions in Industrializing Asia*, London, Routledge.

I would like to thank Sumalee Bumroongsook, Gerard Clarke, Duncan McCargo and Craig Mulling for their helpful comments on this chapter.

The politics of economic governance

David Martin Jones

8.1 The governance of economic development

Accounts of the extraordinary economic transformation of East Asia in the post-Second World War era are often crudely polarized, overemphasizing the role of economics or politics, states or non-state actors. While a consensus on the final balance of causal factors has yet to be settled, it is likely that the most convincing accounts will start from the assumption that all of these factors have been influential. The task is to describe how in particular societies a range of social forces and conditions have initiated and shaped economic change. In short, how has economic development been governed? In the case of East Asia this chapter argues that key state institutions and economic bureaucracies have been at the core of a web of economic governance, but the strategies pursued by those bureaucracies, the power resources available to them, their mode of rule and their relationships with political elites, business corporations and other social groups are very variable. In this chapter I look at three key differences in modes of economic governance. First, what have been the core bureaucratic institutions of economic governance and what strategies have they pursued? Second, what economic and political resources have they had available to them? Economic resources might include access to national savings accounts, or the ability to control significant tax revenue from resource extraction or powerful leverage over the policy of the banking sector. These in turn allow bureaucracies to shape and direct infrastructural and other investments. Political resources might include an entrenched system of legal controls over business, or access to a steady stream of highly educated personnel or culturally ingrained patterns of hierarchy and deference. Third, what is the overall political context in which these bureaucracies have operated and how insulated have they been from the demands of social groups and political elites. In this chapter I explore the importance of authoritarian politics to economic development; the nature of the relationships between bureaucratic elites, politicians and business, and the capacities of these key actors to exclude others from the process of economic governance. Above all, I look at how labour has been marginalized, incorporated or compensated in the process of economic change.

The chapter is organized around a series of case studies. In Section 8.2 I look at post-war Japan, in which the core of economic governance was laid down in the mutually-supportive iron triangle of LDP politicians, economic bureaucrats and the *keiretsu* business groups. The exclusion of labour, economically and politically, combined with a benign international environment, have been the key factors insulating and supporting the Japanese development coalition. In Section 8.3 I examine the cases of South Korea and Taiwan. Both followed elements of the Japanese mode of economic governance, but required much harsher and more exclusionary forms of authoritarian politics. We also find that both states acquired additional sources of governing autonomy. In South Korea the role of the military was significant, whilst in Taiwan the business lobby was weakened by its dispersion into many small firms rather than giant conglomerates. In Section 8.4 I examine economic governance in South-East Asia. There we find much more fractious and diverse development coalitions whose modes of economic governance have been more personalized, informal and clientalistic than in North-East Asia. In addition, these countries have pursued a mode of economic governance much more open to, and reliant upon, international forces. They have also been overlaid by more complex ethnic politics than North-East Asia. In Sections 8.5 and 8.6 I look at two very different cases of economic governance in the region. In the People's Republic of China, economic governance has emerged from a very distinct developmental coalition of senior communists, the military, a nascent private sector and the economic elites of the Chinese diaspora. It is, moreover, a less centralized mode of economic governance than elsewhere in East Asia, with significant power located at the local level. Australia, by contrast to all of these cases, provides an example of economic governance in a liberal democratic state. The political weakness of federal economic bureaucracies and the greater relative strength of Australian civil society and the Australian labour movement has made the kinds of economic governance pursued elsewhere in the region difficult to emulate. Finally in Section 8.7 I sketch some comparative conclusions.

8.2   Japan: the developmental model?

Japan was the first Asian tiger economy both to sustain high rates of economic growth and achieve membership of the OECD in the post-war period and it has served as an example to later developing Asian economies. Government direction of the economy began in the early Meiji era with investment in infrastructure and the nurturing of the textile industry. Support continued in the inter-war period and was directed toward heavy industry and the government linked, family-led conglomerates (*zaibatsu)* such as Mitsubishi, Mitsui and Sumitomo. During the war years, government intervention increased (see Chapter 3, Section 3.4). Total defeat in 1945 and the subsequent US occupation of Japan between 1945 and 1951, transformed the Japanese state and its relationship to the economy. The US occupation initiated a series of reforms, dissolving the influential *zaibatsu* and introducing land reforms designed to displace the old economic elites that had dominated the inter-war Japanese economy. However as the Cold War developed Japan was allowed access to US aid and technology, and a programme of reindustrialization led by those same elites was supported. Perhaps most importantly, the post-war constitution, written by the Americans, facilitated a form of soft authoritarian single party rule; though one tempered by informal institutional checks, party factionalism and the developing balance of power among political, economic and bureaucratic elites. This coalition became the iron triangle of bureaucracy, government and business. The Liberal Democratic Party (LDP) provided the political elite. The LDP governed Japan uninterruptedly from 1952–92 and in coalitional arrangements after 1993. It facilitated the rule of the elite economic bureaucracies. The legislative and judicial branches of government confined themselves primarily to deterring demands from the 'numerous interest groups in society which if catered to would distort the priorities of the developmental state' (Johnson, 1982, p.315). In the 1950s a number of key bureaucracies took the lead in governing Japan's economic development. The Bank of Japan and the Ministry of Finance kept the yen undervalued, domestic savings high and inflation low, all of which facilitated export led growth. Alongside these institutions MITI was the key bureaucratic player, and together with the Ministry of Finance intervened directly to boost advanced steel making technology. MITI not only facilitated infrastructure development favourable to the steel industry for example, but it also extended preferential low interest loans to the industry through the Japanese Development Bank (JDB). A key resource available to Japan's economic bureaucracy was its control of the Japanese postal savings system. The savings system controls assets larger than the world's largest commercial banks which gave the bureaucrats considerable economic leverage (Johnson, 1987, p.148). In addition the bureaucracy had access to a very distinctive instrument of governance – administrative guidance. Administrative guidance required a 'special measures' law that gave the bureaucratic elite the authority to issue directives, requests, warnings, suggestions and encouragements 'to the enterprise ... within a particular ministry's jurisdiction' (Johnson, 1982, p.265). *Amakaduri*, or the procedure of appointing retired bureaucrats to the boards of companies they had previously guided, furthered bureaucratic rule. To underwrite these massive industrial investments, the government protected domestic producers from foreign competition.

For example in 1951, MITI designated automobile manufacture a strategic industry and arranged loans for the Nissan and Toyota marques (Matthews and Ravenhill, 1994, p.46). Simultaneously, the government, manipulated protective tariffs and severely restricted foreign direct investment, to shelter the infant industry from foreign competition. This protection was none the less 'time bound' and the threat of future competition spurred competitiveness, the expansion of productive capacity and the avoidance of excessive price competition. When domestic demand slackened in the early 1970s, these measures facilitated a government sponsored drive into foreign markets. The American market, in particular, became the engine driving the growth of the Japanese auto industry.

The inclusiveness of the iron triangle mode of governance was complemented by its ruthless exclusiveness, and it was organized labour that was systematically excluded from Japanese economic governance. During the occupation radical, communist influenced unions were anathematized and workers were persuaded to join co-operative, enterprise unions. The enterprise arrangement required all workers in a company to join a single union (Yoshihara, 1994, p.149). The bureaucratically managed Japan Productivity Centre (1955) instituted consultations between management and labour, and introduced the zero defect (in products) movement and quality circles. The bureaucracy, in co-operation with management, effectively undermined militant unions notably in coal mining and supported co-operative unions. In return Japanese management offered lifetime employment, seniority graded wages, seniority based promotion, group decision making, group responsibility and the minimization of status differences between managers and workers (Yoshihara, 1994, p.151). This mode of governance drew on elements of Japan's feudal cultural legacy, emphasizing hierarchy, conformity and loyalty to the group.

However, over recent decades this mode of governance has been changing. In the view of Daniel Okimoto, the evolving relationship between business and government has reduced bureaucratic autonomy and created a *network* state. In this arrangement, 'strength is derived from the convergence of public and private interests and the extensive network of ties binding the two sectors together' (Okimoto, 1989, p.145). Rather than a simple triangle – networks are multiple, complex and permeate not only business, government and the bureaucracy, but business itself functions on the basis of established networks of distributors and manufacturers, between small and large scale producers, and between companies through cross cutting share holdings (*keiretsu*). The *keiretsu's* co-operative networks not only make for international competitive advantage, but make it extremely difficult for those without access to their networks to penetrate the Japanese domestic market. However the flipside of such institutional intimacy is the opacity of the relations between the government and the financial and banking sectors. The Japanese state's inability to deregulate the banking sector and make financial dealings transparent has contributed to corruption, bad loans accumulating and growing financial instability (see Chapter 3, Section 3.7).

To summarize, the model of economic governance in Japan consists of a number of interrelated features: externally it required a benign trading environment; domestically it required a high degree of autonomy for key economic bureaucracies to devise and implement policy; the appointment of specific ministries to pick industrial winners; corporatist strategies which promoted indigenous conglomerates and export led growth policies; bureaucratic access to high rates of domestic savings and an educated, cheap, docile and flexible labour force excluded from economic governance.

8.3   Big leadership in South Korea and Taiwan

The Japanese model of economic governance profoundly influenced development strategies in the former colonies of South Korea and Taiwan. Yet, if the Japanese experience of development was softly authoritarian, the South Korean and Taiwanese were much harder. The post-war political defeat of the left, together with the continuing fear of communism, opened the way for strong bureaucratic authoritarian states (Cumings 1987, p.110). The Kuomintang (KMT) occupation of Taiwan after 1949, rapidly facilitated the organization of a single party state on democratic centralist lines creating the degree of state autonomy required to pursue planned development. Thus the KMT's technocratic elite was able to shift the economy from import substitution to labour 'intensive export' oriented growth in the early 1960s and subsequently to higher value added technologies in the early seventies with little political or economic disruption. This was not the case with South Korea. In 1961, the quasi-democratic regime of Syngman Rhee in South Korea collapsed under the weight of declining economic performance and the visible corruption of the regime. It was only under Rhee's replacement, the former General, Park Chung Hee that bureaucratic-authoritarian rule gave the South Korean state sufficient autonomy to move decisively away from a policy of import substitution and towards export led growth.

During Park's regime Korea's economic priority was to expand manufactured exports. Park adopted a 'variety of authoritarian capitalism, in which enterprises were privately owned but the management was shared between the government and the owners' (World Bank, 1993, p.1). An elite bureaucracy consisting of the Economic Planning Board (EPB), the Ministry of Commerce and Industry (MCI) and the Ministry of Finance (MOF) with close links to the Presidency assumed central responsibility for planning industrial policy. Government promoted imports of capital and intermediate goods required by exporters, provided macroeconomic stability by restricting currency trading, maintained an undervalued won and managed the banking sector to ensure that capital flowed into industrial and export expansion (Rhee, 1994, p.66; Patrick and Park, 1994, p.330). Exports, not profitability, constituted the yardstick of industrial performance (Amsden, 1989, p.18). The government favoured economies of scale and rewarded growing companies with better access to credit (Kim and Leipziger, 1993, p.3); particularly the private, family run conglomerates or *chaebol* which were the equivalent of pre-war Japanese *zaibatsu*.

In 1973 Park and the bureaucratic elite decided to reduce support for labour intensive, export oriented light industry in footwear and textiles and instead promote the Heavy and Chemical Industry Plan (HCIP). Again it was the *chaebol* that reaped the benefits of this strategy. HCIP focused on the strategic industries of iron and steel, machinery, electronics, ship building, automobiles and petrochemicals. Apart from a cheap and generally compliant labour market, South Korea possessed no evident comparative heavy industrial advantage. The programme required 'big leadership' by the economic bureaucracies. This was exemplified by the development of the automobile industries. In 1974, the EPB outlined an industry specific plan for automobiles identifying Hyundai, Kia and Daewoo as primary producers (Wade, 1994, p.310). Planning required the primary producers to meet a domestic contents schedule and co-operate in the production of standard parts. Domestic sales were used to subsidize exports.

Despite the successes of this mode of economic governance, a series of economic and political problems developed. Financing this dash for heavy industrialization meant that the government contracted a large foreign debt. This continues to haunt South Korea. Technocratic planning had additional weaknesses both in implementing planned growth and securing the support of business, labour and the middle classes, particularly student groups. State commitment to the dominant *chaebol* meant that investment in light industry and small and medium sized enterprises (SMEs) evaporated. Some sectors, notably finance, SMEs and heavy machinery, stagnated or shrank. By 1980, South Korea had acquired a current account deficit that represented 9 per cent of GNP and a worrying external debt burden estimated at 49 per cent of GNP (*The Economist*, 3 June 1995, p.17). This, together with the second OPEC oil shock of 1979 saw GDP growth cut and inflation spiralling to over 29 per cent a year. The assassination of President Park in October 1979, growing tension within the EPB and MCI over industrial policy, and a breakdown in state corporatist control of labour exacerbated the crisis.

The period 1979–80 witnessed both 'the disorder of political institutions, of policy networks between the state and social groups and of the financial system' and 'the ineffective implementation of economic stabilization policy measures' (Rhee, 1994, p.146). The old mode of economic governance seemed to be collapsing. It was in these difficult circumstances that the military coup staged by General Chun Doo Hwan in May 1980 re-established authoritarian control. The coup also facilitated a radical reform of the economic bureaucracy and a re-evaluation of the relationship between government and big business. In order to legitimize its authority, Chun's regime embarked upon a programme of economic liberalization. The Social Purification Subcommittee's purge of bureaucrats and labour union leaders in 1980 established the political preconditions for the EPB to adjust the heavy industry programme. Administratively guided reduction of business concentration was achieved by 'credit allocation, tax investigation and even naked intimidation by the security agencies as instruments of policy enforcement' (Moon, 1994, p.148). The more compliant conglomerates benefited from the reorganization whilst those who were less co-operative, like the Kukche corporation, collapsed.

Chun's economic reforms changed the relationship between government and big business and created conflict within the bureaucracy between economic liberals and conservatives. The main big business association, the Federation of Korean Industries (FKI), openly criticized the EPB's liberalization programme. These tensions continued through the regimes of Roh Tae Woo (1987–92) and during Kim Young Sam's (1992–97) civilian presidency. The Kim government's decision to increase liberalization and business deconcentration in the seventh Five Year Plan (1992–97) had the unintended consequence of exposing the networks of graft and corruption that permeates government, bureaucracy and *chaebol*. The indictment for treason of former Presidents Chun and Roh in 1996 revealed the extent to which the more compliant *chaebol* went to financially lubricate the government–business nexus. In December 1995, as a direct consequence of Kim's decision to promote fiscal probity, 36 of Korea's leading businessmen, including heads of *chaebol* like Daewoo's Kim Woo Chong admitted donating contributions to former president Roh's billion dollar political slush fund.

Taiwan's development illustrates a similar but more judicious mix of detailed planning, control of access to the domestic market and export oriented growth. As in South Korea, government initiated the shift to export led growth, and the super technocrats of the ESB played the major role. In 1960 the government introduced a Nineteen Point Programme for Economic and Financial Reform together with a new four year plan (1961–64) providing incentives for businesses that produced and marketed for export. In order to guide development the frequently updated Statute for the Encouragement of Investment (1960) co-ordinated investment by foreign nations, the overseas Chinese and local investors. From the 1950s until the late 1980s technocrats with scientific backgrounds like K.Y. Yin and K.T. Li dominated industrial planning. Like their South Korean counterparts, the ESB played a role 'much like that of good traditional Confucian advisors' (Wade, 1994, p.27). Not only did they manage macroeconomic policy and the exchange rate in a manner that promoted exports, they engineered a mutually supportive combination of state and private enterprise. This policy facilitated the emergence of companies like Formosa Plastics. In 1953 K.Y. Yin considered plastics a suitable target for industrialization and identified Y.C. Wang as an entrepreneur with the vision to undertake the project. Thus 'the first plastics plant for polyvinyl chloride (PVC) was constructed under government supervision and handed to Wang in running order in 1957' (Wade, 1994, p.80) In addition to co-ordinating the private sector, the government also extended the range of state owned enterprises. State initiatives in petrochemicals, non-ferrous metals, and the shipbuilding industries date from the move to export led growth in the early 1960s. The international derecognition of Taiwan in 1971 followed by the oil shock of 1973, saw GNP growth slow to 1.2 per cent and inflation rise to 47 per cent. This prompted the government to assert economic leadership even more forcefully during the 1970s. State technocrats proactively developed high technology industries, opening the Hsinchu Science and Industry Park in the late 1970s. In the course of the 1980s Taiwan developed the biggest pool of chip design talent in Asia outside Japan. Personal computers and peripherals, came to constitute a major component of Taiwan's exports, rising from zero to 6.9 per cent between 1980–87. By the late 1980s virtually every major electronics multinational had opened a venture in Taiwan. Domestic firms like Acer, became global names in the personal computers market.

A notable feature of Taiwan's mode of economic governance has been the government's ability to influence indigenous business through its network of connections or *guanxi* with the ruling KMT, and yet to remain relatively autonomous from business pressure. Three factors account for this. First, Taiwan never generated the large industrial conglomerates that could circumvent or challenge the government's management of macroeconomic policy. Second, during the first twenty years of development, government officials were mainlanders and local businessmen were indigenous Taiwanese. When they met officially, it was understood that government conveyed directives to the business associations and not vice versa. Third, the lack of an organized labour movement and the relatively equitable distribution of the wealth created by growth has provided Taiwan's technocrats great room for manoeuvre when trying to adapt the economy to changing market conditions. In the late 1980s, the success of the Taiwanese economy led to external pressure for market and financial liberalization and the revaluation of the won. Characteristically, the bureaucratic elite were proactive, supporting the restructuring of the economy as labour intensive manufacturing and textile industries moved offshore. Taiwan's demand for a source of cheap labour fortuitously coincided with the opening of special economic zones in the People's Republic of China. By 1989, Taiwan's direct overseas investment had increased to US$6.95 billion or 4.6 per cent of GNP and many small businesses relocated labour intensive textile and shoe making operations to Fujian and Guandong in Southern China.

The economic bureaucracies in both South Korea and Taiwan promoted export led growth by combining an outward oriented economic policy with the maintenance of trade barriers in key sectors. A closely supervised and highly regulated financial sector kept inflation low and the currency cheap, which in return promoted export led growth. An enduring feature of the North-East Asian economies consists in the capacity of the bureaucracy through a mixture of financial controls and administrative guidance to manage microeconomic industrial policy. The absence of a political tradition based on the rule of law and contract facilitated highly authoritarian administrative guidance. Firms that failed to comply with bureaucratically determined criteria found their export licenses terminated and their soft loans unrenewed. This was supported by ensuring an organizationally weak and compliant labour force. Before the civilian government of President Kim (1992–97) the succession of military backed regimes outlawed strikes and closed shops. Today, South Korea has the lowest level of unionization in the OECD. Somewhat differently in Taiwan, labour unions have been directly guided by the KMT. Central to the maintenance of administrative guidance, however, has been the state capacity to control the allocation of finance to chosen industries. This has been the case particularly in South Korea where the government has contracted a massive external debt in order to continue funding the *chaebol*.

8.4   The governance of late development in South-East Asia

Thailand, Malaysia and Indonesia possess large rural and resource-rich hinterlands that facilitated their pre-war development as primary product economies. Decolonization and the political instability that engulfed South-East Asia from 1950 to 1975 adversely affected investment and development. These South-East Asian states, adopted economic nationalist and import substituting strategies in order to acquire investment capital in the early 1960s and 1970s. But it was only when they shifted to policies that favoured foreign multinational investment and export led growth in the 1980s that they achieved rapid growth.

Malaysia

In the Malaysian case, communal violence inspired by relatively high unemployment amongst the Malay population and a growing concentration of private enterprise in the hands of the Chinese community, contributed to a major socio-economic rethink and a New Economic Policy (NEP) was introduced in 1971. The NEP policy aimed to achieve growth with equity, eradicating poverty and redressing the economic imbalance between the predominantly urban Chinese and the Malay rural poor. The NEP began an era of state activism in resource allocation primarily through public enterprise trusts like Perbadanan Nasional Bhd (*Pernas)* in order to promote an indigenous or *bumiputra* interest in commerce and industry (Gomez, 1994, p.3). The NEP established affirmative action employment quotas to reflect the ethnic composition of the population and sought to achieve a 30 per cent *bumiputra* stake in Malaysian industry by 1991. The new strategy also sought to promote exports through tax breaks and indirect subsidies to pioneer industries in Export Processing Zones (EPZ). These incentives, combined with the availability of low cost, semi-skilled female workers, attracted the first wave of Japanese, South Korean and Taiwanese foreign investment. By 1980 70 per cent of Malaysia's manufactured exports originated from foreign owned firms located in the new EPZs. Foreign investment in labour intensive semi and low skilled light industrial production resulted in Malaysia becoming the world's leading producer of semiconductor devices by 1978 (Jesudason, 1990, p.174).

The discovery of substantial reserves of oil and natural gas, offshore from Sabah and Sarawak and in Eastern peninsular Malaysia, further boosted economic growth. Buoyed by the revenue derived from the 1980 oil price rise, Mahathir Mohamad, the Prime Minister, launched a state led programme of heavy industrialization under the auspices of the Heavy Industries Corporation of Malaysia (HICOM). Mahathir and UMNO technocrats like Daim Zainuddin looked towards Japan both as a model of state led industrialization and as a source of investment. In the period up to 1985, state run enterprises constituted the vanguard of Malaysian industrialization. But the inefficiency of public enterprises was responsible for an escalation of foreign debt. The UMNO elite then embarked on a programme of privatization and a relaxation of the *bumiputra* affirmative action provision after 1990. In 1990 Mahathir announced a new National Development Policy (NDP) to replace the NEP. The NDP set an annual growth rate of 7 per cent per annum in order to achieve a fully developed Malaysia by 2020. To secure growth targets the government also relaxed the rules governing foreign investment. This coincided with a massive rise in the value of the Japanese yen, and encouraged a wave of Japanese and Taiwanese investment. Japanese FDI, in particular, had the greatest impact on Malaysian industrialization (Ali, 1994, p.105). Between 1986 and 1991 alone, Japanese investment exceeded US$2 billion. By 1995, unemployment had disappeared and UMNO had relatively equitably distributed the wealth created by development. Indeed, the evolving capacity of UMNO technocrats to sustain both growth and infrastructural development and guarantee political stability has attracted foreign investment to Malaysia. This, combined with legal restrictions on trade union activity, a docile and compliant labour force, low inflation and competitive wages 'rated highly in the decision of Japanese companies to locate in the country' after 1985 (Denker, 1994, p.54).

Despite Malaysia's dependence on Japan for FDI, Japanese multinationals have been notably reluctant to transfer technology. Even in joint ventures like the Proton Saga car, Mitsubishi ships ready assembled engines from Japan (Jomo, 1994, p.280). Such practices, combined with an acute shortage of skilled manpower, constrains Malaysia's capacity to move up the industrial ladder to higher value added technologies. Indeed, Malaysia's success in courting Japanese investment aid could prove self defeating. Malaysia, like Thailand, South Korea and Taiwan, runs a growing trade deficit with Japan. Moreover, the growth through borrowing and foreign investment strategy pursued since 1985 has created a burgeoning foreign debt that remains over US$23 billion. The rise in imports to sustain rapid growth has pushed Malaysia's current account into deficit. In 1994 the deficit stood at US$4 billion or about 7.7 per cent of GDP and rose to 8.3 per cent of GDP in 1995. This together with external debt amounting to 39 per cent of GDP has rendered the Malaysian ringgit, like the Thai baht, susceptible to currency meltdown.

These factors together with growing inflation, high interest rates and the murky relationship between politicians and indigenous business groups gives some credence to the view that Malaysian style capitalists are 'paper entrepreneurs' who relentlessly pursue 'opportunities for acquisitions, mergers, restructuring and leveraged buy-outs' (Yoshihara, 1988, p.4), at the expense of developing indigenous manufacturing and technology. The development process, whilst marginalizing the smaller indigenous Chinese entrepreneurs has promoted big Malaysian Chinese trading conglomerates like Quek Leng Chan's Hong Leong Group, the Robert Kuok Groups and Vincent Tan's Inter Pacific which functions as 'business proxies' to key figures in the UMNO elite (Gomez, 1994, pp.37–9). Such arrangements ensure that the UMNO elite's business activity occurs 'outside the purview of the party' (Gomez, 1994, p.43). Although the UMNO party state has astutely manipulated domestic and foreign investment since 1985, the shadier aspects of this strategy have generated a disturbing air of insubstantiality indicated by the growth of imports, mounting foreign debt and rising inflation.

Thailand

In Thailand a military backed bureaucratic polity moved after 1971 from a strategy of economic nationalism to a policy of import substitution that favoured capital intensive manufactures, like automobiles and discriminated against both labour intensive agriculture and labour intensive manufactures. The strong import substituting strategy had a marked effect on the profile of the Thai economy with protected heavy industry contributing 42.6 per cent of value added to the GDP by 1979. However, these industrial developments absorbed a comparatively small proportion of the labour force. While industry's share of GDP increased steadily from about one-quarter in 1970 to one-third by 1988, 'nearly 70 per cent of the labour force was still in agriculture, producing 17 per cent of GDP' (World Bank, 1993, p.6). The import substitution policy, exacerbated by the impact of the second oil shock after 1979, distorted Thailand's pattern of industrialization and culminated in a slump in growth and a ballooning current account deficit in the early 1980s. To remedy this, after a period of incoherent quasi-democracy between 1973 and 1976, the authoritarian leadership of General Prem and the technocrats at the Board of Investment (BOI) organized the post-1981 export promotion drive. The government established export processing zones, streamlined customs procedures, abolished unnecessary regulations to expedite export ship-ments and substantially reduced tariffs on capital goods, automobile imports and computers. This policy dramatically affected growth. Direct foreign investment played a major role in the export boom period (1985–95) as firms from the recently developed North-East Asian economies moved labour intensive manufacturing to the Bangkok region. Between 1980 and 1988 direct foreign investment more than tripled. By 1993 more than half of Thailand's total exports were manufactures, mostly established directly by foreign investors or in the form of joint ventures. In particular Japanese producers have increasingly selected Thailand as a key offshore production base in their global network of export oriented manufacturing.

By the early 1980s moreover, a number of the larger Thai firms, supported by the leading commercial banks, had developed into large, vertically integrated, business conglomerates like Saha Union, Shinawatra, Dusit Thani and Chaeoren Pokhpand. Thai economic governance significantly differed from that pursued in North-East Asia. Technocrats were not guided by a strategy of picking winners but succumbed to patronage and rent seeking (Laothamatas, 1992). The shift from military tutelage to quasi-democracy after 1992, increased the opportunities for rent-seeking and patronage in government–business relations. Under the predatory and incompetent administrations of Banharn and Chavalit (1995–97) fiscal policy loosened and exposed the Bank of Thailand to increasing speculative financial pressure. At the same time indifference to a consumption and credit boom allowed inflation to rise in 1995. As the boom ended the Thai economy had developed a worrying combination of a trade deficit amounting to 8 per cent of GDP and foreign debt corresponding to 46 per cent of GDP, occasioning the departure of a series of finance ministers between 1996–97 and the meltdown of both the currency and the inflated Thai stock market in July 1997.

Thailand's evolving financial crisis, coincided with the economy moving from a position of dependency on cheap labour to dependence on capital goods and more advanced technology. Layoffs in the textile industry have prompted the formation of increasingly aggressive labour unions. Here once again government planning proved ineffective. The state provides only six years of compulsory education, so that Thailand encounters difficulty in providing skilled workers for higher value added technologies and industries. This limits Thai industrial exports to 'processed primary products, garments, textiles and other labour intensive products' (Yoshihara, 1988, p.117). Consequently, when Thai wages increase, 'Thailand cannot develop new industrial exports and thus upgrade the composition of its industrial products' (ibid.).

Indonesia

In Indonesia economic governance has been plagued with similar problems of patronage and rent seeking. Like Malaysia, Indonesia was 'born with a classic colonial economy based on plantation estates producing for export' (Macintyre, 1994, p.246). Its development, however, has been more troubled. After the 1965 coup and counter-coup, the New Order government moved quickly to introduce market minded reforms. It had to. Per capita income actually fell by 15 per cent between 1958 and 1965. Inflation accelerated to 1,000 per cent, foreign borrowing had risen to US$2 billion and interest repayments on debt exceeded export earnings (Schwarz, 1994, p.52). Debt rescheduling afforded the Indonesian government access to capital. Under the guidance of Berkeley trained technocrats like Widjojo Nitisastro, the New Order cut spending, loosened trade barriers, and overhauled investment laws. The technocrats removed most domestic price controls, returned some nationalized enterprises to private ownership and passed a balanced budget law in 1967 prohibiting budget financing through foreign borrowing or money creation. By 1969 this fiscal policy reduced inflation to a manageable 20 per cent per annum. The economy produced double digit growth for the first time in 1968 (Hill, 1994, p.61). With the economy stabilized the focus shifted to long-term developmental planning. The first five year plan, REPELITA 1 (1969–74), emphasized agriculture – particularly rice farming – and infrastructure. The windfall tax revenues afforded by the oil price rises of 1973 and 1979 offered further scope for planning and a reversal of market-oriented policies.

The evolving corporatism of the New Order was built on links between the centres of military bureaucratic power and domestic corporate conglomerates (Robison, 1990, p.104). Despite official commitment to indigenous or *pribumi* entrepreneurs, the corporate giants that emerged after 1975 were Chinese with close ties to the army in general and President Suharto in particular. Thus Liem Sioe Liong's *Salim* group, with interests in 'everything from cement to noodles' dates from Liem's relationship with Suharto in the 1950s. Significantly many of Salim's ventures involve at least one of Suharto's children and the group is deeply embedded in Suharto's patrimonial network (Schwarz, 1994, p.113). Indeed, Suharto's children own the only indigenous conglomerates of substance. His second son Bambang's *Bimantara* group and eldest daughter Tutut's *Citra Lamtoro Gung* group are on a par with the Chinese conglomerates in terms of size and capitalization. As Andrew Macintyre observes, 'the business careers of Suharto's children highlight the fundamental importance of clientalistic connections as the key to gaining access to state generated rent taking opportunities and thence to commercial success' (Macintyre, 1994, p.254).

The decline in oil revenues after 1981 exposed the weaknesses of Indonesia's development strategy and mode of economic governance. Intent on diversification away from dependence on the oil sector, the economic technocrats, attempted to reassert their power at home and create a more attractive climate for foreign investment. The National Planning Agency, Bappenas, introduced an export incentive package and a series of trade reforms in 1986 (Hill, 1994, p.70; Bhattacharaya and Pangestu, 1993, p.31). Almost immediately, the stabilization and adjustment programme boosted manufacturing output, exports and investment. The opening of Indonesia to FDI, as in Malaysia and Thailand, coincided with the appreciation of the North-East Asian currencies and facilitated an influx of foreign investment capital. Japan, in particular, took a keen interest in Indonesian primary resources. Natural resource-based products still formed over 30 per cent of Indonesia's manufactured exports in 1991 (Hill, 1994, p.83). Indonesia thus moved to labour intensive export led growth at a much later stage than other East Asian countries. Though this has been impressive; GDP growth averaged over 7 per cent per annum between 1992 and 1995.

Indonesian economic development has oscillated between periods of state intervention and economic nationalism and periods of reluctant deregulation. The results of economic governance in the New Order have been mixed. The problem of crony capitalism, the widening gap between the business and military bureaucratic elite and the masses and the disparities between urban workers and rural peasants are acute in contemporary Indonesia. Whilst the GDP per capita of Jakarta had grown to US$1,145 by 1995, that of peripheral, but oil rich, Aceh was less than US$500 per capita. The growing perception of a widening income gap between rich and poor and the absence of an efficient legal framework to deal with labour and property disputes has prompted an intermittent recourse to urban and rural *jacquerie*. Only military intervention suppressed labour riots and wildcat strikes at Tanjung Priok (Jakarta) in 1984, in Medan (Sumatra) in April 1994 and more recently across Java in 1998. Exasperation with Chinese business ownership reflects a wider resentment of the close ties between Chinese conglomerates and the Suharto regime. Deregulation of the economy, moreover, has served the interests of the Chinese conglomerates but increased their popular opprobrium. The perception of Chinese business dominance allied to a burgeoning income gap has prompted contradictory demands both for greater economic liberalization and greater government intervention. At the same time the liberalization of financial services since 1986 was a case of 'too much too fast' (Schwarz, 1994, p.74). The rapid flow of money into the Indonesian banking system after 1989 led to an unsustainable rise in lending by state banks and a growth in money supply. It also led to inflation. Property speculation and an overheating economy required the Ministry of Finance to raise interest rates by 30 per cent in 1991. The state banks are adrift on a pool of bad debt, estimated at US$85.88 billion in 1995. Financial scandal has further eroded faith in the banking sector and the recent government practice of running budget deficits has eroded confidence in an already unstable financial sector. More disturbing still is the level of foreign debt, which by 1995 had risen to US$100 billion. Thus although the Indonesian state has attempted to govern development from import substitution to export led growth, the strategy has serious weaknesses.

8.5   China's transition of governance

In 1978, the People's Republic of China embarked on a series of radical economic reforms. It adopted features of the models of economic governance pursued in North-East and South-East Asia. Given the size of China and its massive population, it was a programme fraught with risks of economic and political instability and the PRC possessed political and economic institutions created to support an entirely different form of development and governance. In the early 1950s the Chinese Communist Party undertook a massive process of institutional change. They laid down 'a vast lattice work of Soviet derived political and economic institutions' (White, 1992, p.4). The Soviet model of development was modified by Mao and his supporters in the CCP to Chinese needs and conditions. A distinctively Maoist model of development was begun with the convulsive

Great Leap Forward (1958) before descending into the social, economic and political anarchy of the Cultural Revolution (see Chapter 2). This left an ambivalent legacy of famine, chaos and a pattern of local economic autonomy that contrasted with the more centralized Soviet model. It was against this background that the post Maoist reformers, led by Deng Xiaoping, embarked upon a course of economic reform in 1978. 'It matters not whether the cat is black or white' Deng remarked in 1980, 'if it catches mice it is a good cat'. The new strategy combined economic liberalization with political authoritarianism and unleashed a process of rapid change.

The liberalization of China's economy required a redefinition of the state's and the CCP's role in the economy. The CCP disengaged from many areas of direct economic control, increased the market accountability of productive enterprises, but retained an integument of socialist political ideas and institutions. Unlike the 'big bang' approach adopted in the Soviet Union and the communist states in Eastern Europe, the leadership of the CCP reached a near consensus that political democratization would not accompany economic modernization. Modernization occurred in two stages. The first step involved the decollectivization of agriculture, reform of the industrial urban sector and a great leap outward that permitted foreign trade and investment. Between 1979 and 1983, rural per capita income increased by about 70 per cent. State enterprises, which dominate the Chinese industrial sector, were permitted greater financial autonomy and the labour market was gradually reformed, allowing state enterprises power to hire and fire. Most significant of all was the creation of four special economic zones on the coast of the south-eastern provinces of Guangdong and Fujian which witnessed a dramatic increase in foreign investment.

However, the dramatic growth in the first phase of market opening was not unproblematic. It created supply bottlenecks in key sectors of the economy, inflationary pressures and a balance of payments deficit. A lack of sophisticated financial controls provoked a series of disintermediation crises poorly handled by the People's Bank of China which exacerbated economic difficulties (Naughton, 1995, p.1098). The difficult business of riding the tiger of economic transition provoked elite conflict in the CCP between conservatives like Li Peng and Jiang Zemin who wanted to control the pace of change and reformers like Premier Zhao Ziyang who increasingly felt the need for political reform to accompany economic reform (White, 1992, p.69). The problem of managerial control over the reform process had reached alarming proportions by late 1988. This managerial problem coincided with growing social and political discontent amongst students and urban elites culminating in the Tiananmen protest of June 4, 1989. In the aftermath the new leadership of Premier Li Peng and Party Secretary General Jiang Zemin attempted to slow the pace of economic reform and reassert the authority of the party-state. Slogans like *yadao yiqie* (stability overcomes all) dominated the media and the endless campaigns of spiritual purification. Since Tiananmen, the economy has grown at 10 per cent per annum. This second phase of development has been characterized by an anxious attempt to plan development and manage growth especially along the booming coastal perimeter from Shanghai to Fujian, without undermining the paramount political authority of the CCP politburo. This has been particularly evident in policy towards state owned enterprises (SOEs). The state sector accounts for 45 per cent of industrial output, employs 107 million workers and provides the CCP with its largest body of reliable support. Central government therefore maintains inefficient state owned coal and petroleum extracting industries which contributed a US$5.7 billion loss to the economy in 1995. Yet not all SOEs are inefficient. In certain sectors, electricity generation, steel making and cigarette production, SOEs are highly profitable. Moreover, central government strategy towards China's 1,000 biggest SOEs, is to transform them into Chinese *chaebol*.

A number of these 'red chip' companies have links with, or are owned by, the People's Liberation Army. The PLA is vital to the maintenance of political stability, this is graphically demonstrated by its role in suppressing dissent in 1989. As we know, policy reform has been premised on the fundamental need to maintain political stability (Nolan and Ash, 1995, p.986). Since 1989, both reformist and conservative elements in the CCP have agreed upon the need to reassert central authority especially in the area of macro-economic control. Consequently, the army has been allowed to reap the benefits of economic development. The PLA has developed a number of enterprises notably in the arms industry, but also in transportation, construction, medical services, hotels and farming. Indeed the PLA has developed its own conglomerates like 999 Corp which controls 39 enterprises in the Shenzhen SEZ (Ching, 1994, p.97). At the same time, Beijing has also promoted inward investment. This has had the paradoxical outcome of weakening central control over the regions. In fact, the local state or region has established considerable autonomy both in terms of revenue gathering and developmental policy. In fact, such local autonomy reflects the institutional legacy of Maoism and the cultural revolution which offered cadres at the local level considerable scope for initiative.

China's transitional economy, therefore, is not composed of an efficient market oriented private and a costly and inefficient public sector. Rather, there is a developing distinction between SOEs that are managed by central government, by the PLA and those that are local state initiatives. In other words the ownership of the 'non-state' sector remains dominated by public ownership and management. As Jean Oi observes, 'within a local corporatist context local officials turn the administrative bureaucracy ... into a free channel for information and resources to facilitate market production' (Oi, 1995, p.1139). Oi terms this distinctive form of governance – *local state corporatism*. It constitutes a hybrid form that utilizes local capacities inherited from the Maoist era, blended with forms found in capitalist developmental states. These local state authorities are most successful when they can draw upon foreign capital or overseas Chinese expertise to facilitate development. This is evident in those coastal areas of South China, that have boomed as a consequence of Taiwanese and Hong

Kong investment. The 1980s witnessed a movement of labour intensive manufacturing to the Chinese special economic zones particularly Fujian and Guangdong. By the early 1990s, 12 per cent of Taiwanese manufacturing jobs and 20,000 small businesses had moved to the mainland (Xu, 1994, p.147). However, because of the troubled relationship between Taiwan and the PRC, much of the financial and plant investment passed through Hong Kong. Between 1979 and 1992 trade between Hong Kong and Taiwan increased at an annual rate of 42.4 per cent. As a result of Taiwanese investment in the mainland economic zones, Hong Kong is Taiwan's second biggest trading partner (Yu, 1994, p.142). Hong Kong has not only laundered Taiwanese investment in the mainland but resumed its historic role as an entrepôt for South China and injected enterprise, capital and technical skills. In 1993 the World Bank estimated that three million mainland labourers worked directly for Hong Kong entrepreneurs (Chew, 1993, p.21).

8.6   Australia: governance in the wrong economy

Australia's mode of economic governance has shifted in the twentieth century from a form of imperial incorporation, to social welfarism to an anxious attempt to integrate into the Asia-Pacific economy. These shifts in economic governance were linked to realignments in domestic policy coalitions. The economic downturn of the 1890s exposed the vulnerability of Australia's colonially dependent, resource-based and pastoral economy to international economic forces. They were cruelly exposed again in the depression of the 1930s. In both cases protectionism was the dominant response. Working class mobilization during the 1930s created a coalition of the Australian Labour Party (ALP) with urban social liberals who forced through a range of welfare measures (Castles, 1985). The federal government established a protectionist blanket around Australia's economy and society. Protectionist urban industrial interests and the urban labour movement combined to defeat rural free traders over the issue of trade protectionism. This Australian Settlement represented social engineering on a grand scale and produced an elaborate system of cross-subsidization, a redistribution of national income that favoured protected industrial interests, and the imposition of 'white Australia' immigration controls (Kelly, 1994). State control at the macro-economic level was combined with an indifference to industrial or micro-economic policy design which came to constitute an enduring feature of Australian economic governance (Bell, 1996, Ch.4).

The Australian settlement held together through the severe depression of the 1930s. After 1945 it was overlaid by a social compact that granted the right of business to manage production, in return labour received full employment and a share of productivity gains from expansion. This postwar compact 'sidelined basic conflict over capitalism and moved the focus of business-labour conflict to the distributional and wages arena' (Bell,

1996, p.92). Central to this new compact was a Keynesian economic interventionism which gave the state an active role in a mixed economy to regulate the uncertainties of the market. Redistribution was lubricated by an accommodating monetary policy and a more liberal credit system premised upon strict national exchange controls.

The arrangement began to unravel in the 1970s. For much of the twentieth century Australia did well on the basis of strong commodities exports. By the 1980s Australia had, as the then treasurer Paul Keating observed, the 'wrong economy'. Indeed, for most of the post-war era the prices Australia received for rural and mineral products fell relative to the prices paid for the bulk of largely manufactured imports. This economic fact combined with burgeoning welfare costs accounted for a current account deficit. After 1974, as the Australian economy became mired in recession, the strength of labour relative to business became increasingly problematic. Wage growth was squeezing profits. In the early 1980s under the ALP there emerged a new mode of economic governance which focused on balancing budgets, reducing inflation through monetary controls, deregulating financial markets and rolling back the welfare state. In fact, the reaction of the Bob Hawke's Labour government (1983–91) to a wages explosion and 11 per cent inflation, represented a distinctively Australian mixture of corporatism combined with incremental deregulation. In order to manage labour, trade unions were brought into a new accord. The accord actually increased the political influence of the trade union movement and its peak body the Australian Council of Trade Unions (ACTU). It enabled the Labour government to use wages as a policy tool. The intention of the accord process was to reduce labour costs and spur employment. The attempt to incorporate the unions coincided with financial deregulation, the floating of the dollar in late 1983, and the abolition of exchange controls that exposed the Australian economy to the test of global financial market confidence (Bell, 1996, p.143). Under Labour policies Australia experienced a brief commodity-led boom in the late 1980s followed by asset inflation and a recession. In the aftermath, Australia seems stuck with a current account deficit and one of the lowest saving levels in the OECD.

A critical factor accounting for Australia's current malaise is the failure by successive governments to sustain a coherent developmental coalition. Evident dissonance exists between powerful economic interest groups. Financial, mining and agricultural interests want further deregulation of the labour market, the tax structure and tariff controls in order to exploit the comparative advantage they enjoy in the post-GATT world trade order. On the other hand, labour and manufacturing interests notably in automobiles, textiles and footwear, resist the opening of the Australian economy. They increasingly demand an industrial policy along East Asian lines to address the worrying decline in Australia's manufacturing competitiveness. Ironically, both mining and agricultural interests which want to accelerate the process of deregulation, and manufacturing and labour interests which want to stop or reverse it, appeal selectively to the Asian experience. Thus in 1989, the influential Garnaut Report argued that economic integration with the dynamic regional economies of North and South-East Asia required Australia to 'enhance export orientation and competitiveness' through a process of 'internationalization and trade liberalization' (Garnaut, 1989, p.23). In this view the protection of domestic manufacturing should be dismantled, whilst participation in international mechanisms like the World Trade Order and the Asia-Pacific Economic Co-operation group would enable Australia to exploit its comparative advantage in agricultural and resource-based products. Others in Canberra's policy elite derived a different lesson from the East Asian model observing that Australian economic governance has histori-cally been particularly weak at the microeconomic level. This failure to design an effective coalition of business and labour in an industrial strategy to develop manufacturing and services contrasted markedly with the Japanese, Taiwanese and South Korean experience. Nowhere is this more evident than in the decline of traditional manufacturing in automobiles and textiles and the failure to exploit the new information technology. As the managing director of IBM Australia observed recently, over the past decade Australia had failed to build 'anything of an internationally competitive scale and scope', a failure which he felt required 'radical changes to federal government policy' (*Australian*, 24 June 1997).

8.7   Conclusion

Chalmers Johnson (1987) has identified six characteristics of the strong developmental state: access to and state control of developmental capital; harmonious labour relations; bureaucratic autonomy; autonomy of the state; administrative guidance and successful state supported conglomer-ates. Despite the fact that all the states considered have developed some or a majority of these features, different states, have given more weight to certain features of the developmental profile over time. For example, whilst South Korea and Taiwan share with Japan the majority of the features of the Johnson developmental profile, South Korea has built multinational conglomerates funded by massive foreign borrowing at the expense of small and medium sized enterprises. Meanwhile Taiwan, whilst also retaining a large state sector, never exposed itself to external debt in the same way as South Korea. Differently again, neither the Chinese nor the South-East Asian economies established the bureaucratic autonomy or administrative guidance with the finesse and long-term planning capacity of Japan, Taiwan and South Korea. Consequently, Chinese and South-East Asian capitalism is largely dependent on foreign, usually North-East Asian investment, and subject to questionable and opaque allocative procedures. Further, to the extent that China and South-East Asia have developed conglomerates, they are dominated by transnational, overseas Chinese business networks. In the path development of these different modes of East Asian capitalism, the autonomy and capacity of the bureaucracy has varied. Thus whilst Taiwan, Japan, and South Korea have established economic bureaucracies with the capacity to implement industrial policy over long periods, this has not been the case in either South-East Asia, Australia or in China.

The sequencing of developmental characteristics also affects the developmental outcome. In the post-war period, Japan possessed a bureaucracy before it possessed a national government and this shaped the bureaucracy driven soft authoritarian coalition that emerged in the course of the 1950s. Taiwan and to some extent, Malaysia, developed strong dominant and autonomous party states relatively early on in their development histories, whilst South Korea, Thailand and Indonesia were characterized for long periods by military driven and sometimes unstable coalitional arrangements. Significantly, the North-East Asian states undertook, under American guidance, land reform and acquired aid packages and technology transfers early in their development histories that facilitated subsequent movement up the technology ladder. South-East Asia and the PRC by contrast developed later, and the financing of their export led growth spurt between 1985 and 1995 depended largely upon investment from the already more industrially developed economies of North-East Asia and Japan. In developing this developmental profile and establishing long-term growth with relatively equitable distribution some states have clearly been more successful than others, and some like Indonesia and to a lesser extent Thailand have signally failed to distribute the wealth generated by a growing GDP in an equitable manner. Instead wealth has been concentrated in the capital cities and in the hands of crony capitalist elites with close links to government and access to soft financial loans. Some commentators have attributed this difference in developmental outcomes to a cultural legacy common to the overseas Chinese and North-East Asians and whose Confucian ethic continues to influence the political and economic practice of contemporary Japan, Taiwan, South Korea and increasingly the PRC. Whether more generally a set of Asian values that privilege the family over the individual, group consensus over self interested materialism, deference to rational leadership over the free articulation of interest and saving and deferred gratification over hedonistic self indulgence, constitute a development friendly Asian ethic has been much debated (Redding 1993; Yoshihara 1988).

The economic problems occasioned by technocratically led development and export oriented growth throughout South-East Asia has led some economists to draw attention to a more general flaw in the character of the Asian developmental model. In the view of neo-classical economists the North-East Asian economies and Singapore have been strikingly effective in mobilizing 'inputs' into the economy that accounts for their rapid growth. However, they have been notably less effective in improving total factor productivity, central for continuing growth in the future. An 'astonishing mobilization of resources,' Paul Krugman avers, 'accounts almost entirely for East Asian growth' (Krugman, 1994, pp.70–1). Mobilization of capital inputs, moreover, turned particularly sour in 1997 as the state-regulated financial sector across the Asia-Pacific collapsed in a sea of illiquidity, non-performing loans and external debt repayments that could not be met. Beginning in Thailand in July 1997, and spreading to Malaysia, the Philippines, Indonesia, South Korea and even Japan, Asian currencies became the subject of speculative attack in the financial markets. The attempt to administratively guide state banks to support either capitalist cronies in Malaysia, Indonesia and Thailand or prop up ailing *chaebol* in South Korea and banks in Japan backfired. Evidently, the far-sighted technocratic planners failed to take account of the possibility of capital flight from the region or the possibility of currency devaluation. Relentless lending on property combined with opaque and underdeveloped account-ancy procedures witnessed banks and financial institutions collapsing from Japan to Indonesia. By December 1997, the International Monetary Fund had been called upon to provide over US$70 billion in credits and currency swaps to bail out the overstretched economies of Thailand, Indonesia and South Korea. At the end of the 1990s, Australia which lacked the strong state capacity to guide capital accumulation and generate an effective industrial policy, but nevertheless retained common law practices of open fiscal accountability and management of public sector borrowing, is least exposed to financial meltdown.

References

Ali, A. (1994) 'Japanese manufacturing and investment in Malaysia' in Jomo, K.S. (ed.)

Amsden, A. (1989) *Asia's next giant: South Korea and Late Industrialization,* Oxford, Oxford University Press.

Bell, S. (1996) *Ungoverning the Economy: the Political Economy of Australian Economic Policy,* Melbourne, Oxford University Press.

Bhattacharaya, A. and Pangestu, M. (1993) *Indonesia Development, Transformation and Public Policy,* Washington, World Bank.

Castles, F. (1985) *The Australian Working Class and Welfare,* Sydney, Allen and Unwin.

Chew, L.C. (1993) *Lessons of East Asia: Hong Kong a Unique Case of Development,* Washington, World Bank.

Ching, F. (1994) *China in Transition,* Hong Kong, Far Eastern Economic Review Publishing Co.

Cumings, B. (1987) 'The origins and development of the North-East Asian political economy: industrial sectors, product cycles and political consequences' in Deyo, F.C. (ed.).

Denker, M.S. (1994) 'The evolution of Japanese investment in Malaysia' in Jomo, K.S. (ed.)

Deyo, F.C. (ed.) (1987) *The Political Economy of the New Asian Industrialism,* Ithaca, Cornell University Press.

Garnaut, R. (1989) *Australia and the North-East Asian Ascendancy,* Canberra, Australian Government Publishing Service.

Gomez, E.T. (1994) *Political Business Corporate Involvement of Malaysian Political Parties*, Townsville, James Cook University Press.

Hewison, R. (1994) 'The economy' in Hill, H. (ed.).

Hill, H. (ed.) (1994) *Indonesia's New Order: the Dynamic of Socio-economic Transformation*, St. Leonards, Allen and Unwin.

Jesudason, J.V. (1990) *Ethnicity and the Economy: the State, Chinese Business and Multinationals in Malaysia*, Singapore, Oxford University Press.

Johnson, C. (1982) *MITI and the Japanese Miracle: the Growth of Industrial Policy 1925– 1975*, Stanford, Stanford University Press.

Johnson, C. (1987) 'Political institutions and economic performance: the government–business relationship in Japan, South Korea and Taiwan' in Deyo, F.C. (ed.).

Jomo, K.S. (1994) 'Malaysian forests Japanese wood' in Jomo, K.S. (ed.).

Jomo, K.S. (ed.) (1994) *Japan and Malaysian Development in the Shadow of the Rising Sun*, London, Routledge.

Kelly, P. (1994) *The End of Certainty*, St. Leonards, Allen and Unwin.

Kim, K. and Leipziger, D. (1993) *Lessons of East Asia: Korea a Case of Government Led Development*, Washington, World Bank.

Krugman, P. (1995) 'The myth of the Asian miracle', *Foreign Affairs*, vol.73, no.6, pp.62–78.

Laothamatas, A. (1992) *Business Associations and the New Political Economy of Thailand*, Boulder, Westview.

Macintyre, A. (1994) 'Power, prosperity and patrimonialism: business and government in Indonesia' in Macintyre, A. (ed.).

Macintyre, A. (ed.) (1994) *Business and Government in Industrialising Asia*, St. Leonards, Allen and Unwin.

Matthews, T. and Ravenhill, J. (1994) 'Strategic trade policy: the Northeast Asian experience' in Macintyre, A. (ed.).

Moon, Chung-in (1994) 'Changing patterns of business-government relations in and regime transition in South Korea' in Macintyre, A. (ed.).

Naughton, B. (1995) 'China's macroeconomy in transition', *The China Quarterly 1995*, pp.1083–103.

Nolan, P. and Ash. R. (1995) 'China's economy on the eve of reform', *The China Quarterly 147*, pp.980–97.

Oi, J.C. (1995) 'The role of the local state in China's economy', *The China Quarterly 147*, pp. 1132–49.

Okimoto, D. (1989) *Between MITI and the Market: Japanese Industrial Policy for High Technology*, Stanford, Stanford University Press.

Patrick, H.T. and Park, Yung Chul (eds) (1994) *The Financial Development of Japan, Korea and Taiwan: Growth, Repression and Liberalization*, Oxford, Oxford University Press.

Redding, S.G. (1993) *The Spirit of Chinese Capitalism*, Berlin, Walter de Gruyter.

Rhee, J-c. (1994) *The State and Industry in South Korea: The Limits of the Authoritarian State*, London, Routledge.

Robison, R. (1990) *Power and Economy in Suharto's Indonesia*, Manila, Journal of Contemporary Asia Publishers.

Schwarz, A. (1994) *A Nation in Waiting: Indonesia in the 1990s*, St. Leonards, Allen and Unwin.

Wade, R. (1990) *Governing the Market Economic Theory and the Role of Government in East Asian Industrialization*, Princeton, Princeton University Press.

White, G. (1992) *Riding the Tiger: the Politics of Economic Reform in Post-Mao China*, London, Macmillan.

World Bank (1993) *The East Asian Miracle: Economic Growth and Public Policy*, Oxford, Oxford University Press.

Xu, Xin-peng (1993) 'Taiwan's economic co-operation with Fujian and Guandong province' in Klintworth, G. (ed.) *Taiwan in the Asia-Pacific in the 1990s*, St. Leonards, Allen and Unwin.

Yoshihara, K. (1988) *The Rise of Ersatz Capitalism in South-East Asia*, Kuala Lumpur, Oxford University Press.

Yoshihara, K. (1994) *Japanese Economic Development*, Kuala Lumpur, Oxford University Press.

Further reading

Deyo, F.C. (ed.) (1987) *The Political Economy of the New Asian Industrialism*, Ithaca, Cornell University Press.

Jones, D.M. (1997) *Political Development in Pacific Asia*, Cambridge, Polity Press.

Yoshihara, K. (1994) *Japanese Economic Development*, Kuala Lumpur, Oxford University Press.

CHAPTER 9

The politics of welfare in East Asia

Gordon White, Roger Goodman and Huck-ju-Kwon

9.1 Introduction

This chapter focuses on the nature of welfare systems and the governance of welfare policy in East Asia, covering one mature industrialized country (Japan); four capitalist 'newly industrialized countries' (NICs) (South Korea, Taiwan, Hong Kong and Singapore); and one socialist NIC (China). We are focusing on these countries because they share certain key characteristics – geographical, historical, political, economic, cultural and social – which distinguish them from other areas of the Asia-Pacific region. These are also the countries in East Asia which have generated growing interest in Western countries over the past decade in consequence of their extraordinary economic performance. This interest started with attempts to explain the success of the post-war Japanese economy, then spread to the 'four little tigers' and still more recently to the 'big tiger' of post-Maoist China. The region's impressive economic performance has promoted business competitors in the West to search for the 'secrets' of East Asian success and Western politicians have also shown increasing interest in East Asia as a source of ideas for resolving their policy dilemmas at home. In the international arena agencies such as the World Bank have acclaimed the East Asian miracle as clear evidence of the virtues of competitive markets and a vindication of the orthodoxy of neo-liberal economics. By contrast, their critics have emphasized the crucial role played by the state in guiding economic development in East Asian societies and cited their success to defend the role of government intervention to promote economic growth.

There has been an accompanying reassessment of the character and significance of the cultural basis of East Asian development, conventionally identified as 'Confucianism'. In an earlier era (the 1950s and 1960s) Confucianism was widely seen, in East Asia and elsewhere, as an obstacle to the developmental ambitions of these societies because of its stress on preserving tradition, its contempt for commercial and industrial pursuits, and its hostility to technological innovation and entrepreneurship. Over the past two decades, however, Confucianism has been rediscovered as a positive historical force. It is now commonly cited as having provided the fundamental cultural underpinnings for East Asian economic success, particularly through its perceived emphasis on the importance of education, family relations, social harmony and discipline and a strong work ethic.

These positive images of East Asia have become part of the rhetoric of Western politicians and business leaders, functioning in effect as a new form of what Edward Said (1985) has called 'Orientalism'. Rather like the Enlightenment thinkers of the eighteenth century who drew on far away societies such as China to initiate change in their own societies, so contemporary commentators in the West are holding up their own particular images of East Asia as a means of talking to and about their own identities in terms of some kind of oriental distinctiveness – encapsulated, for example, in the notions of 'Asian values' or 'Chinese characteristics'. (For a comprehensive analysis of these phenomena, see Goodman *et al.*, 1998 and **Lawson, 1998**.)

While these laudatory Western notions of East Asian experience have centred on political and economic issues, the phenomenon is also evident in the area of social welfare where there is much talk of an *East Asian welfare model*. In the West, neo-liberals point to East Asia's success in achieving high levels of popular well-being – measured in terms of the conventional indices of income, health and education and physical well-being – without high levels of government expenditure and a large welfare bureaucracy. They laud the spirit of individual and group responsibility and the crucial role of the family in providing social insurance and services. By contrast, social democrats have argued that East Asian governments have not only acted to promote cohesion and reduce inequality in society as a whole, but have also taken decisive steps to provide certain key items of social welfare, such as public housing in Hong Kong and Singapore and pensions in Singapore. In East Asia itself there is a similar debate. On the one side, conservative elites have advocated the superiority of putatively indigenous welfare practices, notably Singapore's Central Provident Fund; on the other side, new popular forces given greater voice by the transition from authoritarian to democratic rule in South Korea and Taiwan in the mid 1980s have sought to extend the range of collective welfare provision along Western lines, particularly in the areas of pensions and health insurance.

Clearly, with so many contrasting images of East Asian experience being constructed and so many different lessons being drawn from it, questions must be asked about the accuracy of the pictures presented. In this chapter we shall be using a comparative perspective to examine in detail the welfare systems of five East Asian societies with a parallel analysis of the evolution of the Chinese welfare system in the era of post-Mao economic reforms. Our basic intention is to explore whether there actually exists such a creature as an East Asian welfare model. Our specific questions are the following:

1 What are the key elements of the East Asian welfare system, to what extent are they shared across societies and what are the main differences between different countries?

2 What are the basic factors which account for patterns of welfare provision in different countries – economic, political and socio-cultural?

3 To what extent is East Asian experience relevant to the problems of reforming welfare systems elsewhere?

4 To what extent are East Asian welfare systems sustainable in the context of changing social and economic conditions?

At first thought, it might be considered inappropriate to include the People's Republic of China in a study of the East Asian model of social welfare since discussion of the latter has largely been concerned with the capitalist societies of the region. Mainland China has usually been seen as a member of a sharply contrasting family of social security models, that of communist or state socialist societies, with their distinctive patterns of state, collective and enterprise provision of welfare benefits. However, major changes have been taking place in Chinese society under the impact of the market oriented economic reforms launched in 1978. Despite strong elements of continuity with the previous Soviet-style system, particularly in the political sphere, the changes that have taken place in China's economy and society over the past two decades show strong elements of convergence with her East Asian capitalist neighbours. We are interested here to investigate whether this process of 'growing together' is also visible in the area of welfare.

The central unit of analysis is the *welfare system*, the particular pattern of institutional ways in which a society provides social benefits of two main kinds to its citizens with the aim of enhancing their psychological and material well being:

1 society security/insurance, including pensions, health and sickness insurance and unemployment benefits, and

2 social services/assistance, including provision for vulnerable or disadvantaged groups such as poor people, older people, single-parent households and people with physical disabilities or mental health-care needs.

Different societies organize the provision of welfare goods and services through a variety of institutional channels, the most important of our inquiry being:

1 state agencies;

2 voluntary, non-profit organizations of 'civil society';

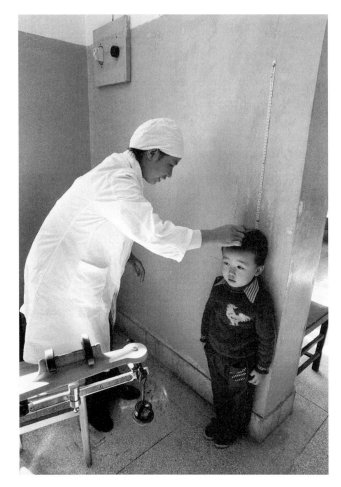

Clinic, Fujian, China, 1986

3   market entities such as insurance companies;

4   local community organizations;

5   families and kinship networks.

The distinctiveness of a society's welfare system rests on the particular combination of these modes of provision and the pattern and level of well-being which it produces.

These systems of welfare provision are very complex and a full analysis lies beyond the scope of this chapter. Therefore, while providing a brief picture of each society's welfare system, we have put our main emphasis on understanding the role of the state in welfare provision rather than that of other elements of the welfare system, such as civil organizations, companies and the family. We shall be particularly interested in identifying the ways in which political interests and ideologies have shaped the evolution of national welfare systems, focusing on the specific ways in which the state is involved in providing welfare, the political governance of welfare policy making and the relationship between welfare and the broader politico and economic trajectories of these societies.

The structure of the chapter is as follows. Section 9.2 will present case studies of the welfare systems of the six individual societies – Singapore, Hong Kong, Taiwan, South Korea, Japan and China; and Section 9.3 will seek to draw conclusions about the distinctive nature of the East Asian welfare experience and the key factors which explain it.

9.2 The welfare systems of East Asia

Singapore: economic protection without social solidarity

Singapore's central welfare institution, the Central Provident Fund (CPF), was created by the country's former colonial master, the British government. The CPF Ordinance became law on 11 December 1953, long before Singapore gained its independence. The CPF was a classic funded scheme with contributions by both employers and employees, with an initial contribution rate of 5 per cent of the wage bill each. (In the language of social policy, a 'funded' social insurance scheme implies that the funds are accumulated over time, rather than being paid out to beneficiaries, as they are paid in by contributors. The latter schemes are referred to as 'pay-as-you-go' systems such as the British basic state pension.) Over the last four decades, the CPF has evolved from a simple compulsory savings scheme to a complex social welfare programme. Its impact on Singaporean society has been profound. Since 1968, when a Housing Scheme was introduced within the CPF, it has been an anchor of various social policies. The Medisave Scheme came into effect in 1984 and other minor programmes such as Edusave followed. As of 1994, the active membership, which means members currently paying contributions, accounted for about 54 per cent of the working population. There were also 163,781 self employed members who had made contributions under the Medisave scheme for the self employed. The CPF contribution rate was 40 per cent of wages in 1994, with employers and employees contributing 20 per cent each (see Table 9.1). Each member of the CPF has three personal accounts which have different purposes: the Ordinary Account for purchasing housing and approved investment; the Medisave Account for hospitalization expenses; and the Special Account for old age pensions and contingencies. Of the total CPF contribution rate of 40 per cent, 30 per cent is credited to the Ordinary Account while 6 per cent and 4 per cent go to the Medisave and Special Accounts respectively. In 1994, contributions during the year amounted to S$11,278.6 million which accounted for 15 per cent of GDP; withdrawals from the fund totalled S$7,292 million, showing a healthy surplus.

Table 9.1 *CPF ratios of contribution (as a percentage of monthly wage income), 1955–94*

Year	Contribution by employee	Contribution by employer	Total
1955	5.0	5.0	10.0
1968	6.5	6.5	13.0
1970	8.0	8.0	16.0
1971	10.0	10.0	20.0
1972	10.0	14.0	24.0
1973	11.0	15.0	26.0
1974	15.0	15.0	30.0
1977	15.5	15.5	31.0
1978	16.5	16.5	33.0
1979	16.5	20.5	37.0
1980	18.0	20.5	38.5
1981	22.0	20.5	42.5
1982	23.0	22.0	45.0
1983	23.0	23.0	46.0
1984	25.0	25.0	50.0
1986	25.0	10.0	35.0
1988	24.0	12.0	36.0
1989	23.0	15.0	28.0
1990	23.0	16.5	39.5
1991	22.5	17.5	40.0
1992	22.0	18.0	40.0
1994	20.0	20.0	40.0

Source: Tremewan (1998)

From a comparative perspective, Singapore's welfare system is anchored around the CPF and has three distinctive characteristics. First, the CDP was arranged in such a way that the state only plays the role of regulator in relation to both the financing and management of the Fund. The CPF Board, responsible for operating the CPF, is a quasi-governmental body to which contributions from employees and employers are paid. These contributions are not a part of formal public expenditures and, as such, do not show up in official fiscal accounts. Despite such financial arrangements, the Singapore government has been able to use the CPF as an effective tool of macro-economic policy and a source of funds for state directed development spending. The colossal amount of funds mobilized through the CPF has been used for building public housing and investing in other government capital projects. In 1994, the CPF fund stood at S$58 billion, which is 73 per cent of GDP in the same year. Of this, S$43.6 billion (57 per cent of GDP) was invested in government bonds and the rest was held as an advanced deposit with the monetary authority of Singapore. In addition, the Singapore government has used the CPF as a means to combat economic fluctuations. For instance, during 1985–86 when Singapore was faced with an unprecedented recession, the government reduced the employers' contribution rate from 25 to 10 per cent in order to stimulate economic activity (Perera, 1992). This policy reduced the level of workers' wages in the long run, but their disposable income remained the same in the short term, which made a hard political decision a lot easier.

Second, the Singapore welfare system grants no entitlement or access to welfare benefits to those outside the CPF system. Singaporeans do not have social rights to a safety net other than their CPF. Only about 2,000 people who pass a strict means test receive public assistance benefits. According to Asher's calculation, the level of public assistance is 25 per cent below the minimum household expenditure for more than one person households (Asher, 1993). This certainly hinders people's inclination to rely on public help, but leaves vulnerable people with virtually no protection other than from their families. It raises the question of whether Singapore's welfare system will be sustainable if the growth rate of the economy becomes much lower than at present, and unemployment increases, leading to much greater pressures on the welfare system. Third, the Singapore government uses housing policy as a measure of ethnic integration and aims at preventing ethnic enclaves. The government's Housing and Development Board regulates the mix of ethnic groups in its housing estates through intervention in both sales and re-sales of public housing flats (Ooi, 1993, p.7). This policy has strong political implications. Even though the Singapore government vehemently denies it, this ethnically oriented housing policy is effectively a form of gerrymandering. Parliamentary candidates who would base their political appeal on ethnic minorities would not have a real chance of winning seats without ethnic enclaves.

Throughout its post-Independence history, the CPF has not only functioned as a key element in the government's macro-economic policy armoury, but has played a key political role. The benefits provided by the scheme have been used positively to bolster the political dominance of the ruling People's Action Party and negatively to undermine the social base and political appeal of opposition forces. At a broader level, it has also been used as a force for integrating Singapore society and creating a sense of national identity in a geo-political context which has at times been threatening.

Hong Kong: a residual system

The welfare system in Hong Kong consists of four main areas of social policy: social security, health, housing and social services. The social security system is very different in its funding and management from that of Singapore. While Singapore's CPF has an active membership of 54 per cent of the working population, Hong Kong's social security system aims only at specific, and relatively narrow, sections of the population. The Comprehensive Social Security Assistance Scheme, introduced in 1971, provides basic income support to those whose income is below a level prescribed by the government. The number of people receiving benefits from this programme was only 140,000 (about 2 per cent of the population) in 1995 and they were mainly older people and people with illnesses or disabilities (Director of Social Welfare, 1996, p.14). This programme was relabelled as the Comprehensive Assistance Scheme in 1993, but despite an increase in the level of benefits, it remains the same as its predecessor which was modelled on British National Assistance (Macpherson, 1993, p.52). Increases in the level of benefits can be most immediately traced back to the 1991 White Paper, Social Welfare into the 1990s and Beyond, which was produced by a Working Party set up by the then Governor David Wilson. In the White Paper, the Working Party claimed that it had attempted to improve social welfare 'without creating the sort of dependency culture that has emerged in some developed industrial societies', resisting thereby any effort to expand the range of welfare benefits along the lines of Western welfare states. Levels of monthly benefits for the major programmes are presented in Table 9.2.

Table 9.2 *Monthly levels of social welfare benefits in Hong Kong[1]*

Scheme	Category	Benefit range in HK$
Comprehensive social security	Elderly over 60	1,505–1,810
	Disabled adult	1,505–3,315
	Disabled child	2,105–3,315
	Able-bodied child	1,505–1,810
	Able-bodied adult	1,045–1,210
Special needs allowance	Normal old age	485
	Higher old age	550
	Normal disability	970
	Higher disability	1,940

[1] The median household income in 1991 was HK$9,964 (Hong Kong Census and Statistics Department, 1992).

Source: Hong Kong Government (1996)

With respect to social services, non-governmental organizations (NGOs) deliver various services ranging from child and youth centres, institutional care for people with mental care problems to residential centres for the elderly. Many of these NGOs have roots in the colony's history in which early missionaries combined religious missions and social services (Hodge, 1981). Some of the NGOs are purely autonomous bodies, but others are not entirely non-governmental since they receive up to 100 per cent of their funding from the government under a fiscal subvention policy. These NGOs are accountable to the government for their output and performance. Other sources of funding for social services are the Lottery Fund, the Community Chest and private donations, but government subvention is still the main source.

While the levels and range of social assistance are very limited, by contrast Hong Kong has a substantial public housing programme. The Housing Authority of Hong Kong is responsible for co-ordinating all aspects of public housing. It has 151 rental estates and has built 122 estates under a Home Ownership Scheme. In 1995, 24.1 per cent of the consolidated public capital expenditure and 4.3 per cent of the consolidated recurrent expenditure of the Hong Kong government were devoted to the development and maintenance of public housing. Rental flats are allocated to applicants according to income bands and housing authority flats are also sold at a price below market value for public housing tenants and families with limited incomes under the Home Ownership Scheme.

While local voices had increasingly called for improvements in the colony's welfare system during the 1970s and 1980s, the lack of democratic access to and influence on the colonial authorities meant that these demands had little effect. However, David Wilson's successor as Governor, Chris Patten, sought to bring significant changes to this welfare system when he proposed an old-age pension programme along with his attempt to break the mould of Hong Kong politics through democratic reforms. In July 1994, the Hong Kong government published a consultation paper, *An Old Age Pension Scheme for Hong Kong*. According to this paper, the Old Age Pension would be a 'pay-as-you-go' scheme in which the present elderly can receive immediate benefits from the contributions of the current working population. It would also have had redistributive effects since the contribution paid would be 5 to 10 per cent of taxable income, but the benefits would be received at a flat rate. As with Patten's political reforms, however, the pension reform came too late and provoked opposition from the Chinese government and their local supporters, particularly among the business community, and it failed to go through.

Due to this failure (and that of a subsequent attempt to introduce a provident fund scheme), the Hong Kong welfare system remains as it has been. It has been shaped by the central political fact that, until very recently, the Hong Kong population may have had considerable freedom, but very little democracy. It is minimalist, targeting only a small section of the population, mainly poor people over 65. Most of the funding for the existing programme is provided by the state. It remains to be seen whether the government of the Special Administrative Region, which was created after 1 July 1997 when the colony reverted to China, will introduce a pension programme which covers or intends to cover all the population. To a large extent, this depends on the impact of ongoing reforms to China's own welfare system.

Taiwan: democracy and the new direction of social policy

The Chinese Nationalist Party (Kuomintang) government fled to Taiwan from the Chinese mainland in 1949. Shortly afterwards, a Labour Insurance programme was introduced in 1950. After that, the welfare system in Taiwan largely stagnated until the 1980s, with only two social insurance schemes: the Labour Insurance and Government Employees' Insurance programmes. Since the 1980s, however, new schemes have been introduced, resulting in a fragmented and complex welfare structure. Up until 1995, when the National Health Insurance programme was introduced, the welfare system had more than 14 different programmes for which various ministries of the central government and provincial governments were responsible, although virtually all of them were, or included, health insurance programmes. Before 1995, health care schemes only covered 59.5 per cent of the total population. The Labour Insurance and Government Employees Insurance programmes included lump-sum retirement payments as well as health insurance schemes, whereas other programmes had only health insurance schemes. The 1995 National Health Insurance programme integrated all these health insurance schemes into a single scheme and is expected to cover nearly all of the population.

These initiatives over the past decade raise two questions crucial to an understanding of the development of the Taiwanese welfare system. First, we need to understand why the Kuomintang (KMT) government first introduced the Labour Insurance programme in 1950, at a time when the island's industrialization had not yet begun. Second, what motivated the state to expand the welfare system in the 1980s and 1990s and extend its responsibility for financing welfare programmes for groups such as farmers and others outside the state sector, the employees of which – bureaucrats, soldiers and professionals – had received privileged treatment in welfare terms?

The Labour Insurance Programme was already a part of the manifesto of the KMT government before it was forced to cross the Taiwan straits. In 1945, in an effort to outmanoeuvre the communists, the KMT launched a social policy manifesto which included: (1) an outline of National Nursery Policy; (2) an outline of Labour policy; (3) an outline of farming policy; and (4) a post-war outline of a Primary Social Security System (Ku, 1995, p.99). This policy launch also reflected the Constitution of the Republic of China, which declares, *inter alia*, that the nation should pursue the idea of the welfare state, following the philosophy of its founding father, Sun Yat-sen. The KMT, however, did not have time to implement the manifesto before they were driven to Taiwan by the communists in 1949. In Taiwan, they were seen as unwelcome outsiders by a large section of the indigenous Taiwanese population The introduction of the Labour Insurance Programme in 1950 must be understood as an attempt to enhance their political legitimacy, not merely to appeal to the indigenous population but also to consolidate their base among the people who had left the mainland with them.

The next major political juncture came in the aftermath of democratization in the mid to late 1980s. This new political environment led to the introduction of the Farmers' Health Insurance programme in 1989 and subsequently the National Health Insurance programme in 1995. These innovations on the welfare front were related to the whole range of socio-economic changes which Taiwan has experienced over the past forty years: its economic development, the growth of a new middle class and the rise of expectations for a higher quality of life undoubtedly played important roles in this development. It was, however, the onset of democratization in 1987 and political competition from the main opposition party, the Democratic Progress Party (DPP), which brought the political momentum for welfare reform. In particular, competitive elections both at local and national levels have forced the main political parties to accept social demands from the population. Political parties have also tried to utilize social policy issues for their own electoral advantage. The KMT, for instance, claims that they are the only party capable of governing the country with responsible social programmes and the KMT government has created a Ministry of Social Welfare to co-ordinate the wide range of welfare programmes. The DPP in turn has been pressing for the introduction of an old-age pension scheme. Thus, Taiwan provides a vivid example of the ways in which a change in the rules of the political game can alter the course of welfare policy and change the structure of a country's welfare system in major ways.

South Korea: the politics of legitimation

The first modern social welfare programme introduced in South Korea was industrial accident insurance introduced in 1963 along with a pilot programme for health insurance. At the beginning, industrial accident insurance covered people in workplaces of 500 employees or more. Since then, the number of people covered has increased gradually, reaching 41.3 per cent of all employed people in 1990. The industrial accident insurance fund is financed solely by contributions from employers. Contributions are related to the safety records of workplaces in a way that the employers of accident prone workplaces have to pay larger contributions than those who have better safety records. There is no state subsidy to help finance industrial accident insurance. Following recommendations from the USA attached to an aid loan in 1975, national health insurance became a compulsory programme in 1977. It started first with large-scale companies, then public employees and private school teachers. By 1987, most employees in the major industrial sectors had access to health care through the national health insurance schemes, while the self-employed, farmers and others who did not have employers fell outside the scheme. This was partly because it was difficult to administer actuarial work for them. Another difficulty in including such groups in the NHI scheme was that they did not have employers who would pay half the contributions. Only in 1989 did the government take on the responsibility for these contributions, thereby ensuring the whole population had access to national health insurance.

A national pension programme (NPP) was first considered in the early 1970s, but implementation was postponed due to the oil shock in 1973. It was eventually reintroduced in 1988, following an election promise by President Roh Tae Woo. It is a typical social insurance programme in which the state only plays the role of regulator. The only fiscal subvention from the state is for the NPPs administrative costs. The most recent welfare programme is the employment insurance scheme introduced by President Kim Young sam's government, which came to office in 1992. It was implemented in 1995 and there is no information available yet on the numbers of people it covers and its financing details. However, it is clear that this is yet another insurance programme in which employers and employees pay contributions and direct state finance is non-existent or negligible.

In a nutshell, these programmes are based on the social insurance principle under which a person has to contribute first before claiming benefits. The role of the state is typically that of regulator. The only exception to the insurance principle in the South Korean welfare system is the public assistance programme which was introduced in 1965 and has provided community and institutional care and income support to those who are defined officially as poor. To be entitled to benefits, one has to show a loss of income-earning ability, and an absence of private support from relatives. One's assets must also be below an official level which the government announces every year. The coverage of the public assistance programme is presented in Table 9.3.

Table 9.3 *Number of people covered by the public assistance programme in South Korea (in thousands)*

Year	Institutional care	Community care	Support for livelihood	As percentage of total population
1965	288	72	3,563	13.7
1970	306	63	2,116	7.7
1975	375	52	904	3.8
1980	330	47	1,500	4.9
1985	282	63	1,928	5.5
1990	340	81	1,935	5.3
1995	307	78	1,369	3.9

Source: So Sang-Mok *et al.* (1981), Korean Government (1996)

In ways similar to Taiwan, the South Korean welfare system has also been shaped by the transition from authoritarian to democratic rule. In the earlier stage, authoritarian regimes were not under pressure to expand welfare schemes and when they did so it was done selectively to garner support and reduce potential opposition. The onset of democracy in 1987 has also changed the pattern of welfare politics, leading to pressures for a wider range of benefits extending to larger sections of the population. Given the lack of a powerful and credible opposition, however, welfare reforms have been relatively gradual and the government has been able to avoid large increases in direct welfare expenditure.

Japan: alternative ideas of social welfare

In its present form, the Japanese welfare system can be divided into four categories: medical care, income maintenance, social services and housing policies. In this section we will concentrate on pension and health care policies. If we look first at pension programmes, 79 per cent of people between the ages of 15 and 64 paid contributions to various pension schemes in 1992, including the employees' pension, the national pension and the mutual aid pension (Ministry of Health and Welfare, 1995, p.288). Calculated against the total working population, pension coverage is slightly over 100 per cent and this means that universal rights to a pension have been established in Japan. Japan had actually achieved a basic level of universal coverage in 1961 when a residence-based national pension insurance (NPI) was introduced (Hoshino, 1988, p.256). The national pension guarantees a basic pension to every Japanese. The employees' pension scheme, which includes various pension programmes, provides pensions which are supplemental to the national pension. These supplements are earnings related.

With respect to health care, the role of the state is somewhat different compared to public pensions. In a broad sense, the Japanese health care system can be divided into two categories of insurance, although it includes various schemes. Work-based health insurance schemes cover people organized in work places, while community based schemes form insurance groups among the residents of each locality. Government managed health insurance covers mainly the employees of small and medium sized companies and society managed health insurance is arranged for those working in large-scale companies. Public employees in national and local government have their own Mutual Aid Associations. (The Mutual Aid Associations are in fact the quasi-governmental public insurance agencies for public employees.) Seamen also have their own insurance system managed by the government. National health insurance covers those who do not have employers, such as farmers, the self-employed and the retired, who were previously insured by work based insurance schemes. One insurance scheme which makes the Japanese health insurance system distinctive is the health service for the aged. This provides health care for those over 70 or those over 65 who are bedridden. Until very recently this scheme provided virtually free medical care to the elderly and has been a major target of reform (Campbell, 1992).

Although the Japanese government, under pressure from mounting political opposition, showed an intention in the early 1970s to emulate their Western counterparts by moving towards a Western-style welfare state, the economic shocks and financial stringencies of the 1970s led the Japanese political elite to repudiate this. They saw the Western welfare state as wasteful and extravagant and sought to seek a distinctive model which Prime Minister Ohira, who came to office in 1978, called a 'Japanese-style welfare society'. This emphasizes the importance of primary reliance on oneself and one's family and community, and seeks to restrict the direct financial role of government to a minimum. Whatever model of welfare adopted, however, they all face a crucial challenge posed by an ageing society, an issue first raised in *The White Paper on the Japanese Economy* in 1985. According to the White Paper, the ageing of the population poses a double-edged threat. First, welfare demands will increase sharply in future, but not all the welfare burden can be passed to future generations. This consideration led the Ministry of Finance to introduce a consumption tax in 1989. It is widely expected that the rate of this consumption tax will rise from the current 3 per cent to 7 per cent (Iwabuchi, 1994). Second, it was resolved that the welfare system should be reformed to ensure that the welfare burden, defined to include not only government expenditure but also individual and employer contributions, should not go beyond 50 per cent of national income in future (Iwabuchi, 1994, p.2). To achieve this aim, the Ministry of Health and Welfare formed an advisory panel, the Council on a Welfare Vision for an Old-Aged Society, which produced a report in March 1994 entitled *Welfare Vision in the 21st Century: For an Ageing Society with Decreasing Numbers of Children*. This report makes, *inter alia*, three main points for the future of social welfare. First, it argues that the Japanese welfare system should improve social service programmes for senior citizens and for working parents with young children. Second, society has to find ways in which people over sixty can find work more easily if they want to work. Third, the report warns that government efforts to contain public spending (including social security costs) under 50 per cent at the peak time of ageing are likely to fail. Given the economic and political uncertainties which have dogged Japan in the early and mid 1990s, there is as yet no clear indication as to how the accelerating problems of an ageing society will be tackled. How to protect the growing number of the elderly and meet the cost is not only dependant upon the demographic structure but also the political balance of power and Japan's economic prospects. In spite of a proposal to deal with the problem through the introduction of a 'Gold Plan' in 1999, whereby everyone over forty would contribute the equivalent of £3 a month to pay for care in their old age, it is likely that this would only cover about 40 per cent of the eventual cost and the state would have to pay the rest itself, probably through taxation.

These growing pressures mean that the Japanese government, however strong its preference for a low spending Japanese welfare state, may find it increasingly difficult to restrict direct public involvement to meet part of the financial burden of welfare. However, with the increased fluidity of the Japanese political scene after the end of the long period of post-war dominance by the Liberal Democratic Party in the early 1990s, it is difficult to predict how these increasingly urgent issues will be resolved.

China: from a communist to an East Asian welfare system

While the range of welfare benefits provided by China's post-revolutionary socialist state was impressive, it only applied to the urban areas, who made up approximately 18 per cent of the population in 1978, the last year before the beginning of the post-Mao economic reform programme. State provided or guaranteed welfare services for the rural population have been relatively marginal, mainly involving small amounts of material relief for particularly impoverished households. Most rural dwellers had to rely on their families or their communities and support from the latter dwindled after the weakening of rural collectives which followed the *de facto* privatization of agriculture in the early years of the reforms. The welfare system thus reinforced existing socio-economic inequalities between the rural and urban areas by subsidizing an already privileged urban population.

The urban welfare system was based on the public work unit – the basic building block of the previous system of central planning – which provided a wide variety of benefits to its employees, including insurance for retirement and medical treatment, as well as various fringe benefits, allowances, subsidies and on-site facilities. Work units also provided perhaps the most basic welfare item of all, a guarantee of lifelong employment. Though the state guaranteed the entire system and specific state agencies were involved in overseeing it, the direct welfare role of state agencies in the cities was a residual one, being confined largely to limited social assistance to a small number of disadvantaged groups who could not be supported by work units.

Post-Mao reformers have criticized the previous welfare system for retarding economic growth by encouraging dependence and complacency among the working population. In their view, moreover, the location of welfare responsibilities in the work unit, combined with the guarantee of lifetime employment impeded labour mobility, dampened work incentives and imposed unreasonable financial burdens on enterprises which increased as their work forces aged. They argued that the responsibility for employment based welfare arrangements should be shifted to other agencies, in the first instance to the state, and that welfare programmes should be redirected towards improving labour productivity and enterprise performance and should involve contributions from their ultimate beneficiaries to reduce the economic burdens of the work unit and the state.

Although the growing impact of market reforms has made welfare reform an increasingly urgent priority, they have also made it a complex and difficult process. As elsewhere in East Asia, the process of governance has involved competition between different interests and institutions, and policy managers at both central and local levels have been forced to seek ways to broker between them and organize a consensus for each specific innovation. It is not surprising, therefore, that welfare reforms have proceeded relatively slowly, lagging behind the pace of economic reform as a whole.

The area of reform which has made most progress has been that of retirement pensions. Pension reform has had to face the double task of making arrangements over the short and medium term for meeting pension entitlements deriving from the previous welfare system and making pro-active provision for the long-term problem of an ageing society into the next century. The main objectives of pension reform have followed those of welfare reforms more generally:

1   to remove the responsibility for financing and managing pensions for the urban workforce from enterprises to external agencies;

2   to share the task of financing pensions between the individual, firm and state to replace the previous system of direct enterprise responsibility;

3   to shift from an unfunded to a partially funded system of financing to allow an accumulation of investable assets;

4   to design a system which contributes to both micro-economic efficiency and social fairness.

The process of pension reform has been marked by disagreement and conflict between three sets of constituencies: institutional, social and geographical. There are a large number of state institutions involved in the design and implementation of new pension arrangements and pension reform is a terrain of institutional manoeuvring as existing organizations seek to protect their bailiwicks and new institutions press for a greater role. The most visible conflict has been between the Ministry of Labour, which oversaw the pre-reform enterprise based welfare system and has the current responsibility for introducing a new pension system for the enterprise sector, and the Economic System Reform Commission, whose role is to supervise the overall process of economic reform in the urban economy and which has been concerned to ensure that any new pension system meets what it perceives as the efficiency requirements of a market economy. The urban population has become more diverse as a consequence of economic reform and different social groups have their particular interests in regard to pension reform: for example, there are divisions between employees in the public sector and in newer sectors of the urban economy which have grown rapidly during the reform era, including private, self-employed, co-operative and foreign invested businesses, and between those in jobs and those who have been cast adrift from the welfare system through unemployment, the latter having to rely on themselves, their personal networks and the market to meet their long term welfare needs. There are also differences between regions and localities over pension reform, particularly between old industrial areas burdened with large numbers of old state industries with large accumulations of pensioners and areas with large concentrations of new economic sectors and foreign direct investment, particularly in the south-eastern coastal regions and the special economic zones.

Pervading these specific interests are broader ideological constituencies with different attitudes to pension reform and welfare reform more generally: a 'socialist' position which emphasizes redistributive fairness as the key principle underlying a new welfare system and the central role of the state in guaranteeing this; a 'reform' position which emphasizes the importance of tailoring welfare schemes to economic efficiency and encourages a greater role for private providers; and a 'developmental statist' position along familiar East Asian lines which seeks pragmatically to design welfare schemes consistent with rapid economic growth, whether by statist or market means.

These various interests and constituencies have shaped the trajectory of pension reform over the past decade. The 'socialist' and reformist' perspectives have been reflected in the two competing models of reform which have dominated the policy process in the 1990s. The first, which can be called the Ministry of Labour model, advocates the principle of social fairness and argues that any pension scheme should be based on mutual help, with a high degree of redistribution through social pooling. The second model, which is associated with the Economic Structure Reform Commission and receives support from the World Bank resident mission in China, emphasizes the principle of economic efficiency, arguing that state organized pensions should be restricted to allow scope for properly funded systems based on individual pension accounts.

While these two rival policy stances could initially be seen as representing differences between the socialist and reform positions, there has been increasing evidence of the emergence and growing strength of the development statist current of thought which exerts influence on the policy process more implicitly. Over time, the balance of power among the three main ideological constituencies has been shifting in favour of the last two and in particular the third. This reflects gradual changes in China's social, economic and political structures and in the balance of regional power. In broad terms, the policy influence of the socialist position is gradually ebbing as the fortunes of the public sector wane, the institutional power of the Ministry of Labour and other agencies such as the All China Federation of Trade Unions weakens and the more dynamic coastal regions assert greater independence from the centre. What appears to be emerging as the dominant policy paradigm is a form of state-led developmentalism along familiar East Asian lines, with the other two positions and their advocates – the redistributive socialist and the market oriented reformist – as ideological outriders. This means gradual movement towards a new welfare system which serves the over-riding priorities of economic growth and economic efficiency, which rewards those groups which contribute to this objective and which minimizes expenditures on 'unproductive' efforts to achieve redistribution or subsidize vulnerable groups.

9.3   The nature of the East Asian welfare experience

In the light of this case material, let us return to our original question: is there such a thing as an 'East Asian welfare model'? This question refers primarily to the first five of our case-societies since the Chinese welfare system has, until recently, been considered alien. We shall begin, therefore, by looking at the experiences of the former and conclude by assessing whether or not the Chinese welfare system is moving in an 'East Asian' direction.

Is there an East Asian welfare model?

We find that in certain respects, welfare systems in the five capitalist East Asian societies analysed do differ significantly from their Western counterparts and to that extent do constitute a distinct welfare experience with shared common elements. In financial terms, East Asian governments are relatively low spenders on social welfare in comparison with Western countries, as statistical evidence such as that provided in Table 9.4 shows. However, state involvement in welfare provision is not as modest as these simple statistics on official public expenditure might suggest. This underestimation mainly reflects the way in which the East Asian state participates in the financing of welfare. The state in these countries is, to varying degrees, a regulator which enforces welfare programmes without providing direct finance, whether based on social insurance schemes or a

Table 9.4   *General government expenditure as proportion of GDP (percentages)*

	1989[1]	*1992*
Sweden	39.5	46.2
United Kingdom	35.8	43.2
Japan	23.5	23.8
South Korea	23.5	25.1
Taiwan	27.1	31.8
Singapore	14.2	16.4
Hong Kong	14.7	13.8

[1] The figures for Taiwan, Singapore and Hong Kong refer to 1990.

Source: *International Financial Statistical Yearbook* (1995); *Japan Statistical Yearbook* (1995); *Korea Statistical Yearbook* (1994); *Statistical Yearbook of the Republic of China* (1994); *Hong Kong Annual Digest of Statistics* (1995); *Singapore Yearbook of Statistics* (1995)

central provident fund (Hong Kong is an exception here). However, even when we broaden our calculations to allow for the state's regulative function, East Asian governments still play a welfare role which is less than their Western counterparts.

There are other common features across these five societies. The notion of state-provided or guaranteed welfare as a social right of citizens is still not well established. Rather, non-state agencies – community, firm and family – have been expected to play a major welfare role in an ideological context wherein self/mutual help is encouraged and dependence on the state is discouraged or indeed stigmatized. Where state-sponsored welfare programmes for basic items of social insurance have emerged, they have tended to take the form of a patchwork of particular schemes for core social groups (Singapore and Hong Kong are exceptions here). Since many welfare programmes – for example, for pensions and health care – initially covered only those who could pay premiums, entitlements to welfare benefits were seen not as a citizenship right for all but as a privilege for certain sections of the population. Among the first groups to gain access to welfare programmes were those in the public sector and big businesses. This was particularly the case in Japan, South Korea and Taiwan during the initial formative period of their welfare systems. Their governments played down the aspect of citizenship rights in their welfare policies. As welfare programmes gradually expanded and came closer to the level of universality, welfare benefits gradually came less and less to be seen as a privilege. Nevertheless, there still exist a large number of separate programmes in specific areas of welfare which cover different categories of people in Japan, South Korea and Taiwan. This fragmentation narrows the range of social risk-pooling, lessens the degree of social solidarity and both reflects and reinforces differentials in power and status in society.

Despite these common elements, however, the evolution of each country's welfare system has had its own distinctive trajectory and in consequence they differ today. National welfare systems have developed incrementally over time and have been conditioned by the structure and dynamics of the social, economic and political conditions in each country. Governance has played a crucial role throughout. For example, social policy in Singapore was a salient part of a political strategy to enhance national solidarity and consolidate the dominance of the PAP. Welfare programmes were also introduced as part of a broad political strategy to build legitimacy for authoritarian regimes (in Taiwan and South Korea), as part of a programme of sponsored democratization (in Hong Kong), or to forestall opposition challenges (in Japan in the early 1970s). As a result of these differences, individual welfare systems have their distinct characteristics: for example, the large-scale public housing programmes in Hong Kong and Singapore and the Central Provident Fund in Singapore. In broad terms, the systemic similarities between Japan, South Korea and Taiwan are more pronounced, partly reflecting the fact that the last two mentioned countries have (un)consciously emulated Japan in constructing their own welfare systems. Hong Kong is a clear outrider because its welfare system has a different structure from the rest and the government plays a more direct role in financing it. Singapore is also distinctive through its adoption of the Central Provident Fund. Given these differences, it is misleading to think in terms of one homogeneous, over-arching East Asian welfare model common to these five societies.

How does one explain East Asian welfare experience?

The reasons for the development of this distinct experience are complex, but political factors are paramount. At the most general level, it is one element of a broader East Asian pattern of state-sponsored development, whereby welfare arrangements have been shaped to fit the strategic priority of rapid industrialization. Rather than being 'wasted' on 'unproductive' welfare expenditures, financial resources have been concentrated on economic development; governments have sought to keep expenditures on social assistance down and to design funded systems of social insurance which could provide financial resources for investment in industry and infrastructure. In consequence, these might be called *developmental welfare systems*. At another level, the East Asian welfare experience reflects a particular pattern of political forces and institutions in which conservative elites have been dominant and authoritarian political regimes have been the norm until recently (even including Japan which had a one-party dominant system of democracy until the early 1990s). Welfare programmes were overwhelmingly introduced by those in power rather than as a result of popular demand. The motives of those in power have focused on the priority of rapid industrialization, partly for reasons of domestic stability and partly in response to geo-political pressures, notably the need to compete with threatening neighbours in a Cold War world. In all five countries, forces which have influenced the evolution and governance of Western welfare systems – notably labour unions and social democratic parties – have not had a significant influence on the making of social policy.

Is East Asian welfare experience a model for other countries to emulate?

Western politicians have recently been looking to East Asia for answers to their welfare dilemmas. It is easy to see why this experience might appear attractive: first, it promotes an ideology and practice which subordinates welfare, particularly in the form of progressive redistribution and a wide-ranging and generous benefits system, to the over-riding priorities of economic efficiency and growth. Second, it is relatively cheap in financial and personnel terms, allowing the diversion of financial resources to directly productive purposes. Third, it creates a welfare environment (in which publicly provided safety-nets are weak or non-existent) which creates both positive work incentives and negative pressures for work discipline. Fourth, it discourages dependency and makes full use of available social resources, including community, firm, group and family. Fifth, funded social insurance schemes provide substantial financial resources which can be used for developmental purposes under state direction, notably through investment in social and physical infrastructure.

On the other hand, the East Asian experience as it is currently constituted has a large 'downside'. First, the heavy reliance on the welfare role of the family has serious implications for gender relations and the position of women. The model rests implicitly on a context in which women are the main carers within the family and therefore potentially imposes an extra load on top of their 'double burden' of housework and paid employment. Second, its welfare systems tend to reinforce socio-economic inequalities. If you are weak, vulnerable or poor, you are not only in trouble but even stigmatized for being so. Third, the lack of institutional integration until recently in these fragmented social insurance systems (notably in the three countries of North-East Asia) poses high efficiency costs in terms of management and co-ordination. Fourth, welfare policy has reflected the political logic of conservative dominance and/or authoritarian institutions and has been established and maintained on this basis. More generally, moreover, it is important to situate any comparative evaluations of welfare systems in the context of more precise meanings of 'cost' and 'welfare'. East Asian welfare systems may appear cheaper than their Western equivalents, but this judgement is usually measured in monetary terms and usually means cheaper for government. However, substantial financial resources are being expended by other agents in society (notably through social insurance contributions) and a substantial amount of the welfare services provided – in the household and community – are non-monetized costs. Moreover, what does welfare mean in different societies? For example, the options available to a person with disabilities in Britain or the USA, where a substantial network of state support exists, may be greater than in a welfare system where the only or main provider is the family and the state plays a residual role. The latter welfare systems may be cheaper, but are they producing less welfare, both in terms of quality and quantity? These weighty issues need more investigation.

Are East Asian welfare systems sustainable?

There are serious questions about the sustainability of the East Asian welfare model in the light of several fundamental trends. Though the extent to which these welfare systems have contributed to economic growth may be debatable since there are many other ingredients of successful economic performance in East Asia, their viability depended on the maintenance of high-growth economies with full or nearly full employment. If these conditions falter, as they have over recent years, first in Japan and then in Korea, there may be intolerable pressures on welfare provision. These welfare systems (including Japan until recently) have been built in 'young' or 'very young' societies and are threatened by the onset of rapid societal ageing and may be undermined to some extent by changes in family structures. By 2030 Taiwan, South Korea, Hong Kong and Singapore will have a higher proportion of citizens over 60 than the USA in 1990. In Singapore, the figure is estimated to increase from 8.5 per cent in 1990 to 29.4 per cent in 2030 (Caplen, 1995). While these welfare systems have been constructed within a matrix of authoritarian politics, the challenges of democratization (in South Korea and Taiwan since the late 1980s; in Hong Kong under Patten; in Japan after the end of the LDP monopoly) are changing these political parameters by giving space for new voices and creating greater pressures for more comprehensive welfare provision. There is also pressure for the state to play a more direct financial role rather than acting merely as a regulator, or to extend its range of direct provision from particular groups to all citizens. Finally, the current process of globalization exerts pressures on companies to 'downsize' domestically or to export jobs to maintain international competitiveness and on erstwhile *dirigiste* regimes to liberalize their commercial, financial and labour systems. These trends may be undermining the socio-economic and institutional conditions which have underpinned existing welfare systems. Let us briefly summarize our argument in this section. While they share certain common features, East Asian welfare systems are not homogeneous and one should be cautious about over-simplification; they have serious deficiencies as well as strong points; and they have relied heavily on distinctive social, demographic, political and economic conditions which may not be present elsewhere and are under threat in East Asia itself.

Is China's welfare system moving closer to those of its East Asian neighbours?

China's pre-reform, state socialist welfare system was very different from those of China's East Asian capitalist neighbours. The ideological basis of welfare, rooted in communist notions of class solidarity and decommodification, was clearly different, as was the institutional matrix of provision through public enterprises and rural collectives; and the range of benefits to the urban population at least was remarkably comprehensive. But these differences should not blind us to certain similarities. First, the welfare system played a handmaiden role in relation to a programme of rapid industrialization organized by a developmental state aiming at high levels of accumulation and unwilling to spend large amounts of funds on welfare benefits which were not directly productive. Second, formal welfare arrangements were focused on a small percentage of the population, mainly the key groups which were deemed important both developmentally and politically – industrial workers and technical, professional and administrative personnel. People outside these sectors of society, mainly the rural population, had to see to their own welfare needs, either through their families or their local communities. Third, as elsewhere in East Asia, welfare functioned as a tool whereby an authoritarian regime could reinforce its authority and control by winning support or at least securing acquiescence from strategic groups.

Now that China is moving towards a 'social market economy' and appears to be abandoning much of the form and substance of socialism, is the Chinese welfare system growing still closer to other East Asian patterns? In certain ways, it is. First, there is a clear preference for contribution-based, fund-managed social insurance systems for health and unemployment as well as pension insurance, as opposed to 'pay as you go' systems financed through taxation. Though the idea of a social security tax has been mooted by the Ministry of Finance, senior politicians regard it as unfeasible in current circumstances, not the least because of an apparently widespread aversion to increasing taxation among the general population. Thus there is a strong preference for the state to play the roles of regulator and manager, rather than direct fiscal provider.

Second, while there is much rhetoric about the citizenry in a socialist society, having a guaranteed right to basic forms of social welfare, the government is clearly unwilling to use large amounts of public money to provide these, rather preferring that individuals and households themselves play a greater role in welfare provision, either through contributions to government-managed schemes, purchase of commercial insurance or reliance on relatives to provide care for disabled or older people. More than other East Asian societies, where democratization is more advanced, the notion of citizenship in any sense of the term – civil, political or social – is empty in the Chinese context. To the extent that social goods and services are provided by the state, this is still officially perceived as the result of state benevolence rather than as a response to the legitimate demands and rights of citizens.

Third, as in other East Asian societies, there is a clear split between the two welfare spheres of social insurance and social assistance. Social insurance schemes have been given high policy priority because they are mainly linked with politically important urban groups. To this extent, the benefits provided by government-sponsored social insurance schemes are socially regressive; they tend to reinforce existing inequalities, as in other East Asian societies, notably in Japan, Korea and Taiwan. Chinese governments are reluctant to spend money on social services and material assistance which they perceive as politically and economically unproductive, such as aid to poor people or vulnerable groups such as the older people, orphaned or abandoned children and people with disabilities. Over recent years there has been a tendency toward official acceptance, if not sponsorship, of the notion that people should not be dependent on the state, with an implicit stigmatization of this kind of welfare recipient as potentially parasitic and feckless. The similarities to welfare ideology elsewhere in East Asia are clear. Fourth, there has been a growing but still circumscribed recognition of the role of market agencies, such as insurance companies, in the provision of welfare in a direction comparable with their role in other East Asian societies.

Whilst these similarities are increasingly in evidence, there are also some significant differences rooted in recent Chinese history and contemporary political realities. First, one can expect there to be significant local/regional variations in emergent new welfare systems in China, depending on variations in the political, social, economic and demographic profiles of specific areas. Second, the potential welfare role of intermediate civil society organizations such as NGOs has not received adequate recognition or been allowed adequate operational scope and, in this respect there is a marked contrast with other parts of East Asia, particularly Hong Kong which relies heavily on this sector of provision. Given the reluctance of governments to spend fiscal resources on social assistance to vulnerable groups, however, there are growing incentives for them to allow greater scope for welfare NGOs of various kinds, both domestic and international. Third, though there has been much talk about expanding the welfare role of urban communities, with approving glances towards the Japanese experience, the urban community – rooted in the neighbourhood offices and residents committees – is still very much dominated by government and rests on a weak financial basis which is being undermined by the rapid commercialization of the urban economy.

To the extent that there is some degree of convergence in the welfare area, it reflects wider similarities in general development strategy and a growing integration of an increasingly commercialized Chinese economy with the rest of East Asia. This has been reinforced by the fact that Chinese welfare reformers have sought to draw on East Asian welfare experience in designing new systems. For example, developmentalist statists have found the Singapore experience based on a Central Provident Fund congenial to their aspirations. Both reformists and developmentalists have condemned Western welfare models as wasteful and inefficient, in ways redolent of Singapore's Lee Kuan Yew and conservative spokesmen in Japan, Taiwan and South Korea. Overall, this means movement towards certain familiar features of other East Asian welfare systems, but within limits set by China's immense size and diversity and the particular political and institutional heritage of state socialism. Welfare reformers of all hues agree that no particular foreign model fits the Chinese situation exactly and any new system must represent particular Chinese conditions and be distinctively Chinese. However, China is a complex and changing society in which notions of what is Chinese are themselves diverse, contested and fluid. The exact meaning of a post-transitional welfare system 'with Chinese characteristics' is still to be worked out.

References

Anderson, S. (1993) *Welfare Policy and Politics in Japan: Beyond the Developmental State*, New York, Paragon House.

Asher, M. (1983) 'Planning for the future: the welfare system in a new phase of development' in Rodan, G. (ed.) *Singapore Changes Guard: Social, Political and Economic Directions in the 1990s*, Cheshire, Longman.

Barr, N. (ed.) (1994) *Labour Markets and Social Policy in Central and Eastern Europe: The Transition and Beyond*, Oxford, Oxford University Press.

Campbell, J. (1992) *Policy Change: The Japanese Government and the Elderly*, Princeton, Princeton University Press.

Caplen, B. (1996) 'Working welfare?', *Demos Quarterly*, no.6, pp.31–3.

Castles, F. G. (1996) 'Needs-based strategies of social protection in Australia and New Zealand' in Esping-Andersen, G. (ed.) pp.88–116.

Deacon, R. *et al.* (eds) (1992) *The New Eastern Europe: Social Policy Past, Present and Future*, London, Sage.

Department of Health, Republic of China (1994) *Toward the Goal of Health for All: A Health White Paper*, Taipei, Republic of China.

Director of Social Welfare (1996) *Departmental Report 1993–1995*, Hong Kong, Hong Kong Government.

Dixon, J. (1981) *The Chinese Welfare System 1949–1979*, New York, Praeger.

Esping-Andersen, G. (1990) *The Three Worlds of Welfare Capitalism*, Princeton, Princeton University Press.

Esping-Anderson, G. (1996) *Welfare States in Transition: National Adaptation in Global Economies*, London, Sage.

Goodman, R. (1997) 'The delivery of personal social services and the "Japanese-style welfare state"' in White, G. and Shang, X. (eds) *Reforms in Chinese Social Assistance and Community Services in Comparative Perspective*, Brighton, Institute of Development Studies, pp.109–18.

Goodman, R., White, G. and Kwon, H.J. (eds) (1998) *Welfare Orientalism: Social Policy in East Asia*, London, Routledge.

Hodge, P. (1981) 'The politics of welfare' in Jones, J. (ed.) *The Common Welfare: Hong Kong's Social Services*, Manila, United Nations Social Welfare and Development Centre for Asia and the Pacific.

Hong Kong Government (1995) *Annual Digest of Statistics*, Hong Kong, Hong Kong Government.

Hong Kong Census Department (1992) *Hong Kong 1991 Population Census*, Hong Kong Government.

Hong Kong Government (1996) *The Five Year Plan for Social Welfare Development in Hong Kong – Review 1995*, Hong Kong, Hong Kong Government.

Hoshino, S. (1988) 'Perspective of the Japanese' in Robert and Morris (eds) *Testing the Limits of Social Welfare: International Perspectives on Policy Changes in Nine Countries*, Hanover, Brandin University Press.

International Financial Statistical Yearbook (1995) Washington DC, IMF.

Iwabuchi, K. (1994) 'Social security today and tomorrow', *Economic Eye*, vol.15, no.2, pp.2–4.

Japan Statistical Yearbook (1995) Tokyo, Japanese Government.

Kato, J. (1994) *The Problem of Bureaucratic Rationality: Tax Politics in Japan*, Princeton, Princeton University Press.

Korean Government (1994) *Statistical Yearbook*, Seoul, Government of the Republic of Korea.

Korean Government (1996) *Statistical Yearbook*, Seoul, Government Publishing Office.

Ku, Y. (1995) *Welfare Capitalism in Taiwan: State, Economy and Social Policy 1895–1990*, Ph.D. Thesis, Manchester, University of Manchester.

Lawson, S. (1998) 'The culture of politics' in Maidment, R. and Mackerras, C. (eds) *Culture and Society in the Asia-Pacific*, London, Routledge in association with The Open University.

Macpherson, S. (1993) 'Social security in Hong Kong', *Social Policy and Administration*, vol.27, no.1, pp.50–7.

Ministry of Health and Welfare (1995) *Annual Report on Health and Welfare 1993–1994*, Tokyo, Ministry of Health and Welfare.

Ooi, G.L. (1993) 'The Housing and Development Board's ethnic integration policy' in Ooi, G.L., Siddique, S. and Cheng, S.K. (eds) *The Management of Ethnic Relations in Public Housing*, Institute of Policy Studies, Time Academic Press.

Perera, A. (1992) *Authoritarian State Capitalism and Late Industrialization: The Case of Singapore*, unpublished M.Phil. Dissertation, Oxford, University of Oxford.

Republic of China (1994) *Statistical Yearbook*, Taipei, Council for Economic Planning and Development.

Said, E. (1985) *Orientalism*, Penguin, Harmondsworth.

Singapore Government (1995) *Yearbook of Statistics*, Singapore, Singapore Government.

Skocpol, T. (1994) *Social Policy in the United States: Future Possibilities in Historical Perspective*, Princeton, Princeton University Press.

So Sang-Mok *et al.* (1981) *The Situation of Poverty and Policies for the Poor*, Seoul, Korean Development Institute.

Tremewan, C. (1998) 'Welfare and governance: public housing under Singapore's party-state' in Goodman, R., White, G. and Kwon, H. (eds).

Tyabji, A. (1993) 'Social security in the Asian-Pacific region', *Asian-Pacific Economic Literature*, vol.7, no.1, pp.53–72.

United Nations Development Programme (1997) *Human Development Report 1997*, New York, Oxford University Press.

Further reading

Ehtisham, A., Dreze, J. and Sen, A. (eds) (1991) *Social Security in Developing Countries*, Oxford, Clarendon Press.
A standard work on welfare systems in developing societies, with case-studies of South Asia, China, Latin America and Sub-Saharan Africa.

Esping-Anderson, G. (ed.) (1996) *Welfare States in Transition: National Adaptation in Global Economies*, London, Sage.
A review of the ways in which national systems of social welfare are changing in the response to economic globalization, with a wide range of regional case-studies.

Goodman, R., White, G. and Kwon, H-J. (eds) (1998) *The East Asian Welfare Model: Welfare Orientalism and the State*, London, Routledge.
A comparative review of welfare systems in East Asia, with particular emphasis on politics and the role of the state, with case-studies of recent developments in the welfare policies of individual countries (South Korea, Japan, Taiwan, Hong Kong, China and Singapore).

Leung, C.B. and Nann, R.C. (1995) *Authority and Benevolence: Social Welfare in China*, Hong Kong, Chinese University Press.
An overall perspective on changes in the Chinese welfare system. A broad-ranging comparative review which contains a case-study of Hong Kong.

Skocpol, T. (1995) *Social Policy in the United States: Future Possibilities in Historical Perspective*, Princeton, Princeton University Press.

CHAPTER 10

Environmental politics and policies in the Asia-Pacific

Rowland Maddock

10.1 Introduction

In September 1997 smog from forest fires burning in the islands of Indonesia blanketed large areas of South-East Asia. At one time the fires, which raged across more than 1.5 million acres of forests, affected up to 70 million people in six countries. The consequences for the region ranged from mild inconvenience to economic catastrophe and long-term health hazards. The most immediate impact was the effect on South-East Asian tourism; for a brief period business dropped by over 90 per cent in some tourist areas. Airports closed and flights were cancelled and production of some foodstuffs was forecast to fall. The largest cost however may well be to long-term health with an increase in the incidence of respiratory diseases and cancer. Exceptionally large scale, the 1997 catastrophe was in fact a repeat of past forest fires in Indonesia. Many of the fires ignited accidentally, but a long period of drought had increased the vulnerability of the forests to accidental conflagration. Indifferent management of forest resources by the Indonesian state and by international logging companies had left brushwood and commercially valueless trees strewn on the forest floor which acted as tinder in the long hot months.

The role of human agency was more than merely indifference. The Indonesian state, despite claiming ownership of the forest areas, either could not or would not provide the resources to monitor the activities of the logging companies. Thus what was nominally common property was transformed into an open access resource where no-one had an incentive or was required to take responsibility for the proper management of the forests. Many fires were started deliberately by logging companies and by small-scale slash and burn cultivators. For the logging companies the decision to burn and clear the land reflects the inefficient pricing of environmental resources in Indonesia, as indeed is the case elsewhere. In societies where value is monetized, resources which are not priced have no value. From the perspective of profit-seeking companies it is entirely rational to avoid spending money on conservation which, to them, has no value. Proper land management is expensive, burning valueless trees is

At the height of the smog, Jambi, Indonesia, October 1997

cheap. For the slash and burn farmers, burning is a traditional method of clearing the land prior to preparation for cultivation. However, over a number of decades the population in Sumatra, Kalimantan and some of the other inner Indonesian islands had increased beyond sustainable levels. To manage population pressures and facilitate development in the inner islands, particularly Java, the Indonesian government sanctioned trans-migration to the outer islands. Farming techniques which were sustainable with a small population ceased to be so when numbers increased beyond the forest's carrying capacity. The careless exploitation of the forests reflects the failure to account for ecological capital in national accounting systems. Unlike its man-made equivalent the destruction of environmental capital is often seen as a benefit to the society where it occurs, but the costs are largely neglected. So an apparently rational cost-benefit calculation of development strategies gives distorted signals to even the most environmentally conscious developer or government official.

The fires reveal who in Indonesian society benefits from modern development and who loses. The beneficiaries are the political elites, members of the government and the bureaucracy who allocate logging concessions and who are often directly or indirectly implicated with national and international logging companies. The losers are indigenous people who lack access to political power (see **Young *et al.*, 1998, pp.303–32**). The fires illustrate, as do few other examples of environmental degradation, the cliché that the environment recognizes no political boundaries. In an interdependent world where conventional notions of sovereignty cannot stand up to critical scrutiny, environmental degradation is increasingly transboundary in origin and in consequence, beyond the capacity of one country to manage.

This chapter examines the issues introduced in the opening paragraphs and is divided into six sections. Section 10.2 describes the major environmental problems faced by the Asia-Pacific countries. Section 10.3 explores the social and structural origins of environmental degradation in the region and is followed by a more detailed investigation of one of the main causes of degradation, population pressure, in Section 10.4. Section 10.5 looks at different forms of national environmental governance, while Section 10.6 looks at international governance and environmental questions and 10.7 looks briefly at non-governmental organizations and grass roots resistance to environmental change.

10.2   Environmental problems in the Asia-Pacific

The Asia-Pacific is not a homogenous ecological region, weather, geography, vegetation and settlement patterns vary enormously. There is little in common between cold, largely empty Alaska and hot, humid and crowded Java, or between small and poor Vanuatu and the wealthy USA or populous China. Some countries are capitalist with an unshakeable belief in the efficiency and equity of the market; others remain, at least nominally, socialist. There is no single paradigm which can encompass such variety. Nevertheless this chapter is informed by a perspective that sees environmental outcomes as reflecting a complex interconnection of structure and agency. The dominant structure is international capitalism with its particular array of values, institutions and processes which favour some at the expense of others. Some agents have easy access to power, others are effectively excluded. Power in this instance is the degree to which an actor is able to control its relationship, and that of other actors, with nature. Power is therefore contextual, though clearly some actors have consistently more power than others. Some countries are more powerful than others, for example, the USA as compared to Tuvalu. Some institutions are more powerful than others – multinational logging companies compared with slash and burn farmers. The values and norms of powerful agents carry more weight in national and international environmental politics than those of the marginal and the vulnerable. As a consequence profit is often more important than conservation.

Ecological political economy, the degradation and regeneration of nature, connects four different spatial levels: the local, the national, the regional and the global. Environmental change in the Asia-Pacific is the outcome of a political economy shaped by structures which are global in scope, and by a rich array of local, national and regional geographies, histories and cultures. For example the potential flooding of the small South Sea islands owes little to the preferences and policies of the islanders themselves. The increase in the level of the oceans, if and when it occurs, will be a consequence of climate change brought about by global rather than local circumstances. The response to that catastrophe, if and when it occurs, does give some leeway to local politics. In the Solomon Islands English and French speaking political parties have different priorities on the development/environmental trade-off, but national parties, however committed, have a negligible direct impact on the ultimate outcome. Their influence is limited to the degree to which they are effective in persuading more powerful actors to establish an international regime to reduce the emissions of global warming gases. The USA on the other hand is economically and politically so dominant that the balance of national and international cause and effect is quite different. Moreover although the excessive rate of deforestation in the Solomon Islands is critical to the well being of its citizens, the consequences for the region are minimal. For a large country such as China its environmental outcomes have consequences which far transcend the national.

In South-East Asia the destruction of natural resources has assumed such proportions that in few other regions of the world are the imperatives of economic growth and environmental degradation on such a direct collision course. High population growth, and poor resource management associated with weak ecological protection have undermined the physical basis of many important activities to the point where they threaten irreversible change in the region's economic and ecological resources. In some developing countries environmental degradation is associated with rapid development and rising per capita incomes. In others it is the consequence of extreme poverty sometimes, as in the case of Cambodia, aggravated by war. In the rich, diversified and developed countries environmental problems though far from negligible do not pose the same threat to security and material well being. Indeed in the USA, Japan, Australia and Canada many domestic environmental indices are improving. Emissions of sulphur dioxide have fallen in all countries and in Japan emissions of nitrous oxide as well. Many water quality indices are improving. In the USA after two centuries of almost continuous decline the area covered by forests stabilized in the early 1990s.

In many areas pollution of the atmosphere, of rivers and the disposal of human and industrial waste has increased to crisis proportions. In East Asia while the economies were growing by 100 per cent every ten years or so, pollution was increasing by a factor of eight to ten. *The Chinese Daily* recently reported that five of the world's ten most polluted cities are Chinese and are becoming worse (*Environmental Digest*, 1995a, p.12). In 1996 respiratory disease was the main cause of death in China's rural areas. Thailand's export oriented development has led to a rapid rise in environmentally destructive and hazardous waste generating industries with a shift from biodegradable residuals to more complex and poisonous pollutants. In Japan pollution levels in large metropolitan areas such as Tokyo and Osaka are unsatisfactory. Dioxin levels from some Japanese incinerators exceed the limit set by government, and are becoming an issue of much concern. Taiwan's landscape has been seriously transformed by economic growth, air quality, soil contamination and radiation leaks are serious problems. The South Korean environment also has serious problems in terms of per capita carbon dioxide emissions and waste disposal. Japan has an acute, and South Korea a growing, problem with the operation of nuclear power plants and the disposal and transport of nuclear waste. Japan's nuclear industry suffered a series of major setbacks with a leak of sodium coolant in the Monjou fast breeder reactor in 1995 and a fire at the Tokaimura reactor in 1997. Botched attempts to conceal the extent of the damage, along with other disclosures of flawed practices, have seriously undermined confidence in the nuclear industry. Nuclear issues are not however limited to the major powers. Recently the government of the Marshall Islands commissioned a US company to conduct a study on the feasibility of establishing a nuclear dump on the island.

In China over 90 per cent of urban ground water and 25 per cent of fresh water is contaminated. Water pollution is a problem for both South Korea and Taiwan, and Tokyo Bay has been declared biologically dead. Water pollution is partly the result of inadequate investment in urban and rural waste disposal services, but also the consequence of high rates of deforestation experienced throughout the region. Tropical deforestation in South-East Asia threatens to destroy in a few decades the ecological legacy of millennia. Comparative data published by the FAO show the rate of deforestation to be particularly rapid in Asia and the Pacific. In Indonesia 50 per cent more logs are cut than is sustainable. In Cambodia the forest cover has decreased from 74 per cent of the land area in 1974 to less than 35 per cent in 1997. In Vietnam deforestation (and illegal poaching) is doing more to destroy the nation's wildlife than 50 years of war. In the Solomon Islands the rate of extraction has trebled in the past few years. The current rate of deforestation so exceeds the long term sustainable rate that the island's forest resources cannot last much beyond 2000. In El Salvador the forest cover has been reduced to only 2 per cent of the land area.

Table 10.1 *Forest cover and annual deforestation by region*

Region	Forest cover (1990)	Annual deforestation (1981–90)	
	million hectares	million hectares	per cent
Asia and the Pacific	310.6	3.9	1.2
Latin America and the Caribbean	918.1	7.4	0.8
Africa	527.6	4.1	0.7
Total	1,756.3	15.4	0.8

Source: Brown (1995, p.116)

For small South Sea Islands, some of which also suffer from unsustainable rates of deforestation, the major environmental concern is flooding and a rise in the level of the oceans due to the predicted global climate change. For the islanders the cause of the potential catastrophe is not of their own making nor is the solution in their own hands.

As well as specific national problems there are regional concerns, some of which are due exclusively to poor resource management within the region while others are due as much to economic activity and political decisions further afield. The South China fisheries have been described as calamitous, and South-East Asia's seas in general are almost exhausted of fish stocks. Industrial waste is dumped into offshore seas with little concerns for marine pollution. The Asia-Pacific countries are also major contributors to global warming. The USA, China, Japan, South Korea, Canada and Australia between them account for almost 50 per cent of global warming gases. Although still in the realm of conjecture, projections of the climatic consequences of global climate change identify South-East Asia and the South Sea Islands as amongst the most vulnerable regions. Some small islands may completely disappear. Populous estuaries could be flooded, others polluted by intrusion of salt water. Tropical storms may increase in incidence and destructiveness.

10.3   Causes of environmental degradation in the Asia-Pacific

The environment is often described as a 'soft issue'; one to which people and governments pay lip service but is too easily discarded when the traditional concerns of wealth, status and security intrude. Its perceived value varies between communities and countries in the region. In many indigenous Third World communities nature has great social and religious as well as economic meaning, but most people view the environment as instrumental. It is a resource which adds to the quality of life. So when faced with a choice between development and conservation, people and governments seldom choose the latter. Some World Bank economists argue that the relationship between the degradation of environmental resources are correlated with the level of economic development and the growth of per capita income. Initially, as countries grow richer the environment deteriorates but, after a certain level of income has been reached, any further increase is associated with an improvement in the environment. In an independent study Grossman and Krueger (1994) estimate that the turning point occurs when the per capita income level is around US$8,000 to US$10,000 p.a. Levels of environmental stress are of course high in absolute terms but the trend is beneficial. Although the precise relationship varies according to local circumstances (in any given country), it does direct attention to the importance of income, in this instance as an index of development, on environmental outcomes. The Pacific nations can be divided into two groups: those with a per capita income above, and those with a per capita income below, the crucial turning point. In the first group are the USA, Canada, Japan, Australia and Singapore, and rather more marginally Taiwan and South Korea. All the other Asia-Pacific countries are in the second group. For the small group of developed nations environmental outcomes are the consequence of wealth and affluence, for the second group they are the consequence of poverty and, crucially, efforts to escape from that poverty.

Rush hour on the Ratcha–Pararop road, Bangkok, 1995

There are good reasons why national environments eventually improve as income increases. High incomes tend to be associated with, and usually are the consequence of, easy access to advanced technologies. Many technologies such as catalytic converters in road vehicles or denitrification equipment in power stations reduce environment/output ratios but are expensive to develop and install. Rich countries with healthy surpluses above subsistence levels can afford to invest in such technologies. Rich people have a varied and sophisticated array of tastes and preferences. After a certain level of income has been reached additional material goods yield diminishing returns. Non-material goods on the other hand, like an improved environment, become more highly valued. Moreover, those who are better off have the time, energy and the organizational skills to bring political pressure on governments which often respond slowly to changing values. Other than a small number of resource rich countries, high income levels tend to be associated with relatively decentralized market systems which despite their many shortcomings are more environmentally benign than centrally directed systems. High income and advanced technologies are not entirely environmentally benign of course. Both encourage and facilitate consumption of, access to, and therefore production of, an increasingly wide range of raw materials and manufactured goods.

Moreover macro data show that rich societies consume a disproportionate share of the world's environmental resources. Nevertheless although for every rich country the relationship between income, level of development and environmental outcome differs, the basic relationship between the two does seem to hold.

Japan's per capita income is over US$21,000 p.a. Since its first air pollution laws in 1962 its domestic environmental regime has become one of the strictest in the world. As early as 1966 MITI financed a large-scale project to develop efficient desulphurization technologies and both the state and private industry have invested heavily in pollution abating technologies. Flue gas desulphurization has been progressively installed in all large emission units since the early 1970s since when emissions have steadily fallen. Japanese firms on average allocate up to 14 per cent of industrial investment to pollution control and at one time accounted for 75 per cent of the world's installed desulphurization and denitrification capacity. Japan accounts for 15 per cent of the world's GNP but emits less than 5 per cent of the world's emissions of carbon dioxide. South Korea, which is on the cusp of the income/environment turning point, has a far less developed environmental regime. Only 0.5 per cent of South Korean GNP is allocated for environmental improvement. However even in South Korea priorities are changing. In 1994 the Ministry of the Environment's budget accounted for 0.09 per cent of the national budget, by 1995 this had increased to 1.35 per cent.

If social forces and political pressures are brought to bear, rich countries can mobilize sufficient economic and technological resources to effect dramatic improvements in local and national environments. Countries in the second group cannot afford, as they see it, the luxury of foregoing increased living standards today for uncertain environmental benefits tomorrow. It is unlikely that relationships between income and environment concerns will remain unchanged. Less developed countries can access more advanced technologies than income levels alone might warrant. International institutions and non-government organizations facilitate the spread of new values and norms, and late comers can learn from and avoid the mistakes of early developers. Nevertheless development and income levels do matter. Poor people discount the long-term future. Environmental sustainability requires the sacrifice of current consumption for future rewards, and for poor people and poor countries the present is all important. It is all very well for the government and citizens of Cambodia to be told that current rates of forest depletion cannot be sustained beyond the early decades of the next century. That is in the future. Meanwhile with a very low per capita income the present needs of a materially poor people have a high immediate priority. Less developed countries choose to allocate such resources as are available to investment or consumption to stimulate development and alleviate poverty. Waste disposal facilities or desulphurization scrubbers are expensive, do not add directly to growth or exports and are therefore low in the priorities of key elites and government bureaucracies. When development and environmental protection conflicts, employment, income, foreign currency dealing and consumption normally take priority. The views of elites in the developing world who understand the choice between development and environmental protection in stark zero sum terms are summarized by Fidel Ramos the Philippines President. At a recent regional environment conference he argued that 'it would be a terrible irony if the agreement [to take action to reduce emissions of greenhouse gases] would freeze the Third World in a state of underdevelopment' (*Environmental Digest*, 1995b, p.8). Although his remarks were directed towards a specific issue over which the South-East Asian nations themselves have little control, they reflect a strong belief that the prominence of environmental issues on so many of the world's agendas is a hurdle deliberately foisted on the developing world, by the developed countries, to reduce international competition. One senior Chinese official has recently argued that pollution is no threat to the world's environment, but is merely rumour and sensationalism designed to maintain existing Western monopoly of resources (*Environmental Digest*, 1997, p.16). Given such beliefs governments easily justify prioritizing development over the environment.

10.4 Population, development and the environment

Historically poverty is positively correlated with high rates of population growth. For some this is the most important of all environmentally destructive trends (see **Hull, 1998, pp.39–64**). In some Asia-Pacific countries the outstanding problem is a large current population, in others it is rapid growth in population. The four most populous countries in the region China, Indonesia, Vietnam and Mexico together have a combined population of almost 1.5 billion people. Although, with the exception of Vietnam, population growth has been reduced below 2 per cent per annum, in the next ten years over 100 million more people will be added in these countries. In other countries the greatest threat is population growth. In the Solomon Islands population is currently increasing at a rate of 3.3 per cent per annum, which will double the number of people by 2015. At the same time it is predicted that the country's forests will be exhausted by then. But a crude focus on demographic trends without analysis of why and where they occur misses the political issues to which they are inextricably linked.

Theory and evidence show there is no intrinsic need for population growth to destroy the environment. The interconnection between population, development and environmental outcomes depends critically on the social structure within which it occurs. When, as in most developing countries, these are inequitable and coercive then population growth is destructive of the environment. In many South-East Asian countries population pressures on fragile ecosystems are associated with the appropriation of land from indigenous communities by elites pursuing economic development and trying to avoid the political costs of agricultural reform. Sustainable agricultural practices have been undermined by government sponsored internal migrations which have overturned traditional common property regimes. Population pressures cannot be divorced from the key issue of who benefits and who loses. Moreover even when environmental destruction is located in poor developing countries, the real catalyst is elsewhere, rich consumers with real economic power in developed countries, often linked to local elites through transnational corporations. Aggregate data show that a comparatively small number of rich northern consumers are considerably more environmentally destructive than the much larger number of poor southern people. This is not to deny the very real problems that exist in many countries, the analysis of and solution to which however is as much political as it is demographic.

In many Asia-Pacific countries infrastructural investments, such as dams, destroy environmental capital. Countries have sought to harness their water resources for flood control and irrigation. China has an ambitious dam building programme, the largest of which, the Three Gorges Dam will, when complete, form an artificial lake 600 kilometres long. Thailand, Laos, Cambodia and Vietnam have recently revived the long dormant Mekong River Commission to harness the Mekong by building a series of dams throughout its length. Laos alone plans to build 58 dams on its stretch of the river by 2020. Dam building, usually financed by foreign capital, not only destroys forests and productive agricultural land but requires the forcible removal of large numbers of local people. In Malaysia the Bakun Dam will flood an estimated 700 million square miles of rainforest and require the relocation of nine to ten thousand tribal people. In China the Three Gorges project may displace between one and one and a half million people. Almost invariably resettled people are worse off after forcible migration. 280,000 people were forcibly moved in China to facilitate the Sanmexia Dam, over 50 per cent of whom remain in dire poverty.

The adverse effects of development, poverty and population pressures are aggravated by environmentally faulty economic policies and poor management. Markets cannot efficiently price open access environmental resources because property rights cannot be allocated or made effective. In a world where price determines value the environment has no price and therefore no value. Environmental resources will tend to be mismanaged. Some countries, such as the USA, have sought to overcome this by artificially creating markets in environmental resources. In the poorer countries, where markets are less effective, politically sanctioned pricing decisions are environmentally destructive. In China and Vietnam socialist prices do not signal scarcity in the environment. Producers and consumers have no knowledge of the environmental costs of their decisions and no incentive to economize in the use of scarce environmental resources. Even in nominally capitalist countries governments pursue pricing policies which invite unsustainable exploitation of ecological resources. In Indonesia the rental which international logging companies pay the state, known as stumpage, is well below the true commercial value of cutting, transporting, treating and replanting trees. Tax, royalties, concessions and subsidies so distort the real price that profit-seeking logging companies have no incentive to husband timber resources. Species which are not valuable to the company but are none the less 'free' are cut without compunction to expedite access to and transport of the species which do have value. In some areas up to 40 per cent of the forest may be destroyed to access the 10 per cent of commercially valuable species. It is estimated that the Indonesian government undercharges foreign firms by around US$500 million, each year for logging rights. However even market efficient prices fail to internalize the non commercial benefits which forests provide. These range from stabilizing water tables and preventing soil erosion to undervaluing non-timber forest products. Nuts, berries and genetic material for the world's medical, pharmaceutical and beauty industries are only beginning to be exploited for the real values they embody. It has been estimated that the value to society of yet undiscovered drugs from species in tropical forests could amount to US$147 billion. A truly efficient valuing system would not only transform cost-benefit calculations, and therefore the pace and pattern of economic development, but also the pattern of winners and losers in the development process.

Poor pricing policies are aggravated by equally faulty management decisions. Determined to maintain ultimate sovereignty over the nation's resources, governments grant logging rights to private companies for a limited period of time, typically 20 to 25 years. While this meets the government's sovereignty objective the period is shorter than the time replanted trees take to reach maturity. Logging companies have no incentive to finance expensive replanting programmes from which other companies might benefit. In Indonesia replanting is less than one-third of current logging rates.

Technical pricing and management decisions are not independent from the dominant economic and political interests of developing countries. Financial profit is conducive to attaining and maintaining political power, which in turn facilitates access to profit making opportunities. A key issue in environmental politics is that of property rights, who owns or has the right to determine how specific resources are utilized. For some environmental resources it is difficult to allocate ownership rights. Other resources such as closed forests are vested in the state which claims the right to manage them for and on behalf of the people. There are however always competing demands on such resources. On the one hand, rapid exploitation of forest, mineral or energy resources generate profits and in its wake political power for particular elite groups. The incentive is to use the resources as rapidly as possible. On the other hand, indigenous peoples who draw their economic livelihoods as well as social, cultural and religious meaning from forests or other well defined ecosystems, have every reason to manage them in a quite different manner, one which is environmentally sustainable. Partly because of social norms, but also because of appropriate technologies indigenous forest dwellers have good reason to ensure that trees remain standing. It is not necessary to idealize the ways of life of hunter-gatherers or slash and burn farmers to appreciate that there are two conflicting concepts of how best to use the forests. Thus who is given the legal right to use the resources has a significant impact on how they will be used. This is necessarily a political decision. Governments of developing states are not on the whole sympathetic to indigenous people who they regard as standing in the way of progress, and who they often argue are the major environmental villains. They are inclined to reject customary land rights which cannot be documented in favour of commercial exploitation which generates government revenue, facilitates modernization, provides political resources for the state and profits for elite groups. In 1994 the Malaysian state of Sarawak announced that it was taking over large tracts of land in the Borneo rainforest and making them available for logging. In theory native rights are protected, but formal titles to land have been issued to only 10 per cent of the affected land.

10.5   Environment policy and the national governance of the environment

This interpenetration of commercial and economic interests makes it difficult for decision makers, with the best will in the world, to distinguish between their own interests and those of the nation they claim to represent. In some developing countries the state is often decisive in the resource allocation process. It decides upon the relative priority of security, development and participation objectives. It determines the appropriate development model and adjudicates between competing economic and political demands. It is the state, through various political and bureaucratic bodies, which allocates logging, drilling or mining concessions. Yet despite its overweening presence the state in many countries is weak and cannot free itself from the influence of strong sectional interests. Development is distorted because of the interests of such groups. In some countries the process is overt and blatant, in others more subtle and circumspect. Even in nominally democratic countries such as the Philippines the political system and therefore economic and ecological outcomes have been dominated by the landed oligarchy.

Ideology makes little difference to the degree to which national environments are degraded. Governments in socialist states such as China and Vietnam have assumed a direct and largely destructive role in their respective countries' environmental decline. Elsewhere weak democratic accountability covers covert or open corruption. Global Witness, a western environmental group, claims to possess evidence that the Cambodian government is heavily implicated in the illegal export of that country's forests. In Thailand members of parliament and senior officials in the Royal Forest Department and the state owned Forest Industrial Organization have been involved in a number of land scams. Politics and personal enrichment so intrude into environmental governance, that some states are facilitating the degradation of their own environments for purposes which are intrinsically uneconomic and which inhibit rather than stimulate true development.

All countries now have in place environmental laws and regulations, monitoring programmes and penalties for transgressors. In some Asia-Pacific countries such as Japan and Australia government leadership is decisive. But even in countries traditionally hostile to environmental concerns governments are coming under pressure from domestic and international, inter-governmental and non-governmental organizations, and are being obliged to modify their historical indifference to national environmental destruction. Papua New Guinea and Vanuatu have banned the export of logs. The Indonesian government aims to decrease its timber harvest by 33 per cent by the end of the century. As a result environmental groups have recently changed their traditional policy of confrontation with the government to a more conciliatory one of working with it, citing a more sympathetic approach and a better appreciation of environmental concerns. In the Philippines post-Marcos governments have been more sympathetic to environmental NGOs, and in consequence these have become more vocal and effective. China plans to increase forest cover from 14 per cent to 20 per cent in the next 50 years or so and the government has forcibly closed nearly 50,000 small factories which were said to be responsible for major pollution.

Despite real progress in environmental learning it is still all too easy for environmental programmes to be overturned. The election of a new government in the Solomon Islands resulted in a more aggressive approach to resource exploitation. Taxes on log exports were halved, a previously announced policy to ban the export of logs from 1997 was rescinded and the government's own environmental monitoring agency shut down. Moreover if indeed environmental concern is negatively correlated with material well-being, economic and financial turmoil as experienced by the Asia-Pacific countries in 1997 and 1998 cannot but re-enforce short-term development horizons to the detriment of environmental sustainability. Many, though not all, environmental resources are 'public goods'. In formal economic theory public goods have strict and well defined properties but they can for present purposes be usefully described as resources to which no-one can claim effective sovereignty. It is for instance not possible, short of war, to prevent citizens or firms in one country using the column of air which extends upwards over another's territory. The same is true of many water resources. Individual consumers, farmers and businesses who seek to minimize the costs of production and consumption perceive such resources as free. They cannot be charged for using them as sinks for the disposal of the unwelcome by-products of modern economies. The costs to business of allowing noxious gases to escape into the atmosphere is low compared with the costs incurred to install technology to treat the gases before they are released into the atmosphere. For much the same reasons it is easier and cheaper for farmers to allow pesticides to run off into nearby streams. Individuals who do not have to account for their own actions easily dismiss as unimportant their small but cumulative pollution of local environments, either the costs of clean up can be left to a higher and more distant authority or the resource can be allowed to degrade. Many users of public goods 'free ride', for they are not obliged to confront the environmental consequences of their decisions and actions.

Carrying toxic waste, Mindanao Island, Philippines, 1994

The incentive to 'leave it to others' is re-enforced by an awareness that one consumer or farmer or firm will almost certainly make an insignificant contribution to environmental destruction, and by the same token to environmental regeneration. Even if a rational decision maker is environmentally aware and concerned there remain powerful incentives not to internalize the environmental consequences of actions because the environmental benefits will be minimal while the economic or other costs could be great. The cost benefit calculus is, for most decision makers, environmentally disadvantageous. This cannot be true for the collective however. If the environment is perceived to be free for each individual it is most certainly not so for society as a whole. It is difficult to estimate the true costs of environmental destruction for most countries, although for China they have been estimated at 10 per cent to 15 per cent of national income (Homer-Dixon, 1994).

In most Third World Asia-Pacific countries traditional land and resource rights are based on communal ownership which is often embodied in small-scale self-help common property regimes to manage local environmental resources. For example, in the Indonesian *adat* land rights system, land is regarded as the common property of the community and can not be bought, sold or leased. In the Philippines the *zanjera* irrigation communities were highly labour intensive property systems which gave a central role to small scale communities of irrigators to determine their own rules, choose their own officials, guard their own systems and maintain their own canals. At one time over 600 such regimes existed in the Philippines. Modernization, the intrusion of the developmental state and transnational capital have seriously undermined such common property organizations especially where their historical rights to their lands and resources are challenged by cosmopolitan loggers and mining companies.

Governments, which are notionally the embodiment of collective values and interests within nation-states, are the agents which internalize the environmental costs external to the individual producer or consumer. But in a wider geographical space countries also free ride, where possible, passing on to others the costs of development and modernization. In the Asia-Pacific region there are numerous examples of countries exporting their environmental costs to their neighbours. The mechanics of this transboundary exchange can be quite varied. Vietnam is concerned that Thailand draws excessive amounts of water from the Mekong in the dry season. Smoke from forest fires in Indonesia harms health, ecology and the economies of Malaysia, Singapore, the Philippines and other countries in the region. Up to 65 per cent of acid rain deposits on Japanese soil originate from China and South Korea. Japanese and Korean investment in heavy industries in East Asia, pollute other countries in their host environments. Overfishing in the South China Seas by fishermen from a number of countries reduces fishing stocks for all. Although the structural characteristics may be similar, the domestic and international politics of each case is quite different.

Although far from sovereign, and in many respects environmentally dysfunctional, states are the critical environmental actors. Domestically states are both the site of social competition and the embodiment of national values and preferences. They are juridically sovereign, but states are seldom coterminous with organic bio-regions which embody ecological rationality. They are simultaneously too large and too small. Bureaucrats are usually distant from the consequences of political decisions taken in national or regional capital cities. Urban elites have little sympathy with local property arrangements or sustainable agricultural practices. At the same time states are too small to manage transboundary environmental public goods. These typically require collective solutions but fragmented sovereignty inhibits effective co-operation. None the less national governance is important, and below we consider three different forms that national environmental governance takes.

The USA

In the USA environmental politics is the outcome of a policy process characterized by high levels of distrust between the interested parties. Unlike many countries the USA eschews self-regulation by polluting industries in favour of imposing environmental standards determined by an often adversarial process. The USA is a litigious society which determines the style as well as the content of environmental politics. Many environmentally concerned groups are rich, well organized and skilled at using the legal process to attain their objectives. Environmental NGOs such as the Sierra Club have been successful over many years in imposing minimum environmental standards on often hostile industries and in limiting commercial access to public lands. American non-governmental organizations have also effectively mobilized congressional and public opinion on inter-governmental organizations such as the World Bank to impose American environmental norms on other countries. But the USA is also home to the most well funded and effective industry and citizens groups campaigning against legal restrictions to environmental resources. The Wise Use Movement, an umbrella organization for a number of citizens' groups, and the Global Climate Coalition, funded by commercial interests, have mobilized against what they consider excessive government regulation.

But despite its rule bound culture the USA has been more willing than most countries to seek innovative solutions to emerging environmental problems and to experiment with new modes of environmental governance, from political dialogues to regulatory negotiations, from environmental dispute resolution to consensus conferences and science courts. In particular Americans show a national preference for market mechanisms where feasible. The USA pioneered the emissions trading system under which power stations are given a permit to pollute. They are allowed to emit a pre-determined quantity of sulphur dioxide into the atmosphere. Power stations that invest in technology to reduce emissions below the legal limit gain credits based on how many tons of sulphur dioxide they do not release into the atmosphere. These credits can be sold to less efficient power stations which in effect have to pay a levy to continue operating, and which therefore have a financial incentive to reduce emissions. Only a part of each ton of emissions saved can be sold on thereby over time reducing total emissions into the atmosphere. Credits have been sold on the open markets for about US$100 a ton, and in the first two years of operation the amount of sulphur released into the atmosphere has been reduced by seven million tons. The USA proposed a similar international trading system for emissions of carbon dioxide at the Kyoto conference on global warming in 1997, reflecting both its preference for economic rationality and its great buying power. Internationally the USA has been unable to exercise consistent leadership. It was a leading country in the negotiations which created the international regime to regulate emissions of CFC gases and has been influential in other overseas regimes such as international whaling, but it has consistently refused to endorse environmental regimes which could adversely affect its commercial interests. It failed to sign the biodiversity treaty at the United Nations Rio conference, and its position over emissions of carbon dioxide and other global warming gases has been strongly criticized.

Australia

In Australia the seven states are, constitutionally, the major environmental legislators. They have the legal responsibility to legislate against pollution and to protect natural habitats and wildlife etc. In fact the intrusive role of the modern administrative state and the importance of central funding for environmental projects, for data collection and for providing scientific expertise have given a strong boost to the role of the federal government in environmental governance; especially at the juncture at which domestic and international politics converge. As the importance of international environmental governance has increased in importance, the federal government has become the key actor. The states remain jealous of their rights and obligations and the degree of freedom available to the federal government is often severely constrained. Unresolved jurisdictions between states and the federal government, reflected in disputes over competence have hampered the process of agreeing to international regimes.

The Australian environmental movement is well established and effective but like those of other countries exists in an uneasy relationship with state and federal governments. It must make its way in a political system dominated by government while at the same time espousing values hostile to it. In some respects the bifurcation between the state and the federal level has benefited the environmental movement. The federal government has courted the environmental movement seeking to utilize its cosmopolitan values and local concerns in its disputes with the states. At the international level the federal government is undoubtedly dominant. Since it is the federal government which agrees obligations on behalf of the nation, it naturally enough seeks the authority to ensure that the domestic response is consistent with its formal international obligations.

Australia is a major exporter of metals, minerals and food, industries which are environmentally destructive and which are often in conflict with environmental groups. As with the USA environmental politics and policies lack a clear and consistent direction. On some issues, such as how it deals with environmental impact assessment, Australia is far ahead of most countries. On others the commercial lobby, as in the USA, inhibits effective progress. Australia, a not insubstantial emitter of greenhouse gases, rejected emission reducing targets in the Kyoto conference in 1997, arguing that this would impose unacceptable costs on key mining and mineral industries. The final agreement allowed Australia to increase emissions by 8 per cent, the second largest of any developed country, an outcome which was bitterly criticized by Australian and other environmental NGOs.

Indonesia

In Indonesia environmental governance is the outcome of a complex interaction of uniquely Indonesian elements and the manner in which, in common with other developing countries, it is incorporated into the international capitalist system. Together they determine who, in Indonesian society, benefits and who loses from the development process, but also to what purpose successful groups use their power. The winners are elite groups and the losers marginal and vulnerable communities, but there is nothing new in this. What gives a uniquely Indonesian flavour to this process is the ethnic composition of winners and losers. The Javanese are culturally dominant and politically powerful not least because of their presence in the armed forces. Java is also the political centre of administration and development.

The national parliament is composed of the People's Consultative Assembly and the House of Representatives. In theory the former is the highest authority in central government. However it rarely meets and more than half its members are appointed by the government. The latter is politically weak since neither the President nor ministers are members. In practice therefore legislation is initiated at the executive level. Opposition parties exist but are strictly controlled. Effective political authority is shared between the military and Golkar the political movement led by President Suharto who is himself a retired general. The President has direct powers over the military which is strongly represented in the bureaucracy and in local and regional government. All civil servants must be members of Golkar. Javanese social norms honour family and kin according great importance to mutual and reciprocal obligations and claims. In a society characterized by networks of close knit groups, and lacking a strong democratic tradition, kinship and family obligations can easily tip over acceptable social practice to become systematic corruption, especially given the participation of the military drawn from the same ethnic and social groups.

The objective of the Indonesian state is capitalist development in which the environment is viewed as a valuable resource to be exploited for rapid growth and personal enrichment but which is ultimately expendable. Since the 1970s the government has invited foreign capital to develop Indonesia's rich natural resources under a joint profit sharing scheme. Initially Japanese but also transnational companies from other countries have systematically, but often inefficiently, exploited resources for profit and personal gain. The government justifies its environmentally destructive development strategy by deflecting the blame for the degradation of ecological resources onto indigenous people. It is they, with their primitive agricultural techniques, who destroy forests and other natural resources. This is in part true, but the accusation ignores the context in which this process occurs. Upwards of nine million people may have migrated from the inner Indonesian islands to the outer islands, particularly Sumatra and Kalimantan, some as part of a government sponsored programme, but others independently. The transmigration programme also had a social dimension, the extension of Javanese hegemony to islands and communities which historically had been hostile to Java, a process which has been described as internal colonization. Javanese norms towards the forests was at odds with those of indigenous people and transmigration rationalized a process of de-legitimizing traditional land owning rights.

In many respects Indonesia is a typical developing country in its dependence on exports of raw materials. Economic development of necessity had, initially at least, to be based on exploitation of Indonesia's rich ecological resources. While it is true that developing countries by and large have little control over terms at which they are incorporated into the international economic system, Indonesia as a large, regionally important and potentially rich country was not wholly powerless in this respect. The combination of rapid development and personal enrichment of a comparatively small segment of the Indonesian population dictated policies and programmes that had little long-term economic rationality but almost guaranteed massive destruction of ecological resources. The government has bowed to recent pressure to create the Indonesian Environmental Impact Management Agency to promote better environmental practices, but this new organization has advisory powers only and is weak compared to the long established resource departments.

In such a centralized authoritarian state the environmental movement is largely emasculated. Recently passed legislation allows the government to keep troublesome pressure groups in check. All non-governmental organizations must register with, and all sources of funds must be approved by, the state. The law even permits the state to ban non-governmental organizations without explanation. Environmental groups do exist and are active. Over 400 such groups are linked together through The Indonesian Forum for the Environment (WALHI) an environmental umbrella organization which played an important role in bringing the country's first law suit against the government for diverting funds intended for rainforest preservation. The suit was however later abandoned and provoked much disagreement within the environmental movement. Despite its best efforts it is difficult to avoid the conclusion that WALHI has not been effective in protecting the environment against the predation of so many entrenched interests.

10.6　Trans-Pacific environmental regimes

Trade and investment is an important and growing dimension of the trans-Pacific economy, as must therefore be environmental outcomes for good or bad. US food and mineral companies have long invested in Central America with adverse consequences on that region's environment. Japanese logging firms have been a catalyst for deforestation in South-East Asia. As timber resources are exhausted in traditional logging areas transnational companies migrate around the region seeking profitable concessions. South Korean and latterly Malaysian companies have become important internationally. Logging companies from Malaysia have in recent years trebled their rate of extraction from Papua New Guinea and the Solomon Islands, as well as being active in Laos.

Many environmental issues cross boundaries and are solvable, if at all, only by co-operation between two or more states at regional or sub-regional level. China and South Korea between them account for 65 per cent of acid rain deposits on Japanese territory. However effective its domestic programme Japan cannot eliminate acid rain from its land without the co-operation of China and South Korea. Similarly conservation of fish stocks in the South China Sea is feasible only by a regional solution to overcome the free riding characteristic of open access resources. Although lax environmental laws are not in themselves decisive in determining the location of foreign direct investment, the economic dynamics of the product cycle induce firms headquartered in developed countries to locate environmentally destructive industries in countries at lower levels of development, an example of environmental power.

Sustainable development strategies are often more feasible at regional or sub-regional level even for resources which are not strictly transboundary public goods. Nations which are competing for income, jobs, exports or inward direct investment are unwilling to incur costs unilaterally which could put them at a competitive disadvantage with their economic rivals. In this case it may be necessary to construct regional regimes to persuade nations to collectively behave in an environmentally responsible manner (see **Ravenhill, 1998, pp.247–70; Woods, 1998, pp.271–88**). This is especially true of many East Asian countries which still exhibit high levels of animus towards neighbours and are unwilling to put themselves at a competitive disadvantage. In North-East Asia, despite a history of intense interstate conflict and no habit of dialogue, a number of regional regimes to regulate transboundary environmental damage have recently been concluded. These include the North-West Pacific Action Plan, the Inter-governmental Oceanographic Commission and the North-East Asian Environmental Programme. Critical issues of regime effectiveness of course remain, in particular those of capacity building, monitoring, verification and financing. What is significant about this regime building process is the manner in which the issue of mutual environmental destruction has induced states at least to start the process of breaking down barriers to co-operation. In the South Pacific fifteen members of the South Pacific Forum agreed to tighten control collectively on the predation of foreign logging companies. Indonesia and Malaysia have approved a plan to establish the world's biggest wild life sanctuary in Borneo.

Whether they wish to or not Pacific countries will inevitably be drawn into international regimes to protect the environment. Global pressure is already being exerted in a practical fashion through the changing aid policies of important bilateral donors and of intergovernmental organizations such as the World Bank and the IMF. The World Bank and other aid agencies are giving higher prominence to environmental criteria in their lending policies. This is apparent in the Bank's attitude towards aid for dam building. With a more effective environmental assessment department much greater attention is given to the environmental and human consequences of dams. Where these are deemed to be unacceptably high the Bank will refuse or withdraw lending. The highest profile example is the Bank's withdrawal of support for the Three Gorges Dam in China, but the new policy is not limited to dams. The IMF and the World Bank have recently withdrawn loans to Cambodia in response to the country's failure to halt illegal logging. The Asian Development Bank has recently published new guidelines because of its concern with the high rates of deforestation, according to which it will no longer support rural development projects which have as a component the destruction of forests.

International environmental regimes are more likely to be successful if there is a leader prepared to invest material and political resources to bring about international co-operation. Leaders perform two functions. They articulate a model which reconciles the often conflicting objectives of follower states, and they are in a position to deploy material resources to translate nascent possibilities into actual collective strategies. The USA has consistently failed to provide international environmental leadership. At a relatively small scale Australia agreed to take over US$2 million of the overseas debt of the Solomon Islands in exchange for a commitment by that country to a more sustainable logging programme. But without doubt the nation most able and willing to bear the burden of regional environmental leadership in the Asia-Pacific is Japan. Although its own environmental record is not without blemish, it more than any other country possesses the two characteristics which make it feasible for it to play a leadership role, which could indeed become important in a Japanese bid for regional hegemony. Hegemons are not countries which simply possess a preponderance of power. An underlying pattern of common interests is also critical between the hegemon and potential or actual followers. Changing circumstance alter national interests and validate different leadership qualities. New issues open up political space to political entrepreneurs. Japan is still not trusted in East Asia and the end of the Cold War exposed it to an uncomfortable legacy of bad relations with its neighbours. One of Japan's most pressing foreign policy tasks is how to balance its legitimate national rights and obligations against regional fears of an imperial resurgence. The most promising leadership route is as a de-militarized power through the active and creative application of an environmental inclusive, comprehensive security policy. At one level this can be construed as simply protecting its own environment from the transboundary externalities of other countries, but Japanese leaders have on numerous occasions expressed their determination to make Japan a regional environmental leader. Japanese government and business leaders, who identify the environment as a source of economic profit as well as status and prestige, have made commitments to prioritizing the environment, commitments which not long ago would have been unimaginable. According to the Director General of Japan's Environmental Agency, by 2010 Japan will be second to none in its active concern for the environment (Coughlin, 1993). Critical to Japan's bid for leadership is environmental aid. Environmental aid now amounts to over 12 per cent of total aid disbursements, and increased funding has been matched by institutional reform including an attempt to expand the involvement of NGOs.

10.7 Social movements and the politics of environmental policy

States are inherently conservative, reluctant to address new issues particularly when these clash with traditional concerns of welfare, status and security. The task of putting the environment on the political agenda therefore falls to a considerable degree on local, national, regional and international NGOs. Environmental NGOs link two critical dimensions. They connect the local with the international and the biophysical with the political. As biophysical processes become politicized traditional international politics, a nationally oriented process where states mediate among conflicting interests, becomes less effective. Moreover although the international dimension is important, environmental change is always local in origin. Hence the two-fold linkage which makes environmental politics so different. States have failed in their role as stewards of the environment and business exploits the environment for profit. The NGOs alone cherish the environment as a consequence of which they espouse a politics of value rather than a politics of power or of interest. They lack the access to the coercive powers of the state and the economic resources available to national and international business. NGOs therefore draw legitimacy from a strong moral position which government and business may lack. They seek no material rewards, status or power. Indeed many of their members willingly accept considerable personal privation and cost. What is radical about environmental NGOs is that their concerns require them to reject exclusive loyalty to the state. However NGOs depend on states for the right to exist, criticize and act. In some developed Asia-Pacific countries such as the USA, Canada and Australia NGOs play a prominent and largely acceptable political role. In others, such as Japan, they are less successful.

Developing country NGOs are in a more difficult position. They are younger and poorer than their counterparts in the developed countries and exist in a more hostile environment. They have to reconcile three key relationships – with their respective national governments, with richer northern NGOs and with local grass-roots activists. Despite being aware that local environmental issues are nested within a wider agenda most developing country NGOs limit themselves to national concerns and campaigns. This reflects the importance of their own governments in the national environmental process and also the fact that other NGOs have more resources to campaign and bargain at the international level.

NGOs increase their effectiveness by active networking in national federations which enables them to pool resources and information. In the Philippines the Green Forum-Philippines links a number of local organizations, in a similar way to the WALHI in Indonesia. Some groups become so effective in articulating alternative values and mobilizing local opinion that many states now find it in their interests to work in partnership with NGOs on environmental campaigns. For example, in the Philippines non-governmental links with forest communities is an important dimension of the government forest programme.

Target for an environmental NGO? rubbish dump in Manilla, Philippines, 1996

The progressive role of NGOs cannot be overstressed, but it is also important to recognize the very real constraints they face. However effective their advocacy and however valid their arguments, powerful economic and political interests would be seriously compromised if the policies they advocate were put into practice. So despite a greater willingness by governments to listen and even to work with them, NGOs are usually allowed to exist only on sufferance. Many Asian NGOs are government sponsored and are therefore not sufficiently independent to be truly critical of government policies and politicians (see Chapter 7). The lack of effective oppositions at national level makes their message more muted, one that governments can ignore when it is convenient for them to do so. In some countries such as Vietnam they are highly constrained. Elsewhere they can be closed down if they become too inconvenient to the government, as was the Institut Pengajaram Kominiti which opposed the building of the Bakun Dam, in Malaysia. NGOs are also active on a regional level. Regional networks such as the Asia-Pacific People's Environment Network, an association of over 150 NGOs, offer national movements international support and a wider horizon than otherwise would be the case. Easier communication across the globe and the growing wealth of many Northern NGOs facilitate the interconnection of the local with the international.

The costs and benefits of environmental change are not borne equally. The losers are the marginal shifting cultivators, small-scale farmers and fishermen, hunter-gatherers and the like, and within these communities the most vulnerable of all are usually women and children. Although lacking formal power such communities seldom accept the consequence of environmental change without protest, sometimes covert but in recent years more open and overt. Grassroots actors deploy a number of coping strategies. Sometimes these require a degree of compliance with local and national political authorities, but often they sanction direct action against the forces of modernization which undermine their traditional claims to land and resources. Thus in Sarawak the Penan have blocked access to logging areas and have destroyed the machinery of logging companies. This is not new, but recent politicization of grass root action has transformed such resistance in many countries into a political force which national leaders can no longer ignore. The politics of grassroots resistance is of course different, precisely because of the lack of the formal instruments of power, but skilful local leaders, often associated with NGOs, have learnt to exploit local and international media to publicize their plight and resistance to the loss of their livelihoods. Change in the rhetoric of international environmental politics confers a legitimacy to the grass roots actors. The UNCED process explicitly recognizes the key role of indigenous and women's groups in the process of local empowerment. In many parts of the South-East Asia community, forest organizations have been set up in villages to exclude outside political and economic agents.

The publicity and material support which grassroots groups gain alters domestic environmental governance in many countries, but the intrinsic limits of such actor's power should not be ignored. Success depends on the existence of local leaders who can effectively publicize their plight in an unfamiliar and often hostile environment. They lack conventional sources of power and depend on pricking the conscience of national or international actors to respond positively to their plight. This may often occur, but ethical indignation is not usually a powerful and long lasting impetus for radical change in international politics. However well-publicized and even effective at a local level, grass roots actors do not alter the fundamental distribution of power which is the essential explanation of environmental change in the modern world.

10.8 Conclusion

It is perhaps not wholly fanciful to believe that at the present time the Asia-Pacific region is poised precariously between environmental salvation and catastrophe. There are certainly good reasons for optimism. Environmental awareness has increased at both popular and elite levels. Media coverage of environmental catastrophes, such as the forest fires in Indonesia have swept away some of the ignorance about environmental affairs. Even in a country like South Korea, not noted for its environmental awareness, surveys have found that 85 per cent of people considered environmental protection more important than development. Greater awareness of environmental issues is partly a consequence of a determined push by activists to put the environment on national and international agendas, but it also reflects a more general process of citizen empowerment. Elites have exercised control through a monopoly of information and knowledge. The explosion in the methods of communication means this is no longer feasible. Rosenau argues that popular access to information is one of the most significant modern trends (Rosenau, 1995), and this is as true for environmental governance as for any other aspect of civil society. Environmental awakening is not limited to activists and threatened communities. Governments too, are facing up to the long-term economic, social and security consequences of unsustainable development, as environmental issues have forced their way on to the political agenda. At the international level environmental regimes proliferate. These have not solved the problem of inadequate interstate co-operation, but they do begin the process of establishing dialogue between states, exchanging information and increasing awareness of the interests and concerns of others which should reduce the virulence of the security dilemma.

The international level is however not wholly benign. Environmental sustainability is not the only intellectual game in town. The collection of theories, paradigms and policy prescriptions which is described as neo-liberalism has attained a degree of intellectual hegemony in political and economic circles, which may have negative environmental consequences. From nominally socialist China to the IMF markets are deemed effective and government involvement in economic affairs malign. The intellectual justification for markets and a reduced role for governments is associated with a material transformation of the world economy popularly under-stood as globalization. One consequence of this is a transformation in the relative bargaining power of international capital and the state. Globalization benefits mobile (transnational corporations) at the expense of fixed (state) institutions. So states lose a degree of autonomy. They are less able to protect the vulnerable elements of society, one of which is the environment. More efficient markets will go some of the way to improving environmental calculation and choice, especially if environmentally destructive subsidies and other financial practices are withdrawn. The state need not reduce support for all public goods to the same degree and there may be an increased protection of the environment in some developed countries. But in Third World countries, which could become less competitive in a globalized capitalist economy public goods may well be sacrificed. Although they were destructive, the fires which burned out of control in Indonesia in the autumn of 1997 may yet produce some long-term benefit in highlighting the centrality of nature to human well-being. If they do, it will act as a spur to environmental action and may bring some benefit to a region poised delicately on the brink of environmental catastrophe.

References

Brown, L. *et al.* (1995) *Trends that are Shaping our Future*, London, Earthscan.

Coughlin, A. (1993) 'The green empire', *New Scientist,* p.48.

Grossman, G. and Krueger, A. (1994) 'Economic growth and the environment', *National Bureau of Economic Research*, Working Paper no.4634, p.19.

Homer-Dixon, T. (1994) 'Environmental scarcities and violent conflict', *International Security*, vol.19, no.1, p.24.

Hull, T. (1998) 'Population' in Maidment, R, and Mackerras, C. (eds) *Culture and Society in the Asia-Pacific*, London, Routledge in association with The Open University.

McGrew, A. and Brook, C. (eds) (1998) *Asia-Pacific in the New World Order*, London, Routledge in association with The Open University.

Ravenhill, J. (1998) 'The growth of intergovernmental collaboration in the Asia-Pacific region' in McGrew, A. and Brook, C. (eds).

Rosenau, J. (1995) 'Governance in the twenty-first century', *Global Governance*, vol.1, no.1.

The Environment Digest (1995a) 'China choking on industrial pollution', *The Environment Digest*, no.1, p.12.

The Environment Digest (1995b) 'Asia-Pacific conference calls for urgent carbon cuts', *The Environment Digest,* no.2, p.8.

The Environment Digest (1997) 'China denies pollution threat', *The Environmental Digest,* no.1, p.16.

Woods, L.T. (1998) 'Regional co-operation: the transnational dimension' in McGrew, A. and Brook, C. (eds).

Young, E., Hunt, C. and Ward, R.G. (1998) 'The environment, traditional production and population' in Thompson, G. (ed.) *Economic Dynamism in the Asia-Pacific*, London, Routledge in association with The Open University.

Further reading

Boardman, R. (1990) *Global Regimes and Nation States, Environmental Issues in Australian Politics,* Ottawa, Carleton University Press.

Bryant, R. and Bailey, S. (1997) *Third World Political Ecology,* London, Routledge.

Burnett, A. (1992) *The Western Pacific: Challenge of Sustainable Growth,* London, Elgar.

Clad, A. and Siy, A. (1996) 'The emergence of ecological issues in South-East Asia' in Wurful, D. and Burton, B. (eds) *South-East Asia in the New World Order,* London, Macmillan.

Colchester, M. and Lohman, L. (1992) *The Struggle for Land and the Fate of the Forests,* London, Zed.

Dowie, M. (1991–92) 'American environmentalism: a movement courting irrelevance', *World Policy Journal,* vol.IX, no.1.

Hayes, P. and Zarsky, L. (1994) 'Environmental issues and regimes in North-East Asia', *International Environment Affairs,* vol.6, no.4.

Karliner, J. (1989) 'Central America's other war: the environment under siege', *World Policy Journal,* vol.6, no.4.

Maull, H. (1992) 'Japan's global environmental politics' in Hurrell, A. and Kingsbury, B. (eds) *The International Politics of the Environment*, Oxford, Clarendon.

PART 3

Riding the Juggernaut: Political Change

CHAPTER 11

Sayonara to the strong state: from government to governance in the Asia-Pacific

William Case

11.1 Introduction

During the decades after the Second World War, many countries in the Asia-Pacific built up strong state apparatuses which possessed significant capacities for intervening in their economies and societies. They constructed them in a variety of ways: communist states in China, Indo-China and North Korea; developmental states in Japan, South Korea, Taiwan and Singapore; neo-patrimonialism or bureaucratic polities in Malaysia, Indonesia, Thailand and the Philippines and bureaucratic-authoritarianism in Mexico, Chile and Peru. Today, the strength of these states appears to be on the decline, either because of their policy failings or, paradoxically, because of their policy successes. These states have been overshadowed by global trading systems and world cultures, then undermined locally by powerful economic elites and feisty civil societies. Yet it is too soon to say that state strength has dissipated entirely. None the less, one can detect enough new constraints, both external and internal, to suggest that most states in the Asia-Pacific region have lost at least some of their strength. It may be that as state strength declines in East Asia and Latin America their polities are beginning to look more like those of the Anglo-American countries in the region: the USA, Canada, Australia and New Zealand. Not all observers celebrate this convergence. In the Asia-Pacific, national leaders like Mahathir Mohamad and Goh Chok Tong lament that their societies are 'going the way of the West', encrusted with new welfare expectations, unruly labour organizations and undisciplined patterns of personal and political behaviour. In the Anglo-American countries of the region many neo-conservatives and neo-liberals regret the loss of the natural hierarchies and untrammelled entrepreneurialism that they believe still to exist in Asia (Robison, 1996, pp.3–28).

This chapter is divided into three main parts. Section 11.2 explores the different dimensions of state strength; a precondition of measuring its accumulation or loss. Specifically, it examines the concepts of *coherence* and *insulation*; traces state strength across some political, economic and societal arenas; and offers some empirical illustrations. It also considers state strength in Anglo-American countries, which provides a benchmark of weak, though still viable, states. Section 11.3 groups key countries in the Asia-Pacific into four geographic regions, which correlate conveniently with distinct patterns of regime type and state strength: China, and its rapidly changing central planning state; North-East Asia and Singapore and their developmental states; South-East Asia's neo-patrimonialist states; and the bureaucratic-authoritarian regimes of Latin America. These regional patterns of state strength and decline are then compared. Finally, Section 11.4 offers some general discussion about the kinds of international and local pressures that limit state strength in the Asia-Pacific irrespective of state forms. The chapter concludes that states find it difficult to maintain their strength amid globalized production and flows of instant global communication. Simultaneously those states face societies that are more autonomous and activist.

11.2   Dimensions of state strength and decline

State strength can be thought of as the capacity of state actors and state institutions to autonomously devise and implement public policy; shaping the preferences and interests of other actors; intervening in and transforming economic and cultural structures. State strength can be mapped out in terms of bureaucratic *insulation* and policy-making *coherence*. Specifically, bureaucracies that are sufficiently insulated from societal and international forces can impose coherent interrelated and mutually supportive economic and social policies, devised by elite-level pilot agencies. These might include state leaders and bureaucrats adopting different industrializing strategies, restoring societal discipline, resolving ethnic imbalances and inspiring nationalist sentiments. On the other hand, these aims may amount to no more than leaders and bureaucrats wishing to cling to state offices. But whatever the motivations of those who operate them, what specifically do strong states look like?

In political terms, strong states tend to be authoritarian regimes. Of course, authoritarianism comes in many different forms that run on a continuum from the totalitarianism of Communist China and the hard state of Park Chung Hee's South Korea to the exclusionary corporatism of Latin America, semi-democracies in South-East Asia and the soft authoritarianism of Japan. But whether using state terror or more artful processes of hollow electoralism and co-option, these states all remain politically insulated from the demands and interests of the mass of the population. The decline of state strength becomes plain in politics when states are forced to democratize: legalizing opposition parties; making existing elections more competitive; allowing electoral results to turn into a change of government. Countries in the Asia-Pacific that have undergone a recent process of democratization include South Korea, Taiwan, Thailand, the Philippines, Peru and Chile (for more details, see Chapter 12). Other states have prolonged their authoritarianism, but in ever diminishing parts of their country. In China, for example, the national government has stoutly resisted democratization, yet has decentralized control over production and finance to local officials, managers, and township and village enterprises. Having yielded local economic administrative control in pursuit of economic success the central Chinese state now faces coastal provinces spurning directives, the appearance of warlords in the interior, labour uprisings in Sichuan, and rogue units of the PLA engaging in extortion and piracy. In sum, states may be weakened in politics by democratization or decentralization, that is, the intrusion of mass electorates or the dispersion of administrative agencies. Either way, insulation and coherence are lost as bureaucracies are forced to take more interests into account and state strength diminishes.

In economic terms, strong states are characterized by either their deep and systematic interventions into the economy or, conversely, their steadfast refusal to intervene despite special pleading from powerful interest groups. Insulation is the key to both strategies because state leaders and bureaucrats need to rebuff those societal interests who would have them perform differently. The economic policies pursued by strong states range from the rigid central planning and quotas once imposed by China to the administrative guidance and industrial policies dispensed in North-East Asia. Malaysia, Indonesia and perhaps Peru also attempted to implement industrial policies during the 1970s and early 1980s. All except Peru were able to finance their state enterprises and development projects during the period with windfall petroleum revenues. In contrast, the colony of Hong Kong adhered doggedly to its formula of positive non-interventionism, long preserving what has been regarded as the freest major trading economy in the world. Likewise, the Philippines under Marcos during the 1970s and Thailand during the 1980s claimed to be undertaking market reforms.

The loss of state strength in the economic arena is revealed in a number of ways. Most obviously, the pilot agencies charged with broad central planning or more focused industrial policies are reined in. In Japan, for example, the activities of the Ministry of International Trade and Industry (MITI) have been sharply curtailed in recent years. Further, many of the state enterprises that were created may be privatized or closed down, having gained new efficiencies (like Pohang Iron and Steel in South Korea and Indosat in Indonesia) or grown heavy with deficits (like Perwaja Steel in Malaysia). On this score, China presents an interesting case. Its many insolvent state enterprises are steadily draining the national coffers. China has therefore restructured some of its smaller enterprises, but it has been unable to close most of the larger ones for fear of tens of millions of workers striking and exacerbating social tensions. China seems caught in a vicious circle, its enterprises so fiscally weakening the state that the state cannot deal with its failing enterprises or with the social costs of closing them down. State weakness in the economic arena is highlighted by an inversely buoyant private sector, bristling with business groups and dynamic small companies that the state had in some instances once fostered. In Japan, MITI rebuilt business networks known as *keiretsu* after the Second World War. Today, many Japanese businesses are organized into a peak association known as the *Keidanren* which, through its campaign contributions and lobbying, has an influential role in shaping public policy. In South Korea, Park Chung Hee built up business groups known as *chaebol,* concentrating the country's industrial structure. Today, however, *chaebol* leaders resist the state in a variety of ways, extracting cheap credit, circumventing regulations, investing offshore, and, in one instance, directly contesting the presidency in a general election. In Thailand, the relationship between the state and business has tilted from extensive state controls during the 1970s to a more evenly balanced, consultative partnership during the 1980s. In the 1990s business freely organizes political parties and gains control over ministries.

Another indicator of state weakness in the economic arena involves changing state attitudes toward foreign investment. For example, China had long emphasized industrial self-reliance, a policy that reached its apogee during the Great Leap Forward (see Chapter 2). Japan, South Korea and to a lesser extent Taiwan also shunned foreign investment, striving to maintain the integrity of their industrial policies. Mexico boldly nationalized banks during the 1980s, while Peru adopted redistributive policies that distinctly alienated foreign investors. Today, all of these countries have been forced by the failure or limits of these policies or pressures from international agencies to open their doors to foreign investors. This has inevitably compromised the autonomy of their economic policy making. Under pressure from GATT (General Agreement on Tariffs and Trade) and subsequently the WTO (World Trade Organization), Japan has lowered its formal barriers to merchandise and capital imports. South Korea began easing restrictions on foreign investment, even before it began negotiations to enter the OECD (Organization of Economic Co-operation and Development). Like South Korea, Mexico reopened its banking sector in 1997 as a precondition for receiving assistance from the International Monetary Fund (IMF) in propping up its beleaguered currency. Indeed, in 1997 Mexico set up an agency called Fobaproa with the express purpose of purchasing bad debt from failing banks, thereby making them more attractive to foreign investors (*The News*, 9 November 1997).

In the social arena, strong states have mostly geared their policies toward promoting and supporting their political and economic aims. In general, strong states have tried either to mobilize their societies behind elite organized projects or failing that they have tried to depoliticize their societies. This has entailed recruiting the public into mass-based parties and industrializing campaigns, or politically suppressing them in order not to distract them from their industrializing tasks. South Korea under Park Chung Hee provides a good example of steady social mobilization with workers exhorted to 'fight while working, work while fighting'. 1966 was declared the 'Year of Hard Work' and 1967 the 'Year of Progress' (Clifford, 1994, p.102). In contrast, Indonesia under the New Order offers an example of depoliticization. Indeed, its ideologues explicitly characterized society as the 'floating mass'.

For many strong states education has been the key arena for social policy initiatives. In particular states have sought to educate the managers, engineers, technicians and accountants who can perpetuate growth (see **Hawkins, 1998**). In the Asia-Pacific, universities have also commonly dispensed much moral education and discipline. However, tertiary education has a tendency to spill over from the development of technical skills and the inculcation of moral values to spawn new forms of social inquiry and unrest, particularly during periods when so many graduates are produced that the economy has difficulty in absorbing them. It is no coincidence that South Korea, where the state has done much to build up local universities and sponsor overseas education, has often produced more graduates than it needs, and now experiences high levels of student alienation and militancy.

Strong states in multiethnic societies have sometimes pursued policies, either to redress imbalances between ethnic communities or to suppress the resentments that such imbalances can create. In Malaysia, for example, after severe ethnic rioting between indigenous Malays and 'overseas' Chinese in 1969, the state built up new strength in order to promote Malay supporters, especially in business. However, many beneficiaries have since used this largesse to win posts in the government and ruling party, thereby tapping back into and enervating state strength. In Peru during the late 1960s and early 1970s, the state attempted to redistribute wealth from the coastal elite, frequently with European ancestry, to highland peasants, usually Indian. But the partial successes of this policy seemed either to embolden or frustrate the indigenous populations, prompting them finally to organize a number of peasant-based guerrilla movements that have tested the Peruvian state's capacity to control its own territory. In contrast, the government in Indonesia, while nominally favouring indigenous business people, has more substantively promoted the minority Chinese, providing the biggest business people among them with state contracts, licenses and protection. Over time, however, indigenous grievances have grown and today confront the state with potentially explosive pressures. Of course, more neutral policies of multicultural tolerance are no guarantee that states can avoid such pressures. Indeed, enthusiasts for this approach have been sobered by the impending break-up of Canada and the mounting antagonisms in Australia and New Zealand over indigenous land rights and Asian immigration (see Chapter 5). Similarly, where states have used their strength to promote particular religious groups, they sometimes find this creates new challenges to state autonomy. The Malaysian state, for example, after supporting the formation of Islamic banks, universities, pilgrimage funds and other institutions in an effort to undercut the appeals of more strident Islamicists, now finds that these Islamicists are steadily gaining new supporters. During the 1990s, one watched in fascination as the federal government and the government of the north-eastern peninsular state of Kelantan attempted to 'out-Islamicize' each other, driving the latter to propose the introduction of *syariah* law and the *hudud* code of punishments.

Finally, strong states often seek to arouse nationalist pride and instil social discipline amongst their population. Japan thus preserves imperial rituals, pageantry and many sacred sites. The South Korean state invests heavily in supporting traditional villages, handicrafts and folk music. Malaysian leaders refer regularly in their speeches to traditional patterns of ethnic Malay obeisance, celebrating, for example, the legend of Hang Tuah's loyalty to his sultan. The Thai government has elevated traditional orientations into a contemporary ideology of 'nation, religion and king'. The governments of China and Mexico celebrate the legitimacy they derive from their revolutionary origins and egalitarian myths. Yet, after using national pride to mould societies into willing work forces, the prosperity that results seems to awaken new interest in Western culture, especially in terms of consumption and entertainment. Accordingly, the state in Malaysia bemoans the new *lepak* culture of indolent urban youth, hanging about Kuala Lumpur's new shopping malls with baseball caps, baggy trousers and skateboards.

An ironic indicator of declining state strength is the new assertiveness in foreign affairs shown by states in the Asia-Pacific. North-East Asian countries have launched cultural initiatives overseas and fund research in US universities (so long as these proposals do not clash with the agendas of their own donor agencies). In China and South-East Asia, however, where states have weakened, yet whose past contributions to growth enable them now to purchase surrogate symbols of strength, military modernization programmes are underway, and threaten territorial conflicts. Today, China spends more on armaments, even as it loses control over the PLA's regional units. It is also pressing large claims in the South China Sea. Many South-East Asian countries have responded with their own programmes of weapon upgrading, giving militaries that were once deployed almost entirely internally the capacity to project threats and power externally. Inadvertently, old territorial disputes between South-East Asian countries seem now to be resurfacing; for example, Malaysia is involved in disputes with Indonesia over the islets of Sigitan and Lipadan and with Singapore over the rocky outcropping of Pedro Branca. Questions persist too over Malaysia's precise border demarcation with Thailand and claims to its eastern state of Sabah made by the Philippines. Many analysts have argued that the USA has assumed an aggressive diplomatic and military posture precisely because of its internal weaknesses. With its fund-raising politicians, divided institutions, checks and balances, and legal constraints, the US state has been riddled with special interests, and its domestic policy failings and scandals have been trumpeted through a free press. It is to compensate for this that the USA has tried to project its strength overseas. In a lesser way, the same might be said of Australia. The extent to which states elsewhere in the Asia-Pacific are driven in a similar direction to respond suggests both a decline in state strength and worrying implications for the possibility of international co-operation.

In sum, the loss of state strength can be measured in politics by the slippage from authoritarian regimes to more democratic ones, or from highly centralized apparatuses to ones that are more fragmented. In the economy, states once committed to central planning, developmentalism, or bureaucratic authoritarianism sink into more ad hoc interventions (some of which may involve privatization). Business groups, meanwhile, operate more autonomously, or restore close relations with the state, by taking the upper hand. In terms of social policies (like education, ethnicity, religion and culture), favoured groups may rise finally to challenge the states that have promoted them. Conversely, the resentments of excluded groups may grow so severe that they too mount challenges. Either way, societies become more differentiated and sceptical of official cultures and ideologies. In consequence, states in the Asia-Pacific appear to be losing much of their bureaucratic insulation and policy coherence across a number of arenas, thereby coming to resemble the Anglo-American states of the region.

11.3 Sub-regional patterns of state strength and decline

Countries in the Asia-Pacific are incredibly diverse in terms of their political regimes, levels of economic development and social structures. None the less, one important trajectory shared by many has been the acquisition of state strength, followed by its gradual decline To map these patterns and make comparisons between them, these countries can usefully be grouped into four categories, namely, China, North-East Asia, South-East Asia and Latin America.

China: the central planning state

Through war and social revolution, the Communist Party and the state it created swept aside the old political and socio-economic order, enabling it to assert great power over Chinese society. In politics, this strength is indicated by the intensity of China's totalitarian experience. China's economy was centrally planned and collectivized. Its social policies were geared to perpetual mobilization, ideological control and redistribution. But while the state in China appeared immensely strong several elements of its make-up contained the seeds of future weakness. The revolutionary fervour that had made totalitarianism possible faded slowly over time, leaving behind an ideology that looked increasingly threadbare, inspiring less commitment than lip service and cynicism. Observers often remarked that among party functionaries, careerist ambitions had supplanted revolutionary ideals. Hence, additional mobilizing campaigns and purges became necessary to re-energize their commitments, though these upheavals seemed afterward to leave China exhausted.

In the economy, although central planning had succeeded in establishing much infrastructure and heavy industry, it depended on large and continuous investments of resources, indicating that China's industrialization, though rapid, was highly inefficient. Once established, China's sustained economic growth necessitated a transition from self-reliance and heavy industry to exported consumer goods. Cumbersome central planning was unable to achieve this transition as state production quotas, utterly disconnected from price signals and consumer tastes, failed to refine and extend growth. Impediments were posed also by China's social policies. China's collectivization and redistributive policies eroded managerial decision making and worker motivation. Collectivized agriculture failed to produce enough food to sustain China's urban populations, and state factories produced great quantities of inferior manufactures for which there were no buyers.

Deng Xiaoping initiated economic reforms in 1978, first de-collectivizing agriculture by issuing family-based leases, then restructuring industry by devolving decision making over manufacturing and finance to managers and local officials (see Chapter 8, Section 8.5). In addition, though Deng professed to extend communist social policies – most evident in the retention of state enterprises – he in fact stripped away many social guarantees. What Deng sought to leave unchanged, however, was his party's monopoly on state power. Indeed, his policies were intended to restart economic growth precisely in order that the Communist Party's hold on state power might be left intact. In other words, state officials began retreating from economic affairs in order better to insulate their grip on political offices.

Whether this model of authoritarian politics and free markets can be maintained, is the central question about China's future. Samuel Huntington observes that whether authoritarianism promotes economic growth or fails to, pressures build inevitably on authoritarian regimes, causing them either to democratize or assume some new authoritarian form (Huntington, 1991). Of course, the state in China retains many resources with which to insulate itself. Ideologues have set to work papering over seeming contradictions between politics and markets, coining slogans such as 'market socialism'. They encourage also a pride based on the country's recent economic gains, which often swells into a strident sense of nationalism. Further, when ideological appeals fail, the state remains able to impose its rule by coercion, as the outcome of the Tiananmen Square demonstrations attest.

In sum, as the weaknesses embedded in China's central planning state became clear, the state retreated to a more defensive posture. Its aim has been to blunt political challenges by fomenting economic growth. However, whether the state can defend even this leaner position seems doubtful. State managers and officials to whom economic power has been devolved, are not content merely to accept new responsibilities. Increasingly they defy central directives while probing new markets. Further, while China's army grows preoccupied with business dealings, it may cease to faithfully do the central state's bidding. Hence, if Huntington is right about societal upsurge – whether motivated by new aspirations or smouldering impatience – local officials and security agencies in China may merely stand by when next it takes place. One is thus left to speculate that the once strong state in China, having already lost so much of its strength, stands to lose more (see Chapter 6, Section 6.5).

North-East Asia: developmental states

The developmental states of North-East Asia adopted far more nuanced strategies than central planning states did. In politics, their postures ranged from a soft authoritarianism in Japan to a hard state in Park Chung Hee's Korea (Johnson, 1987). Singapore and Taiwan adopted more middling postures, preserving respectively some parliamentary forms and local elections. Developmental states were most celebrated, however, for their economic policies which enabled them rapidly to industrialize and export (see Chapter 8). These policies were market conforming rather than market avoiding, using state power to accelerate the growth patterns that free markets would have realized only gradually. This involved the formation of pilot agencies (MITI in Japan, the Economic Planning Board in South Korea, the Council of Economic Co-operation and Development in Taiwan, and the Economic Development Board in Singapore), the recruitment of bureaucrats from top universities, the adoption of active industrial policies, the provision of administrative guidance to selected business groups aided by various forms of subsidies and protection, and applying strict performance standards with which finally to make the transition from import substitution to export oriented industrialization. This is the transition that central planning states were not able to carry out. Finally, developmental states adopted explicit social policies, initiating land reforms and sustaining socio-economic equality, thereby pre-empting sharp political resentments. Worker commitment was steeled by Confucianist appeals, then charged with nationalism and regular reminders of threats to national economic and military security.

But developmental states contained weaknesses too, exposed in part by their very successes. Most importantly, the disciplined relationship between state bureaucrats and business leaders – one in which bureaucrats served as senior partners – often deteriorated into more normal forms of bureaucratism, collusion and corruption. This has raised questions about how development states were set up in the first place and how their ruling coalitions have been maintained for so long. Analysts have found no good answer, but one notes that pilot agencies and committed bureaucrats emerged in the wake of severe upheavals and national devastation: in Japan after the Second World War, in Korea after the Korean War, in Taiwan after the KMT's flight from the mainland, and in Singapore after its expulsion from Malaysia. With the exception of Singapore, developmental states appear to have lasted for about twenty years, the time frame of a single, traumatized generation. Hence, as memories gradually dimmed of national devastation and the need to rebuild, bureaucratic commitment eroded. In

Japan, under Prime Minister Tanaka during the 1970s, many ministries were drawn out of their administrative guidance roles into new 'iron triangle' relationships, which rather than promoting new industries colluded with existing business groups. Accordingly, policy concerns shifted from national industrialization to back-scratching and mutual enrichment. Ministries, especially those involved in public works and construction, now allocated resources to entrenched business interests rather than dynamic new industries. In return, Japan's main business association, the Keidanren, passed on campaign contributions to key factions within the ruling Liberal Democratic Party. The LDP, finally, offered information and promises of party positions to bureaucrats, the latter contemplating their 'descent from heaven', that is, their retirement from the civil service. Needless to say, much state strength was lost as Japan's developmental state mutated into the iron triangle, its policy making coherence and bureaucratic insulation having been stripped steadily and dismantled (see Chapter 6, Section 6.2).

One detects much the same erosion in South Korea and Taiwan, though commencing perhaps a decade later. In South Korea, after the assassination of Park Chung Hee in 1979, General Chun Doo-Hwan seized state power through a military coup. Then, to establish legitimacy quickly, he promised to distance the bureaucracy from Korea's large business groups, perceived by many, especially small business owners, to be unfairly promoted. But while promising reforms and even closing down one *chaebol*, many bureaucrats and indeed, Chun's own family members continued quietly to arrange cheap loans for key business groups. Using state banks as conduits, they pushed through credit, then took kickbacks in return. In Taiwan, state favours more often took the form of public works contracts, often awarded to companies linked to the ruling KMT itself.

At the same time, the economic growth that developmental states had brought about began sharply to transform societies in North-East Asia, producing new middle classes of highly educated professionals. As modernization theorists would expect, these middle classes grew more interested in democratic procedures. Because of the corruption into which erstwhile developmental states were now descending, North-East Asia's middle classes were handed an issue that prompted them finally to act joining NGOs, supporting opposition parties, and mounting demonstrations. In South Korea, they were joined by workers who now wanted greater rewards for the sacrifices they had made, and students whom momentarily at least, grew more interested in political change than corporate placement. Thus, during the late 1980s, South Korea and Taiwan began their democratic transitions. A former opposition leader, Kim Young Sam, was elected finally as president of South Korea in 1992. Taiwan's president, Lee Teng-hui, was first popularly elected in 1996, and even Japan gave greater content to its nominally democratic regime by turning out the LDP – at least for a time – after a long series of scandals.

While declining developmental states in their corrupt old age needed to be held more accountable, democratization seemed unable to ensure it.

The South Korean State deploys its strength at Myongdong Cathedral, Seoul, January 1997. The trade union protester is separated by riot police from leaders of the Korean Confederation of Trade Unions who have taken refuge in the cathedral after leading three weeks of strikes

South Korea's Kim Young Sam, for example, made a promising start to his administration. He purged the state apparatus of corrupt generals, imposed a 'real-name' transaction system on bank deposits, and forced the *chaebol* to sell off some of their downtown land holdings. Yet he found later that his advisers, and even his son, had become deeply involved in corrupt practices. Indeed, new forms of corruption may even have been exacerbated by democratic procedures as ruling party politicians approached business more boldly for campaign contributions. In Taiwan, even more nefariously, it appears to be organized crime that has been best poised to exploit the new democratic openness. Regional policy-making bodies have come frequently to be dominated by politicians with gangland ties. They have established a strong presence in the Legislative Yuan too. While operating in these arenas, they are better able to shift public works contracts to the companies they favour. Japan, during Hosokawa's brief term of office, enacted reforms meant to reduce the LDPs intra-party competitiveness, and thus the party's great reliance on campaign contributions (see Chapter 3). After extended bargaining, the Diet's multi-member districts were converted into a combination of single member districts elected by a system of proportional representation. It is unclear, though, whether this has done anything to diminish the cost of waging electoral battles in Japan.

Perhaps recoiling from the sight of its fellow developmental states' stumbling in these ways, as well as the inability of democracy to prop them back up, Singapore has followed its own course. Indeed, through dynamic national leadership, sustained bureaucratic commitment, pseudo-democratic politics and careful ethnic policies, Singapore has maintained the initial strength of its developmental state. It could be argued that Singapore's industrial policies have been modest, confined largely to screening and integrating foreign investors rather than nurturing local business groups. Moreover Singapore's bureaucrats have made policy mistakes. During the early 1980s, for example, they dramatically increased wages, hoping to attract multinational investors with more advanced technologies, thereby propelling Singapore into its second industrial revolution. The timing was poor, however, occurring during global recession, forcing them to push wages back down. Further, an attempt to counter 'Westernization' among young people by introducing religious knowledge classes, especially Confucianism, into secondary school curricula provoked fears among ethnic Malays and Indians of Chinese cultural dominance. Hence, after investing considerable resources in these classes, the government abruptly terminated them in 1990. None the less, while Singapore has made policy mistakes and though its successes have stimulated new societal challenges, its state probably remains the strongest in the Asia-Pacific region.

South-East Asia: neo-patrimonialist states

In South-East Asia, states sought to gain strength rather later than they had in China and North-East Asia. This is sometimes attributed to the comparative abundance of natural resources in South-East Asia, the sale of which enabled countries there to gain some revenues without making hard choices about industrializing. However, when finally they did choose to industrialize, it was high commodity prices during the 1970s that made it possible. In particular, Malaysia and Indonesia benefited from petroleum exports and revenues, enabling their states to begin building infrastructures and establish state industrial enterprises. To a lesser extent, Thailand benefited from higher prices for its rice exports, enabling the state to carry out at least some mild import substitution. The Philippines, in contrast, with fewer resources and having to import petroleum, chose to open its markets to freer competition – or so its President, Ferdinand Marcos, often claimed.

In politics, then, these countries adopted a variety of regime forms, but ones that at root were all authoritarian. During the 1970s, Malaysia could be characterized as a semi-democracy, Indonesia as an even less competitive pseudo-democracy. Thailand had a military government during at least the late 1970s, and the Philippines was a personal dictatorship. Social policies were then designed to reinforce these regimes with mass-level compliance. For example, the state in Malaysia emphasized regularly the need for orderly politics, Malay unity, and societal harmony; especially as it promoted rapid industrialization in tandem with cross-ethnic redistribution. Indonesia's leaders, meanwhile, revived the five principles of Pancasila, similarly stressing tolerance and harmony amid the structural inequalities that they otherwise made little effort to redress (see Chapter 4).

But despite most South-East Asian states growing more authoritarian during this period, and despite their new interest in industrialization, they never acquired the strength that states possessed in North-East Asia. Firm insulation against special interests was never established, perhaps because bureaucrats remained undisciplined by any war-time devastation and lingering security threats. Nepotism, cronyism, and occasional populism remained embedded across the region. Nor did their policies gain much coherence. Real technical expertise seldom filtered below the topmost levels of state apparatuses. The Indonesian state's erratic interventions into the economy fuelled tensions between upstream and downstream industries, long frustrating the export of anything but petroleum and plywood. Malaysia's industrial policies were perhaps better articulated, but then were muddled by ethnic quotas. Accordingly, many observers have characterized states in South-East Asia as neo-patrimonialist during this time. They were large, authoritarian, and intervened deeply in their economies and cultures, but as much to favour family members and cronies as to promote national unity and development (Yoshihara, 1988).

During the mid 1980s, however, a period marked by global recession and eventually, sharp falls in commodity prices, states in South-East Asia commenced a strategic retreat, scaling back their industrial policies and, in the case of Malaysia, holding its social policy of ethnic redistribution in abeyance. Bureaucrats then hurriedly looked about for new engines of growth. They chose to deregulate their economies, unleash local entrepreneurism, and invited the return of foreign investors. In displaying this restraint, they demonstrated a new kind of strength, insulating themselves against rent-seekers in order to let free markets work. In the late 1980s these market reforms paid off, triggering new flows of manufactured exports and making South-East Asia's economies into some of the fastest growing in the world. States in the region thus increased their budgetary resources, while societies were empowered by new wealth. Ironically, this tended to erode the new strength that states had acquired.

At the elite level, rather than rebuffing rent-seekers, state bureaucrats could again afford to indulge them. Poorly co-ordinated industrial policies sometimes also reappeared, the best example of which was Indonesia's campaign to develop a national car industry. This project bore great costs, alienating Japan and testing the World Trade Organization. It was directed for a time by President Suharto's son 'Tommy', a figure with no experience in the automotive industry and who had finally to import his first run of 'national cars' from the true manufacturer, Kia Motors in Korea. In Malaysia, where the state has attracted much attention for its privatization campaign, one must caution against this being mistaken for state strength. Rather, much of this privatization appears to have been carried out in neo-patrimonialist ways with state assets quietly transferred to favoured recipients. The state-owned Heavy Industries Corporation of Malaysia (which includes Proton, the country's national car maker) offers one example. While on board a plane to a trade meeting in Burma/Myanmar, Malaysia's highly influential former finance minister, Daim Zainuddin, was approached by a young Malay entrepreneur about the possibility of the latter's acquiring Proton. Diam responded casually that the entrepreneur should instead take the entire holding company, using the proposed acquisition as collateral for loans (*Far Eastern Economic Review*, 1996, p.68).

While the state in South-East Asia has lost much insulation and coherence at the top, it has been increasingly pressured from below. This must be qualified, recognizing that South-East Asia has been identified as the geographic area most resistant to democracy (Emmerson, 1995). But societal demands for political change have none the less been mounting (see Chapter 12, Section 4). People power pushed democratization through in the Philippines in 1986 thus ensuring that a weak state became weaker still. In Thailand, the urban middle class helped topple the military government during 'Black May' in 1992, though they evidently have strong doubts today that public policy has improved. In Indonesia, rivalries between the president and military leaders allowed student groups and a critical press to peep through in the early 1990s, heralding a brief period of openness. In Malaysia, factionalism within the country's dominant political party caused it first to be officially de-registered, then openly divided, allowing at least the general election of 1990 to be unusually competitive.

In sum, states in South-East Asia have historically been large and authoritarian, but flabby and undisciplined, conditions made tolerable by the economic cushion of commodity exports. Even during the 1970s when these states were motivated by sharp rises in commodity prices to start industrializing their economies and restructuring their societies, they pursued their programmes in neo-patrimonialist ways. Hence, it was the collapse of commodity prices that induced states in South-East Asia at last to gain strength. And throughout the 1980s then, these states reined in their industrial policies and social engineering. However, with economic recovery during the 1990s, some states have resumed their neo-patrimonialist methods. Others have been confronted by societal forces, causing them to democratize their politics. But either way, whether again indulging cronies (as in Indonesia) or making democratic concessions to mass populations (as in Thailand and the Philippines) many states in South-East Asia have lost much of the insulation from social pressures they had momentarily acquired.

Latin America: bureaucratic-authoritarian states

During the 1960s and 1970s, most countries in Latin America abandoned their democracies and adopted new forms of authoritarianism. To explain these democratic breakdowns – some of which occurred in the region's richest countries – Guillermo O'Donnell (1973) developed an important analytical model he called bureaucratic authoritarianism. He suggested that the import substitution policies of the previous decades had stimulated production and consumer demand, thereby placating local business people and industrial workers. In these circumstances, democratic procedures could sometimes peacefully persist. However, with the exhaustion of the import substitution strategy, marked by low quality consumer goods, saturated markets and a paradoxically greater dependence on imported capital equipment – new efficiencies and industrial capacities had to be found. To do this, states throughout the region forged alliances between the military and the state bureaucracy, tightened their political regimes and suppressed organized labour, thereby building new forms of bureaucratic insulation and policy coherence. Further, economic policies were designed to attract foreign investment and technologies, and then link them to local businesses in order that capital equipment could finally be locally produced. Bureaucratic authoritarianism differed in important ways from the developmentalism practised in North-East Asia. First, it relied on foreign investment to deepen local industry. Second, it rarely succeeded in sparking the transition from import substitution to export competitiveness. Hence, as frustrations gradually mounted, Latin America's strong states were subject first to internal factional strains, then finally to societal upsurges.

The bureaucratic authoritarian model applied most clearly to Brazil, Argentina and Uruguay. However, so powerful did the model's explanatory power seem to be that analysts extended it to some Latin American countries on the Pacific coast: Mexico during the 1970s and 1980s, Chile after 1973 under Pinochet, and Peru after 1968. The precise guise of bureaucratic authoritarianism that these countries adopted and the economic and social policies they pursued diverged in some ways. Mexico essentially perpetuated the corporatist structures it had already in place, enabling the state to deal with the exhaustion of import substitution and the need for economic modernization. Chile, after the violent removal of its elected president Salvador Allende, adopted a very stark form of authoritarianism geared mostly to economic rationalization and Peru, while attempting also to revive its economy, showed interest for a time in a cross-ethnic, trans-class and spatial redistribution of wealth. But whatever their policy differences, these countries were all marked by the accumulation of greater state strength, or, in the case of Mexico, an intensified use of existing state power.

Over time, it appeared that the state in Mexico had deepened its corrupt practices more than its industrial base. During the 1980s, factionalism within the country's ruling party sharpened over the spoils of office, while opposition parties stirred the societal discontents that resulted. Amid growing tensions between ruling party factions and between them and opposition parties there arose appalling revelations of state-sanctioned assassinations and drug running. While the state in Mexico was able to resist the full democratization of national politics, it could not prevent the emergence of opposition parties in local assemblies and important mayoralty races. It was challenged also by ethnic secessionism and guerrilla movements in the country's southern regions. Finally, during the mid 1990s, it appeared that the state in Mexico had lost so much strength that it was unable even to follow the course of economic liberalization it is now charting, suffering current account deficits and currency collapses that came elsewhere to be known as the 'Mexican disease'.

Efforts in Chile to accumulate state strength and revitalize the economy were far more successful, even if its market reforms meant foreign investment and commodities production rather than industrial deepening and manufactured exports. But whatever their limitations, these comparative successes enabled Chile's leader, General Pinochet, to cling to office and retard his country's democratic transition, even as he faced a resurgent middle-class public and rejuvenated political parties. A civilian was finally elected president in 1990, but Pinochet kept much control over military affairs. The military was also able to maintain a 10 per cent levy on all foreign exchange gained through the export of copper. Still, these reserve domains should not be understood as retention of bureaucratic-authoritarianism or state strength. Instead, state power was now divided between the ruling coalition, the bureaucracy and intransigent elements in the military, setting the stage for rivalries and constitutional crises. And to the extent that democratization had taken place, it meant that the public's demands had to be factored into state policy-making too. By the late 1990s, while Chile had carried out far-reaching economic reforms, its political transition had not yet been completed, creating an uncertainty that eroded state strength further.

Peru, finally, has displayed yet another pattern, briefly gaining state strength during the mid 1970s, losing it thereafter, then appearing recently to regain some. Specifically, Peru's military seized state power from a populist government in 1968. It then found populist pressures to be so great that it attempted to manage, rather than curb the import substitution and redistributive policies that were already in place. Later, when economic contradictions had at last to be reconciled, the military mounted a counter-coup. The military rationalized the economy during the late 1970s, and democratized politics towards the end of the decade, allowing a succession of elected governments to follow. Taken together, Peru's democratic governments performed disastrously, first perpetuating economic rationalism, later lapsing back into populism and finally suspending democratic procedures under President Fujimori. But Fujimori managed to create a new form of state strength. He undergirded his authoritarian approach to populism with military support, and then lifted economic growth rates. One must be cautious, however, about concluding that Peru's new progress defies this chapter's thesis. When placed in context, one recognizes that Peru's new state capacity and economic performance have emerged from a very low base.

11.4   New threats to state strength

This section conducts a more general discussion of the factors that constrain states in the Asia-Pacific in the late 1990s. It begins by exploring international factors, then returns to domestic forces. Briefly, it contends that countries have only been able to use strong state strategies during specific phases of political, economic and social development, that is, before international trade partners are so antagonized, local business firms so competitive, and broader societal forces so activated that they are able to resist strong states.

Globalized production, finance and technology

During the past decade, much has been written about capitalism's triumph over other forms of social and economic organization. In short, with the removal of many ideological obstacles, capitalism has extended its global reach. Production, investment patterns and technology transfers have all become global. Industries now source materials, components, assembly work and finance from the countries that can most cheaply provide them. They market their products in the countries that can most afford them. In these ways, proponents suggest, capitalism has achieved new economies of scale and levels of growth. Accordingly, these global exchanges are better conducted by transnational corporations than by individual states. A transnational firm based in New York may establish its regional headquarters in Hong Kong, carry out its research and development in Taiwan, source components in Thailand, carry out final assembly in China, then market finished products back in the USA, Canada and Mexico. Alternatively, a common pattern set wholly within the Asia-Pacific involves Japanese companies exporting sophisticated components and capital to production sites in South-East Asia, overseeing assembly, then re-exporting products back to Japan. Thus, in acquiescing to the more globalized trade patterns that foster these efficiencies, strong states in the Asia-Pacific find that possibilities for coherent national industrial policies are eroded.

In addition to freer trade, strong states have been confronted by pressures for foreign investment – something that many had avoided in the past in order to keep control over economic planning. In part, these pressures have come about through the development of new electronic technologies, transferring capital round the globe in seconds. Moreover, these transfers are not necessarily productive, often arriving in the form of portfolio investment – so-called 'hot money' – which is easily withdrawn from a country. This can fracture the long-term decision making of corporations as readily as that of states. But when foreign capital takes the form of direct investment, it can bring with it new technologies and production facilities that many host countries would otherwise find hard to replicate. Technological development makes this new or revived form of dependence clear. Strong states, especially in North-East Asia, once subsidized research and development, providing much funding, training and laboratory sites. And as late as the 1970s, strong states were able to refine, reverse engineer and in some cases purloin existing technologies, thereby breaking into the automobile parts and electronics industries. But as technologies have grown more complex – like bio-technologies, integrated circuits, microelectronics and special materials – their development has become more difficult. Late-industrializing countries must therefore turn to the transnational firms that innovate or control them. South Korea, for example, must still import from Japan some key components for its automobile industry. Malaysia, in order to manufacture dynamic random access memories (DRAMs), has formed a joint venture partnership with Hitachi to set up a silicon wafer foundry. A Thai company, Alphatec Electronics, has done the same by buying a subsidiary of Texas Instruments. In short, late-industrializing countries that today seek to advance their position in the global economy, must gain new technologies, and to the extent that they must attract transnational firms for this purpose. When they do so, state coherence and insulation diminish.

At the same time, while attracting foreign investment, many countries in the Asia-Pacific find that they must themselves invest overseas, either to carry out some of their own production more cheaply offshore, to circumvent lingering barriers to overseas markets, or to exploit new markets for services. MITI first permitted Japanese corporations to invest their capital surpluses overseas during the late 1960s. A second wave of Japanese foreign investment followed the Plaza Accord in 1985, an international currency agreement that pushed the value of the yen – and the costs of production in Japan – sharply upward. But even as Japanese capital flowed to South Korea and Taiwan, South Korean and Taiwanese capital began filtering into South-East Asia, then to the USA, Europe and the *maquiladoras* in Mexico. South-East Asian companies then followed this trend. A Thai transnational, Chaeoren Pokhpand, has become the single largest foreign investor in China. Malaysian companies have been investing heavily in banking, hotels and gaming in China, Cambodia and Vietnam. On the other hand, Indonesia is probably experiencing less a repatriation of profits and more a capital flight, with ethnic Chinese-owned firms and Suharto family members preparing for presidential succession. In any event, most states in the Asia-Pacific are today enmeshed in more globalized patterns of production, investment and technology transfer. State officials hope this will extend or renew economic growth, though they recognize that globalization risks creating losers as well as winners. But whether foreign capital comes in the form of direct or portfolio investment, whether it brings new technologies and production capacities or it fails to, and whether capital then leaves with the promise of repatriating profits or engaging simply in flight, economic globalization is eroding the strong state.

US trade pressures

Somewhat distinct from the issue of economic globalization is the issue of free trade and open markets in the Asia-Pacific. In many cases, it was the USA that had supported the development of strong states in the Asia-Pacific, politically defending authoritarian regimes, dispensing much infrastructural aid, providing contracts for war-time production, and opening its markets for consumer exports (see **Gangopadhyay, 1998, pp.20–54**). It did this, of course, because of security concerns over communist expansion. Hence, authoritarian but fiercely anti-communist national leaders like Chiang Kai-shek, President Marcos and General Pinochet received a great deal of US support. During the Korean War, Japan gained contracts from the USA for troop carriers and walkie-talkies, laying the basis later for its automobile and consumer electronics industries. During the Vietnam War, South Korea, Taiwan and Singapore gained similarly, while Thailand, as a 'front-line country', received enormous infrastructural assistance for road networks, port facilities and power grids. The USA calculated that sound economies made for good allies with whom to help wage the Cold War. It thus provided developmental assistance, then opened its domestic markets, even without getting trade access in return.

After the Vietnam War the USA grew less worried about threats posed by communism and more worried by the hollowing out of its industrial base and rising levels of unemployment. Its confidence was shaken also by the economic volatility of the 1970s, a decade marked by the break-up of the Bretton Woods system of fixed currency valuations, followed by sharp increases in petroleum prices. Hence, the USA began demanding reciprocal trade access with the strong states it once supported. Then, when denied such access, it ushered in a period characterized by some analysts as the new protectionism, featuring new forms of bilateral, non-tariff barriers to trade. Finally, the USA returned to demanding free trade, punishing those who resisted in opening their markets or honouring intellectual property rights. Bureaucratic insulation and industrial policy coherence are denied to states in the Asia-Pacific, though this time because of political pressures posed by the USA as much as the functional requisites of globalized production. Because the USA still offers the world's richest market for consumer exports, its commitment to free trade counts for much. Other countries in the Asia-Pacific recognize they stand to gain little by defiantly protecting their economies and subsidizing their businesses. Accordingly, they have agreed gradually to abandon key policies that allowed them to effectively intervene in their own economies.

Challenges from local business

In addition to being confronted by the USA over their economic successes, strong states often find themselves challenged by the local businesses they had promoted. This is particularly likely where bureaucrats operating developmental states have begun to languish, their nationalist commitments flagging. In Japan, as we have seen, after perhaps twenty years of development business has gained more influence in politics, while politicians have gained ascendancy over the bureaucracy. Accordingly, Japan's economic policy making has lost some of its coherence, emerging now as the upshot of three-way interactions between business groups, factions of the LDP, and sundry agencies in the bureaucracy. These exchanges, characterized as the iron triangle are not unlike the political and business relationships forged in the USA. The levels of corruption that facilitate such exchanges have been made plain in Japan by the extensive bid-rigging associated with public works projects, as well as televised images of gold bricks being carted from the home of the LDP leader, Shin Kanemaru, in 1991.

In South Korea, after the assassination of Park Chung Hee in 1979 and the emergence of Chun Doo Hwan, the state's orientation toward the *chaebol* began to shift. Specifically, Chun sought to mobilize political support by appealing to popular resentments over state subsidies given to the *chaebol*. While reducing the subsidies that had accelerated economic growth, Chun began to squeeze the *chaebol,* extracting large financial contributions with which to shore up political support. One *chaebol* leader, Chung Ju Yung of Hyundai, responded by directly contesting the presidency in Korea's 1992 election challenging the ruling Democratic Liberal Party. The state made clear it still possessed the upper hand, denying Hyundai state contracts, subjecting Chung to stiff tax audits, and detaining and interrogating his sons who served as company directors. Despite its disciplining of Hyundai, the state has relaxed its controlling hand over businesses, allowing them to find their own place in a more dynamic global economy. Daewoo, the country's fourth largest *chaebol*, has since shown the way, plunging into markets from the USA and Vietnam to Romania and Kazakhstan.

In Taiwan, the state has directly operated some key enterprises, and while the ruling KMT has run a vast stable of companies, the state never wielded full control over the country's dynamic small and medium-sized businesses. During the 1980s, its control slipped further, with businesses freely avoiding tax liabilities, business regulations, copyrights and trademarks, engaging in a style of business that Lam and Clark (1994) have described as 'guerrilla capitalism'. Moreover, many business interests have filtered their resources back into politics, passing contributions to presidential candidates at the national level, while gaining fuller control over local assemblies and state contracting processes. Even in Singapore, the state has relaxed its control over business. While the state continues to guide the country's globalizing strategies and still modulates foreign investment, it was so chastened by the world recession of the mid 1980s that it recognizes now the value of more regional strategies too. Moreover, state officials believe that their highly formalized, bureaucratic approach is less appropriate for tapping into the Overseas Chinese business networks than the style of their own local business people.

Elsewhere in the Asia-Pacific, new business associations have arisen. In Indonesia, these associations have occasionally lobbied effectively to free up markets, and in Thailand they have deeply infiltrated ruling political coalitions. In the Philippines, powerful families with business interests have historically dominated the national congress, while top entrepreneurs in Malaysia have regularly snared posts in the dominant party. In China, the sons and daughters of high Communist Party officials have emerged as new 'princelings', using their connections to make off with state assets, then mediate transfers to regional markets in return for commissions and kickbacks. Many observers fear that these business methods, which pose profound challenges to state strength, will filter into Hong Kong.

Finally, on Latin America's Pacific Coast, one finds that business in Mexico has been regionally divided, colluding with the ruling party in the country's central areas while steadfastly supporting opposition parties in the north. The state in Mexico, through its state enterprises and marketing agencies long held a presence in the economy sufficient to make or break any firm. The corporatist, broadly disaggregated nature of Mexico's political system has meant that industrial policies have dissolved in piecemeal rent-seeking, turning mostly on import and operating licenses. Firms located away from the centre have been able to wage some quiet resistance. The policy failures that inevitably have accumulated in Mexico have galvanized mass discontents. In Chile, business has weakened the state in another way, not by piercing the authoritarian state's insulation in order to snatch rents, but by refusing to co-operate with a democratic government, thus limiting policy coherence. Specifically, business in Chile has remained close to its erstwhile protector, the military. This posture contrasts sharply with business behaviour in Brazil, Argentina and Uruguay during the 1980s, countries in which the bourgeoisie joined finally in democratizing coalitions, or at least stood idly aside as democratization took place.

In sum, as economic growth has gathered pace in the Asia-Pacific, local businesses have acquired new resources and greater organizational autonomy, enabling them to evade state controls. Business has occasionally been able to round on the state, when leading business people have made direct bids for office at national and local levels. In some cases, this has been economically productive, where business has needed to free itself from the state in order to more flexibly develop new product lines and exports. It has sometimes produced a new transparency in legal structures and financial systems, helping to enhance competition, regularize business life and generate new sources of funding. However, in using its new autonomy, business has been able to act in less productive ways too, gaining favoured access to uninsulated state officials and skewing allocative processes. Either way, whether productive or parasitic, new business activities have greatly diminished the state's bureaucratic insulation and policy-making coherence.

Civil society and cultural challenges

Rapid economic growth, and the uneven opportunities posed by globalization have done more than awaken local businesses. These forces have animated civil society in the Asia-Pacific. Modernization theory predicted that as societies grew richer, their populations would become more participatory, an impulse that could best be accommodated by democratizing politics. However, one finds that throughout the Asia-Pacific, there have been great delays in this opening. Unlike in the Anglo-American countries, upon whose experiences modernization theory was based, the strong states were responsible for the creation of the new middle classes that emerged. Consequently, while accumulating small grievances during everyday transactions, they have been unlikely to oppose openly the state that had promoted them. Indeed, even where they wished to share in state policy making themselves, they have been wary of democratizing politics more fully, risking the empowerment of the working classes and peasantries who outnumber them. In short, many new middle classes in the Asia-Pacific have avoided the democratizing role assigned them by modernization theory.

Further, in South-East Asia, but also in Taiwan and Peru, societies have been fragmented by ethnic sentiments, preventing them from challenging the state. Korean and Mexican societies, though more ethnically hom-ogenous, have long been strained by regional identities and differences. Of course, societies fragmented in these ways help to make state controls more difficult to impose, but such fragmentation helps also to prevent society from opposing the state more squarely.

Thus, while many new middle classes in the Asia-Pacific have been constrained by their statist origins, and civil societies have been fragmented by their class, ethnic and regional identities, they have none the less succeeded occasionally in limiting state power. Much of this is attributable to deep structural changes brought about by rapid economic growth, but one detects also some cultural changes of attitude. Old patterns of unequal, relations between leaders and followers, bureaucrats and petitioners, patrons and clients have been increasingly contested. Civil societies are challenging the patterns of deference and fatalism that underpinned old social hierarchies. Simultaneously non-government organizations, neigh-bourhood associations and self-help groups have mushroomed across the region. Women's groups have challenged family policy in the Philippines, Singapore and Mexico; environmentalist groups in Japan and Taiwan have blocked new industrial projects or forced them offshore, youths adopt punk fashions in Seoul and grunge looks in Kuala Lumpur, and there is a gay activists network across Indonesia.

11.5   Conclusion

In the Asia-Pacific, the rise of strong states has been attributed to a variety of political, economic and societal factors. The central planning state emerged out of a communist revolution in China and deployed its political autonomy in pursuit of heavy industrialization and new levels of social equality. Developmental states emerged in Japan and North-East Asia more expressly to promote economic growth. South-East Asia's neo-patrimonialist states, though possessing less state strength, also pursued industrial policies and social restructuring. So too did at least some of the bureaucratic-authoritarian states of Latin America.

But that strength has come under pressure from internal and external forces. Internally, state apparatuses have withered, their internal discipline evaporating as memories fade of wartime dislocation, poverty and nationalist commitment. Close relationships with business have deteriorated from administrative guidance, steeled by performance stan-dards, into more commonplace corrupt exchanges, institutionalized sometimes as iron triangles. Alternatively, business groups, often promoted by state policies, now defy the policies that states lay down, even competing politically for state offices. Middle classes too, though mindful of their dependence on the state, have sought increasingly to test authoritarian regimes. And civil societies, animated by instant communi-cations and organizational know-how, have mounted a variety of political and cultural challenges. At an international level, the USA insists that its trade partners in the Asia-Pacific now accept US exports in return for exporting to the USA, sharply diminishing the possibilities for protection-ism and nurturing infant industries. The end of the Cold War and the globalization of markets has intensified trade and investment flows, thereby elevating the power of transnational corporations relative to nation-states. For all these reasons, then, the strong state, so long a feature of the Asia-Pacific, is perhaps on the wane.

However, it is far too soon to count the state out entirely. Don Marshall has argued that while private forms of wealth creation have replaced those organized by the state, there remain some essential functions that only states can perform (Marshall, 1996). While transnational corporations may steadily elude the jurisdictions of particular countries, they still need states to arrange national security, operate infrastructure, maintain currency systems and provide legal frameworks for property rights and contracts. The fact that the state is called upon to tax private dealings in order to fund infrastructure, to back the currencies that facilitate transactions, and to punish the local and international violators of property rights shows that states still retain considerable authority. While globalized production and distribution will surely perpetuate economic growth, relative social inequalities will persist, even deepen. Just when capital mobility and globalized production appear to diminish the power of organized labour, global information and communications technologies are helping disseminate grievances and forge new transnational identities and solidarities, making new kinds of labour organization more likely. The owners of capital, even when celebrating free markets, will continue to rely on the state to contain the unrest that their activities unleash coercion is one response, welfare is another. There are indications that some countries in East Asia, while articulating 'family values', are pondering new welfare commitments as family structures erode (see Chapter 9). But whether the challenges of globalization are met by coercion or welfare, they each signal an enduring role for the state. In consequence, while many states in the Asia-Pacific have doubtless lost strength in politics, the economy and society, one cannot yet say *sayonara* to them altogether.

References

Clifford, M. (1994) *Troubled Tiger: Businessmen, Bureaucrats and Generals in South Korea*, Armonk, New York, M.E. Sharpe.

Emmerson, D.K. (1995) 'Region and recalcitrance: rethinking democracy through South-East Asia', *The Pacific Review*, vol.8, no.2, pp.223–48.

Far Eastern Economic Review (1996) 'On a platter', May, p.68.

Gangopadhyay, P. (1998) 'Patterns of trade, investment and migration in the Asia-Pacific' in Thompson, G. (ed.) *Economic Dynamism in the Asia-Pacific*, London, Routledge in association with The Open University.

Hawkins, J. (1998) 'Education' in Maidment, R. and Mackerras, C. (eds) *Culture and Society in the Asia-Pacific*, London, Routledge in association with The Open University.

Huntington, S. (1991) *The Third Wave: Democratization in the Late Twentieth Century*, Norman, University of Oklahoma Press.

Johnson, C. (1987) 'Political institutions and economic performance: the government–business relationship in Japan, South Korea and Taiwan' in Deyo, F.C. (ed.) *The Political Economy of the New Asian Industrialism*, Ithaca New York, Cornell University Press, pp.136–64.

Lam, D. and Clark, C. (1994) 'Beyond the developmental state: the cultural roots of "Guerrilla Capitalism" in Taiwan', *Governance*, vol.7, no.4, pp.412–30.

Marshall, D.D. (1996) 'Understanding late-twentieth-century capitalism: reassessing the globalization theme', *Government and Opposition*, vol.31, no.2.

O'Donnell, G.A. (1973) 'Modernization and bureaucratic-authoritarianism: studies', *South American Politics*, Berkeley, Institute of International Studies, University of California.

Robison, R. (1996) 'Looking North: myths and strategies' in Robison, R. (ed.) *Pathways to Asia: The Politics of Engagement*, St. Leonards, NSW, Australia, Allen and Unwin, pp.3–28.

The News (Mexico City) (1997) 'Government bailout of banks for 48 billion'.

Yoshihara K. (1988) *The Rise of Ersatz Capitalism in South-East Asia*, Singapore, Oxford University Press.

Further reading

Doner, R. (1992) 'Limits of state strength: toward an institutionalist view of economic development', *World Politics*, vol.44, no.3.

Dunning, J.H. (1993) *The Globalization of Business*, London, Routledge.

Goddard, C.R. *et al.* (eds) *International Political Economy: State Market Relations in the Changing Global Order*, Boulder, Lynne Reinner.

MacIntyre, A. (ed.) (1994) *Business and Government in Industrialising Asia*, St. Leonards, NSW, Australia, Allen and Unwin.

Marshall, D.D. (1996) 'Understanding late-twentieth-century capitalism: reassessing the globalization theme', *Government and Opposition*, vol.31, no.2.

Stopford, J.M. (1996) 'The globalization of business' in de la Mothe, J. and Paquet, G. (eds) *Evolutionary Economics and the New International Political Economy*, London, Pinter.

CHAPTER 12

Pressures for change: capitalist development and democracy

Jacques Bierling and George Lafferty

12.1 Introduction

The great upheavals of defeat and victory, revolution and independence that swept the Asia-Pacific at the end of the Second World War left behind them an enormously diverse political landscape. One of the key variations in political life in the region, then as now, was the form and degree of democratic politics that existed within states and the variable strength and power of authoritarian and democratic political movements. The Anglo-American states of the region remained, for their white citizens at any rate, liberal democracies. They were characterized by regular free and fair elections, universal and equal suffrage, competitive multi-party politics, accountable representative government and diverse legal freedoms and entrenched rights. Significant barriers to political participation and formal and informal exclusion from the suffrage persisted for African-Americans in the Southern states of the USA and for indigenous peoples in all of these states. In China, and the northern halves of Korea and Vietnam, people's democratic republics had been declared by victorious communist parties, who created regimes which combined both extraordinary mass participation and mobilization and intensely regulated authoritarian polities. Across the rest of non-communist Asia-Pacific a complex pattern of regimes emerged from defeat, occupation, civil war and independence struggles. The reconstructed Japanese state possessed a pristine, US drafted, liberal democratic constitution. None the less, like its US counterpart, the political system that emerged alongside this constitution managed to secrete very significant powers away from democratic and popular accountability. Sygmann Rhee's South Korea, also possessed a democratic constitution and often highly undemocratic and exclusionary politics. Thailand's military rulers were similarly authoritarian in outlook and practice. Hopes for democratic politics were stronger in the newly independent states of Indonesia, Malaysia and the Philippines, yet all of them fell at some point in the decades after independence to personal authoritarianisms or the fierce politics of ethnic exclusion. It did not appear that the Asia-Pacific would prove a very fertile environment for democratic politics and democratizing social movements. Yet for all the limits of the liberal democratic models available in the Anglo-American states and the strength of authoritarian politics and culture in many states in the region, the Asia-Pacific continues to display consistent and powerful pressures for democratization. Why should this be?

In the five decades since the end of the war the region has been transformed by an extraordinary wave of economic dynamism. This has taken many forms and exhibited many variations. It has turned the USA into a post-industrial economy of unprecedented size. It has made East Asia the third pole, alongside North America and Europe, of a global industrial economy. Economic dynamism and change have swept through South-East Asia and flooded the coastal plains of Asia's communist economies. Even in the distant islands of the Pacific Ocean and in the hermetically sealed communist kingdom of North Korea, the currents and eddies of economic transformation are swirling. It is hardly surprising that the political systems and modes of governance and rule that stabilized at the end of the Second World War have subsequently come under pressure. However, since 1989, the tidal forces of economic change have been combined with the end of the Cold War in Europe. The struggles and conflicts of the Cold War era had decisively shaped the political life and interests of every nation in the region. The end of the Cold War signalled a profound reorientation of international relations, military forces and security issues in the region. Old justifications for emergency powers and martial law began to evaporate; American and Soviet support for compliant regimes receded and the power and prestige of the military in every state was diminished at a stroke. Of course the Cold War remains frozen on the Korean demilitarized zone (DMZ) and its impending termination heralds new tensions and conflicts in the region. Yet it has simultaneously lifted the lid on the pressure cooker of political change that had been building up such a head of steam in the region.

As a glance at the European and North American experience of democratic political change suggests, capitalist development with or without a relaxation in international tensions, has an ambiguous political implication. The simple equation of capitalism and democracy is not tenable, but there are a powerful set of connections, for capitalist development is socially as well as economically voracious. Capitalist development tends to create new wealth and powerful new social classes who challenge old elites and old exclusionary political systems. It tends to create new urban classes of workers, blue and white collar, as well as larger groups of students all of whom may protest at their political exclusion and domination. In short, capitalist development creates mass, educated and organized publics who almost invariably, although rarely in unison, begin to demand their inclusion within the political process at some level, and who are powerful enough to sometimes succeed. Democratization is not always inclusive or successful, but in capitalist societies it is rarely off the political agenda.

The purpose of this chapter is to explore the impact of these forces and pressures in the Asia-Pacific over the last couple of decades. In Section 12.2 we outline some of the key theoretical models that have been advanced to explain the relationship between capitalism and democracy. These theories have been devised with liberal democracy as their normative model or preferred political destination (modernization theory) or even where they have doubts about the enduring worth of liberal democracies their empirical focus or has been on the formation of liberal democracies in Europe, Australasia and North America (structural theory). Not surprisingly these models bear the marks of their origins and are in many ways crude instruments for investigating the experience of East Asia. None the less, it may be that these models can emerge from an engagement with the experience of the Asia-Pacific transformed in their argument but ultimately strengthened. Recognizing the diversity of political experience in the Asia Pacific region we tackle the narrative and explanation of democratization on a sub-regional basis. In Section 12.3 we outline the recent state of democratic politics in four sub-regions, the Anglo-American states, North-East Asia, South-East Asia and Oceania. In Section 12.4 we seek to apply the models developed in the earlier part of the chapter to explain the differential progress of democratic politics in different regions and different states. We focus in particular on the way in which capitalist development has transformed the political landscape of states, and created pressures for democratization. In the conclusion to the chapter we draw up a balance sheet of explanations and political responses to the immense pressures for political change that the Asia-Pacific has experienced.

12.2   Democratization: theoretical models

The rich and diverse literature on democratization has thrown up two broad schools of thought: modernization theory and structural theory. Beginning in the 1950s, modernization theorists – predominantly American political scientists – proposed a model of democratization that barely concealed an explicit normative and political programme for the transformation of 'backward' societies into 'modern' societies; from variants of authoritarianism and communalism to liberal democracies. Modernization theorists argued that, broadly speaking, there was an empirical relationship between the degree of economic development in a state (usually measured as GNP per capita and levels of literacy) and the extent of democratic politics. More development meant more democracy. How would this come about in developing states like those of the Asia-Pacific? They argued that intensified economic relations with the rich states would stimulate socio-economic development throughout developing countries. But crucially, capitalist development would encourage the formation of a bourgeois elite with a modernizing, democratic political agenda. The bourgeoisie would transform the state apparatus mimicking the rich countries. This would facilitate further investment from the developed world and economic growth. These new economic and political institutions would sponsor the dissemination of European legal-rational norms to a populace previously dominated by kinship and patronage relations. As legal-rational norms percolated down from these institutions through everyday life, the working class would experience the benefits of democratic co-operation and learn to organize their own affairs. Working class co-operation and self-control would nourish organized labour movements with a stake in further capitalist development. The middle classes would grow as people saved enough money to establish their own business. This increasingly dense civil society would eventually dominate the polity and ensure the establishment of a bourgeois liberal democratic system familiar to the citizens of the West.

In contrast to the linearity of modernization theory, Rueschemeyer *et al.* (1992) propose a more complex structural model of the relationship between capitalism and democracy. They argue that the relationship between capitalist development and democracy is close, but not because of the political largesse of new economic elites or the beneficial effects of legal-rational bureaucracies. Rather, they argue that capitalist development tends to shift the balance of political power in societies from predominantly authoritarian classes and social groups to those more democratically inclined. Capitalist development, for example, tends to diminish the power of old landlord classes and aristocracies who, not surprisingly, have rarely been democratically inclined. Simultaneously capitalist development creates new classes of industrial owners (the bourgeoisie) as well as mass middle and working classes. However the changing balance of class power is insufficient to explain whether democratization takes place or not. In addition they argue that the relationship between state and civil society must be taken into account as well as the impact of transnational factors like war and international military alliances. 'Capitalist development is associated with democracy because it transforms the class structure, strengthening the working and middle classes and weakening the landed upper class. It was not the capitalist market nor capitalists as the new dominant force, but rather the contradictions of capitalism that advanced the cause of democracy' (Rueschemeyer *et al.*, 1992, p.7).

Capitalist development creates dense, complex civil societies, and aids the spread of urbanization, literacy, new means of transport and of communication. It provides the means for more social groups to politically and socially organize themselves, articulate their interests and put pressure on dominant elites and state institutions. A dense civil society provides the counterweight to state power under the control of landed elites and it forces the state to establish relations with other power groups throughout society. Such relations enable groups to gain support from external interests who bring pressure to bear on the state apparatus for further democratic transformation.

How well can this model be applied to the Asia-Pacific? In their survey of democratic transitions in Europe and Latin America, Rueschemeyer *et al.* found that the role of peasants and rural labourers in the push for democracy was less important in systems where patronage relations dominated. While rural labourers had much to gain from democratization, webs of patronage relationships, personal control and minimal organizational resources made dependent peasants unlike candidates for membership of democratizing social movements. In the Asia-Pacific, this argument is borne out by the quiescence of much of the rural population in the Philippines. By contrast the more autonomous peasants and rural labourers were, as in Thailand, the more they joined democratizing class coalitions in urban centres. The ruling elites, primarily composed of urban landlords and large rural estate holders as in South Korea and Japan, consistently opposed democratization or attempted to undermine democratic advances; a clear parallel with the aristocratic elites of Europe. The urban working class, as in Taiwan, was the most steadfastly pro-democratic of classes and played an important role in the push for democratic reform.

Goran Therborn (1983), like Ruschemeyer *et al.*, has argued that capitalist development is central in accounting for democratization. However, his account of democratization places particular stress on the impact of war on political outcomes. He shares Ruschemeyer *et al.*'s focus on the importance of changing class coalitions, but argues that it is only in a very few cases that democracy has emerged by internal development alone (for example, in the cases of Australia and New Zealand) (see Chapters 1 and 5). More often than not the achievement of liberal democracy has required the impetus and push of war. He cites two particular mechanisms of democratization; democracy by national mobilization and democracy by defeat. In the case of the former, democracy is the price that ruling elites have had to pay to ensure successful national mobilization during war time. After all, it is very difficult to obtain large sacrifices from a population in the inferno of total war while simultaneously excluding them from the suffrage. Democracy by defeat, occurs when the legitimacy and power of ruling elites is destroyed by defeat in war and often active exclusion from politics by victorious and occupying powers. While these routes to democracy were tested by Therborn in the context of European and North American history, they have some purchase on the experience of the Asia-Pacific. Japan, for example, falls into the category of democracy by defeat fairly clearly, while democracy by national mobilization has some purchase on the experience of the US Civil Rights movement during the Vietnam War. However war and preparation for war are not always beneficial for democratization as the history of the Asia-Pacific indicates. Preparation for war and concerns over national security in South Korea, for example, were an important element in maintaining the legitimacy of an authoritarian civilian–military coalition for over three decades. By contrast, Taiwan's precarious relations with the People's Republic of China ensured accelerated economic production and a demand from the middle class for wider political representation. The threat of Communism and insurgency movements unleashed considerable authoritarian forces in Malaysia, Singapore, the Philippines and Indonesia.

What can we tentatively conclude on the basis of our reading of these different models of democratization and an initial glance at the experience of the Asia-Pacific? On the one hand, capitalist development in the region should have been a major force for democratization. It should have diminished the power of landed elites and aristocracies, created potentially pro-democratic bourgeois, middle classes and urban working classes. Capitalist development should also have stimulated urbanization, literacy, new communications and an increasingly dense civil society from which challenges to authoritarian state power could have been mounted. However, those states which have been dominated by an aristocratic and/ or military elite have been least amenable to change despite the increasing strength and density of modern civil society. While the size of the middle class has substantially increased in East Asia, this class has generally aligned itself to dominant political parties controlled by landed and capitalist elites. Sections of urban labour are organized in many countries, particularly in the manufacturing sector, but levels of unionization are small compared with those of the developed countries. Industrial restructuring has steadily eroded solidarity within the broad labour movement, while a history of union repression has worn down organized resistance.

Moreover, external factors have been important in determining political outcomes. From the late 1950s to the late 1980s, the Cold War stimulated a reorganization of political and economic life throughout much of East Asia. Sustained hostilities ensured that many societies were on a permanent war footing, maintained capitalist production at fever pitch, encouraged rapid consumerism, which led to calls for civil freedoms. However, the democratic implications of the Cold War were combined with authoritarian implications: the dominance of military elites; the crushing of dissent; the rise of powerful secret services. From the late 1980s, socio-economic transformation was intensified through regional organizations like APEC (Asia-Pacific Economic Co-operation), PEC (Pacific Economic Co-operation), and ASEAN (Association of South-East Asian Nations), encouraging a rising technocratic class to reorient parochial economic and social institutions towards international norms and agendas. Such changes, however, were not uniformly extended to full democratic participation or negated the recurring problem of civil rights abuses against organized labour. Thus both capitalist development and war have been ambiguous in their relationship to democracy and democratization. In the following sections we begin to sketch how these complex and often contradictory social forces worked themselves out in the many regions and states of the Asia-Pacific.

12.3   Structures and modes of governance

What are the broad features of democratic governance in the region? Our model of democracy, as defined by Therborn, is: '(1) a representative government elected by, (2) an electorate consisting of the entire adult population, (3) whose votes carry equal weight, and (4) who are allowed to vote for any opinion without intimidation by the state apparatus' (Therborn, 1983, p.264)

Our formal definition is limited in that while the basic attributes of such a system appear to describe most polities, there are obvious differences in the democratic process from country to country.

The Anglo-American states

In general, the constitutional bases of government in the Anglo-American states have changed little since independence. Legal systems in Australia, New Zealand, Canada and the USA are primarily based on English common law. Except for New Zealand, two houses of parliament pass legislation reviewed by the judiciary. The executive includes leader, deputy and cabinet. Suffrage is universal and political participation is articulated through large centralized parties. In addition to relative structural uniformity, the Anglo-American states also demonstrate increasing similarities in modes of governance. The executive leader formulates policies to sell to the electorate. Such policies are then shaped into bills by the cabinet, and passed to both houses of parliament for debate. Since the 1980s however, the growing complexities of the pluralist political systems of the Anglo-American states means that independent representatives or politicians lobbied by interest groups, frequently exercise their power to impede the passing of legislation (see Chapter 5). As a result, advisory panels or 'think tanks', including government representatives, entrepreneurs, and academics, specifically design bills to cater to the intricacies of relations in Congress or Parliament. In other words, governance in the Anglo-American states has shifted from an emphasis on executive control to executive management. Governance in the Anglo-American states generally demonstrates a diversity of power centres, the separation of state from civil society, and an impersonal structure of power that guarantees genuine political competition. Executive leaders are focused on capturing public confidence since the leader's populist appeal is crucial to the electoral success of one party over another. Members of the executive team assume personal responsibility for the day to day running of government. Technocrats are responsible for government planning and politicians take considerable pains to ideologically distance themselves from day to day institutional decisions except in the broadest terms.

North-East Asia

The constitutional bases of government in North-East Asian countries were formulated after the Second World War. They are subject to amendment, revision or suspension. Legal systems are based on English, French and American law but have also been subject to local custom, Confucian and communist thought, and civil precedent. One house of parliament passes legislation not universally reviewed by the judiciary. The executive includes a leader and cabinet but not always a deputy. Suffrage is universal but political participation in the case of China is restricted to one party (see Chapter 2). In countries where conspicuous consumption may be as respected as religious asceticism, governance balances traditional communitarian social relations with Western competitive individualism. Competitive individualism was most encouraged by relations with the USA. US economic support for Japan, Taiwan and South Korea during the Cold War generated a system of sub-regional governance that placed strong emphasis on economic growth through formal planning, facilitating the expansion of a state managerial class supportive of private capital. The expanding middle classes have won a greater share of political power, especially in Japan. Organized labour in the manufacturing sectors of Japan, Taiwan and South Korea, has also established formal representative organizations. At the same time, traditional relations that stressed the value of informality modified the strict separation of state and civil society advanced by Western institutionalists. The traditional–Western mix means that governance combines both formal and informal networks of communication between capital and the state. Except for the communist states of China and Vietnam, most countries in North-East Asia demonstrate a diversity of power centres. There is less emphasis, however, on the strict separation of state and civil society. Furthermore, personal relations between key players encourage informal networks of communication that does affect genuine political competition. As a result, politicians in countries like Japan, Taiwan and South Korea are continually exposed to charges of corruption and nepotism.

South-East Asia

The constitutions of most governments in South-East Asia were formulated during the colonial period and based on laws derived from England, Spain and the USA, local custom and Islamic teaching. Indonesia's constitution was formulated during its struggle for independence from the Dutch. There is no review of legislation in Indonesia. An absolute sultan rules in Brunei. The executive generally includes a leader, a deputy and cabinet. Suffrage is universal, from age 15 in the Philippines to 21 in Thailand and Malaysia. Except for Brunei, all are nominally multi-party states. Modes of governance in South-East Asia were profoundly shaped in the neo-colonial period because of the instability generated by internal division, ongoing insurgency and border disputes. As a result, since the 1960s military governments have largely ruled states such as Indonesia and Thailand. Malaysia and Singapore have developed a style of governance based on a mix of authoritarianism, corporatism and competitive individualism. The Philippines, the most democratic country in the sub-region in the 1960s, is now the most elitist. Capitalist development has deeply rearranged social relations in the urban centres of these states but has made less impact in rural areas, where traditional village organization, based on patterns of agrarian production, developed during the colonial period continues to dominate. As a result, urban centres are divided along class lines and demonstrate a diversity of political representation while patronage relations dominate political representation in the rural areas. Ethnic and kin loyalties are most important in Malaysia and Singapore, patronage is most relevant in Indonesia and the Philippines, whereas social and economic class is increasingly important in Thailand. In sum, countries in South-East Asia demonstrate less diversity of power centres than elsewhere in East Asia. There is no sustained tradition of separation between state and civil society. Furthermore, while genuine political competition is evident in most urban centres it is relatively absent in the countryside where ethnic, kinship and patronage relations limit representation. As a result, democratic change in South-East Asia has tended to be more conservative than in North-East Asia.

Oceania

The constitutions of most states in Oceania emerged during the transitions from colonial rule to independence between the late 1960s and the 1980s. Legal systems are primarily based on English common law, modified by local custom. The president is generally a traditional leader whose control over government organizations is legitimated by his position in the indigenous hierarchical system. The cabinet is often drawn from the local aristocracy. Suffrage is not always universal and few Oceanic states are multi-party. Governance is based on the fusion of traditional power relations and hierarchies with the new values and institutions of the post-colonial settlement. The history of governance throughout the Pacific Islands has passed through three phases. Before European colonization in the nineteenth century, power was exerted in largely agricultural communities through rigid hierarchical personal relations. These were dominated by big men in Melanesia, and an aristocratic class of chieftains who controlled the land in Polynesia and Micronesia. In the long plantation phase that followed, governance was based on complex and co-dependent relations between indigenous power holders and European companies that had taken land for the production of commercial crops like sugar, coconuts and timber. The plantation system acutely disrupted traditional communal life in many parts of the Pacific. From the post-war period, however, social dislocation fuelled political demands for independence. In the third phase of governance from the late 1960s, a post-independence indigenous technocracy, many of whom were educated in Australia, New Zealand, the UK or the USA, assumed control of colonial institutions, labour organizations and many aspects of economic life. This neo-colonial phase of governance was undertaken by an alliance of traditional power holders, state technocrats and modern corporate organizations, primarily based in Australia, New Zealand and the USA, but also in East Asia. Contemporary governance in Oceanic countries, given their small populations, is often an idiosyncratic process based on personal relations between the executive, the educated technocracy and foreign corporate representatives in the capital. Government technocrats have encouraged investment by foreign corporations and they have inevitably exerted considerable power over the small island. Thus oceanic states demonstrate little diversity of power centres. The state is intimately connected with civil society. The impersonal structure of power is weak and genuine political competition is rare.

12.4   Pressures for change

We begin this section by analysing the response of the Anglo-American states to pressures for democratic change that emerged during the 1950s and 1960s. We then examine the pressures for democratic change that gathered pace in East Asia and Oceania from the 1960s to the 1990s. We argue that our comparative survey shows that the models of democratization presented by structural theory have some purchase on events in all regions. In particular, we find Rueschemeyer *et al.*'s focus on the destabilizing impact of capitalist development, the transformation of class structures, and the increasing political power of labour and the middle class particularly useful. Therborn's focus on mobilization for war, and the need of authoritarian elites to seek support from the middle and working classes is also useful.

The Anglo-American states

During the 1950s and 1960s, the USA was both directly and indirectly at war. Young men were conscripted. Dissent was limited by the hysteria of McCarthyism. Economic development created a military-industrial complex. Public accountability was sacrificed to the expansion of secretive organizations like the CIA. The USA was on a permanent war footing. Labour organizations backed the state in exchange for higher wages and better conditions, the middle classes reaped the rewards of economic growth – unabated consumerism. However, this new phase of US capitalist development increased the size of the middle class and realigned class power relations. During the 1960s, the children of the new middle classes responded to the defeats and contradictions of US liberal democracy, helping form a series of radical social movements that challenged the status quo, including the anti-Vietnam movement and radical feminism. Simultaneously, capitalist development in the post-war USA had transformed the conditions and geography of African-Americans. Explosive industrial growth in the north and west of the country had seen a huge exodus of African-Americans from the south. Distanced from the patronage relationships and systematic institutional racism of the South, black

Americans were able for the first time to extensively socially and politically organize. In the South a new generation of religious and social leaders emerged from the painstakingly created institutions of black education. Together they provided sufficient social weight and inspired leadership to launch the Civil Rights movement in the early 1960s. The government initially responded to such movements with the armed force of the National Guard, police and its secret service organizations, but US democracy was sufficiently resilient to absorb pressures for change from civil society. The effective exercise of the franchise was extended to African-Americans at the same time as the Vietnam War ended through declining public support for mobilization. During the 1970s, feminism transformed the nature of public thought and institutions. This flourishing of social movements and the development of a denser civil society was repeated in the other Anglo-American states. In Canada, Australia and New Zealand the democratic agenda has been more focused on the extension of civil, political and social rights to indigenous peoples (see Chapter 5).

In sum, we find that mobilization for total war in the Anglo-American states required political and economic elites to mobilize the public. A concerted ideological programme focused on a common enemy accompanied mobilization. Support for the war footing was secured through the extension of working class social rights and increased prosperity. The rising middle classes and excluded ethnic groups challenged the political status quo with some success.

North-East Asia

In developing North-East Asian states like Taiwan and South Korea, democratic institution building has undergone three distinct stages. The first stage involved initial resistance to democratization and concerted attempts by landed and military elites to maintain control. The second stage was a phase of rapid capitalist economic development with strong economic and military support from the USA. This saw the new middle class and labour organizations integrated into a corporatist project driven by state elites. The single-mindedness of the USA in containing the communist threat, meant that the USA often overlooked concerns over human rights abuses by authoritarian elite regimes. Issues of democratization came second to the construction of reliable anti-communist North-East Asian regimes. In the third phase, the economic transformations of earlier eras, created sufficient pressures for change that the old authoritarian status quo began to give way.

In the first stage of democratization, Taiwan was a military state controlled by the Kuomintang (KMT) without a free press or an independent judiciary. In the second stage from 1950, the executive Yuan, composed of the Kuomintang military elite, maintained the island in a permanent state of mobilization for war with the People's Republic of China. Before 1951, Taiwan was an overwhelmingly agrarian economy. However, US sponsored aid to strategic industries between 1951 and 1965, encouraged the generation of an export-led economy focused on manufacturing. From the late 1950s, the Taiwanese government promoted capitalist economic expansion and focused on infrastructure planning and management to assist the export sectors. The government also instituted land reforms that won the KMT support from tenant farmers. Land reform prevented the monopolization of capital by a rentier class, forced the rural bourgeoisie to invest their capital in enterprise, and improved rural income distribution. The KMT essentially integrated the rural bourgeoisie into its plans for rapid economic development. The middle class dominated Taiwan's economy from the 1960s following the adoption of an export-oriented labour-intensive policy for capitalist development by the KMT. The KMT developed strong links with capitalist elites and encouraged foreign investment and high domestic savings. A competitive labour market held wage rates in check but labour was difficult to organize. Domestic production focused on small to medium sized business that primarily employed members of the extended kin group or affiliated members. Political opposition during this period primarily came from native Taiwanese, resistant to the domination of mainland politicians and technocrats. By the 1970s, Taiwan had a sizeable and prosperous middle class with a booming domestic market for consumer goods. The push for democratic change in the 1970s was associated with a decline in US financial and ideological support for Taiwan. Taiwan was expelled from the UN in 1971, and a USA–China communiqué exacerbated its insecure position in 1972. The death of Chiang Kai-shek in 1975 and US derecognition in 1979 made matters worse. Such actions fuelled growing opposition to the regime from native Taiwanese, the intelligentsia and some labour organizations, but the opposition was fragmented, and public dissent was forcefully repressed including a number of riots that were sparked by charges of KMT electoral corruption in the late 1970s. However, the transformation of Taiwan from a one-party state to a one and half party state had begun. Martial law was maintained until 1986 and ensured the absence of a competitive electoral system. Opposition leaders primarily drawn from the native Taiwanese professional class were routinely arrested and imprisoned, though elections were held in 1983 to satisfy international and domestic demands for greater liberalization. In 1986, the small political opposition to the ruling KMT mobilized sufficient support within the ranks of urban labour and the petty bourgeoisie to mount a campaign against the KMT in both state and local elections. The election process itself forced the fragmented political opposition to form a new party, the DPP (Democratic Progressive Party). The DPP was tolerated by the KMT primarily to avoid renewed international and domestic criticism though the KMT did pass three new laws — the National Security Law, the Assembly and Parade Law, and the Civic Organization Law — to curtail the activities of the opposition. The new laws expressly forbade political activities who advocated separation or communism. Nevertheless, the DPP doubled its national vote between 1983 and 1992 and achieved 30 per cent of the vote in local government elections in 1989, gaining six of the potential 21 seats.

Support for the DPP was built around a comprehensive democratic reform programme, that stressed social provision, government support for small businesses and formal independence from the People's Republic. The electoral backlash against the KMT forced the premier to declare an amnesty for political prisoners. In 1990 the KMT phased out the official dissident blacklist, reviewed bans on the movement of opposition student leaders and intellectuals, and transferred the power to dissolve any political party from the National Assembly to the judiciary. Furthermore, the premier initiated proceedings to terminate the life-membership terms of National Assembly members who possessed the power to elect and recall the president. As a result, the electorate showed renewed confidence in the KMT and the DPP lost ground during the 1991 elections. Further reforms included the abolition of emergency provisions except in specified cases, amendments to the constitution guaranteeing a multi-party state, and a separation of powers between the president and premier similar to the French model. The president controls foreign policy and defence, while the premier is in charge of domestic affairs. By the mid 1990s the KMT had largely reconstructed its role as guardian of stability and manager of an extremely successful economy with the largest trade surplus in Asia.

During the first stage of democratic transformation in South Korea, the country was occupied by Japan. The Japanese broke up the power of the Korean landed aristocracy, prohibited a free press and limited civil and political association. After the Korean War the South remained on a permanent war footing. Its leadership was primarily drawn from a cadre of pro-military pro-development civilians who depended on the USA for military and economic aid. Authoritarianism grew in a political climate that associated political opposition or dissent in any state intervention in all areas of life with anticommunism, though the government received support from the rural electorate because of land redistribution and from economic elites because of significant state support for business.

Throughout the 1960s, permanent mobilization for war ensured that some 30 per cent of GDP was devoted to defence spending (37 per cent by the late 1970s). National Security legislation legally curtailed the formation of a political opposition. President Park utilized the skills of a sophisticated economic bureaucracy to promote export industries. Cheap labour, government spending on infrastructure and control of the banking system generated high rates of productivity enabling conglomerates (*chaebol*) to develop markets in clothing, automobiles and steel both at home and abroad. All political opposition was banned in 1975. Martial law was imposed in 1980 as a result of the president's assassination by the head of his own intelligence bureau. Demonstrations against martial law by dissident members of the intelligentsia and students were forcefully repressed and justified the formation of a military government. Political opposition was fragmented.

The third stage of democratic transformation began in the mid to late 1980s. The ferocity of anti-communism abated and generated a new political and social milieu that encouraged peaceful dialogue with the North. At the same time the US intensified its anti-protectionist trade policy, while competition between the NICs intensified and the *chaebol* forged new production niches in China, South Korea's ideological enemy, and throughout South-East Asia. Lower rates of economic growth from 1987 resulted in unemployment and encouraged widespread dissatisfaction with the army-backed Democratic Justice Party (DJP). Economic downturn stimulated the emergence of a broad range of opposition interest groups representing the concerns of an insecure labour force and radicalized students. Renewed opposition was accompanied by street protests in 1987 and forced the DJP to elections. Without a history of solidarity, however, the fragmented political opposition was unable to gain power, though it forced the government to initiate significant democratic reforms, including rights to political organization and a less restricted press. In 1990, however, some opposition parties merged with the Democratic Liberal Party (DLP) to win a majority of seats in the local elections of 1991. In the national elections of 1992, in which both the DJP and the DLP based their political platform on efficient economic management and further civil reforms, the DJP lost its majority in the legislative house. The DLP triumph appeared to usher in a new stage of democratic change; a stage that has been consolidated by the triumph of the veteran leftist dissident Kim Dae-Jung in the 1997 presidential elections.

Democratic pressures in the communist states followed on from the end of economic isolationism and war. In China, state and elite energies focused on ideological enemies during the 1950s and 1960s, in East Asia the USA and within China itself. The turmoil of both industrialization and the cultural revolution left little political space for the emergence of institutionalized opposition. East–West *détente* in the 1970s began the end of isolationism. Energies devoted to internal party struggles turned to a programme of economic reform. During the 1980s, economic liberalization gained considerable momentum and was associated with transformation of living conditions for a sizeable portion of urban populations in the capital and the south. Liberalization, however, also generated inflation and considerable social dislocation. The ageing leadership cadre of Communist Party leaders appeared to lack the skills and strategy for controlling the social and political consequences of economic change; for economic change created losers as well as winners. Small-scale farmers who bought land following the privatization of communally held property, found that tax burdens increased and saw the income ratio compared with urban workers fall from 1:1.7 in 1985 to 1:2.4 in 1992. Tens of millions of poor rural migrants flocked to the coastal cities competing for work and driving wages down. Tiananmen dashed the aspirations of intellectuals for political reform in 1989.

In Vietnam, land reform and US aid before 1970 stimulated a different economic trajectory in the south to that of the north, where collectivization and small-scale industry was the norm. Throughout the 1980s, in a unified Vietnam, the southern mode of production has gained ascendancy over the country. Collective agricultural production devolved into a system of private contractual arrangements between household units and the commune that appropriated a share of production. Surplus was sold to the state or on the market. Such contracts were extended to encourage private investment and now provide a substantial portion of household income. Most collective assets were sold and the role of collectives shifted from management of production to support for production via credit, services, advice and marketing facilities. Foreign investment and the accumulation of substantial pools of private capital stimulated the privatization of public enterprise. Vietnam now possesses a substantial market economy driven by petty bourgeois entrepreneurs and middle class family businesses. While economic transformation generated growing income inequalities, conservative local governments offset the destabilizing effects of such disparities through relative income redistribution, social provision and differential barriers to open market competition. As a result, the country is divided into an ambitious rising middle class, including state technocrats who demand further economic liberalization, and a conservative wing of the state bureaucracy supported by Communist Party elites who continue to dominate national and local politics.

In sum, we find that mobilization for war, US support, and rapid capitalist development were crucial factors in the early stages of democratic transformation in Taiwan and South Korea. The decline of military threat, mobilization and US support stimulated economic restructuring and more active opposition from a now enlarged intelligentsia, labour movement, and petty bourgeoisie. In these latter stages, the elite controlled state apparatus gave ground, resulting in a more democratic society. This picture is different in communist states that have only experienced the early stages of capitalist development democratic transformation. In China and Vietnam the end of civil disorder and war made possible a period of economic reform. Economic restructuring and growing income disparities have led to disaffection amongst labour and rural landholders in China and the middle class and technocrats in Vietnam. In both China and Vietnam, a repressive state apparatus currently mutes pressures for democratic reform though there are some signs that the struggle between an emerging middle classes and the Communist Party may emerge.

South-East Asia

In South-East Asia, pressures for democratic reform have been less disruptive to the status quo than in North-East Asia. The first stage of democratic transformation occurred in the early period of post-colonial independence during the 1950s. The second stage began with the development of authoritarian regimes in the 1960s and 1970s characterized by persistent struggles between elected governments and rebel insurgents with a radical communist agenda. Inter-communal conflict in the Malay Peninsula and Indonesia resulted in draconian legislation allowing governments to detain suspected communist and communalist agitators (see Chapter 4). Such laws were also used against government critics, activists and dissidents. Thailand, Malaysia, Singapore, the Philippines and Indonesia have experienced significant levels of capitalist economic development from the 1980s, but development has not been clearly correlated with less authoritarian government.

Thailand experienced the promise of democratic transformation from the early 1970s. In 1973, student and urban labour protests against the military regime resulted in democratic elections though the civilian government was toppled by the military in 1976. Civilian government was only restored because of dissension between military factions. Some radical officers were dissatisfied with the corrupt links between the armed forces, big business and civilian politicians. The pro-democrats in the military insisted on a longer period of democratic tutelage to accustom civil society to free elections. The conservatives emphasized traditional values and the integrity of existing institutions against demands for change, which they regarded as threatening the national interest. Government in Thailand is now nominally democratic with two houses of parliament. While free elections determine the make-up of the Lower House, the National Peacekeeping Council (NPKC) primarily composed of military leaders, nominated representatives to the Upper House or the Senate. The non-elective nature of the Upper House is justified because of the NPKC's stated role in ensuring social stability, the achievement of socio-economic developmental goals and the elimination of corruption within the ranks of civilian politicians. The NPKC views itself as the guardian of moral purity and public confidence. Free elections were held in 1988 and resulted in the election of a civilian prime minister, though the government was toppled in a military coup in 1991. The new constitution of 1992 gave the Senate, and therefore the NPKC, veto powers over Lower House legislation and permanent control over future election results.

Thailand experienced dramatic levels of capitalist economic development between the 1960s and the 1990s. Civil society today embraces a dominant capitalist ethos in an increasingly cosmopolitan nation that embraces modernization and foreign investment with some vigour. The small number of industrial conglomerates that control much of the Thai media and big business have politically and ideologically supported this breakneck mode of capitalist development. Resistance to military authoritarianism, however, is less focused. A large sector of the population, particularly in rural areas, associates civilian control with widespread corruption. At the same time, the displacement of many rural people through large energy and industrial developments sponsored by the military-dominated government has disrupted and weakened organized communal resistance. Critics of the state include a sizeable cadre of students and intellectuals. An expanding education sector has ensured relatively high rates of participation in South-East Asian terms (93 per cent literacy rates compared with 78 per cent in Malaysia and 77 per cent in Indonesia) and students have played a significant role in the movements leading to the army massacre of pro-democracy demonstrators in 1992. A significant force of radicalized labour in the urban centres, agitating for basic union rights, social provision and industrial legislation to ensure employer compliance to rules governing awards, conditions and safety, has also opposed military authority. Labour organizations were significant in the democratization struggles of the 1970s and early 1990s, but many of their proposals have been ignored or sidelined by civilian and military rulers. The Labour Act of 1975 excludes a large number of workers in state enterprises from joining radical unions and the Social Security Bill proposed in 1990 was rejected by the Upper House. The united pro-democracy push of the intelligentsia between the 1970s and early 1990s has gradually fragmented so that pragmatic intellectuals are now aligned with the dominant conservative army clique. Many Thai workers no longer believe that existing labour organizations can achieve much. Only 1 per cent approximately of the workforce is unionized. Big business representation in government has grown to the point where approximately half the cabinet is composed of business leaders. Yet the numerous business councils have demanded greater democratization to ensure more middle class control over economic liberalization and government planning policy. The rapid expansion of the provincial petty bourgeois also means that business lobby and interest groups influence the pro-democracy push. However, Thai conglomerates are firmly aligned with the conservative elements of the military. Such groups, largely controlled by Chinese–Thai banking families, direct much of the nation's capital disadvantaging the interests of small-scale entrepreneurs. In parts of the country, the NPKC have initiated large-scale development plans to secure the loyalties of the *nouveau riche* but at the same time have alienated traditional small businesses through displacement caused by such developments. Thus despite challenges to the status quo by a combination of forces, the military retains tight control over the political process.

Class divisions in Thai society were amply demonstrated at the beginning of the currency crisis in late 1997. The intelligentsia aligned with the government to propose a variety of economic and political reforms to be carried out over the following decade. Their plan involved micro and macro economic restructuring, a renewed emphasis on cultural nationalism, smaller government and community led development schemes financed by the World Bank and the IMF. Intellectuals opposing such plans argued that Thailand must shift from dependence on foreign institutional loans for accelerated development to appropriate development based on capacity to raise funds at the domestic level and existing skills and technologies. The middle class facing economic uncertainty was divided between those who marched in the urban centres demanding the resignation of the government, and those wary of seeing a repeat of the chaotic events of 1976 and 1992. While the Prime Minister called for a state of emergency in the capital the armed forces remained circumspect, waiting for events to play themselves out as the cabinet resigned and the Prime Minister stepped down. Opposition parties were similarly reticent to take an early stand and focused their energies on preparing for fresh elections. Only the Thai economic elites were united in blaming the currency crisis on external investors rather than their own mismanagement of the banking system. During the most critical moment of Thailand's recent history, there was little coherence amongst the forces pushing for democratic transformation.

In Malaysia, the National Front (*Barisan Nasional* or BN), dominated by the Malay Party UMNO, has held majority political support since independence. Its principal partners within the Front include the MCA (Malay Chinese Association) and the MIC (Malaysian Indian Congress). Because electoral representation has traditionally followed ethnic lines, UMNO's control over the BN is assured at the national, state and local levels. Although the MCA has some leverage, it is predominantly composed of representatives from the minority Chinese business community that controls some 45 per cent of the nation's equity capital. The National Front also controls thirteen of the fourteen states in Malaysia and minority parties must gain membership of the coalition to achieve any genuine political voice in the country. The National Front policy is to incorporate political rivals into what is called the 'BN family'. While political activities were curtailed during various states of emergency between the 1950s and late 1960s, restrictions were lifted after the early 1970s and public debate is officially unrestricted. The BN does, however, exert considerable economic and social pressure to ensure loyalty to the existing dominant-party regime. Over the past twenty years, it has used the Internal Security Act of 1976 and the Sedition Act against its own dissident coalition members. It has silenced government critics, ousted a legally elected state government in Kelantan, and harassed union leaders. The Official Secrets Act was tightened in 1977 to prevent a free and open press from criticizing government representatives or members of the ruling aristocracy. Furthermore, the government has intervened in the constitutional and legal frameworks of the states.

The New Economic Policy of 1969 set the country firmly on the road to capitalist development and is associated with the rapid expansion of the Malay middle class which supports UMNO. Spectacular economic growth during the 1980s transformed traditional society; created a unionized labour force and a new middle class who accounted for some 35 per cent of the population. UMNO rural support fell dramatically due to loosening of loyalties that linked village headman to national political representatives. Despite political competition from unions that represent an expanding class of urban proletariat UMNO's urban constituency has expanded. The labour movement is particularly subject to censure in designated sensitive industries like electronics, and is officially denied the right to organize a nation-wide union. Cheap labour is considered the country's chief asset in attracting foreign investment. In the electronics industry, for example, Malaysian workers are paid roughly one-third to one-quarter of the wages paid to comparable labour in Singapore. The Malaysian intelligentsia is particularly vulnerable to BN patronage in obtaining employment and the government regularly monitors universities and schools. In essence, BN has managed to develop a regime that combines features of both authoritarian and democratic rule mixing political freedom and restriction. Pressures for democratic reforms are diluted through channels of ethnic representation that associate all forms of dissent with an attack on majority interests.

Since Singapore's formal independence in 1959, the People's Action Party (PAP) has dominated political life. PAP was founded on socialist principles but from the late 1960s justified an authoritarian politics that could pursue centralized economic planning, curb communal ethnic violence, and ensure Singapore's sovereignty in the face of Malaysian and Indonesian belligerence. In the early 1960s, a grassroots socialist movement composed of Chinese labourers and intellectuals did attempt to generate a two-party system. However, numerous arrests of organizers and representatives of the broad left, as well as the deregistration of the Singapore Association of Trade Unions, prevented the emergence of a politically viable opposition. From the late 1960s, Singapore conformed most closely to the model of a corporate state, in which sectional interests are submerged, allowing the state to focus on uniform socio-economic development at the expense of political diversity. The possibility of a strong opposition was further limited by the 1987 Internal Security Act that associates active political dissent with anti-state activities. From the early days of government, the PAP linked its interests with that of state bureaucrats, and spread its influence over every section of the state, including a government-controlled media.

The success of the development plans impacted on conservative PAP control over civil society. Between the 1960s and the mid 1980s, the party secured almost 75 per cent of the popular vote in free elections. A sizeable electoral swing against the PAP in 1984 signalled a change in the party's direction though did little to diminish its representation in the parliament given Singapore's first-past-the-post voting system. The swing denoted a generational shift in Singapore. The PAP's constituency was previously based on a conservative majority that had experienced Singapore's rise from peripheral to 'tiger' economic status. By the late 1980s, approximately one in four Singaporeans was a technocrat, the number of people in higher education had almost doubled during the decade, and half the island's population was under 35. This young middle class demanded significant changes to PAP's policy, particularly in the repression of political diversity and the maintenance of strict controls over everyday life. As a result, the PAP attempted to broaden its constituency and appeal to a younger generation by consulting representative interest groups, liberalizing some restrictions on media, and subsidising the arts. While PAP's emphasis on consultation has gained the party some renewed support with the younger generation, it continues to maintain the divide between government and civil society. The one-party state is so deeply embedded in the history of Singapore's spectacular economic development that many citizens associate political diversity with an attack on contemporary living standards and opportunities. The large middle classes may be discontented with many features of PAP hegemony, from its control over the critical press and its links with economic elites, but they offer little resistance to the existing system. As a result, the regime continues to be intolerant of dissent and the critical media, while broadening the criteria for detention.

The Philippines and Indonesia have both experienced great political upheavals. Communist insurgency in the 1960s did little to propel either nation towards liberal democratic reform. On the contrary, it entrenched authoritarian rule and greatly limited aspirations for change. Perhaps the most promising nation in the region for liberal democratic transformation was the Philippines. Between the 1930s and 1960s, the country established a number of precedents in South-East Asia, including land tenure reform, a court of industrial relations, and a social justice programme to ameliorate work and living conditions for the majority of tenant farmers and wage labourers in the agricultural sector. Median living conditions rose substantially until 1960. The state's major political dilemmas concerned ethnic secessionist movements, but successive governments retained the class loyalties of the dominant large landholders and an enlarged urban upper middle class until the 1960s.

Party politics in the post-war period did not really represent diverse class interests but focused on charismatic figures primarily drawn from the landowning and industrial elites. The radical student movement of the 1960s, drawn from the lower middle class, was associated with a broad shift to the left. Urban labour unionized and the Communist Party of the Philippines (CPP) extended its constituency among the ranks of rural labour. In response, President Marcos, who was elected to office in 1965, declared martial law in 1972. Under martial law, the constitution was declared invalid, political activity was banned and the press was muzzled. The New Labour Code of 1974 deregistered unions. The dictatorship, however, won few supporters, either within the ranks of the landed aristocracy which was left without the power to shape government policy or the urban middle classes that saw their economic gains slowly eroded through cronyism. While Marcos restored the electoral process in 1978, and was officially elected with the support of the landowning and middle classes, he kept his powers of decree and strengthened the power of the executive over the legislature.

Economic decline in the 1970s and early 1980s was exacerbated by a growing national deficit. Unease spread through most sectors of civil society, culminating in the push for democratic reforms and the People Power demonstrations of 1986. The overthrow of Marcos and election of Cory Aquino to office did not result in a broad-based government. Rather, Aquino's power base rested on the support of the same sectional interests who had supported Marcos; the large landholders and urban upper middle class. As a result, the new Constitution of February 1987 retained the prescriptive industrial relations fostered by Marcos that limited the ability of unions to organize. Land reform programmes were shelved, striking workers and trade union leaders were arrested.

Between 1986 and the contemporary period, pressures for democratic change in the Philippines were muted. In general, a decline in participation may be associated with a general recovery in the economy and the focus of national energy on pursuing immediate economic gains. Economic liberalization and renewed transnational investment in the Philippines after 1992 have primarily advantaged industrial and landholding capital. An uneven pattern of economic development has reinforced class divisions, labour unrest has been largely depoliticized through the construction of an enterprise-based bargaining system through regional wage boards that have fragmented labour solidarity across economic and regional sectors. The present Ramos regime deals more leniently with radical elements in the labour movement than past governments, but such leniency is primarily designed to maintain the appearance of industrial stability for foreign investors. The state retains the power to mobilize coercive force against a truculent working class.

The republic of Indonesia achieved independence in 1945 after more than 300 years of Dutch colonial rule. In the post-independence period, the numerous ethnic and religious divisions within the archipelago were incorporated within a political and ideological state structure that legitimated centralized rule. However, liberal democratic governments throughout the 1950s were unable to gain a broad constituency. The success of the Communist Party of Indonesia (PKI) threatened the interests of landed elites, the middle class and business, who supported a military take-over in 1965. In 1968, General Suharto assumed the presidency and has maintained power to the present. While elections in Indonesia are nominally competitive, only a selected number of parties are permitted to compete. Their activities are limited to the election period and the military state itself dominates elections through its own party, Golkar. Golkar legitimizes its control over the electoral process by claiming to maintain order and the constitution. Over the past 30 years it has clearly defined national goals and aspirations – stability, discipline, communal values and religious tolerance. Political competition is constructed as inimical to guided development and therefore against the national interest.

As such, the ruling junta has strongly repressed pressures for change from a variety of sectional interests including orthodox Muslim groups, the rising technocracy, portions of the middle class, and fragmented elements of the working class. Authoritarianism in Indonesia is deeply entrenched but counter tendencies have eroded the unquestioned power exerted by the president and his family. During the late 1980s, ruptures developed between sections of the armed forces and civilian advisors to the president concerning the appointment of public officials. Capitalist economic development, particularly in large cities like Jakarta, has resulted in the emergence of a significant middle class who support the president but not necessarily the army hierarchy. Ruptures between moderates and hard-liners within the military itself has led to cautious discussion for a less conservative stance by the armed forces. In Indonesian terms, such discussions are quite revolutionary but were diverted through the 1990s by the debate over economic reforms. Economic deregulation benefited some sections of the middle class because of increased transnational investment. Mass bourgeois disquiet with the regime, however, was fostered by awareness that new found wealth was strongly shaped by a military-bureaucratic regime associated with widespread corruption. Economic liberalization may benefit the few not necessarily the many. However, the middle class has not played a significant role in post-independence politics, with little political organization or clear political agenda. With the currency crisis of 1997–98, the hold of Suharto seems more tenuous, but what political system could replace his rule is uncertain.

Oceania

In the numerous republics and kingdoms of Oceania, the pressure for democratization has come from a bureaucratic technocracy, the small indigenous bourgeoisie, labour and the intelligentsia. However political opposition to elite rule is still fragmented. The primary source of disruption to traditional aristocratic control has come from intensified economic relations between Oceanic states and the developed countries, particularly the USA and Australia. Intensified economic engagement combined with tied development aid has cemented Oceanic dependency. Recent capitalist development has seen the extension of transnational control over land and maritime resource extraction. Traditional elites, however, remain at the apex of political power in most countries. In countries like Tonga, elite rule is most deeply entrenched and a majority of the representatives in the Legislative Assembly are either appointed by the king or elected by the nobles. In general, the absence of a united challenge to elite rule means that political parties are often pragmatic alliances between powerful sectional interests rather than broad popular parties with a coherent ideological and political agenda. An electoral system based on class interests was inherited from the colonial period, but Oceanic societies are still dominated by complex clan and lineage alliances in often dispersed communities. Political life demonstrates features of both instability and stability. In Papua New Guinea, for example, approximately half the members of parliament lose their seats at every election as a result of clan rivalries. The few elite politicians who do survive the tumultuous electoral process form a stable core of political leadership but such long-term representatives have inserted their influence over every aspect of government impeding any meaningful democratic separation of powers. As a result, successive PNG leaders are besieged by allegations of corruption.

The domination of the political process by elites has been modified by the emergence of a technocracy that has sought stronger control over public policy in order to achieve development goals and encourage external investment. Few public resources are allocated to state organizations charged with maintaining political accountability and a fear of reprisal tempers the ability of critics to satisfactorily ensure open government. Development is associated, nevertheless, with the rise of a small middle class and localized labour organizations, which have tried to transform traditional hierarchical relations. The intelligentsia, primarily educated in Australia and New Zealand, often speak for local communities concerned with environmental over-exploitation, but are also associated with state technocrats and labour organizations. Public criticism of the political status quo, however, has led to increasing limitations on free speech. In Papua New Guinea, for example, draft media laws require the state registration of journalists and enable the government to fine and deregister journalists judged in contempt of parliament. While such laws are accompanied by a Freedom of Information bill, the government has the power to declare media investigation as infringing national security. Throughout the 1990s, journalists were detained, arrested and jailed in Tonga for reports criticizing members of parliament, detailing corruption, and asserting the undemocratic nature of parliamentary rule. In Samoa, the political opposition is banned from gaining access to the state-controlled radio service.

The most serious challenge to Oceanic liberal democratic development occurred in Fiji. Before 1987, two major political parties had competed for power in a relatively stable political environment. The Alliance Party (AP) had maintained parliamentary control since independence but was supported by ethnic Fijians, European and Chinese minorities, as well as part of the bourgeois urban Indian electorate. The opposition National Federation Party (NFP) was primarily supported by Indian labour in both rural areas and urban centres. The formation of the Fiji Labour Party in the mid 1980s, however, challenged the nature of electoral competition from traditional allegiance to party based on lineage, family or extended group association, to political appeals based on class. The Labour Party drew support from poorly paid ethnic Fijian and Indian workers in the large towns, particularly in the new industrial centres where working conditions in the textile industry were harsh. In 1987, a coalition between the Labour Party and the smaller Fijian Nationalist Party under Dr. Bavadra, an ethnic Fijian, won the national elections. The new government initiated a programme of democratic reform. An army coup led by Colonel Sitiveni Rabuka deposed the government. A civilian government was re-elected in 1992 following substantial revisions to the constitution. Under the new constitution the president is elected by the Council of Chiefs and appoints the prime minister, usually the leader of the ethnic Fijian party. The prime minister advises the president on the appointment of the cabinet, and the president is also charged with appointing the leader of the opposition. In other words, ethnic Indian Fijians are constitutionally excluded from political control and subject to the dictates of the indigenous Fijian aristocracy. Electors may only vote for candidates from their own ethnic group. Rabuka led the first post-coup civilian government from 1992. National and international criticism, as well as continued pressure from the Fijian bourgeoisie, forced the prime minister to include Indian representatives in the cabinet, but the most important outcome of the coup is a decline of the Labour Party and class-based politics.

In sum, we find that disruption to aristocratic control is primarily associated with capitalist economic development resulting from economic links between the island states and developed countries. Development is facilitated by an emerging technocracy often critical of conservative governments who focus on maintaining elite privileges. Development has resulted in growing income disparities and stimulated a politics based on class rather than clan or lineage loyalties. However, political opposition remains fragmented. Although pressures for change have resulted in limited negotiation by traditional elites, attempts at organizing opposition along class lines by the intelligentsia and labour organizations are often countered by increasing state repression.

12.5   Conclusion

Our brief survey of democratic struggles and patterns of democratization in the Asia-Pacific suggests a number of broad conclusions. First, capitalist development has been a major force for social and political change. Capitalist economic development comes in many forms but almost universally it transforms the social structure of societies; weakens old classes and generates new ones; creates changing interests and aspirations amongst many social groups. Second, capitalist development can help create the conditions for democratization. It is probably a necessary but not sufficient condition of democratization, but it is no guarantee of reform. The ways in which old elites and new political actors respond to the pressures and opportunities of capitalist development is very variable. Old elites may transform themselves and cling to power, new elites may throw in their lot with the old order, prosperity can dampen dissent, oppositions can fragment. Third, one of the most significant additional factors in explaining the endurance of authoritarian systems in the Asia-Pacific of rule in the midst of economic transformation is war and international relations. External powers may choose for security reasons to support authoritarian regimes. Security threats bolster the legitimacy of the military including an active role in political affairs. External threats can legitimize emergency powers and the control of dissent. The end of wars and the diminishing of international threats can provide opportunities for democratization – but are no guarantee of their success either. Given these broad causal relationships what explains the different responses of different state elites to pressures for change? In the last part of the conclusion we look at how flexible and innovative political elites have been in the different regions of the Asia-Pacific when faced with pressures for change.

Perhaps the most flexible system among developing states was that of Taiwan. Taiwan experienced the most dramatic changes between the 1980s and 1990s. Foreign and internal pressure for the end of martial law generated a competitive party structure in 1983 and the formation of the DPP as a focal point for intellectual, small business and labour dissatis-factions with the KMT. The ruling KMT bowed to electoral pressure and modified its own stance on a number of issues including the legalization of political parties, regular elections and formulated electoral rules, greater legislative control over government policy and a more open press. As a result, the KMT regained its clear majority in the 1991 elections and the KMT has captured the democratic agenda. The primary forces that facilitated this transformation were Taiwan's dense civil society, the expansion of bourgeois representation in the political system and a unified active opposition to the status quo drawn from the intelligentsia, labour organizations and the petty bourgeoisie.

Factors associated with moderate flexibility by political systems in the face of pressures for change include the absence of major security threats, a divided opposition and ruling political parties capable of expanding their support as old social forces decline and new ones emerge. The best example of such a system is Malaysia, which experienced incremental moves towards democracy in the 1980s and 1990s. This process was primarily associated with a change in grassroots support for UMNO. A rising middle class no longer supported the conservative policies of UMNO stalwarts though it still supported the UMNO leadership under Dr. Mahathir Mohamed. Mahathir retained their support because of the leadership's success in sustaining economic growth. Organized labour, still subject to repression of strikes and demonstrations, argued for a change to the status quo. The Malaysian labour force was increasingly skilled, average wages increased steadily after 1993, and there was a labour shortage in many parts of the country throughout much of the 1990s. But the Malaysian labour movement has yet to convert economic power into political power. Control over democratic transformation, remains in the hands of UMNO and a young urban middle class.

Democratic transformations were more limited in polities where elites sought to retain direct control over the political and economic process; where the corruption of state offices and privileged links between the state and elite interests permeated politics. Indonesia best exemplifies the limits of capitalist development's capacity to force democratic transformation. The regime changed little between the 1980s and 1990s. In the mid 1990s the strongest forms of resistance had emerged from within the ranks of the urban intelligentsia, the new technocracy and organized labour. Technocrats offered tacit political support to opposition leaders like Megawati Sukarnoputri precisely because of the conservative nature of the existing regime. Sukarnoputri did not promise a radical reshaping of Indonesian society, but she did support land reform, environmental issues and improved wages and labour conditions. In response, the regime tempered its economic liberalization politics and arrested labour leaders and dissident members of the intelligentsia. Furthermore, the president devolved some of his powers directly to members of his family to ensure succession and maintenance of the status quo.

Capitalist development in the Asia-Pacific has created a diversity of power centres, a greater separation of state-civil society and a more impersonal power structure in many developing countries between the 1960s and 1990s. But democratic transformations have then been limited and frail. Throughout much of East Asia and in Oceania too, the middle class has achieved substantial political gains, but labour and rural workers are still largely excluded, fragmented and disorganized. The intelligentsia have made few inroads on civil society. The petty bourgeoisie are primarily focused on economic improvement. Even in the most dictatorial regimes, however, strains between political conservatives and technocrats do signal potential shifts. The new urban technocracies, which support both economic liberalization and political accountability, is generally young, better educated and more international in its outlook than earlier generations. It is this group, drawn from established middle class and skilled working-class families, that may initiate the next stage of democratic transformation.

References

Rueschemeyer, D., Stephens, E.H. and Stephens, J.D. (1992) *Capitalist Development and Democracy,* Cambridge, Polity Press.

Therborn, G. (1978) *What Does the Ruling Class Do When it Rules?: State Apparatuses and State Power under Feudalism, Capitalism and Socialism*, London, NLB.

Therborn, G. (1980) *The Ideology of Power and the Power of Ideology,* London, Verso.

Therborn, G. (1983) 'The rule of capital and the rise of democracy' in Held, D. *et al.* (eds) *States and Societies,* Oxford, Martin Robertson.

Therborn, G. (1995) *European Modernity and Beyond: The Trajectory of European Societies 1945–2000*, London, Sage.

Further reading

Bierling, J. (1995) 'The developing powers: Thailand, Malaysia, the Philippines and Indonesia', *Current Sociology*, vol.43, no.1, pp.97–114.

Beasley, W.G. (1990) *The Rise of Modern Japan*, London, Weidenfeld and Nicholson.

Bello, W. and Rosenfeld, S. (1993) *Dragons in Distress: Asia's Miracle Economies in Crisis*, London, Penguin Books.

Burnett, A. (1992) *The Western Pacific*, Sydney, Allen and Unwin.

Hewison, K., Robison, R. and Rodan, G. (1993) *Southeast Asia in the 1990s*, Sydney, Allen and Unwin.

Higgott, R., Leaver, R. and Ravenhill, J. (1993) *Pacific Economic Relations in the 1990s*, Sydney, Allen and Unwin.

Hill, H. (1994) *Indonesia's New Order: the Dynamics of Socio-Economic Transformation*, Sydney, Allen and Unwin.

Klintworth, G. (1994) *Taiwan in the Asia-Pacific in the 1990s*, Sydney, Allen and Unwin.

Morris, J. (1991) *Japan and the Global Economy: Issues and Trends in the 1990s*, London, Routledge and Kegan Paul.

Trood, R. (1993) *The Future Pacific Economic Order*, Brisbane, Centre for the Study of Australia–Asia Relations.

Van Fossen, A. (1995) 'Corporate power in the Pacific Islands', *Current Sociology*, vol.43, no.1, pp.115–33.

Acknowledgements

Grateful acknowledgement is made to the following sources for permission to reproduce material in this book:

Tables

Table 9.1: Goodman, R., White, G. and Huck-ju Kwon (eds) (1998) *The East Asian Welfare Model: Welfare Orientalism and the State*, Routledge; Table 10.1: from 'Forest Resources Assessment 1990: tropical countries', Forestry Paper, vol.112 (Rome, 1993) in *Vital Signs 1995 – The Trends that are Shaping Our Future*, Food and Agriculture Organization of the United Nations.

Illustrations

Cover: Hulton Getty; pp.14, 17, 20, 54, 61 and 84: Getty Images; p.32: © Wu Yinxian/Magnum Photos; pp.37, 38, 48, 71, 77, 92, 117, 222 and 260: Popperfoto; p.101: © Danny Lyon/Magnum Photos; p.102: © Bob Adelman/Magnum Photos; p.198: Sean Sprague/Panos Pictures; pp.227, 234 and 243: Still Pictures.

List of contributors

Jacques Bierling is a Lecturer in the School of Humanities, Faculty of Arts, Griffith University, Nathan, Queensland, and specializes in the political economy of developing countries with a focus on democratic development in East Asia. His recent work is in the field of socio-economic changes in the rich and emerging states of the Pacific Rim, including publications in *Current Sociology*. His current research is in the process of democratization in the Philippines after 1992.

William A. **Callahan** is a Lecturer in the Department of Politics at the University of Durham, UK. Formerly the Head of the Philosophy, Politics and Economics Programme at Rangsit University in Thailand, Dr Callahan has also lectured at the University of Hawaii and been a visiting professor at Seoul National University, Korea. He is the author of *Imagining Democracy: Reading the Events of May 1992 in Thailand* (1998, ISEAS), *Poll Watching, Elections and Civil Society in Southeast Asia* (1998, Ashgate), and numerous articles. His current research considers the identity of politics in Greater China and the discourse of Asian democracy.

William Case has been a Senior Lecturer in the School of International Business, Griffith University, Brisbane, since 1995. He has a Ph.D. from the Department of Government, University of Texas at Austin and has worked also at the Australian National University and the University of Malaya. His research covers the politics of South-East Asia, especially Malaysia and Indonesia. His recent publications include *Elites and Regimes in Malaysia: Revisiting a Consociational Democracy* published by the Monash Asia Institute, Victoria, Australia, in 1996.

Robert Elson teaches the history and politics of South-East Asia in the School of Modern Asian Studies at Griffith University, Nathan, Queensland. He has written widely on the issues of social and economic change in South-East Asia including several books and numerous articles on Javanese social and economic history in the nineteenth and twentieth centuries. He was a contributor to the *Cambridge History of Southeast Asia*. His most recent book, *The End of the Peasantry in Southeast Asia: a Social and Economic History of Peasant Livelihood, 1800–1990*, was published by Macmillan in 1997. He is currently researching a biography of President Suharto of Indonesia.

Frank Gibney is Director of the Pacific Basin Institute, Santa Monica, California. He is an established scholar of US–Japanese relations and author of numerous works on Japan, and US–Asia-Pacific relations.

David Goldblatt is a Lecturer in the Government Discipline of the Open University and is the author of *Social Theory and the Environment*, Cambridge, Polity, 1996. He lives in west London with Sarah and Molly.

Roger Goodman is University Lecturer in the Social Anthropology of Japan and a Fellow of St. Antony's College, University of Oxford. He specializes in the study of

Japanese educational and welfare systems and is the author of *Japan's 'International Youth': the Emergence of a New Class of Schoolchildren* (Oxford University Press, 1993) and co-editor (with Gordon White and Huck-ju Kwon) of *The East Asian Welfare Model: Welfare Orientalism and the State*.

Huck-ju Kwon is Senior Lecturer at Sung Kyun Kwan University, Seoul and is currently working on income distribution in East Asia. His publications include *The Welfare State in Korea: the Politics of Legitimisation* and *The East Asian Welfare Model: Welfare Orientalism and the State* (co-editor).

David Martin Jones is Senior Lecturer in the Government Department at the University of Tasmania. Between 1990 and 1995 he lectured in the Political Science Department at the National University of Singapore. Whilst there he co-authored *Towards Illiberal Democracy in Pacific Asia* (Macmillan/St. Martin's/St. Anthony's, 1995). His most recent book is *Political Development in Pacific Asia* (Polity Press, 1997).

George Lafferty is Senior Lecturer in Industrial Relations, Graduate School of Management, University of Queensland. He has published in the areas of social and political theory, Australian and comparative politics, industrial relations, tourism policy and higher education policy. His current research projects include the future of socialist theory, the reorganization of academic work, the international political economy of tourism and the growth of homeworking.

Duncan McCargo is a Lecturer in the Department of Politics at the University of Leeds. He received his Ph.D. from the School of Oriental and African Studies, University of London, and has also lectured at Queen's University, Belfast and Kobe Gakuin University, Japan. Dr McCargo is the author of *Chamlong Srimuang and the New Thai Politics* (Hurst and St. Martin's, 1997) as well as many articles. His research interests include contemporary Thai politics, the comparative politics of South-East Asia, and politics and the media.

Colin Mackerras is Professor and Head of the School of Modern Asian Studies at Griffith University, Brisbane. He has also published some fifteen scholarly books and nearly 90 scholarly articles on Chinese and other East Asian affairs. His main academic research has been on China's minorities and theatre. His most recent major scholarly publications are: *China's Minorities: Integration and Modernization in the Twentieth Century* (1994); *China's Minority Cultures: Identities and Integration Since 1912* (1995); and *Peking Opera* (1997).

Rowland Maddock is Senior Lecturer in the Department of International Politics, University of Wales, Aberystwyth. He is a graduate of the University of Wales and taught at the Universities of Keele and Lancaster. His major research interests are international political economy and international environmental politics. His most recent publications are in the area of environmental security.

The late **Gordon White** was a Professorial Fellow of the Institute of Development Studies at Sussex University; he was a specialist on China and development issues. His many books include: *Riding the Tiger: the Politics of Economic Reform in China* (1993); *In Search of Civil Society: Market Reforms and Social Change in Contemporary China* (1996, co-author); and *Democratisation in the South: the Jagged Wave* (co-editor, 1996).

Index

P33